When
JUSTICE
PREVAILS

DEDICATION

To my Mom and Dad for giving me the chance.

YORKVILLE PRESS
NEW YORK, NEW YORK

Library of Congress Cataloging-in-Publication Data

Yerrid, C. Steven.
When justice prevails / C. Steven Yerrid.
  p. cm.
ISBN 0-9729427-0-X
1. Yerrid, C. Steven. 2. Lawyers--United States--Biography. 3.
Trials--United States. I. Title.
KF373.Y47A3 2003
340'.092--dc21'

                                        2003006648

Designed by Tina Taylor

Printed in the USA
jes 10 9 8 7 6 5 4 3 2 1

When
JUSTICE
PREVAILS

C. STEVEN YERRID

YORKVILLE PRESS
NEW YORK, NEW YORK

*"To the truth and those who seek it,
to justice and those who achieve it . . .
but mostly, to the innocent
who are often left without both."*

■ ■ ■

— C. Steven Yerrid

Contents

Introduction

Chiseled in stone on the entrance to the United States Supreme Court are the words "Equal Justice Under Law." They represent America's promise to every person and embody the spirit of justice. It is in the courtrooms across this land that justice must prosper in order for that promise to be fulfilled.

Unfortunately, the truth about life is that justice doesn't always prevail. Too often, the outcome of our most important struggles is influenced by money and power. Surely it is indisputable that the more fortunate among us have the best advantages in life. When disease strikes, the quality and extent of the treatment provided are often affected by who we are, and the difference between living and dying can depend on who can best afford the price tag.

On occasion, the American justice system operates in much the same way. The affluent have access to the best attorneys and the best resources, and as a result they also sometimes have the best chance of prevailing--regardless of whether or not that is justice.

When I was a young man, my father taught me the realities of the world and the very large differences between those who "have" and those who do not. He provided me with invaluable counsel on the human treasures of life such as integrity, honesty, and compassion for people as well as causes. From my mother I learned firsthand about unconditional love and the sacrifices a young, attractive, single parent makes when raising a boy into a man. On city streets I learned about fighting, fear, and the qualities of courage, faith, and one of the best assets of all--determination. It was that determination and those values instilled by my parents that took me through law school at Georgetown, and launched my career in the legal profession.

I became a trial lawyer to make a difference. The opportunity to help guide the hands of justice--when people's lives have been destroyed, families ruined, dreams lost, or widespread societal change and reform are needed--is the fulfillment of my life's ambition. When I take a case and enter the courtroom, it is with the confidence that our system is capable of finding the truth and delivering justice for my clients.

In the courtroom, we are engaged in the most vital of human affairs and matters of utmost importance, where the outcome can bring relief and vindication for shattered lives and seemingly lost souls. For me, there always exists the chance to be a champion of ideas, principles, and causes I believe in. And I also have the privilege of carrying the banner of people who believe in me. No one could ask for more.

WHEN JUSTICE PREVAILS presents eight compelling cases involving many different areas of the law, including medical malpractice, product liability, maritime catastrophe, premises liability, the wrongful exploitation of intellectual property, and the State of Florida's landmark case against Big Tobacco. The stories are dramatic, the cases are powerful, and often their impact is far-reaching. Actual testimony and the text of closing arguments are presented throughout the book.

The people and occurrences in the book are real. The compassion, warmth, love, and determination of the human spirit found within these pages are neither imagined nor contrived. Because of these clients and many others like them whom I have represented over the years, I have become a true believer in that human spirit. The cases I share with you entail the personal crusades and telling journeys of what it means to seek justice in an American courtroom.

I have tried to capture the lessons of life that I have learned as a courtroom lawyer. After many years of seeking truth and justice as a trial attorney, the jury is no longer out with me. I finally have become convinced of who I am, and I have begun to understand, in my own way, the passages of life. I marvel at its seasons, bound with both joys and sorrows that come and go so damned unpredictably.

My run in this world has convinced me that goodness has an overwhelming power. Once I find the goodness in a situation, the confusion of life fades. My choices become clear, my course easily charted. When I do things for the right reasons, that is the goodness in itself. I no longer worry greatly about the result. More and more, what matters most to me is the principle at issue and whether I have put forth my very best efforts. These are the standards by which I measure success.

In spite of all the suffering I have seen my clients bear, each instance of heartache has led me in the direction of learning and caring. My clients and their causes have inspired me to be a better lawyer and, more importantly, a better person. I have seen goodness, compassion, and mercy in their purest form. I have experienced unconditional love, trust, and absolute faith. Of course, I have seen the other side as well . . . hatred, envy, and cruelty in their most vile forms. Still, it is the good that I have chosen to let dominate my life. More often than not, the quest for the truth has succeeded in delivering justice, and that has been enough reward for me.

■ ■ ■ ■ ■

Mayday! Mayday! The bridge is down! Stop all traffic!
The Sunshine Skyway Bridge is down!

■ ■ ■

—Captain John Lerro of the 608-foot *M/V Summit Venture*
Transmission to the United States Coast Guard, May 9, 1980, 7:34 a.m.

I just saw the cars come down, almost rippling in slow
motion, tumbling off the bridge, one by one. No matter
how hard I yelled, no matter how hard I struggled, no
matter whom I tried to get to stop, no one…nothing
…would stop. And they kept coming…they kept
coming over the tear in the bridge and falling like toys
in slow motion.

■ ■ ■

—John Lerro
Trial Testimony, October 24, 1980

CREDITS

CHAPTER ONE

Skyway to Heaven

The earsplitting crack of thunder sounded as if lightning had struck my bedroom. The storm's intensity and violence awakened me quickly and fully. Rain pounded the flat roof of my bedroom and the rumble of thunder trembled the glass panes in the skylight above my head. The pelting of the hail, mixed in with the downpour, filled my ears. Glancing at the clock on the nightstand, I saw that it was 7:30, just fifteen minutes before the alarm had been set to go off. Better the sounds of rain than that damned buzzer.

Morning storms in Florida, especially those in the spring, display the raw power of nature's force. Their startling brevity makes them particularly impressive. The unexpected thunderstorm raging outside this morning would undoubtedly lead to the inevitable traffic jams and flooded streets. Still, I would enjoy the drive into town; the extra time it would take because of the rain would allow me some quiet time before the frenzied pace of the workday ahead. I accepted the fast pace and high pressure—there was absolutely no reason to expect anything less. It was all included at no extra charge in the life of being a trial lawyer.

After a quick shower and even quicker breakfast, my car was slicing through the standing pools of water that had accumulated on the narrow streets of downtown Tampa. For part of the drive, there had been lulls in the storm, but as I approached the parking garage of the twenty-two-story white building housing our law firm, the sky had turned an angry midnight blue and the wind-driven rain was in a full downpour. As I entered the parking garage at the Exchange National Bank, the abrupt halt of the blowing sheets of water cleared the windshield. The brightness of the overhead fluorescent lights seemed even more intense than usual.

Finally, I was out of the weather and in the dark quiet of my parking space. Grabbing my briefcase, but leaving behind the umbrella I never used, I walked quickly to the elevators that would take me to the thirteenth floor.

The Exchange Bank was one of the law firm's oldest and most reliable clients. The towering building with the bright red X on its front was the bank's main headquarters, and it also served as the Tampa office of Holland & Knight. With over a hundred attorneys and countless support staff, the law firm was one of the biggest and most talented in Florida. As the premier institutional law firm in the state, it offered legal expertise in virtually every specialty of law and was considered to be one of the leading firms in the entire South. In the mid-1970s, when the firm was smaller, with just over fifty lawyers, I joined its litigation department upon graduation from Georgetown University Law Center in Washington, D.C. I had my pick of firms when I got out of school—as they had their pick of graduates. As it was turning out, the firm and I had made the right choice. From the start I was given quality trial work and as much responsibility as I could handle. The challenges and rewards were exceptional. The firm had recognized my energy and provided the freedom for an unleashed ambition to be the best I could be.

Now, four and a half years later, when I pushed open the heavy wooden door to the office, I was surprised to see the receptionist's desk unattended. That meant it was still before 8:30, the time when the office would start to come alive with dozens of lawyers, paralegals, and support personnel of all kinds. Good. I would have a few more minutes to further prepare for a deposition I had scheduled that morning.

To some lawyers, depositions are boring, a routine—yet necessary—aspect of trial work. But having a person sworn under oath and taking his or her testimony fascinated me. Each deposition presented the opportunity to examine and cross-examine witnesses. As a young lawyer, I was not yet worn down by the tediousness of legal work, and taking deposition testimony was another way to hone my skills and polish my style.

I moved toward my office and no more than subconsciously noted the plush but conservative décor of the firm. The furniture was traditional, not modern—burnished browns and tans dotted over a dark chocolate carpet—and here and there were sprinklings of brass decorative accessories that shone under just the right amount of muted, indirect lighting. The best of the 1970s, expensive grass cloth covered the walls.

While the richness of the reception area wasn't strikingly obvious, at times I was acutely aware of my surroundings and how far I had come from the dirt-poor hills and hollows of West Virginia. Chuckling to myself as I set my briefcase down, I thought of Holland & Knight and how I referred to them as the "Yankees." Whether recruiting graduating law students for possible employment or just in everyday conversation, I referred to the firm as the Yankees of the legal world. It wasn't because of any northern origins or reference to nicknames based on the Mason-Dixon line. I used the label because of my view that the firm shared in the New York Yankees' tradition of having an established history and the confident pride in being perennial winners. The best of the best: I liked that comparison, and it seemed to fit.

Within the next few minutes, I gathered the materials for my deposition, and then started down the hallway toward the conference room, where the witness was already seated. Halfway there, I stopped when I saw Paul Hardy and Gregg Thomas huddled together in front of the long rows of maritime books, where the latest publications of Lloyd's Register of Vessels were kept. Paul was dressed in the traditional big-firm uniform: a dark blue Brooks Brothers suit—two pieces, never three—a white shirt, club tie, and black wingtip shoes. In his forties, Paul was completely bald on top, and his short salt-and-pepper hair surrounded his ears in neatly coifed tufts. He held a pipe in his mouth so much of the time his lips should have been permanently creased.

When I joined the firm, Paul was *the* admiralty department and operated as a one-man show. But as the Port of Tampa's business increased, the need arose for more manpower to handle the growing maritime law practice. Within my first few weeks at the firm, Paul had asked me to help out by being a "boat lawyer," at least part time. I accepted without hesitation. I had always loved being around the sea. Big ships and the floating cities of an international maritime community fascinated me. So did the strength, magnificence, and sheer force of the ocean. For two of my summers in college, I had worked on a dredge in St. Croix. I had good memories of the Virgin Islands and treasured my experiences there. To anyone who would listen, I talked often about my time in paradise: fishing for deepwater red snapper, diving for the big Caribbean lobsters with the alien antennae, and swimming among the barracudas and car-sized sharks.

Not once after accepting Paul's offer had I ever regretted the decision. He became a great friend who was both loyal and smart. Over time, I became his protégé. Countless hours of unselfish counseling and guidance on his part had ultimately produced a confidence that served me well as a very young trial attorney in a very old world of nautical tradition and the most conservative customs of legal practice. My inexperience was countered by a willingness to do the unexpected and, in doing so, to exploit a trial lawyer's best weapons—surprise and unpredictability.

Paul and I were close friends with a mutual respect for each other's talents. We worked together with both ease and efficiency. The arrival of Gregg Thomas—the youngest associate lawyer hired as a member of the maritime law team—had done nothing to change that. Paul had the voice of reason and a consistently low-key approach. My eagerness, brashness, and limitless supply of energy added fire and enthusiasm. Gregg gave us young talent to train. He was a tall, heavily built athletic type who wore gold-rimmed glasses—the "Ben Franklin" look. He sported a reddish beard that was scraggly and had more than a few bare spots, but he was damned proud of it. Like a lot of young turks, Gregg went at everything with an aggressive, almost bulldog enthusiasm. He had spent three years clerking for two federal judges, and he was accustomed to working hard and watching others get the glory. It's amazing how many landmark judicial opinions are actually conceived and authored by aspiring law clerks just like Gregg.

He had one trait that particularly amused me. When he became excited, his cheeks blushed a bright red. That morning, when I stopped in the hallway on my way to the conference room, Gregg's face was a solid crimson.

In genuine disbelief, I listened as Paul explained that a large bulk freighter had slammed into the Sunshine Skyway Bridge during the same thunderstorm that had awakened me earlier that morning. The whole center bridge span had come crashing down and an unknown number of innocent people were missing and presumed dead. I could not even comprehend the nightmarish scene he was describing. How in the hell could this be true? The bridge gone? People killed? I had fished under that bridge most of my adult life—it was just too damned big to fall. How could something like that happen?

Paul, in a low and worried voice, said, "Come on into my office and I'll tell you everything we know so far."

As we moved quickly into his office, our footsteps silent on the plush carpet, my mind conjured up images of the bridge. The Sunshine Skyway Bridge was in effect the gatekeeper for Tampa Bay, a steel and concrete sentry standing guard over the entire Tampa-St. Petersburg-Clearwater area. It spanned the landmasses otherwise separated by the expansive waters where Tampa Bay met the Gulf of Mexico. Actually, two spans made up the Skyway—one carrying two lanes of northbound traffic, the other two lanes southbound. The colossal concrete piers and steel superstructures that made up the maritime freeway looked very much like two side-by-side versions of the Golden Gate Bridge in San Francisco. At its highest point, the twin structures stood over twenty stories tall. Its causeways and huge spans ran several miles across the shimmering waters of the Tampa Bay channel that connected the nation's seventh largest shipping port to the rest of the world. Depending on the weather, season, or time of day, the glassy waters beneath the Skyway could transform from a stunning transparent sheet of blue to a soft shimmering green, or turn snow white from the crested caps of the diffused gray mountains of waves that the storms of Florida created.

Driving up the incline of the mammoth structure at its main span was like inching up a roller coaster at an amusement park. The anticipation of reaching the top, the long drop to the water below, and just the experience of being so high up…I had never liked crossing the damned thing, and each time I did, I felt an uneasiness that I couldn't control— and a welcome relief when I reached the other side. It was like coming out of the sky and clouds and landing back on dry, flat land.

As Paul described the accident, I tried my best to absorb what he was telling me. From his understanding of the facts, the ship had made impact with the bridge's primary anchor pilings. According to the initial reports, the concrete of the towers had literally exploded, instantaneously sending a powerful rippling effect to the steel-grated and concrete roadway above. The roadway had shuddered, then begun tearing itself apart, sending tons of screeching, twisting metal and pavement to the deck of the ship and into the water below. Jumbled inside the wreckage of the bridge were cars, a pickup truck, and a Greyhound bus that was thought to be fully loaded with passengers. I was stunned, then overwhelmed, as the enormity of the tragedy took hold. Looking out of the window behind Paul at the still rainy and darkened sky, I asked in a low voice, "How many aboard the ship were killed?"

Paul's reply was as bizarre as almost everything else I had heard. "No one aboard the ship was even hurt. The southern span of the bridge has entirely collapsed, and I have been told part of it is still draped across the ship's bow. No one knows how many cars were on it or drove off it after the span was down. But all hands on board have been accounted for, and no injuries have been reported."

"Is the ship ours?" I asked. As I waited for the answer, my heart pounded. There were only two law firms in the port representing the world's shipowners, and Holland & Knight was one of them.

Paul replied evenly, showing none of the emotions that were raging inside me. "No." His answer struck me almost as violently as the thunderbolt that had startled me from sleep that morning.

"We have to be sure. Are you sure?" I asked as I realized the stupidity of the question even as the words came out.

Rather than taking offense, Paul kept his composure. He knew the importance of the moment, and the almost unbelievable magnitude of it

The *Summit Venture*, with a portion of the fallen roadway on its deck, lies at anchor at the foot of the ruined southern span of the Sunshine Skyway Bridge.

all. "She's the *Summit Venture*, a bulk freighter of Liberian registry. It looks like the ship's owner is a Fowler White client." Fowler White was Tampa's other large maritime law firm.

The sharp ring of the telephone on Paul's desk grabbed my attention. The Merchant Officers Protection Syndicate (MOPS) was calling from New York. We would not be retained by the shipowner's underwriter, but the pilot had insurance as well. MOPS was the large underwriting corporation that provided insurance coverage for the maritime pilots of Tampa Bay on the most valuable of their possessions: their licenses. A pilot's license wasn't easy to get. The shipping industry was dependent on a pilot's knowledge of the local waters and skills in navigating giant vessels from the open sea into and through the winding harbor channels to the safety of the port's docks. The pay was excellent, almost two hundred thousand dollars a year for the more senior mariners. But the pressure and constant tension of the job made even the most accomplished pilots occasionally question whether it was worth it. With mammoth ships navigating in outdated channels and docking at old facilities, there were bound to be accidents. Whether a matter was a minor "fender bender" or major casualty, MOPS was the company that would hire the lawyer if ever the state or Coast Guard tried to revoke a pilot's license on allegations of negligence or incompetence. Each pilot paid an insurance premium for coverage, and in return the underwriter provided the best legal talent money could buy.

Shortly after the world began to wake and learn that the Sunshine Skyway had collapsed, MOPS found out that Captain John E. Lerro was the pilot aboard the *Summit Venture*. Lerro had paid his premiums and now it was the syndicate's obligation to protect his interests. Dick Hrazanek's voice filled the room when Paul put the phone on speaker. "I guess you've heard about the Skyway. Our assured was one of the newer pilots. His name is John Lerro. We believe there may be another licensee on board as well, riding as an observer. We just don't know yet. But we are sure about Lerro. He's still on the *Summit Venture* and the Coast Guard is already aboard. We need to have a lawyer out there immediately. Can your firm take the case?"

Several years before, Paul, along with a few other partners, had decided that the law firm shouldn't represent the pilots any longer. With the increase in the port's business and the number of ships calling on Tampa, conflicts of interest arose all too frequently. The firm was obligated both financially and historically to take the side of the shipowner. Sometimes, this meant taking sides opposite the pilot. Regardless, I knew that the enormity of this catastrophe and the legal war it would create made it something special. Maybe the firm would make an exception… Whoever the hell Lerro was, he needed help now—a *whole* lot of help. I tried to picture the scene taking place less than twenty-five miles away from our office at the crippled Skyway bridge.

Paul glanced at me before he broke the silence with Dick Hrazanek, and I could see that he wanted to say yes and give me the opportunity and challenge of a legal lifetime. The horror of it all and the tragic loss of innocent lives were almost overwhelming. Paul had never hesitated to send me into trial. From the beginning, he had believed in me. As the victories mounted, so did his confidence in my abilities. Time and again I was given the more difficult and "pressured" assignments that had been historically handled by the more senior lawyers in the firm. After four and a half years of being battle-tested, I had acquired the confidence to believe that I could take on a case of this magnitude and deal with a client who was in such desperate need of help. Gregg Thomas would further complement the defense team Hardy had obviously already begun considering.

"Dick," Paul said into the receiver, "it's all over the news and I'm afraid it's a very bad situation. Huge damages and a tremendous loss of life. I appreciate your position and my inclination is to take the case, but I'll have to clear everything with the firm's executive committee. I can get back to you within the next few minutes."

"I understand, Paul. We'll stand by," Hrazanek replied.

Paul's calculated words were self-explanatory. It was the way large firms operated. Because of the magnitude of the case, and the political ramifications to the institutional clients we invariably represented, Paul needed to discuss the matter with the most senior lawyers of the firm, ones who were consulted only in the most serious of decisions.

I reflected on what was occurring. Paul had told Hrazanek that it was his "inclination" to take the case. As the head of the maritime department, his recommendation would weigh heavily in whatever decision the firm made. After Paul's conversation with Hrazanek ended, he asked me to stay close in case I was needed. *Stay close?* I thought. *Who the hell could tear me away?*

"Okay, Paul. Let me know as soon as you hear something," I answered. "I have a deposition scheduled, but I'll make sure my secretary interrupts. Convince them we can do this. That pilot needs our help."

The interruption came less than fifteen minutes later. Just as the deposition got started, my secretary knocked on the conference room door. Pausing only briefly, she came to me with a folded note in her hand. The message—from the office of John Germany—was simple: "See us immediately." Being summoned to the office of John Germany could only mean one thing—a decision had been made.

John was the partner in charge of the entire Tampa operation of Holland & Knight. Reared in the small town of Plant City, twenty miles from downtown, he was an original, founding partner of the firm and had established a reputation of excellence, accomplishment, and integrity. After receiving his law degree from Harvard, John had gone into private practice and become politically active. He briefly left the practice of law to occupy a key role in the administration of Governor Leroy Collins, one of the best known and most popular politicians in Florida's history. During the 1950s and 1960s, he had been one of the main players helping Florida take its place in the inner circle of national power and prestige. But John could not choose politics over the law, and Governor Collins appointed him as the youngest circuit court judge to ever take the bench in Florida. After several years, in 1968 he left his judgeship to join several other high-powered lawyers in founding Holland & Knight, becoming the undisputed leader of the firm's growth and presence in the booming development of Tampa. His closely cropped gray hair and traditional dark suits were often accompanied by a bow tie and a smile that showcased his goodness. John was a leader who commanded respect. His displeasure was not welcomed by anyone in the firm, and when he spoke, everyone listened. More importantly, he had become my mentor and we had also become the best of friends. Even with our age difference, I did not have a closer relationship with anyone else in the firm.

Early on, John had given me assignments involving his own most prestigious clients. His personal clients read like a corporate Who's Who: Tropicana Orange Juice, Tampa Electric Company, Quaker Oats, Fisher Price Toys, Lloyd's of London, and on and on. One of the chief rainmakers and power brokers in the firm, "Judge Germany" was known for the extraordinary quality of his law practice. As with Paul Hardy, the legal tasks I worked on were small at first, but as his confidence in me increased, I was allowed to be involved in some of the most important and significant cases Holland & Knight handled. John's reliance and trust in my abilities fueled my desire to excel.

That's the way it is in big firms. Like salmon swimming upstream, some associate lawyers make it through the rapids and over the waterfalls, and even more don't. Worse, young aspiring trial lawyers sometimes fall victim to personal demons or self-destruction from the unyielding stress and nonstop competition. But I had been fortunate. I had successfully navigated the treacherous waters of becoming a real trial lawyer and, at least so far, had not been eaten by the bears.

After arranging with the opposing attorney for an "emergency hold" on the deposition that had been scheduled that day, I hurried down the hall to John's spacious corner office. Paul and John were both seated as I walked in. John spoke quietly, but with an air of authority. "Sit down, Steve. We have to talk. Earlier this morning, the governor called. The firm has been asked to represent the State of Florida in the Skyway tragedy. Before committing, I was having a routine conflict of interest run when Paul came in and told me of MOPS's request that we represent the pilot involved. I don't know this pilot, John Lerro. Anyway, it seems obvious to me that we couldn't go wrong representing the state. The bridge certainly didn't move in front of the ship."

If his words were an invitation for levity, nobody was going to crack a smile. I sat expressionless as a sick feeling of disappointment began to sink in. "On the other hand," John continued as he looked directly at me, "the defense of the pilot will also be difficult and the case probably cannot be won." He didn't wait for a response and went on in a matter-of-fact, flat-toned logic. "This case will receive worldwide attention. If the pilot's defense is lost, everyone would expect it. But if…well, you probably have earned the opportunity to see what can be done. I doubt anyone believes you can win and maybe you can't, but it's yours, if you want it, Steve. Paul and I have agreed to give you the case."

It was happening! It had happened! I felt the rush go through every fiber of my body, but I kept my acceptance simple. "I can't promise I'll win," I said with all the calmness I could muster. My eyes locked first with Paul's and then John's. "But I believe you both know that I'll give it everything I've got. I'll do my best to make you proud. And you —"

"Steve," John interrupted, "we know all of that. Now, get going. I'm sure this Captain Lerro must be getting pretty desperate by now."

In an instant, I was gone. I practically fell as I left the chair and half ran out of John's office and down the hall to my own. I was stuffing my briefcase with pens and legal pads when Paul walked in. While I finished gathering my things, he explained that MOPS had first called Roger Vaughan. Roger was an excellent trial attorney who was well respected, well known and, most importantly, tough as nails. He was a graduate of the Kingspoint Merchant Marine Academy and knew maritime law as well as anyone around. In the past, Roger had acted on MOPS's behalf and represented Lerro on a couple of minor matters. Paul let me know that Roger had turned the representation down earlier in the morning. Of course, MOPS knew why: The company had been in the insurance business a long time and the pattern was usually the same. In the aftermath of tragedy, the living quickly retain the best lawyers, especially when huge money damages are inevitably sought on behalf of the dead. Roger Vaughan would bide his time, keep his options open, and then make himself available to the families of the victims and the big money recoveries the case would bring.

Okay, so I was second choice. We had the case and that was all that mattered. We knew we had to get aboard the *Summit Venture* quickly. The crippled freighter and the broken bridge were both in the middle of Tampa Bay. A boat would be too slow. There was only one way: by helicopter. I didn't particularly like flying, and especially not in a chopper. There had been a few times when I had been forced to charter a helicopter, fly miles out over the ocean, and land on the deck of a waiting ship. While buzzing around in a helicopter may have a certain James Bond flair to it, it scared me to death.

Immediately, we made telephone calls to the various air charter companies. All of the helicopters in town had already been hired by television and newspaper crews, or anyone else who had the money and wanted to see firsthand the tragedy at the Skyway. Out of desperation, I offered to double the normal going rate the media would pay for a charter, and more calls were made. The idea worked. I was told a charter company would have its best pilot and helicopter on the grass field by the downtown Holiday Inn in less than ten minutes. Paul, Gregg, and I were there in five.

We piled into the helicopter, and I took the front seat by the pilot. Our ascent into the still gray and cloudy skies was swift and straight up. A full view of Tampa and its surrounding bay soon emerged even through the murkiness. Even though the air was heavy and overcast, it wasn't bad enough to make me worry. It was going to be a quick trip, a few minutes at the most, out to the mouth of Tampa Bay where the Skyway and John Lerro waited. Under the guidance of the pilot, Vietnam veteran Buddy Knotts, the chopper skirted with ease and efficiency around the lingering rain showers still dotting Tampa Bay. I knew Buddy fairly well and had used his services before. He was a skillful and extremely professional pilot, and most comforting of all, his safety record was impeccable.

Soon we were whirring over downtown St. Petersburg, just across the bay from Tampa. The clearly etched water line along the shore was littered with debris and seaweed that had been torn up from the bottom of the bay by the wind-whipped storm. In the next few moments, the elegant Don CeSar hotel and beach resort came into view, the massive yet majestic building dominating the waterfront. Built in the 1920s, it had been restored, revitalized, and then painted a brilliant pink with the whitest of trim. Even with the dismal gray-sky backdrop and the haze of light rain, the posh hotel was a beautiful sight. Almost three years before, I had attended my ten-year high school reunion there. It had been a fitting place for remembering the old days. The Don CeSar stood in grand defiance of age, oblivious to the passage of time and, it seemed, an almost certain landmark for the future. My eyes were focused on the full rich colors of the resort when the chopper began a sudden rocking as though an immense hand had begun shoving us from side to side. I turned to look at the sea.

Before us, a solid dark sheet of driving, windblown rain, its presence like a monster's maw, was coming ashore from the Gulf of Mexico. Before I could alert Paul and Gregg, we were swallowed deeply into the middle of the thunderstorm. There was no chance of skirting or dodging the violent winds and rain, and the chopper began twisting and buckling in a sudden blackness that seemed to have no up or down. Desperate for some sense of normalcy, I searched the horizon for the comforting view of the Don CeSar, but it had disappeared. Every building, every image had been enveloped by the darkness of the storm front and the violence that was trying to bat us out of the air.

Turning to Gregg and Paul in the back, I yelled to make myself heard above the noise. "Let's get the hell out of here!" When the two of them vigorously nodded their heads in agreement, I was already tapping and shoving on Buddy's shoulder. He didn't respond; he was focusing on the obliterating rain, with most of his attention directed toward the radio headset he wore. Funny thing about pilots, he seemed to be completely removed from the nervousness consuming me and the others. Several seconds passed before he finally turned his eyes in my direction and lifted the headset from his ears. Again, my voice was loud. "Nobody gets paid enough for this! Set this thing down, or turn back, but get us the hell out of this storm!"

Buddy smiled in agreement, and explained he had already radioed the control tower and received clearance to land at Albert Whitted Airport near downtown St. Petersburg. While the airport wasn't the deck of the *Summit Venture*, at least we would be a lot closer to John Lerro than we had been twenty minutes before; and, thankfully, we would be out of the fury that was now erupting in the skies.

Even before the rotor blades stopped spinning, I could see the media had shared our failure to reach the ship. The airport runway was littered with helicopters, all grounded. We hopped out of Buddy's chopper, and I thought of John Lerro on the bridge of the stricken ship. Nearly three hours had gone by since the giant bulk carrier had brought the Skyway crashing down. Still, no one was there for him. I couldn't remember when

I had felt so frustrated—nor could I imagine how alone Lerro must be feeling. Those thoughts vanished as Paul, Gregg, and I concentrated on sprinting across the tarmac to the dryness and safety of the terminal.

Inside, it was crowded with people dripping and sloshing in their wet clothes and shoes. The media had landed. In one glance, I saw that all of the pay telephones were tied up. Cell phones had not been invented and I was fresh out of carrier pigeons. I was desperate to call the Tampa Bay Pilots Association.

"Excuse me," I said to a young lady behind a rental car counter, "I think we'll be needing a rental car. But first, I would like to use your telephone. May I?" Probably every reporter in the terminal had made the same request, but I had seen no one using the bright red phone sitting on her desk. "Listen, it's really important. I'm trying to get to the ship. There's a man out there who really needs our help." She looked at me for a moment and seemed to appreciate my sincerity.

"All right. But don't be long." She pulled the telephone onto the counter.

When the operator of the Tampa Bay Pilots Association answered, I quickly told him of the aborted helicopter ride and our backup plan. We would rent a car and drive to Hubbard's Pier. There, I explained, we would rendezvous with the pilot boat that would take us to the mouth of Tampa Bay where the crippled *Summit Venture* lay anchored beside the fallen bridge. I asked the dispatcher to pass one singular message to Lerro: *Keep quiet and hang on. We're almost there.*

Soon after we left the airport in the rented car, the drenching rain slowed to an irritating drizzle and traffic was returning to normal. I turned on the radio, and the airwaves were filled with coverage of the Skyway disaster. During the drive to the pier, we learned from the newscasts that at least one man, whose name was reported as Wesley McIntyre, had survived the fall from the bridge. When the ship slammed into the bridge and the roadway ripped out from underneath him, McIntyre hadn't been able to stop his pickup truck. The truck had sailed off the shattered bridge into nothingness. Its plummeting free fall was broken when it bounced on the forward deck of the ship, which had pushed its way under the span that was no longer where it should be. By landing on the deck of the *Summit Venture*, elevated some sixty feet above the water's surface, the truck had its death dive prematurely halted. McIntyre's truck had quivered on the edge of the freighter for just an instant, and then pirouetted off the giant ship and continued its fall into the storm-churned waters of the bay. Within seconds, his pickup had sunk through the murky water and half-buried itself in the silt and sand of the bay's bottom, more than fifty feet below.

In subsequent television interviews, he described rolling down his window, pushing his 220-pound muscular frame through the narrow opening, and frantically swimming with all of his strength to the surface. His eyes teared and he began to break down when he talked of how he thought his lungs would burst before he finally reached air. McIntyre was a tough son of a bitch. Fittingly, he had a tattoo etched on the bulge of his large biceps that read, "Tough Old Bird." But even his toughness did not prepare him for what he was about to see.

After breaking the surface, he had grabbed and clung to a steel girder jutting out from the watery grave of the fallen Skyway, where he hung on for dear life. Utter devastation and views of death were all around him. He was in the water less than ten timeless minutes before he was spotted and rescued by the crew of the *Summit Venture*. According to the early news reports, he was the only known survivor among the large number of people believed to have fallen from the bridge. We continued to listen to the morning broadcasts and I realized that the extent of the horror and the death toll would be worse than anyone imagined.

When Paul, Gregg, and I pulled up to Hubbard's Pier, the pilot boat was still not there. The rain had started again, and we took refuge in a small bar and grill located across the street. The one-room restaurant was crowded even though it wasn't yet eleven o'clock. We ordered some coffees to go, and I listened to the conversations filling the room.

"I told the wife this morning that was a killer storm," an old salt announced in a crackling voice. "That's what I told her, even 'fore I knew what happened to the Skyway. That's what I said, all right. The wind liked to have blown me down when I went to take the garbage out this morning. Storms like that one always do bad work. They was made to do bad."

A younger man with shoulder-length hair slugged his beer and looked into nowhere as he answered the old man's rumblings. "Yeah, it was bad all right, but that sumbitch of a ship captain never shoulda took that ship near the bridge in weather like that."

"Maybe. Maybe not," another man with the word Jimmy inscribed on his cap chimed in. "But that damned storm hit awful fast and nobody knew it was comin'. I was on my way down to the docks and it wasn't so bad—then BAM!—thought my van was goin' to get swept right off the road. Wind musta been blowin' close to sixty, maybe eighty knots. Then, quick as the sumbitch came, it was gone. Just like that!" He snapped his fingers.

Before we left the bar, I made my way around the room and for the price of a few beers, gathered names, addresses, and telephone numbers of the people who had been discussing the storm. It was clear the weather would play a crucial role in the defense of John Lerro, a man whom I had never met nor even seen but who, for better or worse, was already my client.

By the time we walked the short distance to the end of Hubbard's Pier, the dark and angry black sky of the early morning was gone. The brilliant blue and the brightness of the new day made me squint as my eyes adjusted. There wasn't a cloud left in the powder-blue ceiling of a picture-perfect spring morning in sunny Florida. The waters of the bay were glassy and calm, and bore no resemblance to the storm-driven whitecaps of Lerro's nightmare. Not far across those tranquil waters John Lerro still waited on the bridge of the *Summit Venture*, fully enveloped in his own hellish ordeal aboard the once-proud ship that lay helplessly alongside the collapsed Skyway.

"Good morning," the boatman said as we boarded the small pilot boat, the *Egmont*. "I have already radioed Captain Lerro. He knows you fellows are on your way." The sturdy thirty-foot vessel resembled a small tugboat, but equipped with high-powered engines it was much faster. These pilot boats served as the water taxis for the harbor pilots and were designed to be used in all types of weather to bring the pilots to and from the large international fleet of mammoth vessels that called upon the Port of Tampa.

As we found seats on the boat, Paul spoke to Gregg and described the layout and channel network of the bay that surrounded us. Paul always made an effort to impart his experience and knowledge to the younger lawyers in the firm. I admired that about him. He always gave everything he had to give. Other, less secure attorneys taught young lawyers much differently. They chose to tell the new blood almost but not quite everything, showing only some of the tricks of the trade. This was a classic example of a popular survival strategy: By holding back, keeping some of the knowledge to themselves, the older lawyers reserved an advantage that they could call on if ever the youngsters of the firm became too aggressive for power or position. But not Paul Hardy. He shared his inner thoughts and uncensored knowledge as only a devoted teacher would for his most deserving students.

Riding out across the water to the bridge on that May morning, I realized that Paul was giving me something else: center stage. He and John were handing me the lead in Lerro's defense for as long as I could handle it. I had outwardly expressed total confidence and begged for the chance. Still, I wondered inside if everything I had would be enough.

We were quiet as the *Egmont* cut powerfully through the now placid water. We passed Tarpon Key shoals, and began our final approach to the center span of the bridge. Our eyes began straining against the brightness of the sun to see the ship and the Skyway—or at least what was left of it. Slowing to follow the channel, the boat rounded the final bend and we entered the open bay.

Nothing had prepared me for what I saw. The blood in my veins turned to ice water, and chills ran the length of my spine.

The freighter and the stricken bridge lay beside each other—centerpieces in a grotesque tableau that looked like a special-effects scene from a movie. The Coast Guard was keeping all boats at least two hundred feet away from the ship.

At first, my mind couldn't comprehend what my eyes were seeing. The missing span of the bridge kept being made whole again in my imagination. And then, as the seconds passed, reality seeped through and the horror before me began to crystallize. Most of the mammoth steel superstructure of the southern span of the bridge was gone. The concrete piers that had supported the roadway above the deep blue water now stood awkwardly alone against the backdrop of the Skyway's untouched, undamaged northern span. One of the anchor piers that had rooted the southern span of the bridge to the bottom of the bay was broken off and shattered, barely visible above the water line. The metal reinforcing rods that had been embedded in the concrete mass were now fully exposed and jutted skyward from the battered remnants of the pilings as if deadly steel fingers were beckoning the remainder of the bridge to the water's surface.

When the pilot boat pulled closer, I saw an automobile stopped at the end of the broken span that was hanging 150 feet above us. At first, the car seemed to be teetering up and down, ready to drop into the bay, but then I looked more closely and could see that it wasn't moving. Somehow, some way, the driver had managed to bring the car to a halt only inches from the death plunge others had made into the waiting sea. The extent of the tragedy began to sink in. My stare focused on the sus-

A car teeters on the edge of the remaining roadway above the *Summit Venture* and the bridge's damaged anchor piers.

pended car, and I wondered how many others who were crossing the bridge that morning had met death.

"This is the United States Coast Guard." The radio came alive loudly and without warning, causing me to jump at the sound of the man's firm voice. "Identify your vessel and your business. You are proceeding into a rescue zone. This area is restricted to authorized marine traffic only."

Rescue zone? The span had collapsed *hours* earlier! From listening to the radio reports during our ride in the rental car, we understood that there had been no survivors to rescue, with the exception of one. In the first few minutes following the collision, the sole survivor had been plucked from the water by the ship's crew. That had to be McIntyre. Almost certainly, the grisly fate of anyone else who had been hurled into the bay had been sealed long ago.

My attention was suddenly riveted to a police boat off the port side of the *Egmont*. Two scuba divers were struggling against the currents to hold the lifeless body of a man against the stern. The crew of the police boat seemed preoccupied with another large bundle that was already aboard. From the distance, the bundle looked like an army-green pup tent, but I had seen body bags before, and I knew, with a sickening feeling creeping into my gut, what the plastic container held. The death count had begun and at least two people would never see their families again.

"My God! Look at that!" Gregg's stunned voice broke my stare. My eyes followed to where his fingers were pointing: the bow of the *Summit Venture*.

Jesus. My lips formed the word, but no sound came out.

Draped across the front of the ship was part of the roadway that had been caught by the ship's deck as the Skyway came crashing down. Dangling across the bow with only its frayed and torn ends betraying the appearance of an otherwise intact segment of highway, the asphalt was dark and eerie. The scene was surreal and reminded me of the crazy look of a Dali painting. The bright yellow paint of the midline dashes of the road was undisturbed, a piece of highway that led to nowhere.

In the background, I heard the professional voice of the *Egmont* pilot. "Coast Guard, this is the pilot boat *Egmont*. We have the attorneys for

Captain Lerro aboard and request permission to proceed to the *Summit Venture*." Seconds passed without a reply. The boatman reduced the engines and waited for clearance. The silence continued and my anger began to rise. Why was there a delay? What difference did another boat make anyway? There were already scores of other private motorboats scurrying in and out of the area where the *Summit Venture* lay anchored. Helicopters filled the sky. Some were hanging motionless, hovering just above the ship. Planes circled overhead like a flock of hungry buzzards. Restricted area my ass.

After a few more long, tense moments, the reply finally crackled over the radio. "*Egmont*, this is the Coast Guard." The voice was unhurried and authoritative. "You have permission to come ahead. Please put your party aboard the port side."

"Roger, Coast Guard. We'll look for a gangway on the vessel's port side," the boatman answered. He hung up the microphone and brought the engines ahead. Instead of my tension easing, my nervousness increased as I was moments away from finally meeting John Lerro. The boatman glanced at us. "Almost there."

"Looks like they're waiting on us," Paul answered as he, Gregg, and I made our way to the bow of the *Egmont*. The pilot boat drew nearer to the *Summit Venture*. The waters of the bay were flat and calm enough to use a gangway to climb up to the deck of the ship. Just before I stepped off the *Egmont* and onto the gangway stairs, I glanced up to the wheelhouse of the *Summit Venture*. Crowded at the window were fifteen, maybe twenty faces, their eyes watching our every move.

Standing on the deck at the top of the gangway was the ship's officer whose job it was to greet us. He said hello, and shook our hands. Even though he had an Asian accent, his English was almost perfect. He led us up six flights of stairs to the ship's bridge, where people were crammed into every available space. Normally, there were perhaps four people to command and run the ship from its bridge. I estimated at least a couple of dozen had crowded into the wheelhouse located in the middle of the ship's bridge.

The wheelhouse usually served as the quiet control center of the vessel. When I took the few short steps across the bridge's deck and entered the wheelhouse, it sounded instead like the trading floor at the stock exchange. It seemed that almost every person there was talking. Neatly dressed, blue-uniformed investigating officers who had been dispatched from the Coast Guard seemed oblivious to the chaos and were busily checking the ship's steering gear, electronic course recorder, radar, engine telegraph—and just about everything that even looked like it was checkable. Out of the corner of my eye, I could see that several men dressed in dark suits were also clustered in tightly packed but separate groups that filled the wheelhouse and spilled out the doorways onto the bridge deck. Each group appeared to be deeply involved in its own heated conversation.

Among the throng, I also saw the shipowner's lawyers. I recognized Dewey Villareal and Carl Nelson of the law firm of Fowler White, intensely engaged in conversation with the Coast Guard's investigative officer. His name was Lieutenant Peter A. Popko. I was sure he would be in charge of the investigation, at least in the initial stages. The three of them abruptly stopped talking as I approached. "Hello, Dewey. Carl. Good morning, Lieutenant," I said pleasantly. "Do you know where Captain Lerro is?"

Dewey spoke first. "He's inside, Steve. I think the helicopters were getting to him." Over six feet four, Dewey, who was in his sixties, had an athletic build and a handsome face. With his snow-white hair, impeccably dressed in his customary blue pinstriped suit, he towered above the surrounding group of people. He had an outstanding reputation and was regarded as one of the best admiralty lawyers in the United States. Even as an adversary, he had befriended me early on, and we had respected each other from the start. He understood the law, but he also knew compassion. Whatever his professional role, he knew Lerro needed help. We were adversaries, but in our hearts we each had kept our humanity. Standing on the bridge of the ship that morning, surrounded by death, we silently shared and understood the profundity of the tragedy and the legal warfare that awaited us.

My eyes lifted to the several helicopters circling overhead, television cameras visible through their open doors. My gaze shifted back to the deck. The media had not been allowed aboard. With all of the activity in the air and the water, I fully appreciated Lerro's choice to remain under the cover of the wheelhouse rather than in camera view on the open deck. It was a feeding frenzy—live and up close and playing on television sets throughout the world.

As I turned to go inside, Lieutenant Popko lightly placed a hand on my shoulder. I had dealt with him on several occasions in the past, and he had been nice enough. In fact, I'd grown to like him. But we had never been exposed to this type of situation and whatever our previous relationship had been, it was now off the table. Popko was in his early thirties and looked exactly like the kind of man you would expect to see on a recruiting poster. He had straight dark hair that was cut short and well groomed, and he sported a neatly trimmed mustache. He was dressed in a uniform of dark blue pants and a flawlessly pressed light blue shirt that carried a number of colorful medals and ribbons.

Over the past couple of years, during the times we had been legal adversaries, Lieutenant Popko had been professional, fair, and honest. I wondered if center stage at one of the worst maritime disasters would change all that. Lieutenant Popko had tended to be aggressive in his investigations, and that character trait was plainly evident as he began our dialogue. "Mr. Yerrid, we would like to ask Captain Lerro a few questions—that is, unless you have an objection." The words and mannerisms were formal and were said in a tone as crisp as his starched blues. On this morning we both knew there would be no casual conversation.

My answer was polite but firm. "I'm sorry, Lieutenant. Not today. We'll be happy to make him available to the Coast Guard sometime later, but not here and not now. It's important that he leave the ship and get some rest. It's been one helluva morning for him and everybody else."

There was nothing left to say. Without waiting for his reply, I turned and started for the wheelhouse where Lerro waited. Before I could make the few steps there, I was stopped again. This time, though, I didn't mind. It was another pilot.

Captain Bob Park was one of Tampa's most able and experienced pilots. He had been taking ships in and out of Tampa Bay for over twenty years. His face was weathered and tanned by years of work at sea. His body was trim and hard. Although he was of normal size and height, he projected a bigger presence and carried an air of control and confidence. I was sure Captain Park had been there to bolster Lerro during the longest morning of his life. I looked into his face and experienced a feeling of relief for the first time that day. No doubt Captain Park had assisted in securing the *Summit Venture* and bringing the ship to safe anchorage. I was also certain that he would have kept the Coast Guard, and anyone else for that matter, from talking to Lerro until his legal team arrived.

"Mornin', Steve," he said as he shook my hand. "I already spoke to Paul Hardy. He asked me to tell you that Captain Lerro is in the wheelhouse. We have everything under control here, but you'd better get John—Captain Lerro—off the ship. More and more people keep coming aboard and everyone wants a piece of him."

"Thanks, Bob. It was damned good you were here," I replied. Captain Park was our client and my friend. We trusted each other and he had confidence in me. Despite my success in representing many of the local pilots, many of the more senior mariners still tended to deal primarily with Paul on admiralty matters. Paul's gray hair and years of experience filled clients with security and confidence that younger attorneys had yet to earn. In the legal world of the ocean, gray hair and years of experience meant a great deal. Fortunately, both Paul and Captain Park had always chosen to disregard my age. That was probably because I was constantly promising them that I was getting old as fast as I could.

Entering the doorway of the wheelhouse, it was easy to pick out John Lerro. He was standing off to the side, isolated from everyone and everything. He was staring out of the west window—the one facing the open sea and away from the fallen Skyway. He seemed to sense my presence, and slowly turned as I moved toward him. He was handsome, and much younger in appearance than I had expected. He had a square chin, high cheekbones, and a full head of raven-black hair. His Hollywood looks reminded me of Al Pacino, and his somber mood furthered the impression. *Italian*, I thought, *Italian through and through*. Lerro was clean-shaven, and his dark brown eyes dominated his face. Captain John Lerro looked straight at me, but his eyes seemed lifeless, as if his spirit had been ripped from deep inside.

I think it was at that moment I fully realized just how alone he was. An overwhelming, uncontrollable sadness filled me and made my

John Lerro at his hearing.

determination to speak to him seem awkwardly callous. I chose my words carefully and I spoke gently. "Hello, Captain. I'm Steve Yerrid, from Holland & Knight. Paul Hardy and Gregg Thomas are out on the ship's wing. I'm sorry we couldn't get here sooner. We have been trying to reach you all morning."

"Yeah," he answered lightly, "I got your message." His New York accent wasn't heavy, but it was enough to instantly separate him from the good ol' boy twang that many of the local pilots used to communicate. He was a New Yorker, probably Brooklyn or Queens. Regardless of his accent, his few words and tone had a sense of resignation, and I began to wonder just how much of himself he had left inside. I could only hope that it was enough to travel the long road of investigations, hearings, and the trial that I knew lay ahead.

"We have the pilot boat standing by. We're going to get you ashore and away from here." I made sure my voice had no hesitancy in it. A case started here. It always did. Clients need someone to trust and share the burden. The special relationship between a trial attorney and client that must exist needs to be established properly and immediately. First impressions are only made once.

Lerro cocked his head slightly. "What about the Coast Guard? Do I have to talk to them now?"

"No," I said quickly as I laid my hand on his shoulder. "Get your gear. We're leaving." The tiniest glint of life flickered in Lerro's eyes. Right or wrong, he knew I was capable of making a decision…and, more importantly, he didn't have to decide anything else. Maybe the look on his face was simply caused by finally knowing he was leaving what had become a deadly nightmare. I didn't care what the reason was, the poor bastard had shown something, and for now, that was enough.

"Have you talked with Bruce yet?" Lerro asked as we started moving out of the wheelhouse.

Bruce? Who in the hell was Bruce? "I don't know who you mean, John. Who is he?" I asked as we kept up our hurried walk to the pilot boat.

"I thought you knew. Bruce Atkins was riding as an observer pilot on the trip in. There he is, over there." He pointed toward Paul, Gregg, Captain Park, and a fourth man who seemed to be the center of the group's attention. Ah! So there *were* two pilots aboard the *Summit Venture* that morning. Good. Bruce Atkins's presence would be useful. Two sets of eyes, two men experiencing and witnessing the critical events of a catastrophe, would help bring things together and corroborate the guts of our defense.

Once we all boarded the *Egmont* for the ride back to Hubbard's Pier, an eerie quiet enveloped everyone on board. It was the silent passage of moments that could not, would not, tolerate anyone's interruption. And no one said a word. Not one. Everyone seemed to welcome the ride back to land as a soothing respite from the ordeal we each had experienced that morning in our own separate way.

I had a million questions and thoughts racing in my mind, but the command of silence held. I would not break into the space where Lerro had fled. His faraway stare into nothingness was all I needed to see. There would be ample opportunities for questions, and more than enough time to wait for the answers. I would allow our small group to treasure the quiet for as long as possible. Those few minutes on the water, between the mangled Skyway and the waiting pier, created a feeling of tranquillity. As the *Egmont* split through the waters of Tampa Bay, reality was already pounding at the door, and I knew that all too soon this small moment of peace would be swept away for good.

Harvest of Souls

· · · · · · ·

The facts are unchangeable, as they always will be, locked forever in John Lerro's heart, his memory, and seared into the depths of his soul. My role was simple enough—prove it wasn't his fault. A moving ship hitting a stationary bridge? That glaring fact, coupled with his own self-conviction, did not exactly inspire confidence. The case was awfully tough and damned near unwinnable. I knew that much. But we had a shot and if nothing else, maybe I could give Lerro a reason to forgive himself. The road to his redemption, if it existed at all, would be long and winding, its final destination perhaps even unreachable.

When we began to piece together the events of May 9, 1980, I found the morning had started out like any other. The previous night, John had piloted a ship *out* of Port Manatee, so the next morning it was his turn to go "back to town," a term the pilots used to describe going back *in* to port. His ship, the Motor Vessel *Summit Venture*, an empty Liberian-registered freighter, was more than two football fields long. The 608-foot bulk freighter was just in from Houston. The ship would be loaded with phosphate in Tampa and sent back out to sea, bound for South Korea. On its arrival for the inbound trip, it would be riding high in the water, with its tall sides fully exposed to the wind like giant metal sails. The reason? Money. It was pure, basic economics.

Everyone knew that vessels like this one were much more maneuverable and under control if they were loaded. With most of its hull submerged, the ship barely felt the effects of any wind. But if bulk cargo like phosphate was to be picked up in Tampa, it made better business sense to keep the ship empty as it entered port. Seawater was always available as loading ballast, and it could be put into the cargo hold and allow the ship to sit low in the water, making for easy navigation. The seawater ballast could then be pumped out at the loading dock. Of course, that would take additional time and effort. Time meant money.

In the end, profit usually wins over safety. The modern-day world of maritime commerce is no different. The ships calling on Tampa and ports throughout the world invariably come in empty, and the "light" freighters arrive dockside immediately ready to be filled with cargo. The hours saved could be worth tens of thousands of dollars. The pilots have virtually no say in the matter. The decades-old business practice was so routine that John didn't give the situation a second thought. Even so, he had checked, double-checked, and triple-checked the weather. Nothing significant popped up, and no marine weather warnings or watches of any kind had been given. The wind should not be a concern on the exposed hull of the ship.

As the ship began its inbound voyage into Tampa Bay, the storm's assault on the unsuspecting Florida coastline was well under way. In the middle of the Gulf of Mexico, less than one hundred miles west, a treacherous squall line was gathering energy. Packing killer winds of extraordinary strength, it began making a headlong dash directly east toward Florida's western shore. The renegade storm roared across the Gulf with surprising speed and caught the huge freighter from behind. It unleashed a frenzied fury that quickly reduced visibility to zero as the rain and wind ripped through the channel and engulfed the ship. In the following weeks, investigations would reveal that the winds had gusted as high as ninety-two miles per hour. The fury of the storm had hit just when the *Summit Venture* was approaching the channel's turn into the main ship channel of the Sunshine Skyway Bridge where the ship would pass under the massive spans, then proceed north into Tampa Bay.

The waters instantly became a churning sea of whitecaps as the *Summit Venture* approached the last set of buoy markers that signaled the eighteen-degree turn into the deep channel that would lead the ship under the Skyway. Even with the storm on top of him, Lerro was able to sight and mark the buoys and use them to make the final turn of the vessel's approach. As the vessel drew nearer to the bridge, the violent storm unleashed its full hell. Lerro had cut the ship's speed as the walls of water beat against the wheelhouse, its glass windows blinded by howling winds and driving horizontal rains. He had ordered a lookout to the bow but it had done no good. A person looking into these elements simply could not see.

The radar now became the ship's only vision. Despite numerous proposals and suggestions over the years, the State of Florida had declined to place any navigational equipment or even a honing beacon on the main spans of the massive superstructure that stood ahead. The *Summit Venture*, its crew, and Lerro were on their own.

With disbelief, Lerro and Atkins watched the ship's radar as the yellow clutter created by the intensity of the driving rain spread rapidly across the entire scope. Both men stared at the solid color of nothingness. The ship's navigational eyes were now as blind as their own. The turning buoys, already lost from visual sight, were now lost by the ship's radar.

Lerro's mind raced through the available options as the seconds ticked on and the giant freighter drew nearer to the Skyway. Turn out of the channel and try to bring the vessel around before the bridge was reached? He could not turn left. He knew another ship was approaching from the opposite direction and would be on the port side. Based on radio communications, he knew the *Pure Oil*, under the direction of Captain John G. Schiffmacher, a fellow Tampa Bay pilot, was outbound in the immediate vicinity. It carried a full load of jet fuel. Certainly plenty enough to blow up both ships, both spans of the bridge, and a whole lot of whatever else was around. Turning left was out of the question.

Turn right? Lerro discarded that notion quickly. Taking the vessel into a right turn would put the *Summit Venture* broadside into the face of the savage wind. Empty and with its freeboard riding high in the water, the ship would be "set" sideways into the Skyway, and nearly impossible to control.

Too many seconds were passing—without the location of the critical turning buoys, he could no longer maintain his intended course. Visually blinded and with the ship's radar occluded, he ran through other options. Drop both anchors and at least lessen the speed of the vessel before it reached the span ahead? He quickly realized that could not be done. By the time the length of the anchor chain ("shots") ran out, the anchor caught on the bottom ("fetched up"), and the anchor line came tight, the ship would be right on top of the bridge. Not only would it strike headfirst, but very likely the ship would also be swung around and slammed into both of the Skyway's spans. If that happened....

His mind raced as the walls of wind continued to batter the ship. In the two-minute period since the storm arrived, the intensity of the powerful wind gusts had caused Lerro to "steer into" the direction where the gale forces originated. It was similar to a person leaning into the wind to remain upright. By oversteering the course and leaning into the southerly wind, if he judged his speed and the distance just right, he could put the *Summit Venture* exactly where he intended—through the gaping hole between the main supports of the Sunshine Skyway Bridge. John later told me he had sometimes thought of ancient mariners passing through the enormous legs of the Colossus of Rhodes and majestically entering its glistening port at the center of the world.

Suddenly, the voice of Bruce Atkins stopped him cold. He shouted that the radarscope had cleared. With the buoys located, Lerro didn't hesitate another instant. In a stern command, he ordered the turn for the steerage to the proper course and alerted the bow watch to stand by the anchors.

The Chinese helmsman repeated Lerro's order and simultaneously turned the wheel from the ship's eighty-one-degree course that had been steered and steadied up on the sixty-three-degree course that would lead the vessel down the main navigational channel and into the center of and through the Skyway's enormous spans. With no navigational beacons, the superstructure of the bridge appeared as a broad, steady line drawn across the radarscope. For a few moments, the torrents of wind and rain unleashed the full fury of the maverick weather cell that had seized their fate. The souls aboard the *Summit Venture* united in silent prayer and anticipation as the ship moved forward. Everything seemed to be in control and for several precious moments Lerro sensed that all might be right.

Then his worst nightmare became a reality. As if turned off by a switch, the renegade storm was gone as quickly as it had come. The ship emerged from the blackness of the blinding rains and howling wind and entered a world of blue sky, sunshine, and clear visibility.

That is when he saw it. He unconsciously widened his eyes in complete and utter disbelief. Directly ahead, less than two ship lengths, was the massive glistening steel of the Skyway's superstructure. But instead of the entrance to the main channel, he saw the anchor piers of the support system that were located almost three hundred feet from the center of the safe passage he had sought. Lerro would never forget what he saw or what he felt at that moment…

How? In God's name, how?…immediately followed by a wonderment that shook his entire being—*Why?* The questions would haunt him for the remainder of his life. But right then—he had to act.

Somehow the freighter had been wind-driven out of the channel, and just a few hundred yards away, the Sunshine Skyway's secondary concrete piers emerged through the slackened rainstorm and grew menacingly larger as the ship drew nearer.

In that horrible moment, everyone aboard knew there was no way the *Summit Venture* could be stopped before it crashed into the looming Skyway. But John Lerro—Captain Lerro—knew in that one savage instant that he had to try. At once, he barked the orders to reverse the engines and shouted the command to drop both of the ship's anchors.

But it was too little, too late. The *Summit Venture* and all of her vast tonnage came out of the fierce winds into the surreal Florida sunshine and tranquil skies and drove fully into the bridge in a muffled explosion.

The Skyway was designed and built as a cantilevered bridge, which meant that every element on it depended on all of the other elements for support; when one portion of the bridge failed for whatever reason, the rest of it would fail, and all too quickly. When the bow of the *Summit Venture* hit the anchor piers, the overwhelming force of the blow instantly sent massive hunks of concrete and dust from the towering pier flying in all directions. Almost immediately, the roadway above the water began to shudder, strain, and moan in protest to the collision. The snow-white concrete of the anchor piers exploded and the steel girders that held the bridge together abruptly began to buckle and snap from the tremendous pressure. At nearly the same instant, the southern span of the roadway—carrying a steady stream of motorists bound for Manatee and Hillsborough Counties and beyond—cracked and tore at the seams. Literally ripped apart, the remnants of the bridge—in a profusion of steel, concrete, and asphalt—dropped like a falling stack of dominoes onto the ship and into the water, spiraling and twisting and carrying along a chaotic jumble of cars, trucks, a Greyhound bus—and their passengers.

Moments after the freighter made contact and the bridge began to

fall to the water below, John snatched up the radiotelephone and called the Coast Guard. "Mayday! Mayday!" he screamed into the microphone. "The bridge is hit! The bridge is down! Stop all traffic!" He shouted his request several times, and then looked up and saw that the bridge was still falling and more cars were driving off into nowhere.

All told, thirty-six people were inside those vehicles, including those ill-fated passengers bound for Miami in the Greyhound. Only one of those innocent and unsuspecting thirty-six would live to tell his tale of terror. The other thirty-five passengers and motorists probably never knew what caused their death. Suddenly, for the motorists and passengers on their own personal journeys into the morning, the bridge was no longer there. There had been no stopping the vehicles as they plunged off the tattered end of the roadway and into their own darkness of death.

So many times in the days ahead, John Lerro would recount and dream about the scene he viewed from the wheelhouse of the ship. "I just saw the cars come down, almost rippling in slow motion, tumbling off the bridge, one by one. No matter how hard I yelled, no matter how hard I struggled, no matter whom I tried to get to stop, no one...nothing... would stop. And they kept coming...they kept coming over the tear in the bridge and falling like toys in slow motion."

The unending nightmare had begun and so, too, had the harvesting of John Lerro's soul.

* * * * * * *

On the morning of the accident, and in the hours, days, weeks, and months to follow, I learned a great deal about John. He was a sophisticated intellectual who had once studied ballet and dance, and even performed at Carnegie Hall, a feat that many entertainers have envisioned but few have achieved. When I first had the chance to visit him at his home, it was filled with Tiffany lamps and Oriental rugs, and the classical music of Tchaikovsky playing ethereally in the background. He was not a typical ship's captain. John had not been reared on the water; he was a cultured, urban New Yorker. Athletic and well spoken, he had good street sense and a hell of a wit. John also had a good heart and he genuinely cared for people. But the first John

Lerro I encountered was the perpetrator of the tragedy. He believed, maybe more than anyone else, that he was the one who had caused all of those people to die that day. He saw himself as the bad guy, the villain—maybe even a murderer.

John was thirty-seven years old at the time of the Skyway tragedy, married but emotionally separated from his wife, a woman named Sophie whom he had met when they both danced professionally in New York. They had one child, Charles, an impressionable twelve-year-old. By the spring of 1980, John and his family had lived in the Tampa area for almost two years, having moved there from the Panama Canal. He had been licensed as a harbor pilot for three and a half years. His career had been unremarkable and his maritime record was unblemished. Although he had been involved in several minor shipping accidents during his years as a pilot, none of them was found to be his fault.

As his lawyer and advocate, I knew that I had to gain his trust, get inside his head and save him from himself. If not, I knew that he would be utterly destroyed—physically, emotionally, and spiritually.

On the morning of May 9, John Lerro was, at least on the surface of things, the world's greatest loser. It appeared to many that I was going to be a close second because I had chosen to take on the impossible task of proving that he wasn't the incompetent pilot everyone was asserting. Even accusations that he was a murderer were beginning to crop up.

Just days after the accident, N. K. Wittenberg, secretary of Florida's Department of Professional Regulation—the agency that oversees pilots' licenses—issued an "order of emergency suspension," immediately stripping John of his harbor pilot's license. The suspension order stated: "[Lerro] failed to take due regard to the existing circumstances and did not properly react to the foreseeable consequences of piloting in conditions of no visibility and high winds as he approached Skyway Bridge. This demonstrates that John Lerro does not possess the ability to execute command of a vessel in a stressful situation and that should he continue to pilot vessels in Tampa Bay, lives and property will be unnecessarily jeopardized." Secretary Wittenberg also found that he lacked "the necessary skill, judgment, and presence of mind to pilot a vessel in a trustworthy manner," and that his license was suspended because "he represented an immediate danger to the public's health, safety, and welfare."

In a hearing called by the Department of Professional Regulation and the Special Prosecutor's Office in response to the order of emergency suspension, I argued that barely forty-eight hours had gone by since the *Summit Venture* had struck the bridge. Due process was needed and such drastic findings could not have been properly reached so quickly. There had been no time for any conclusive facts to be established. Speculation was, of course, rampant, but nothing had been proven. I stressed the fundamental concepts of fairness and the presumption of innocence. I tried to point out that it was easy but inherently dangerous to cast all of the blame on one person, instead of investigating the as-yet-unexplained chain of events.

It was useless. At that point, the only fact that seemed to matter was that the ship had hit the bridge, and thirty-five people were dead. The Special Prosecutor's Office had charged Lerro with negligence and gross incompetency. Of course, the prosecution would have to carry the burden of proof but so what? The State of Florida had someone to blame other than God. John Lerro was a good target, especially as an "out of towner" in a distinctly Southern city.

Ken Oertel, the special prosecutor, furthered the charge that John was a "danger" to the welfare and safety of others if he were allowed to return to the water, by asserting he "obviously" suffered from some "mental impairment" that must have rendered him incapable of making the decisions necessary to have prevented him from piloting the boat into the bridge. The prosecution was trying its best to hang John Lerro out to dry, daggering his reputation like he was a pin doll with nothing to lose, rather than a human being with a family, a career, and a conscience.

I did not buy any of the prosecutor's outrageous assertions. Those few days after the accident and before the hearing had shown me something much different. It was a tragedy, no doubt about that. But it was not going to become a travesty—not if I could help it. John had no mental impairment. Sure, he had something wrong in his head, but it wasn't a malfunction. He was carrying a truckload burden of guilt and, right then, he did not have a friend in the world. After being around him for long hours that stretched into days, I was pretty sure of that much, even without the benefit of any psychological or psychiatric examination. I knew at some point he would have to be examined, and the expert opinions of medical witnesses would be necessary to prove he was "of sound mind." But I had already been convinced of at least that much. I felt confident that the examining doctors would agree.

The prosecutorial straw man that was being portrayed and set up was a work of fiction. Since the collision, I had spent nearly every waking moment with John Lerro. Already from my numerous conversations with him and countless others who knew him, I had learned that John was a good and decent man, and good and decent men don't go around knocking down bridges and killing people on purpose. While John and I both were furious at Oertel's unfounded allegations, there was little we could do without the benefit of further investigations, and John's license remained suspended indefinitely. We were not going to win in the media or the court of public opinion.

In fact, we were getting killed in the court of public opinion. The newspaper and television media's appetite for eating us alive increased. We weren't doing so well in the courtroom either. The emergency order summarily suspending Lerro from piloting ships had been entered without the slightest hint of due process. No relief would be given. The shock and angry reaction to the devastation of the catastrophe were being utilized to propel an extraordinarily one-sided action. For now, we had to keep our powder dry, no matter how much it hurt—and it hurt a lot. The outcome of the hearing was predetermined. It was only being held for appearances' sake, to avoid any accusation of a lynch mob approach. It took less than an hour for the Probable Cause Panel to affirm the validity and correctness of Lerro's emergency suspension. My client would remain "on the beach" and off the sea until his trial was over—unless, of course, he was convicted, and if that happened, he would never return to the piloting career he loved so much. Given the devastation and the number of lives lost, permanent revocation of his pilot's license was a certainty should we lose.

Obviously, the facts of the accident didn't look good. Hell, they looked worse than bad. It had been fairly easy to assemble a chronology of events because of the ship's own records, interviews with those closely

The Tampa Times

88th Year — No. 107   Tampa, Florida, Tuesday, June 10, 1980   40 Pages—10 Cents   Final City

Lawyer says Lerro 'gambled'

State will investigate pilot

By DAVID DAHL
Times Staff Writer

A three-member panel investigating the Skyway disaster this morning found there is probable cause for a state hearing into the actions of Deputy Pilot John Lerro.

action," Department of Professional Regulations attorney Ken Oertell said.

"He took unnecessary risks, and as a result of those risks the collision occurred."

Oertell asked for the hearing to determine whether the 37-year-old Lerro was at fault when the Summit

ing officer. The panel reviews fact and recommends whether the DPR hearing is justified. A DPR hearing officer could recommend to the full board that Lerro's license be revoked or suspended.

A pilot license has never been revoked by DPR or the pilot board, which has been in existence five years.

ing the 608-foot freighter in the channel.

Lerro, 37, was dressed in a blue suit and was flanked by two lawyers.

In contrast to his emotional testimony to a Coast Guard Marine Board of Inquiry into the accident in May, Lerro appeared composed today as he testified

St. Petersburg Times

VOL. 96 — NO. 320   64 PAGES   Florida's Best Newspaper   ST. PETERSBURG, FLORIDA, WEDNESDAY, JUNE 11, 1980   20 CENTS A COPY

State prosecutor blames pilot for Skyway disaster

> The pilot 'took unnecessary risks and as a result of those risks the collision occurred'
>
> State investigator Kenneth G. Oertel

Weatherman tells of squalls prior to Skyway disaster

By JOHN HARWOOD
St. Petersburg Times Staff Writer

TAMPA — Attorneys for Tampa Bay ship pilot John E. Lerro asked a television weatherman in the witness stand Tuesday in their attempt to show that a sudden squall caused the Sunshine Skyway bridge disaster.

Bill Kowal, weatherman for WTVT-Channel 13 and a meteorologist in the Coast Guard Marine Weather Service, described to the Coast Guard Marine Board of Investigation with reference to photographs, vector diagrams and terms like "mesoscale.

Pilots Recall 'Vicious' Squalls
Raging Minutes Before Crash

By BENTLEY ORRICK
Tribune Staff Writer

Three pilot ships were overtaken by quick succession without warning by powerful, fast-moving, probably torrential laden thunderstorms — the kind sailors call "line squall" — that roared across the mouth of Tampa Bay on the morning of M...

One jogged in place to ride out the blow but vicious thunderstorms — thinking the "prudent" course of action — left the channel and anchored. And one hit the Skyway tumbling 1,200 feet of the southbound span into the bay.

At least eight vehicles — including a Greyhound bus — hurtled about 150 feet into the water along with the...

Wind may have altered
Summit...

By CH...
Sun Sta...

TAMP...
Thursda...
have b...
Ventur...
hundre...
persons...

Lerro...
suspend...
perits...
day to...
"an at...
to str...
bridge...

The...

Possible negligence of ship's pilot cited in bridge collapse

TAMPA, Fla. (AP) — A state review panel has concluded there is probable cause to believe pilot John Lerro negligently handled a freighter which rammed the Sunshine Skyway bridge in an accident that claimed 35 lives.

The three-member marine casualty review board said, in effect, there are grounds for a state hearing against Lerro by the Florida Board of Pilot Commissioners, which licenses harbor pilots.

The commissioners also informally recommended the state suspend Lerro's license pending further investigation.

Lerro, 37, was at the helm of the 608-foot Summit Venture May 9 when it struck a piling, collapsing a 1,400-foot section of the bridge's southbound span. Eight vehicles, including a Greyhound bus, pitched into the water 15 stories below. All the victims were crossing the bridge.

Bad weather cited

Lerro, testifying during the the panel's hearing yesterday, blamed weather for the accident. He said a sudden, fierce thunderstorm struck without warning

less than a mile from the bridge. "Hellacious rains and hellacious winds" of up to 60 knots gripped the vessel and blew it off course into the bridge, he said.

Commissioners asked Lerro why he didn't stop the ship and wait out the storm. Lerro replied he was afraid the gale-force winds would slide him broadside into the bridge or into another vessel that was in the area.

Prosecutor Ken Oertell contended Lerro "gambled and navigated blindly" as visibility dropped to zero on his approach to the towering structure.

"The facts of the collision are not in dispute," Oertell argued. "Capt. Lerro took no action to halt the ship or alter course until collision was imminent. He apparently had no idea where he was."

Oertell called for a finding of "incompetence or negligence." He said that was "an inescapable conclusion. You're left with the conclusion he took unnecessary risks, and as a result of those risks a collision occurred."

Lerro declined comment on the panel's recommendations.

Pilot John Lerro, center, getting advice from his lawyer at a meeting of a Florida marine review board yesterday in Tampa.

A-10   BERGEN   THE RECORD, WEDNESDAY, JUNE 11, 1980

associated with the tragedy, and the scattering of weather reports we were already beginning to compile within days of the collision. But I knew there was something else out there. Somewhere among the pile of rubble and in the murky depths that intermittently gave back the bloated bodies of the dead in the hours and days following the tragedy, the answers to Lerro's questions of "how" and "why" had to be found.

The "Cold Hard Facts"
· · · · · · ·

At 6:25 a.m., on May 9, 1980, John and his pilot trainee, Bruce Atkins, had boarded the *Summit Venture* as it came out of the Gulf of Mexico bound for the Port of Tampa. At 7:06, the giant bulk phosphate carrier, with John at the helm, passed the lighthouse at Egmont Key, near the mouth of Tampa Bay, while the storm continued to gather strength and roar eastward across the Gulf of Mexico. At 7:18, the beginnings of what appeared to be a typical spring rain shower were noted. The real guts of the fury, though, did not strike until almost fifteen minutes later, just as the ship approached the last buoy marker—numbered 2A—which signaled the upcoming eighteen-degree turn into the main shipping channel that cut through the middle of the bridge spans. Less than a half mile from the bridge itself, the *Summit Venture*'s speed of twelve knots meant the vessel would be covering six hundred feet every thirty seconds. It would take less than three minutes to arrive at the Skyway. As the ship moved forward into its last course change before the bridge, the weather was at its violent worst. During those few moments, the radar's visibility was lost for a few critical seconds. The storm pushed the *Summit Venture* some four hundred yards out of the channel, with the ship traveling across the surface like a beach ball blown across a swimming pool. Even though the instruments and steerage showed a proper course was being followed, the vessel's actual route was a crabbing, sideways movement that resulted in a collision course with the anchor piers of the Sunshine Skyway Bridge. At 7:34, the ship collided with and took down over 1,300 feet of the Skyway's main span.

The principal areas of criticism began to emerge almost immediately after the collision. The weather could not have been that bad. Even if it was, why the hell was John Lerro navigating in such severe weather in the first place? Why didn't he stop the ship? Couldn't Captain Lerro simply have dropped the anchors and reversed the engines? Surely he could have stopped, so why did he keep going? Slowly, but inevitably, came the barbs leading up to the poisonous theme already thrust forth nationwide—he must have had mental problems, been drunk, or worse, on drugs. There was even the nastiest accusation of all: Maybe he did it on purpose.

Something extraordinary and beyond the normal realm of our own experience had occurred that morning. A freak, unpredicted small cell of hurricane-like weather had hit the ship at exactly the worst possible time, leaving in its wake of devastation and death the unbelievability of it all, a distinct sense of powerlessness. From my interviews with John and dozens of witnesses, and our team's examination of thousands of documents, including the huge amount of weather data we were able to amass, we were going to take the accusations on—all of them—with one singular defense. The forces of nature had taken over and nothing Lerro could have done would have made any difference whatsoever. Our defense would be an "Act of God."

An Act of God defense is not asserted very often. The reason is simple. In order to prevail, this defense must prove that nothing humanly possible could have been done to change the course of events that occurred. The belief that we are not in control over what will happen in our lives is often very difficult for people to accept. Successfully advocating this defense might be damned near impossible. Who was easier to blame? An Italian from New York or God? Who was I kidding?

If only the storm had waited to unleash its fury for just a little while longer, *if only* it had come just a few moments sooner or later—either one would have made all of the difference between whether or not John would have hit that bridge, and the passage would have been as uneventful as the hundreds of other passages he had piloted before. *If only, if only, if only*…but that was not reality. The accident had happened. Thirty-five people were dead, and John Lerro was being blamed. The swells of anger from the public were building into enormous waves of conviction.

While I was preparing our defense, the government prosecutors working for the State of Florida were having a field day in their efforts to convict John without the benefit of a trial. After the emergency hearing upholding the suspension of John's license, there were meetings, interviews, and phone calls galore. From the outset, the prosecutors seemed to assume Lerro's conviction, and continually urged that I save everyone's time and trouble by pleading John guilty to the charges that had been filed against him.

E. J. Salcines, the State Attorney for the Thirteenth Judicial Circuit, was being urged to indict John for criminal manslaughter. Instead, he withstood the political pressures and after thoroughly reviewing the evidence, made the determination that such a charge was not warranted. (Many years later, his lifetime works of honesty, good judgment, and integrity were rewarded. E. J. Salcines was appointed and still serves as an appellate judge on the prestigious Second District Court of Appeals for the State of Florida.)

Even without such a criminal indictment from the state attorney's office, the political manhunt remained in full swing and no prisoners would be taken. Prosecutor Ken Oertel would zealously prosecute the administrative charges and seek an adjudication that Lerro was incompetent, grossly negligent and needed to be forever barred from the piloting profession. He asserted that John had ignored weather warnings issued that morning by the National Weather Service and that he had intentionally navigated the freighter blindly through Tampa Bay during a hellacious storm. Worse, the prosecution contended, when the visibility cleared a bit from the storm and Lerro saw that the ship was on a direct course for the bridge, he did nothing to avoid the collision. Oertel said that "Captain Lerro took unnecessary risks and as a result of those risks, the collision occurred." As a matter of fact, "gross" negligence was the term Oertel used, but the only thing I saw "gross" was his suggestion that John plead guilty, voluntarily surrender his pilot's license permanently and, in effect, be thrown to the "mercy" of the innumerable wolves howling and tearing at the door.

Throughout the summer before the trial, most of the world had already decided that John was guilty of murdering thirty-five people by ramming the *Summit Venture* into the Sunshine Skyway, and here I was defending him. The only thing I could do was let 'em talk. I believed in John, and I was convinced there was something more to the story than the public outcry that he was incompetent or worse.

Finally, five months after the collision and the tragic collapse of the Skyway, the week of trial came. As John and I settled into our chairs in the courtroom waiting for the proceedings to begin, a bailiff moved quietly behind me and tapped my shoulder lightly. "Mr. Yerrid," he said in a hushed voice, "there is a man outside who wants to see you. His name is Arthur Goodale. Says it's important to your case. He wants to talk to you before the case begins. Says it's urgent."

Intrigued, I quickly excused myself and walked out into the hall.

"Mr. Yerrid," Goodale said as he moved toward me to shake my hand, "I'm Art Goodale. We need to talk, and you need to listen, and listen well."

"Okay, but I can only give you a minute or two. I'm sure you understand that I'm sort of busy right now," I answered as I quickly appraised him. Goodale was in his late sixties and around six feet tall; his gray hair framed an intelligent face, and the weathered creases and wrinkles of his tanned features suggested a lifetime of work outdoors.

The gentleman began to speak in a hurried voice. "Let's just say you're on the *Summit Venture*, with Mr. Lerro at the helm. You have been blown off course during the storm as you come up the bay. Picture the ship as you hit that southbound pier with a glancing blow. The pier collapses, sending not only those cars and trucks off of the bridge, but chunks—huge chunks—of the Skyway to the water below." Art Goodale paused for a moment, took a deep breath, and then continued, "I'm telling you, Mr. Yerrid, the Sunshine Skyway Bridge was so deficient that it wasn't John Lerro's ship that collapsed the bridge. There was a reason the *bridge* couldn't take a blow to that effect."

"What are you talking about, Mr. Goodale?" I asked, incredulous but acutely aware that I had to get back to the courtroom and John Lerro.

He quickly glanced around the empty hallway before answering. "I'm a civil engineer, and I was the general superintendent of the original northbound span of the Skyway when it was first built years ago. When the sister bridge was built right beside mine, the original blueprints were used, but the construction was bad. I was busy building the Baltimore tunnel at the time of the newer span's construction, but I tell you that I know what I'm talking about."

The intensity I saw in his eyes told me he believed strongly in every word he said. He continued, "During that time, the Brooksville area north of here was mining the material for the concrete for the bridge. The mines were depleted to the point that there were deficiencies in the material used to make the concrete. Bad lime rock was used to make that concrete. The lime rock goes into the concrete, along with sand, stone, water, and rock. That mixture, every component of it, all of it, has to be good. There can't be a deficient portion in it because one ingredient complements the other. In other words, the sand is covered with cement, and the rock is covered with cement. The lime rock was not good! As to the main pier on the south side, the one that the superstructure fell through…well, rather than adhere to the design as made by the original contractor, corners were cut. That was wrong, Mr. Yerrid. That crazy bridge was coming apart before Mr. Lerro even hit it. The force of that impact should have never caused that bridge to fall. It crumbled and fell apart because it wasn't built right and the State of Florida knew it."

"So, what you are saying, Mr. Goodale, is simply that the bridge should never have fallen?" I asked, looking nervously at my watch.

"The blow might have sunk the ship by punching a huge hole into the ship. The ship would have taken on water, because it was empty. The bridge would have been damaged, knocked out of line even, but it certainly should have withstood the force of the collision. It would have been jarred by the impact, but it would never have fallen if it had been constructed properly. You've got to listen to me. The builders bypassed the actual soundings—the borings—just to save time and money, and changes were made. Instead of putting pilings down to the original first bridge strata, the hard strata, the state's contractors used a different sort of piling and they shortened them up. In turn, when a load of concrete was put on, it depressed the strata and the pier settled. This pier, when it settled, settled on one end. So, the bolts and everything that held the superstructure up were not in the same location when it finally came to rest; all of the supports moved over. In the middle of construction, the state had to take the structural steel and send it away to have new bearings put on it so it would fit. And actually, there were nine thousand yards of concrete that couldn't be straightened up. When the ship hit the pier, it shook it enough to shift the superstructure in the direction that hadn't settled, toward the north. That's the end of the pier that *hadn't* settled, and that's exactly why the Skyway collapsed."

"Mr. Goodale," I said forcefully. "I must leave now. What you have told me is interesting—"

"I have proof!" the gentleman announced as I turned to go back into the courtroom. "I have confirmation of everything! John Lerro is not responsible for this bridge falling! The State of Florida is going after him only to cover up those deficiencies in the bridge! You have to listen, I have all the documents, and I can show you all the calculations!"

My hand pushed at the door of the courtroom as I glanced back at him once more and said, "Call me later, Mr. Goodale, and we'll talk. Right now, I have to get back in there." I left him standing there in the brightness of the hallway lights, but his haunting accusations stayed with me. I had a sickening feeling every single thing he told me just might be the damned truth—but I knew I couldn't use a word. What happened after the *Summit Venture* struck the Skyway had nothing to do with the case I had to try. The trial was about Lerro's guilt or innocence in the *Summit Venture's* collision with the bridge, not what happened after the bridge was struck. If there was a greater irony, I had not seen it.

Back in the courtroom, with Goodale's words gnawing at my gut, the proceedings began. The entire group of spectators in the packed courtroom stood up when the judge entered, signaling that it was showtime.

The prosecutor's opening remarks were scalding. "We will prove by the greater weight of evidence that Captain John E. Lerro, a relatively inexperienced harbor pilot, overextended his limited abilities and with willful disregard for life and property, ignoring every prudent aspect of his profession and training, caused this calamity to occur and grossly violated our public trust. Further, we will show that Captain Lerro is solely, individually, and unredeemably responsible for this disaster. The bridge was struck. The ship was navigated in a blinding storm with zero visibility, under conditions when radar was inoperable." The condemnation was intense and unrelenting as the next twenty minutes dragged by.

My opening response was brief and to the point. "Our case is very simple. We will prove that John Lerro exercised judgment, professional skill of the highest order, and demonstrated great human concern in the face of a situation that no other human being, let alone he, could have possibly prevented. That he failed is known, but that *he failed at his very best* is not known. Nor is it known against what force he failed. Or why. Those questions will be answered here. That is our only purpose. We will prove this tragedy was caused by an Act of God and that no human action could have altered or changed the course of events."

One of the first witnesses during the trial was Captain Ernest Clothier, a retired harbor pilot who had been hired by the Department of Professional Regulation as a piloting consultant. He was the prosecution's key expert witness, and his credentials were excellent. He was a graduate of the New York State Merchant Marine Academy and had served as president of the American Pilots Association and the International Pilots Association, groups whose memberships comprised virtually all the licensed pilots in the world. Captain Clothier had testified numerous times as an expert on piloting; but our investigation revealed the amazing fact that he had never piloted a ship through the waters of Tampa Bay. I made sure we checked and rechecked that critically important point. It was his Achilles heel, and would provide invaluable ammunition for my cross-examination.

His testimony began with the prosecutor detailing Captain Clothier's extensive credentials. After establishing his expertise in maritime pilot matters, Oertel asked the key question: "Captain Clothier, can you give me your opinion as to whether, from the point of two-tenths of a mile, approaching Buoy 2A, to the time the *Summit Venture* struck the Skyway Bridge, whether it was navigated in a professional and prudent manner?"

"I don't think the turn was made properly in the beginning," Captain Clothier said as he gazed directly into the jammed gallery of spectators. His eyes stopped on the television camera that was operating as the pool broadcast for all of the network stations as he continued. "I think, under the circumstances, if he, Captain Lerro, was in a position that I think he was, that he had to steer without the aid of a radar. In other words, he was steering courses and distances. In my opinion, I think he should have gone around in a more sharper fashion and brought the ship around to the next course immediately, or as soon as possible. He acted negligently and irresponsibly, and his conduct resulted in this maritime casualty."

The questioning wore on, and Oertel did everything in his power to wound our defense. Finally, the direct testimony and the spoon-fed character assassination finished. It was my turn. On cross-examination, I made my words penetrating, like the thrusts of a knife. "Can you think of a person better qualified than John Lerro to become a Tampa Bay pilot?"

"As I understand it, when John Lerro applied to be a pilot, he came with credentials that were flawless," Clothier replied.

"Flawless," I answered, and then paused for a beat before going on. "You don't think he's incompetent, do you, sir?"

"I didn't say he was." Clothier's look had the tiniest hint of indignation to it. The approach and direction seemed to take him off guard.

"You don't think he's mentally impaired, do you, sir?"

"I never said that, either," Clothier responded hastily. At the same time, I could see his eyes dart to those sitting at the prosecution table. The broad, damning brushstrokes of the prosecutor's allegations were not his words, and he certainly didn't want ownership of such drastic condemnation.

Encouraged, I pressed on. But as I did so, I left the podium and walked halfway to the witness stand. Moving laterally, I made sure I blocked the view between his seat and the table where the prosecutors sat. There would be no visual help from them. I became even more insistent in my line of questioning. "Don't you think in a situation like this, there are a lot of opinions?" At once, Art Goodale's words—his opinions—traced across my mind in quick flashes: *corners were cut...deficient lime rock...Lerro not responsible.*

"Certainly," Captain Clothier stated as his eyes flashed and his face flushed in exasperation.

Immediately, I pushed Goodale's words aside as I said, "And you would agree those opinions are often reached after you spend hours in a diagram room and chart rooms, and you map it out and say, 'Well, he could have stopped twenty feet short of that bridge.'"

"That's the case in every accident."

"That's what is called nautical hindsight, isn't it?"

"It's also called Monday morning quarterbacking."

Interesting term he used, I thought. Anyone could give an opinion, and everyone has them, calling the shots after the fact, including Captain Clothier. My tone was crisp, almost angry, when I asked him simply, "That's exactly what you're doing, isn't it, Captain?"

"Correct."

His words had come without pause and the admission had been overwhelming. I wanted to freeze the moment. In a courtroom, it was as good at it gets. I turned to the judge. "I have nothing else."

While there were many who may have thought that John Lerro suffered from some sort of "mental impairment," very few would take the stand and say as much. Captain Clothier would not brand a fellow pilot as a mental cripple, and I had counted on that. The prosecution team had continuously spun that notion and seemed convinced John had mental deficiencies. The prosecutors had wasted no words with the media in making that point time after time. As the allegations were repeated and printed many times over by the media, there seemed to be an endless list of those who assumed John's thinking process had been impaired when the accident occurred. The time had finally come to lay those rumors to rest, as I called Dr. Robert M. Wooten to the stand. (Because of the complexity of the case and the array of both expert and lay witnesses presented by both sides, the usual order of protocol had been discarded. The prosecution and Lerro's defense each interrupted the presentation of the case as various witnesses became available or arrived in town.)

Dr. Wooten was a graduate of the University of North Carolina, where he had obtained his medical degree. Following medical school, he served his internship at the University of Kentucky Hospital in Lexington, and then returned to the University of North Carolina where he taught for two years in the medical school. Soon after, he completed a three-year residency in psychiatry and became board certified in psychiatry and neurology. He was a leading psychiatrist at the nationally renowned Watson Clinic, located in nearby Lakeland, Florida.

I had asked Dr. Wooten, with his exemplary qualifications, to examine John and formulate an opinion about his emotional state at the time of the accident. I also wanted his views as to whether or not John's capacity to think rationally was, in any way, impaired on the date of the tragedy.

Dr. Wooten would be my first witness. He was a practiced expert witness. He would listen patiently after each inquiry I made, pause upon the completion of the question, and then redirect his total attention to the judge. During the most critical parts of his testimony, Dr. Wooten spoke in a slow and deliberate tone. "I felt Captain Lerro was handling this as well as he could under the circumstances," he responded to my line of questioning. "I talked with Captain Lerro extensively about his life, about his past history, his upbringing, his professional career, and his activities in general prior to the accident. It is my opinion that up to the point of this tragedy, John Lerro had functioned well in his capacity as a person, a seaman, and as a harbor pilot. I think of particular importance to me was the fact that being a pilot was of great value to him. He took great pride in doing this."

Dr. Wooten continued, "He also is one of the more candid individuals whom I have run into, and never in our conversations did he attempt to dissimulate or whitewash or rationalize. I think he is exceptionally clear on his ideas about himself and his abilities. I think that he is perhaps a little more credible than the average individual; he's also very blunt. And, as I said, I think that he derived a great deal of satisfaction from his profession and possessed great pride in his proven expertise in being an outstanding pilot. In talking with him, I did not feel that he is a person who would make snap decisions, for example. I think that he always tries to make decisions on the basis of as much information as possible, when that is possible. But particularly, I did not feel that there was any evidence of any underlying emotional disorder that might have impaired him either emotionally or intellectually. As I said, this was only an opinion and some-times it is important to have data to back this up; and because of this, I then took the liberty of referring him to Dr. Leonard Dee, who is a clinical psychologist, for extensive testing and workup. This was carried out, and Dr. Dee's opinions and test results essentially confirmed my opinion."

"And with particular respect to his intellect," I began as I moved directly in front of the witness chair, "was he found to be of high intel-lectual ability?"

Dr. Wooten answered immediately, "Dr. Dee found him to be of above average intelligence, and this was supported, without exception, by all of the objective evaluations. And, as I said, John Lerro is an analytical sort of individual. There was absolutely no evidence of any disruption of his thought processes or mental impairment. He is a logical thinker and there's no evidence to assume that he was not in the past. He still remains a logical thinker."

I took a deliberate and prolonged pause, made eye contact with the judge, and then looked at John Lerro before I asked Dr. Wooten my last question. "Then I'm safe to assume that not only today is he a logical thinker, capable of making rational decisions under difficult circumstances, but on May 9, this man sitting in this chair"—and I pointed at John—"could have made a rational decision under tremendous pressure. Is that correct?"

"That is my medical opinion, substantiated by the psychological tests and all of our clinical evaluations and examinations," the psychiatrist answered.

Witness by witness, the swell of favorable testimony began to build. Circuit Court Judge Mark McGarry, a well-known trial judge who sat on the bench of the Sixth Judicial Circuit, St. Petersburg, Florida, traded his familiar bench for the witness stand. Judge McGarry, a delightful gentleman in the courtroom or out, had been at Fort DeSoto Park during the storm. The broken remains of the once-proud Civil War fortress were located just across Tampa Bay from the Sunshine Skyway. Its ancient ramparts and elevated artillery positions bring thousands of tourists to the historic site each year. Because it contains a campground and recreational vehicle park and is surrounded by crystal clear water full of speckled trout, snook, and redfish, residents and local fishermen make sure the place is always crowded. Judge McGarry and his wife had parked their own trailer there as a weekend getaway. I would use McGarry's testimony to help demonstrate that the wind's direction had changed at a critical moment.

Judge McGarry sat straight and tall in the witness chair as I moved in front of him and began to speak. "Sir, how did the circumstances prevail that you came to be a witness in this case?"

"Well, there have been great differences heard and read about the case," he began earnestly. "I know the importance of opinions about the weather that day, and I know the importance of actual eyewitnesses. So, I called you. I telephoned to let you know that I was there that awful morning and I know exactly what the weather did. I needed to step forward, and so, I have."

"And that's because I understand you were involved in the storm that took place on May 9, 1980?" I asked, smiling at his answer.

"Yes, sir. I was at Fort DeSoto at the time."

"I don't often have a chance to have a judge as a witness, so I'll try to be especially polite. Can you tell us briefly the events that transpired that morning?"

Judge McGarry shifted in his chair, making himself more comfortable. "Well, yes, sir. My wife and I had taken our trailer out there Thursday evening, the night before the storm. Fort DeSoto is a splendid park, and we often go there for long weekends. We have a big trailer, thirty-one foot Avion, and it was parked in a direction of approximately 330 degrees. I woke up about seven in the morning, and it was raining. I was concerned about the storm, but not so much immediately that I thought it was necessary to go pull my awning in for purposes of protection. But as the wind began to gather force, the trailer began to shake in a fashion that was quite unusual, as far as I was concerned. So I thought, 'Well, I'll make the effort to rescue the awning,' which has withstood every storm that it's been in before. When I went to step outside, I felt a great resistance just to get the door open. I put my hand on the trailer awning bar to roll it up, and a gust of wind hit that was so strong that it picked up the awning *and me* off the ground. Fortunately, I had the presence of mind to let go. The awning went over the top of the trailer, pulling it out from the sides of the trailer, tearing the rivets loose and flying almost straight up. I ended up being deposited on the ground. I abandoned any thoughts of saving my awning and thought about saving myself. I made it back in the trailer only after I managed to pry the door open. It was lined up in such a fashion that the wind was holding it shut."

Our best chance was here. If we were going to prove a radical change in wind direction, it was with this witness. Earlier in the trial, from the weather records and other evidence, it had been demonstrated that the prevailing direction of the wind was from the south, 180 degrees.

That was the reason Lerro had oversteered to the south—as a compensation for the wind's effect on the ship. McGarry's testimony demonstrated the critical change in direction. "Could you expound on that a little bit?" I asked. "You said your trailer was parked at 330 degrees?"

"The way we were parked out there, it just happened to be lined up in that direction."

"What direction on a compass heading would that be? Northwest?"

"It would be northwest, a northwest heading. I have a Hobie Cat out there, and it had a wind direction vane on it that I happened to notice at the time when I looked out over the water, because it was fascinating. The bay, the water, was such a series of whitecaps and windblown waves that, well, I have never seen anything like it before. So I did make notice of that. It was strange that it would come with such intensity and for such a length of time, that it would be blowing in what I would consider very strong gusts, extremely powerful gusts broken by lulls of calm. Very unusual. Like I said, I have never seen anything like it before. That's why I made a point of telling several people what I had seen and experienced. I remarked to my wife that the storm was quite a nasty one, and that was before I found out there had been any accident at the Skyway."

"Let me ask you something, Judge, and I feel strange calling you Judge. I feel like I should call you Your Honor, but…"

"Don't apologize, son." His words were kind and reassuring.

"I'm well aware of what a trial judge goes through in the daily rituals of his practice, and I would ask you, many times you're faced with lay witnesses opining as to distances, times, wind velocity, or whatever, but in your mind…how old are you, sir?"

"Fifty-one."

"Fifty-one. You've become pretty objective, I imagine, because of your profession. Can you tell us about how intense you felt that storm was in your own words?"

"I can tell you that it was the most intense I have ever stood out in, and I have lived in Florida for fifty years. I have stood out in hurricanes before, and I have never felt wind any stronger than that particular wind."

"I have nothing further. Captain Lerro thanks you."

There were no sweeter words spoken than those of Judge McGarry.

The direction of the wind and its suddenness and extreme intensity were critical to our defense. The prosecution team had its hands full. We had scored big and everyone in the courtroom knew it.

Ken Oertel then stepped up to the podium and began the cross-examination of Judge McGarry. "How do you know which compass heading you were parked at—facing?"

"Well," Judge McGarry started, "I have camped out there many times, and it seems that when my wife and I sit out in the evening and enjoy the scenery, we always make note of the North Star, which always seems to be in the same place."

"I couldn't figure that out, either," Oertel replied. Whether or not his comment was blatant sarcasm or an attempt at humor, it was terribly out of place. The somber look of Judge McGarry and his unfazed demeanor emphasized the awkwardness of the prosecutor's first salvo.

The tenseness was broken by Judge McGarry himself. "Well, it is. The direction of the North Star would be such that I was able to judge the direction of the wind and the direction of my trailer was approximately 330 degrees."

"I see. Was this the driver's side you stepped out of?"

"Well, it's the only door in the trailer…it's not a motor vehicle; it's a trailer. It doesn't have a motor in it."

"The door was on the left-hand side that you stepped out of?" Oertel asked.

"It was on the right-hand side, I would think. It was on the westerly side of the trailer."

"And the trailer was facing 30 degrees north of due north—well, 30 degrees off due north, 330 degrees—30 degrees off 360?"

Judge McGarry was diplomatic and well-mannered in his answer. "Right, sir."

"And the wind, you say, was keeping the door shut?" The transcript would never show it, but the facial expression of Oertel reflected disbelief and an incredulous half-smile.

Judge McGarry was unbreakable, though, as he replied, "Yes, sir, it was blowing that hard."

"So the wind was coming from about due west?"

"No, sir," the judge answered emphatically. "The wind was coming out of 330 degrees. The trailer was lined up in that direction, and the door opened into the wind, which is awkward. I have always thought that was poor positioning of a door, because if you're driving down the road, if it opens, it slams clear against the side of the trailer. It's just a very poor position of the door. Of course, in this particular instance, if I'd opened it, it could have torn it up that way, too."

"So the wind was coming straight on to your…"

"Right on to the rear of the trailer."

"How far away did you step away from the trailer during this period of time?"

"Oh, no more than ten feet."

"Ten feet," Oertel said firmly. "How far back from the front were you?"

"I was about in the middle of the trailer. Of course, I was moving about some, and I'd put on my rain gear before I stepped out, which was totally useless, as it turned out, and…"

Oertel interrupted before Judge McGarry could complete his sentence. "You really can't be sure of the wind's speed or strength, can you? I mean, you are not familiar with the effect of an air current passing around a solid object? Correct?"

"No, that is not correct," the judge said sternly as he looked directly at Oertel. "I have owned an airplane and had a pilot's license for thirty years. I'm fairly familiar with it."

"So you know that when a current of air is passing around an obstruction, the air gets compressed closer to the sides of the object?"

"I'm not so sure that I agree with that, but if you say so."

Oertel kept up the banter, hoping the witness would falter. "Well, at certain points in its transit, it does get compressed and actually travels faster than it would in an unobstructed passage. You understand that, don't you?"

Several more self-proclaiming questions were hurled before I stood up and faced the presiding judge. "I object, Your Honor. The prosecutor is not asking questions; he's testifying. This may be cross-examination, but it's not supposed to be a testimonial."

"The point has been made," the judicial hearing officer started.

"Actually, Judge McGarry, I suspect, can testify that air perhaps travels faster in the upper surface of a plane than it does on the lower surface on an airplane."

Judge McGarry answered directly. "It does to a certain extent. That may not be the question." Whatever hope the prosecutor had of shaking this witness had long since faded. On the critical estimates of the wind's change in direction and bruteness of force, he had been unflappable. We had established the suddenness of the wind change and its new direction through a damned trailer, an airplane pilot...and one hell of a stroke of good fortune.

"It seems you're besieged by pilots, Mr. Oertel," the hearing officer said with a smile.

Oertel was confused by the comment. "Pardon?" he asked as he glanced from the hearing officer to Judge McGarry.

"You're besieged by pilots on all sides," the hearing officer repeated.

"I know...I know. Thank you, Your Honor. No further questions," Oertel said. The prosecution had conceded the witness, and Judge McGarry's testimony had been pivotal. Judge McGarry had been honest and forthright. Additionally, his expertise as an avid airplane pilot had been an unexpected windfall. Not only was he an eyewitness, but he also possessed extensive technical expertise. The tumblers of everything good were falling into place.

The backdrop of what happened the morning of May 9, 1980, had been set. The storm, with its furious intensity, had lashed out on the *Summit Venture* in an unexpected manner, just as it had lashed out on Judge McGarry's small corner of real estate at Fort DeSoto. In fact, the radical change in the wind's direction had been *dramatically* established.

Our success in eliciting the critical evidence of the storm's violence and strength continued through the next several witnesses. John gained confidence as the storm's existence was singled out from the "lineup" of mysteries surrounding the bridge's collapse. On the other hand, my satisfaction concerning that proof was being quickly replaced by anxiety. The prosecution had one last place to set a deadly trap. Having decisively established the forceful evidence that the storm had actually existed, we figured that the prosecution's attack would be refocused on the recklessness of John Lerro in piloting the huge freighter in the face of "known" severe weather.

When it finally came, the anticipated assault was brutal and direct. The prosecution argued through a number of witnesses that only a madman would have sailed the massive ship into port under those conditions. According to the prosecution, having been "warned" of the terrible risk, Lerro should be held harshly accountable for disregarding safety and the fundamentals of navigation. The prosecution team had been poised to spring its trap. By our own success in establishing the terrible weather that drove the ship into the Skyway, we had actually set the stage for the final attack on Lerro. The charge was simple: Captain Lerro had sailed blindly under severe weather conditions and ignored the weather warnings issued to prevent the very tragedy that had occurred.

Initially, the prosecution had rejected the whole idea that such bad weather had even existed. Before the proceedings were halfway through, however, the evidence overwhelmingly demonstrated an undeniably strong, violent—and very sudden—storm. The prosecution had lost the battle to persuade the court—and the world—that there was no storm to cause the catastrophe. The prosecutorial fallback position would focus on Lerro's disregard of its dangers. The state's case would hinge on another of its key expert witnesses, William H. Haggard.

Haggard was a nationally known meteorologist who operated the Climatological Consulting Corporation in Asheville, North Carolina, which, he stated, was a "consulting firm that specializes in weather analysis and testimony." He formed the corporation in 1976, after retiring from National Weather Record Center—now the National Climatic Center— in December of 1975. He was a recognized authority who spoke on behalf of the National Weather Service. Haggard had been brought in to first refute the severity of the storm, and then take the position that even if it existed, adequate warnings had been given and the weather should never have been transited.

Bill Haggard was based in Asheville, and from the outset, he made a point of asserting that his presence in Asheville—rather than in Tampa— during the storm was not a "handicap" to the forensic investigation he had conducted. On direct examination, he sought to dismiss the issue by stating, "One must have some familiarity with the geography of the area they're concerned with, but the basic weather file is maintained in the National Climatic Center in Asheville, North Carolina, and that resource was particularly available to me in that area." In other words, even though he was a thousand miles away from the storm and relying on records kept in Asheville, not Tampa, his opinions were supposedly sound. The prosecutor emphasized through Haggard's testimony that warnings were issued at 4:39 a.m. on the day of the storm, and a severe weather warning had in fact been subsequently issued, he said, "on the morning of May 9."

Oertel specifically asked Haggard what type of information was given about that particular weather system. Haggard's voice was confident as he answered, "Well, starting at 3:30 a.m., the radar summary statements specifically tracked this line of thunderstorms as they came across the eastern Gulf, and at 3:30 a.m., the radar data—through a special radar summary—was issued for the Tampa Bay area and read, 'at 3:30 a.m., scattered thunderstorms were moving onshore near Cedar Key in Levy and Citrus Counties in western Florida. Local heavy rain, strong gusty wind, and frequent lightning can be expected with these thunderstorms for the next few hours. For marine interests, locally rough seas can be expected near these thunderstorms. Showers and thundershowers extended west and southwest into the Gulf for 150 miles. Moving west to east at thirty-five miles per hour.' At 4:30, there was an update of this."

After a quick shuffle of papers, Haggard began speaking again. "At 4:30 a.m., scattered showers and thundershowers, some very heavy, mixed with rain, continued to develop from Inverness to Cross City and extended west and southwest over the Gulf for more than two hundred miles. These showers were moving east at about thirty-five miles per hour. At 5:30 a.m., a large area of light rain and a few heavy thundershowers continued to spread across the north central part of the state from St. Augustine to Daytona Beach on the east coast to Cross City and Bayport on the west coast, and then southwest over the Gulf for more than 150 miles. Movement to the east at more than thirty-five miles per hour. And at 6:30 a.m....at 6:30 a.m., scattered showers and a few very heavy thunderstorms were imbedded in a large area of rain that stretched across the state from St. Augustine and Titusville to St. Petersburg and Cross

City. Then west and southwest into the Gulf for one hundred miles. Movement was to the east at thirty-five miles per hour. These continued at 8:30, 9:30, and so on through the day."

"Now," Oertel continued, "with regard to those radar summaries, those were what you were just reading, I believe?"

"Yes."

"Can you tell me how they were broadcast?" Oertel asked.

"They were transmitted on the NOAA Weather Wire and they were broadcast on the NOAA Weather Radio. They were available to commercial stations; which carried them, I'm not sure...[The NOAA Weather Wire] is a teletype circuit that NOAA, National Oceanic and Atmospheric Administration, uses to disseminate weather information, and this weather information is carried into a city such as Tampa. And then drops on that wire can be subscribed to by individuals or concerns, radio stations, organizations—whoever has an interest in acquiring weather data on a continuing basis."

After a few more questions, Oertel brought his best heat. "Do you have any opinion as to the intensity of the storm itself?"

"Yes," Haggard answered. "There were some cells—the majority of the cells were level two or level three in the radar scale. There were a few cells at scattered points along the line that reached level four."

Oertel glanced at the hearing officer, and then back at Haggard. "All right. Then assuming we're talking about the possibility at least of a level four storm, were there any greater cells that you detected?"

"Than level four?" Haggard answered with a question, and then said decisively, "Nothing. Not that crossed Tampa Bay. No, sir."

"Okay. Do you have any opinion as to what the prevailing wind would have been from a level four storm in this squall line?"

Haggard responded, "The prevailing wind, the sustained wind during the passage of the squall was generally in the range of thirty to thirty-five knots...thirty to thirty-five knots with gusts to forty or forty-five...these are short-time excursions in the speed of wind...a typical gust would be in the order of five to ten seconds in duration, though they may come quite frequently."

I had listened carefully to Haggard's answers. I began the cross-examination by requiring him to again read aloud the exact wording of the 4:39 a.m. warning. "All right. I said, at 3:30 a.m., Eastern Daylight Time on May 9, a radar summary, special weather statement was issued for the Tampa Bay area. It read, 'At 3:30 a.m., scattered thunderstorms were moving onshore near Cedar Key in Levy and Citrus Counties in western Florida. Local heavy rain, strong gusty wind, and frequent lightning can be expected with these thunderstorms for the next few hours. For marine interests, locally rough seas can be expected near these thunderstorms. Showers and thundershowers extended west and southwest into the Gulf for 150 miles. Moving west to east at thirty-five miles per hour.'"

We had all of that, sure, but it was time for me to pounce on Mr. Haggard. "These were pretty bad storms, is that right?"

"There were some very heavy thunderstorms in this, yes, sir," he answered without looking at anyone but me.

"How would you classify fifty-knot winds as a meteorologist? Would you classify that as extremely heavy, extremely strong?"

"It's a strong wind. It was not . . ." he started.

My words cut off his answer. "What would be an extremely strong wind, sir?"

His reply was short. "Over seventy-five."

"Would that be a hurricane?" I asked, already knowing the answer.

"Yes, sir."

"What's a gale?"

"Thirty-five to forty some knots."

"Okay. What does it start becoming classified at fifty knots? What's a fifty-knot wind?"

"Storm."

I was now in full pursuit of the witness. "Somewhere between gale and hurricane?"

"Yes."

"You'd consider a gale a strong storm, wouldn't you?"

"Not...I wouldn't consider a gale a storm. No, sir. In the technical terminology."

"Have you been in the broadcasting business?"

"No, sir."

"Are you familiar with broadcasting to the general public?"

"Yes, sir."

"Are you familiar with broadcasting to mariners?"

"Yes, sir."

The time came for me to lock and load and take my shots. "Well, then, you must be familiar with the fact that an aviation terminal forecast would not be directed toward mariners, would it, sir?" I didn't wait for an answer, although I heard him mumble, "That's correct," as the next question was already racing from my mouth. "A mariner would not be expected to know what an aviation forecast was reading at any particular time, would he?"

"It would be available to him if he chose to…"

I interrupted him abruptly, "*If* he had a Telex out on the ship, or *if* he could get it from the air, or *if* he was monitoring an air channel?"

"Yes, sir."

"You wouldn't expect a mariner to be monitoring constantly an air channel, would you, sir?" Haggard sat there indignantly, ignoring my question. "Do you understand my question?" I asked forcefully.

"I understand your question! It was available, whether it was monitored or not!" The loudness of the exchange had escalated far beyond normal levels and the face of the witness was turning a bright, almost beet red.

Haggard was obviously angry and becoming increasingly frustrated, but that did not matter to me. I pressed on. "If you got these types of information that you've been asked to read and you have read, would you expect some subsequent actions as far as issuing a radar watch—I mean, excuse me—a bad weather watch? I don't know your terminology or…"

"Severe weather warning or severe weather watch?" He interrupted pointedly, the color in his face beginning to return to normal, but still flushed a dark pink.

"Yes," I answered, "something like that, a marine warning, something like that…"

"These would ordinarily be issued if there was an expectancy of very high winds or of hail associated with it. The severe weather watch and severe weather warning are issued when damaging winds, heavy hail, or the potential for dangerous weather is expected. This storm was not of that severity and such were not issued."

In my mind, I could hear the *pound pound pound* of the hammer smashing the nail on its head, and there I was, loving every second of Haggard's testimony. "So," I asked, mentally listening to the hammer as it went up and down, up and down, "in your opinion, this storm really wasn't significant enough to merit a severe weather warning?"

Like a frustrated teacher to the slowest of students, he suppressed a sigh as he answered the question curtly, "It did not have the ingredients that would qualify it for such a warning."

After a few more questions, I asked, "Would you expect a warning of some type to be issued under those conditions?"

"With a forty-knot wind?"

"Yes."

"Not ordinarily, no, sir."

The questioning wore on, and now was the time, the moment I had been waiting for. With deliberate slowness, I launched my final assault on the prosecution's case. "It seems we've got a situation where an individual allegedly took a ship toward a bridge without ascertaining the weather conditions insofar as the particular authorities were concerned, particularly the federal government and the weather service and what not. But yet, it's your opinion that there wouldn't have been any such warnings on that day. Is that right?"

His forehead pinched in confusion. "I don't understand the question, sir."

"You wouldn't expect a mariner to really be concerned with any of these warnings, take note of them, change his action, stop his navigational intent, because of these types of warnings, would you?"

"It would depend on what his operation was."

"If he was operating a 608-foot bulk carrier through Tampa Bay!" I nearly shouted the words.

Haggard responded as if he didn't understand the question or the significance of the point just made. "I would think that he would be concerned about the severity of the rainfall and the strength of the wind."

Finally, I finished the assault. "John Lerro couldn't very well ignore

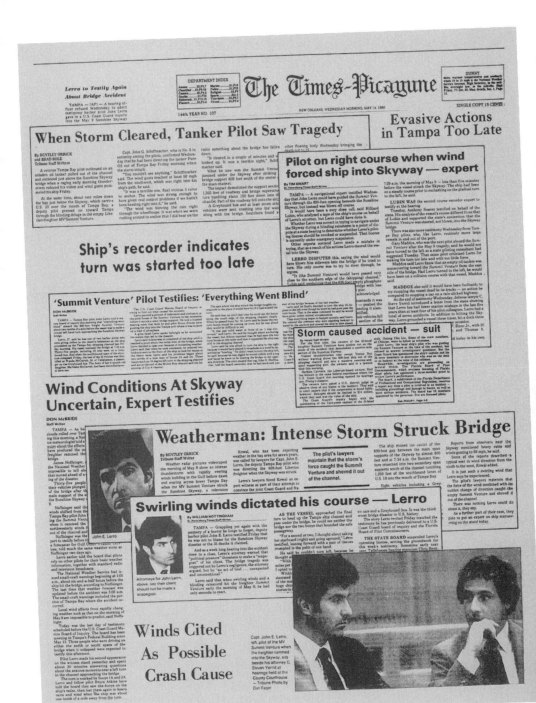

weather warnings that were never issued, could he?"

A long sigh escaped Haggard's lips as he looked down at his hands. When he glanced back up at me, I said simply, "I have nothing further with this witness."

By that time, Haggard looked exhausted and beaten. But the hearing officer had a final question of him. "Mr. Haggard, from your experience, and perhaps you can't, but from your experience, do you have an opinion you can share with us on whether this forecast of this squall line was a common forecast for the Tampa Bay area?"

Taking in a deep breath, Haggard answered, "The general weather forecast was not uncommon in its character. The details of the special radar summaries were sufficiently explicit to be, to point to an unusual event, to delineate the line of showers and their movement and the severity of the very heavy ones imbedded in it. If you were to turn on the NOAA weather radio today, however, the reading would be quite different than it was on this day."

But it wasn't over yet. To end our stellar day, we finished with the testimony of Bill Kowal, who was a well-known meteorologist with Channel 13, Tampa Bay's CBS affiliate. Unlike Haggard, Bill Kowal worked and lived in Tampa Bay, was a television regular, and had experienced the storm firsthand. There were Haggard's—and a thousand others'—suggestions that John had simply ignored reports of severe thunderstorm warnings issued on the morning of May 9. The prosecution keyed on the severity of the storm and disputed that any change at all had occurred in the wind direction.

In a profound and amazing stroke of good fortune, I had learned during preparation for the case that Channel 13 had been experimenting with a new radarscope; it was so advanced for the day that it could visually distinguish wind strengths by displaying different color patterns. Its palette of yellows, oranges, reds, and greens could be interpreted to determine the wind strengths shown on the scope. The fact that it could represent the wind's movement in terms of location as well as direction made this state-of-the-art meteorological innovation the latest and greatest equipment available. A time-lapse view available on printout was the final touch. Remember, this trial was in 1980. Today, Doppler radar is an everyday tool used on virtually all weather broadcasts.

I have found the adage that a picture is worth a thousand words to be absolutely true. We had brought the color photographs of the radarscope and a video still of the complete time sequence of the storm raging through the Gulf of Mexico as it tracked eastward and bore down on its victims at the Skyway. We were even able to produce a spectacular photograph of the radarscope image showing the killer storm sitting on top of the Skyway with the time of 7:32 a.m. imposed on the screen—the same time the *Summit Venture* was being blown into the bridge.

Kowal used his best television demeanor to narrate the photographs and videos of the storm as he described its crossing from the Gulf and explosion onto Florida's coast. As the "weather show" was going on in the courtroom, I would intersperse questions to the meteorologist. "What wind direction is being shown there, Mr. Kowal? As far as the Tampa Bay area is concerned?"

"Southwesterly at 7:00 a.m." That was just over half an hour from the impact of the *Summit Venture* with the Skyway.

"South by southwest?" I asked.

"I would say generally south—well, southwest it appears from the air streams," he answered, and then pointed and began again. "And here, it is plainly demonstrated that the wind direction has dramatically shifted shortly before 8:00 a.m."

"Is that almost a meeting between north and south wave vectors?"

"Here's the 7:00 a.m. vector, southerly winds represented over the Tampa Bay area south and southwest, then by eight o'clock, a marked directional shift."

"This appears to demonstrate an extreme and sudden change in wind direction," I said. "It looks to be mid-state, which would dissect Florida into two parts. Seemingly, the line cuts across the Tampa Bay area and it indicates different wind vectors from both sides of the line. Can you tell us what wind directions were designated in the 7:00 a.m. pictures and then what wind directions were designated in the 8:00 a.m. picture for the Tampa Bay area?"

"Certainly," he began in a matter of fact manner, perhaps not fully realizing the critical impact of his answer. "The flow is southwesterly over

Tampa at 7:00 a.m., and at 8:00 a.m., the winds had already shifted radically toward the west and northwest."

"So the shifting had to take place within that hour?" I asked, my body tensing as I realized he was verifying everything John Lerro had told me at the beginning of our long journey together.

"Yes, I would say so."

"That would be 7:00 a.m. to 8:00 a.m., on May 9, 1980?"

"That's right."

Kowal also noted in a series of photographs of the radar screen that a phenomenon called attenuation had occurred, which, he said, "is a situation when heavy rain comes over a radar site or over your focal point on the radar. It scatters the beam and this gives it a general appearance of the area of rain shrinking." He said that someone viewing the radar wouldn't be able to see areas of rain far to the south or far to the north, because the rain would be cutting out on the radar. In that particular storm, he pointed out, there was a tremendous amount of heavy rain. "And as a professional meteorologist," he added, "the *strange presentation* like this on radar would make me believe that was some sort of mesoscale small low-pressure development within the line or within the area of showers and thunderstorms was taking place."

He also stated that around the time of 7:30 on the morning of the storm, weather observers had recorded winds and gusts from forty to seventy miles per hour, with unconfirmed estimates even higher. Kowal

A radarscope image of the storm cell engulfing Tampa Bay as the *Summit Venture* approached the Sunshine Skyway Bridge.

related one observer even had the roof blown off part of his home and porch during that period of time. Another observer had described the winds as "hurricane force." I asked Kowal one last question. "To your knowledge, did the National Weather Service issue any severe warnings from the period of 6:00 a.m. to 8:00 a.m. on May 9, 1980?"

He answered succinctly, "To my knowledge, no."

The first severe weather warnings had come at 8:15 a.m., forty-one minutes *after* Captain Lerro's ship had hit the bridge…forty-one minutes after thirty-five motorists and passengers plunged to their deaths from the torn end of the Sunshine Skyway Bridge…forty-one minutes too late to save lives and the very nearly mortally wounded soul of John Lerro. It was a bittersweet and overwhelming realization.

We were nearing the end of the trial and we were still standing. The days of the courtroom battle had seemed endless, and the weeklong trial felt more like a month.

Because of my total focus and commitment, I rarely entertained thoughts of losing, and I always strove to give 110 percent. I figured when a courtroom loss came—and sooner or later, defeat comes to everyone—I could better tolerate the sickness and disappointment because I would know that I had done everything I could. Even if my best effort was not enough to prevail, to know that I could not have tried harder or given more was essential if I had to deal with losing.

I didn't know if it was the exertion, the strain of the case, or the enormity of the task, but as I drove home that night, for the first time since the case began I finally felt total and complete exhaustion. I fell into bed, turning on the alarm and wishing tomorrow would wait a while.

When I arrived at the office the next morning, the trial team had already assembled for the final day. Most of our trial papers, exhibits, and pleadings were already at the courthouse. Each day, we carried out only what was needed for that evening's preparation. On that morning, I would only bring three files under my arm. One of the witnesses for the early session was Professor Anthony Suarez, a recognized expert in the area of hydrodynamics, and the star expert the prosecution would call as the cleanup hitter in its grand finale.

In response, I had scheduled Hilliard Lubin. "Hilly," as he was called, was an international authority in the maritime community on the particular specialty of ascertaining the exact path of travel by vessels with devices known as course recorders. These tracking mechanisms installed aboard the more sophisticated and best-equipped ships used a needle to record an ink plotting of the actual course the vessel was making over the ground below the water's surface. Using time and distance markings, Hilly could utilize the data recorded by the instrument to determine almost exactly where the *Summit Venture* had been at any given point in time, regardless of the course steered, the engine speed, the water current or the wind direction.

The last witness called in the case would be John Lerro. The Friday afternoon session of the trial would be reserved for legal argument, motions, and final summation.

On the way out of our offices, I was handed a thick wad of phone messages. At that point, the number of pink-slipped "please call backs" was running in excess of a hundred a day. Mostly media, some witnesses, several concerning my non-Skyway legal practice, and a handful of personal calls. I sorted through the colored sheets and pulled out the personal calls. One of the pink slips was from my mother. She had called to say hello and wish me well. Mom's messages, when I was in trial, carried what she had always given me, which was her unconditional love and support.

Occasionally, Mom drove down to the courthouse and sat in as an unannounced spectator. Usually, though, she preferred to stay away and wait for me to recount the experiences in the familiarity of her living room. Faye "Missy" Yerrid had followed the same pattern during my athletic career. I think she believed her presence would cause me undue pressure. Deep down, I think she felt it might bring me bad luck. For whatever reason, I had enjoyed success and good fortune, and superstition encouraged us both to keep doing what we had been doing for so many years. I would call her back at the end of the long day ahead.

I went on to my next message. It was from my father, Charlie Yerrid. He had been living in Washington, D.C., for the past twenty years, working as a machinist for the *Washington Post*. The battle with the weather experts the day before must have drawn national attention, because my father had called to tell me that a photograph of Captain Lerro and me had run in the morning's *New York Times*. He sent his congratulations and love.

Suzanne Reed, my paralegal, began to gather the materials and the late-night work product we had prepared for the day's testimony as I hastily told her, "Make sure all of our trial exhibits are in order and marked. Also, please return all of the rest of the phone messages. Give the usual explanation: 'I'm in court and unable to call anyone back.' Call Mom and tell her my mug made the *Times,* and that I'll stop by her house after court and show her the newspaper. Call Dad and tell him I got his message…and tell him thanks. In the meantime, you had better order a few copies of the *New York Times*." Suzanne took the frenzied orders without hesitation. She had become an invaluable part of my trial practice and was accustomed to the pace and pressure of the fast lane. As I had ascended the ranks in the law firm and legal circles of Tampa, Suzanne had been at my side. She was one of the best paralegals I had ever seen, and I knew my instructions and anything else that needed to be done would be handled with the utmost care.

"Got it, Steve." Suzanne smiled and used a tone of voice that put me at ease. "Now, all you need to do is go in there and win." Her unconditional support and tireless enthusiasm gave me a jumpstart for the day that lay ahead.

The courtroom was packed. Not only were all of the seats taken, but also there wasn't even standing room. I said hello to a few familiar faces as I made my way to the counsel table through the jammed center aisle. The only island of space on the spectator side of the bar within the sea of people was the five-foot circumference that was roped off for the pool camera of the television networks.

Judge Chris Bentley entered the courtroom promptly at nine. The drama surrounding the Skyway had been going on for months and everyone sensed its conclusion. Judge Bentley looked intense and determined, and I knew that the last day of the trial was going to be serious business and high excitement.

Professor Suarez, the well-known maritime specialist hired by the prosecution, had been a recognized hydrodynamics expert for over forty years. Having taught at a number of prestigious universities, he specialized in maritime catastrophe and had appeared in courtrooms across the country to testify about the effects of wind and water upon vessel movement. I had taken his deposition a month before and discovered the essence of his testimony. His theory of the case was simple and straightforward. Captain Lerro, according to Suarez, had made a late turn in his approach to the Skyway Bridge. As a result, he concluded, the *Summit Venture* had been steered into the Skyway, not blown. And further, Suarez opined, the wind and rain had virtually no effect on the vessel's course and the entire disaster was attributable to human error, not an Act of God.

In the elaborate charts and exhibits the prosecution had prepared for the professor's deposition testimony, I had discovered a fundamental error. A huge timeline that demonstrated the sequence of events illustrated the entire course traveled by the *Summit Venture*. The eight-foot-long chart first listed the beginning of the activities of May 9, 1980, commencing with John boarding the ship. Points in time were then highlighted by dots, with drawn explanation lines describing the location of the vessel and the events transpiring at any particular instance. Every witness and the bridge logbook had consistently had the *Summit Venture* passing Green No. 16, a key navigational buoy several thousand yards from the bridge, at 7:23 a.m. The ship's speed of twelve knots was uncontested. The prosecution's chart had listed the last event of the timeline—the collision of the *Summit Venture* with the Skyway—*as occurring at 7:32 a.m., not 7:34 a.m.*, as we had established from the actual Coast Guard time and Coast Guard record of Lerro's Mayday transmission.

Oertel, Professor Suarez, and the entire prosecution team had picked up the time of collision as it had been erroneously described in the ship's log. Gradually working forward from the beginning of the *Summit Venture* transit, Professor Suarez had premised his opinions on correct times and locations except on the most critical of issues: the time of the collision! When the professor was called to the stand for his testimony at trial, I held my breath as I thought, *Please, God, please, let them bring the same chart.* I said a couple more prayers and shut my eyes for just a few quick seconds. The two young staff members of the prosecution team were setting up the charts on the tripods. In the center was my very favorite chart! The simple, terrible mistake was still there. I will never forget the rush of exhilaration that swept over me. I had them...

When the time for cross-examination came, I was able to embarrass the academic elitist quickly and efficiently. He was hanged by his own sophisticated approach. After several minutes of jousting, I cut to the chase. "Professor Suarez, I see from the time chart you have utilized in forming your expert opinions and testifying this morning that you have noted the *Summit Venture* passing Green Buoy No. 16 at 7:23 a.m., making a speed of twelve knots. Is that correct?"

"Yes, that is accurate," he replied in a professional voice. At seventy-plus years, Professor Suarez had a full head of white hair; black-rimmed spectacles fit his tanned and weathered face perfectly. He exuded confidence and was concise and deliberate in his answers.

"And the timeline has identified the point of the Skyway where the *Summit Venture* struck. Is that right?"

A good expert with years of experience, he was not going to pass up any opportunity to embellish and bolster the prosecution's case. "Yes, and as I understand it, both the bridge and the ship are to scale. The angle of the ship to the anchor pier at the time of the collision is also a hundred percent accurate."

"You mentioned 'the time of the collision,' sir," I pressed on. "Is it correct that virtually all of your assumptions, as well as your expert opinions, are based on the time of the collision at the bridge to be 7:32 a.m.?"

"Correct."

If Professor Suarez was concerned about where his testimony was headed, he sure as hell wasn't showing it. Could I be that wrong on the importance of the time? No, I was sure of myself. The sick surge of that thought was gone as quickly as it had come, and I asked, "Professor, did you ever hear the Mayday transmission recorded by the United States Coast Guard on the morning of May 9, 1980?"

In an unruffled voice, he answered, "Of course I have. I believe everyone has heard Captain Lerro's radio call by now."

"Are you aware the time of the radio transmissions received by the Coast Guard are independently recorded and logged?" I asked.

"I don't doubt it."

"Okay. I want you to assume the Mayday transmission of Captain Lerro occurred at 7:34 a.m., and not 7:32 a.m. I want you to also assume the transmission was made immediately after the time of the collision. That is, within five to ten seconds, sir. Assuming, therefore, that the time of the collision by the *Summit Venture* with the Sunshine Skyway Bridge was 7:34 a.m., wouldn't that make each and every one of your opinions and conclusions about what happened that morning *absolutely wrong?*" As I finished the question, I walked away from the podium and stood no more than five feet from the witness stand and awaited his answer.

The professor no longer seemed confident, and his brow was deeply wrinkled as he said, "I am not sure what you are getting at, Counselor." He sat stiffly and upright in his chair as he stared at me.

"Well, Professor, if the ship was traveling at twelve knots, and we all agree on that, it would be covering roughly twelve hundred feet per minute. At 7:32 a.m., and assuming one calculates time and distances from the last known point of Green Buoy No. 16 at 7:23 a.m., the ship would still be well over two thousand feet from the bridge at the time you opined the collision occurred. Simply put, you are two minutes and a couple of thousand feet off, aren't you? Your calculations compute a description of a marine casualty that could not physically happen. You've made a mistake, and the assumptions underlying all the testimony you have given here today are in error. Isn't that correct?"

Professor Suarez was angry, indignant, and embarrassed as he answered in an almost too loud voice, "I was told the collision happened at 7:32 a.m.! I didn't assume it! I *presumed* I was given accurate information. If the collision time was wrong, I didn't make that mistake, Counselor, someone else did." My work with this key witness was done. Even though it was clear there would be no more questions, the elderly gentleman sat unmoving. It was bizarre. He was staring down at the worksheets he had carried to the witness stand and just sitting there as if he was contemplating his next move.

Finally, Judge Bentley broke the awkward silence. "You may be excused, Professor Suarez."

Still, the old professor didn't move, nor did he look up at either the judge or me. Again, Judge Bentley spoke in a louder, firmer tone. "Professor, you are finished. You may step down." At last, the witness slowly gathered the papers spread before him. He stood up, and as he did, he buttoned his dark gray suit coat. Within a moment or two, he descended the three steps from the witness box, and then walked out of the courtroom without looking at anyone or saying another word.

"For the record," Judge Bentley continued, "I understand that was the last witness for the prosecution. There will be two final witnesses before the case is closed and we commence final argument. You're going to call a Mr. Hilliard Lubin and, of course, Captain Lerro will testify. Is that right, Mr. Yerrid?"

"Yes, Your Honor."

"Please proceed."

Having Hilliard Lubin as an expert witness required little participation on my part. He simply needed to be asked for his name, a description of his outstanding credentials, the basis for his opinions and an explanation of those opinions. He did the rest. It was a one-man show.

Hilly was a colorful and charismatic witness who both charmed and persuaded everyone in the courtroom. His black hair, peppered with streaks of gray, was swept back, and his bushy eyebrows reminded me of Walter Cronkite. But perhaps best of all were his sparkling blue eyes, which always had a devilish, playful glint to them. "Sir Hilliard," as I affectionately nicknamed him, always sported half-rimmed glasses that hung about his neck and were attached by traditional leather "snuggies." When Hilly wore his glasses, he affixed them near the bottom of his nose so he could look over them or shift his focus through the half-lenses to read. He was at least six feet tall and didn't weigh more than 160 pounds. With his knowledge, I considered him an international heavyweight, despite his size.

Perhaps most striking of all of Hilly's traits was that he was so damned articulate. His perfectly proper English was of the style used by American actors back in the early days of the movies. Skilled and experienced, Hilly Lubin, with his splendid vernacular, effortlessly went through his opinions as we had done in preparing for his testimony several weeks before. Unshakable, Hilly illustrated and tracked the course of the *Summit Venture* from the point of collision *backward* to the onset of the voyage when John had first boarded the ship. His calculations and utilization of the course recorder were portrayed on a simple clear overlay, which was placed on a backdrop of an enlarged nautical chart. The colorized chart and its magnification presented a much better image than the timeline and other exhibits put in evidence by the prosecution.

Hilly's testimony was bulletproof. Instead of making assumptions and working forward like Professor Suarez had, he took the known time and place of the collision and worked backward. From the debris field and the actual point of verified impact, Hilly plugged in the 7:34 Coast Guard time of the impact and walked the judge from that point back to earlier on that awful morning.

Without a doubt, he had everyone in the courtroom mesmerized. His profile of the course the *Summit Venture* had traveled confirmed the crablike, sideways movement of the ship. He expertly documented that the vessel had been blown, not steered, into the anchor pier of the bridge. In a remarkably simple way, Hilly's expert opinions removed any remaining doubt that the ship had been directed by the storm. Neither Lerro nor anyone else aboard the *Summit Venture* had determined its deadly path. The cross-examination was ineffective and short.

After Hilly Lubin finished, we took a short break before Captain John Lerro would take the stand as our last witness. The preparation and endless amount of time exploring every detail of the entire incident had been exhausting. In the process, John had gained varying degrees of composure and confidence as he came to realize what had happened. The "trial" of John Lerro and the most ruthless of cross-examinations had already taken place well over a dozen times in my law office. Every shred of evidence, every conceivable point, had been explored, re-explored, and then analyzed again. A universe of prosecutorial theories had been anticipated and rehearsed, and I had often assumed the role of prosecutor in our mock trial exercises. As the weeks rolled into months, John's abilities and confidence as a witness strengthened. With each new threshold of improvement, the intensity of the cross-examination would escalate, and the aggressiveness of my questioning would sometimes end in a heated and emotional exchange between the two of us. I took John to the brink, but tried never to break the belief he was gradually establishing in himself. I doubted any prosecutor would ever muster the attacks I made John withstand. Now, in addition to the pretrial preparation, John had heard each witness and had seen all of the evidence. He was as ready as he would ever be.

John and I sat together at the defense table, side by side, each of us sensing the finality of the moment. The courtroom drama and the quest not only to defend John but actually to prove his innocence had in effect been a much lesser task than convincing him to fight...to survive. We had become closer than I could have imagined. Bound by a friendship that was forged through adversity and relentless attacks on both of us—professionally and personally—we had become isolated from almost everyone and everything. I don't know when it occurred, but we had developed a blind trust in each other. On especially hard days and even longer, more difficult nights, we had shared stories, facets of our lives, and eventually our innermost hopes and fears. Confiding in each other had energized our resolve to fight on, and the strength we found was in our togetherness.

From the beginning, I had known that this case was an opportunity to perform in the legal arena. I knew that if by some chance our defense succeeded, a national winning reputation would be mine. To John, though, it was a much graver matter. If an Act of God was proven, some salvation of his soul was possible. As our time together wore on, his grim determination to find a way to relieve his terrible guilt and self-inflicted condemnation took hold of me as well. I not only began to feel his pain and torment, but also began to lose my professional self. By the last day of trial, the quest had become personal. Totally and completely, we had both put everything on the line. Now we needed to reach down for that special part I believe every good person has deep inside.

"John," I began as we sat so very alone at the counsel table and I placed my hand on his shoulder, "I would like to give you some great legal advice, come up with some inspirational talk, help you with what you are about to do, but I honest to God don't know what to say. We have worked so damned hard and I don't think our side of the case could have gone any better; nor do I believe the prosecution's could have gone any worse. We can win this thing. Do you hear me? We can win—better still, you can win. Now, get up there and just do your damned best. I'll never ask any more of you than that. Go do it, John. I'll be sitting right here until you get back." Nothing else was said after that between the two of us. We smiled at each other, and then clasped hands under the table before he stood up and moved to the witness stand.

John's time on the stand was one of those moments that some athletes describe as being in the zone. Some would call it a perfect ten. No matter the label, John Lerro was tremendous. He wove the testimony presented in the case into his personal narrative. He was calm, almost quiet in his manner, but his resolve and conviction were absolute and obvious. I took John through his entire direct testimony, and not once did the focus of the entire courtroom leave him. As I put question after question before him, his answers were flawless and clear. We augmented his almost perfect recall and recital of the riveting chronological testimony of what had happened with the ship's documents and logbooks, including the chart where the mate on the bridge wrote down the times of the vessel's passage, the engine room logbooks, and the helmsman's notated steerage of the course—with each piece of evidence corroborating everything John said.

There was only one thing that didn't make sense. If everything had worked the way it was supposed to, there was no way that the Summit Venture would have hit the Skyway. That was the puzzlement. John was steering the proper course, at the proper time, at the proper place. How, then? Why? Those had been John's haunting questions as he watched the tragedy unfold.

We had finally proven the answers. No one had taken into account the drastic change of the wind direction. The wind had shifted to the opposite direction, so John was doing what is called "set." The vessel was being steered, in fact oversteered, into a wind with an assumed direction from the south. When the hurricane force storm hit, there had been a drastic increase in the wind speed but more critically, its direction had swung to the opposite side. Ignorant of the radical change in direction, Lerro was no longer steering the *Summit Venture* into the wind. The ship was being steered with the wind. Both its freeboard and its heading magnified the effect of the renegade gale to push the ship sideways through the water and move its course to run with the new wind direction. As the vessel attempted to travel forward, it was really moving laterally. But the navigational instruments and compass still indicated the ship was heading in the right direction—they couldn't account for the sideways motion. It was the ultimate deception.

The questioning came to a close as I asked, "And in conclusion, Captain Lerro, is there anything you wish to add?"

"I really don't think there is anything left to say." John's voice had a finality to it as his eyes fixed upon mine. The silence in the packed courtroom was overpowering.

In the end, the cross-examination was incredibly uneventful. John's many hours under my overly aggressive bombardment of rehearsed questioning paid off. Lerro was untouchable and the prosecutor was not able to lay so much as a glove on him. I was so damned proud of him. He had never, *ever* been as good as he was on that day. When John was finished with his testimony and returned to his seat, I greeted him quietly. "You were outstanding, John, simply outstanding."

The prosecution had aggressively pursued its case against Lerro utilizing two separate charges: one accusing him of incompetence, the other of gross negligence. Against the backdrop of thirty-five innocent lives lost, a finding of guilt on either of them meant an end to his maritime career.

Now it was my turn to speak.

▪ ▪ ▪ ▪ ▪ ▪ ▪

The Closing Argument

MAY IT PLEASE THE COURT, I stood by this podium when this case began, and I suggested the evidence would show many things that I would just like to summarize. First, it has shown through the testimony of Dr. Robert Wooten, a competent medical doctor specializing in the field of psychiatry and neurology, that Captain John Lerro is not now impaired and has never been impaired. It has been established that he has no mental inability that altered or encumbered any decision that he made on May 9, 1980.

For months leading up to this trial, the prosecution has continued to make the devastating allegation asserted for all the world to hear that John Lerro was mentally unfit. It was that blatantly false condemnation that acted as the basis for this man to be declared an immediate threat to the public health, safety, and welfare, and his license to pilot was summarily and unilaterally suspended shortly after the Skyway tragedy. Because of the gravity of the declaration, the nature of the emergency suspension allowed due process of law to be bypassed entirely. It is not until now, over six months later, that this awful falsity has been exposed.

Based upon the prosecution's assertion, the District Court of Appeals would not reverse the emergency suspension by the Secretary of Florida's Department of Professional Regulation, Nancy Wittenberg. That Order of Emergency Suspension was entered on June 17, 1980, rendering my client incapable of performing his professional activity and taking away his livelihood before he was ever afforded a day in court. In obedience to that suspension, this man, a fully licensed pilot with absolutely no previous disciplinary history, has not attempted, nor will he attempt, until justice is done through the restoration of his livelihood, to pilot any vessels. He has not sought any other employment, nor does he have any such intention. He is a pilot—nothing more, nothing less.

We talked about this man many, many times in official proceedings. I never, ever felt that the evidence, the facts, as we learned them, constituted his classification as an "accident waiting to happen"; nonetheless, that as–

sertion has been repeatedly proclaimed to the public and anyone who would listen. We have chosen to remain silent. We have endeavored, to the best of our ability, to withstand the ensuing furor, the public outcry, and the pre-trial condemnations.

We are not the State of Florida. We certainly don't have the resources of a sovereign in that those resources are absolutely unlimited, but we initially focused much of our efforts to first explore that damning assertion, because we believed it had to be addressed up front. That was done, and pursuant to the exhaustive investigation and efforts made known into this record, we have submitted facts from the Panama Canal Company and the United States Panama Canal Commission, which indicate John Lerro had an exceptional record as a federally licensed pilot in Panama. His physical, mental, and emotional evaluations were nothing less than stellar. He was never subject to any disciplinary proceedings. He was never involved in any formal investigative action. He didn't leave there because he was hounded out or because folks said he was a no-good, incompetent, or mentally impaired pilot. Yet, we have heard all of those claims being made.

Directly contrary to the prosecutor's allegations, he left Panama because he had a better job as a state pilot in Tampa Bay, Florida. I would submit that is hardly a reason to classify him as an accident waiting to happen. Nonetheless, we bolstered that particular position by bringing into this courtroom the Department of Professional Regulation's own report, prepared at my request, setting forth the number of casualties which had occurred under the pilotage of the individuals licensed to pilot in Tampa Bay.

We didn't introduce that evidence into the record to show how John Lerro ranked among his colleagues. He didn't want to do that. We didn't try to embarrass anyone by submission of that list, nor was that the purpose or design for that submission. It was offered to demonstrate that this man was comparable to what we have and what we consider here in the State of Florida as being good pilots. His record was not without reported incidents. I believe the only truly unblemished record of the eighteen pilots licensed in the Port of Tampa was Captain V. W. Straigis, who, from a period of October 1, 1975, through the same day, 1980, was fortunate enough not to have experienced any marine casualties whatsoever.

There were others, but basically John Lerro with his seven minor marine casualties, and pilots often refer to those as fender benders, had the same type of instances so common as these other pilots who move those thousands, thousands of tons each day in very confined waters. They do have what is called fender benders, and with a ship six hundred, seven hundred feet long at the dock; such a large ship sometimes causes damage, thankfully almost always causing only minimal damage.

Still, all such incidents must be reported as marine casualties, regardless of fault. But we believe the evidence is clear. There has been no attempt on the Department's behalf to show anything that would substantiate the assertions that John Lerro was a careless pilot or a professional who was prone to be involved in an inordinate number of mishaps. That is because there is no such evidence.

Those blatant assertions of incompetence and unfitness made by the prosecutors were unfounded when they were made, and they are unfounded today. That is not to say all of the terribly damning accusations were made by the Department itself or any of their spokesmen or the prosecutors. I give a certain amount of discredit to the media for that. But the accusations have been made nonetheless. The most vicious of attacks have been aired on television and appeared in newspapers everywhere. As a result, John Lerro's reputation has been destroyed. His career and life have been impugned and irreparably damaged, not just within Tampa among his family, his friends, and his colleagues, but also across the country, and with some hesitation, I must confess, maybe even across the world.

The burden to sustain the most serious charges that the state sought initially in this case, would require proof that John Lerro was incompetent. Because of the nature and severity of the charges, the prosecutor's proof would also be required to demonstrate that John Lerro was grossly negligent. As a fallback position, it appeared the Department of Professional Regulation was forced to refocus its efforts on the lesser charge made under the alternative statutory ground of mere negligence.

Our fundamental defense to all of these charges had been simple and consistent. This catastrophic tragedy was the result of an Act of God.

There's something about an Act of God, which I think people find to be a little hard to accept, or at the very least, reluctant to embrace. Of course, an Act of God does not mean that God must actually come down and act. Rather, it means a force of nature occurs that is unexpected, so intense, and so supervening, as to relieve the human actions taken under the overpowering influence of that force. There could be no finding of negligence, not gross negligence certainly, not mere negligence, as a matter of law, but no finding of negligence whatsoever if there is a finding that this bridge was brought down by an Act of God. Simply put, the evidence introduced during trial has shown that on the morning of this fateful storm, nothing humanly possible could have been done that would have altered or changed the outcome or the course of events that occurred.

That brings us to the testimony that has been produced in this case. I don't believe anyone who has sat through these many exhausting days of trial can say there was no violent storm out there on the morning of May 9. The first theory asserted by the state was simple: The storm never happened, it did not exist. The evidence is absolutely undisputed that a terrible storm occurred on the morning of May 9, 1980. It came without warning, quite unexpected and unpredicted. The horrendous nature of the storm rendered Captain Lerro's vision, both with the naked eye and with radar, virtually useless. That critical fact finally came out through the expert testimony of Captain Clothier, one of the prosecution's key witnesses.

I think Captain Clothier is as fine a person as anyone could find. He has an impeccable reputation as a pilot. However, that does not circumvent the fact that Captain Clothier, the only maritime expert called by the State of Florida with regard to pilotage, has not piloted a vessel since 1964. Captain Clothier had not, nor has he to this day, even through the commencement of this very hearing, piloted any vessel in Tampa Bay, Florida…not one…not ever.

In support of Captain Lerro's case, we brought you pilots who had, Your Honor. We brought you pilots whose credentials are unimpeachable. They were, I believe at one point in time, referred to by the prosecution team as brothers, pilot brothers, as if this is some sort of social club we have down here in Tampa Bay. One must not look very far to determine the fact that these pilots are licensed professionals. They didn't pay any money to join the club. They joined "the club," if you want to call our pilot association in this town and the fine professionals we have a club; they joined that very exclusive and exquisitely talented club as a result of hard work, dedication, and proven skills.

Much of their lives have been spent on the sea, and more importantly, it was only after the Department of Professional Regulation itself saw fit to appoint them to that very, very trustworthy and fiduciary position, that those pilots became members of the Tampa Bay Pilots Association. The State of Florida didn't license these professionals lightly, or without a great deal of thought, evaluative effort, and qualitative analysis. They didn't do it because these individuals are "buddies," or because they would lie for each other. Hopefully, the State of Florida assumes that they have impeccable integrity and that each one of these pilots exerts his very best on a daily basis to ensure that no lives are lost and no property is damaged.

It is inconceivable that the State of Florida, the Department of Professional Regulation, and the prosecutors involved in this case could assert Captain John Lerro was ever incompetent. For that position, by its own admission, would mean that the State of Florida allowed, through the Department of Regulation's malfeasance, this man to pilot ships for three and a half years on Tampa Bay. In sum, it would mean that every motorist crossing that Skyway Bridge, which unfortunately and tragically has been destroyed, was playing russian roulette at the choice—not of his or her own choice, but by the choice of the Department of Professional Regulation. That is unacceptable, and frankly, incomprehensible.

The evidence shows that the pilots called by our defense as witnesses in this trial are competent and extremely skilled. Captain Gary Maddox, who came into this courtroom, and who is the co-manager of the Pilots Association; Captain Cyrus Epler, another expert who testified and is the other co-manager; Captain George McDonald; Captain Earl G. Evans; Captain John Schiffmacher—those last two people were called by the prosecution, not by us—all opined that John Lerro was forced to take the best option he had, under the very worst of circumstances. Virtually every witness has testified that he did not have a lot of good options available. People don't like to "shoot for that hole"—in John's words—don't like to shoot for that narrow hole of the channel's passage, especially without actual vision or the critical sight that radar normally provides.

I submit to you what he is being judged on here has been nothing but nautical hindsight in its most vile form. Captain Lerro has been sitting here and listening to witnesses and experts talk about what he could or could not have done. And that brings me to take a closer examination of the experts who were called. Getting back to Captain Clothier, he said he had no problem with this man's actions, no problem with this man's actions, basically. He said something about the fact that Captain Lerro should have taken times and distances; however, Captain Lerro adequately addressed that criticism. John Lerro testified that he took the time during the entire transit and plotted distances throughout the passage of the inbound voyage the *Summit Venture* attempted to make on May 9. Captain Clothier found fault using a very good catch phrase. He summed up his criticism of John Lerro's actions as being "too little, too late," emphasizing the point that the last crucial turn of the ship was too little and ordered too late to allow safe passage.

I submit every one of our witnesses addressed that critic's opinion with more specificity than I had anticipated. But the one who addressed it most succinctly was the one who actually made the decision as to when, where, and how to turn, and that was Captain Lerro. Captain Lerro said that he made that turn, which would normally be to sixty-three degrees, even though he knew the turn was late, seconds late, I might add, not late in terms of minutes. I again emphasize we are talking about seconds. He made that turn without even waiting for an acknowledgment as to where that "buoy starboard bow" exactly was. At that point, the fury of the storm was all over him and the *Summit Venture*.

He waited as long as he could for the visual sighting of the buoy by the lookout, and when he could wait no more, and then he made the turn regardless, because he knew of all the very limited options, that was his very best one. Our experts took the witness stand and demonstrated exactly how the set and drift of the vessel would have been effectuated had Captain Lerro's assumption of a southwesterly wind at fifty knots or greater been correct. An increased wind coming from the same direction would have affected the vessel in the exact manner as to allow Captain Lerro's navigating successfully the Sunshine Skyway Bridge. At the same time, Captain Lerro's commands would have avoided collision with Captain Schiffmacher, the pilot aboard the outbound vessel *Pure Oil*, which Captain Lerro believed was coming through the Skyway's span from the opposite side.

That testimony is simply undisputed. Captain Lerro had reason to believe, maybe not with certainty, but with reasonable probability, that Captain Schiffmacher was passing through that bridge and his ship was in close proximity, in extremely close range, and far too close for John Lerro to roll the dice, as some people have alleged he did when to took his course of action. Truly, rolling the dice would have been going hard port and taking a terrible chance. What if he proceeded in that fashion? An explosion, and a collision with a fully loaded gasoline tanker that would probably kill all the crewmen aboard and possibly blow up both spans of the bridge. No, not a reasonable option at all. Instead, he took the option that every single pilot who testified said was the single best option available.

What, then, has occurred? Professor Anthony Suarez was summoned to testify by the prosecution. He was the only expert, the only expert, to say that John Lerro would have hit that bridge regardless of wind, regardless of a fifty-knot wind and his thirty-five feet of freeboard, John Lerro would have hit that bridge. The opinion of the state's hired expert witness flies in the face of Captain Gary Maddox and the other expert pilots who have real experience and make those hands-on decisions every day of their professional lives. With all respect, Your Honor, I suggest this type of speculative second-guessing just doesn't wash with the expert testimony of Hilliard Lubin, the world-renowned expert we put on the stand. He corroborates the testimony of the pilots and makes the exact same point: It was the right call. Better put, it was the very best choice he had under the circumstances.

Professor Lawrence Ward—here is a man if ever there was a true, pure witness—if they are out there—if they are still alive. Here is a man who came in here and said, "I have never appeared before in court. I am not a professional witness. I am simply an academic professor." His credentials were above reproach. He is known throughout the nautical world to be unimpeachable and authoritative. He testified unequivocally that without that wind and its unpredictable and dramatic change in direction,

Captain Lerro would have made it. It would have been close, but he would have successfully navigated the main ship channel in the fury of this monster storm—and one of the largest maritime disasters in history would never have happened. The direction and unbelievable speed of the wind on that terrible morning were forces of nature. Not controlled by man—these elements are the essence of an Act of God. Again, we came back to the inescapable notion that nothing humanly possible would have changed or altered the course of events. The terrible sad truth, thirty-five souls were going to be lost that fateful morning, regardless of Captain Lerro's best efforts…or his worst.

What about the prosecution's key expert, Professor Anthony Suarez? Professor Suarez based his entire presentation on a number of very limited and specific premises and assumptions. One, the *Summit Venture's* logbook description of courses and times at all times can be assumed to be precise and accurate. I have a list of a large number of other assumptions that must be made if Professor Suarez is found to be right. Professor Suarez made fifteen separate assumptions to get where he wanted to go. His direct testimony was most revealing; in fact, I specifically wrote down one thing he said. He testified that he tried to satisfy the conditions of the testimony that he was supposed to give. That's a quote; it's in the record. What he did say was, "Well, I assumed always wind from the stern. Now, of course, the wind can vary, but under the assumptions I have made, it can only vary fifteen degrees, fifteen degrees, before the point comes when you have side force on the vessel and the vessel has lateral movement."

Well, that's a great assumption to make, but there was a course change here from eighty-three degrees, eighty-two degrees, which was actually being steered, making a course over ground of eighty-one degrees in Mullet Key up into Alpha Cut, where the channel went to sixty-three degrees. Now, I assume, I must assume Professor Suarez put in that very confined set of working rules and assumptions that this wind was following the *Summit Venture*. Of course, that would be a little different than the prosecution would have you believe.

The prosecution asserts there never really was a wind change. That was all a figment of John Lerro's imagination. What about Judge Mark McGarry? Can we forget the Circuit Court judge who is also a licensed airplane pilot and his firsthand eyewitness account of the weather? I specifically asked him, "Did the wind change?" McGarry, Judge McGarry, a very honored and respected St. Petersburg trial judge who happens to be extremely skilled in ascertaining the speed and direction of wind, said, "Well, I was blown and knocked down by the wind, and it was at 330 degrees northwest." I recall he stated to the prosecutor, "Yes, Mr. Oertel, I know where the North Star is, and I am very sure of the wind's direction. The North Star doesn't move very often." Additionally, the weather testimony, the radarscope, and the actual meteorological computer data all show the winds changed severely and dramatically.

To arrive at his opinions, Professor Suarez assumed while all this was occurring, the wind direction and force remained constant. That is a very nice thing to have in an academic laboratory, constant, constant, fifty miles per hour from the same direction. That is a constant wind force and a wind speed that didn't change. But it is a professor's laboratory version versus what really happened.

The weather experts called by the prosecution came from Asheville, North Carolina. According to these folks, it didn't matter what our local weatherman and a flock of eyewitnesses actually saw. According to the good professor's laboratory analysis and the weather experts flown here from North Carolina, the wind didn't change and its speed never increased.

I submit to you, Your Honor, if that wind direction can be shown in this record by substantial, competent evidence to be anywhere outside that fifteen-degree range from the stern, Professor Suarez's testimony is about worth what I paid for lunch today—nothing, because somebody bought me lunch. What I'm suggesting is that under the confines of this case, and I'm sure the prosecutor paid his experts just like I paid mine, the testimony that this critically important expert who was essential to the prosecution's case came in to give, was based on inaccurate assumptions. I want to be clear on that—this expert testimony was based entirely on inaccurate and demonstrated wrong assumptions. I'm not saying the man came in and lied and cheated. I'm simply saying he was just wrong, dead wrong.

In contrast, Professor Ward, who has a Ph.D. in hydrodynamics, came in and stated candidly, "Well, we're not really sure this assumption may be true, it simply cannot be made"; because if you look at the table it has fifty knots on there, not miles per hour. That makes a substantial difference. It has also obtained various wind speeds; forty, fifty, sixty, forty, fifty, and sixty, this shows a variable wind speed. There are also different degree wind directions that must produce a variable result. That is important, Your Honor, because the one thing Hilliard Lubin and Dr. Lawrence Ward said—unlike Mr. Suarez—was that they could not tell you what speed the vessel was going at any point in time. They could simply calculate their fundamental knowledge of time, speed, and distance. Because they knew how long it took to go from one point to another, groundless assumptions as to the specific speed and any one point in time were unnecessary. Reliable calculations could be made based upon what we know actually happened. I suggest to you that is what this case is all about.

It's about a variable wind speed, which drastically changed both direction and force. Our local weather expert, Bill Kowal of Tampa Bay's CBS affiliate, brought in the television station's computer-generated pictures portraying those wind vectors. They clearly show that in Panama City, Florida, there was a northerly wind at seven o'clock on the morning of May 9. Also demonstrated is a very strong southerly wind vector in the area of Fort Myers. Somewhere in between, and it wasn't clear where, but it seems most likely it is the Tampa Bay area and almost exactly where the Sunshine Skyway Bridge stood, the wind changed, going from that southerly course to a northerly course in a very radical, violent, and dramatic directional shift.

Now, Your Honor, that is the crux of the expert testimony presented; additionally, the record evidence is also in our favor. Two of their lay witnesses, the prosecution's own witnesses, were impeached by Mr. Oertel because he had inconsistencies apparently in the affidavit given during the state's investigation and the very different testimony elicited under oath in this courtroom. Also, even one of their pilotage experts, Captain Schiffmacher, ultimately was disowned by the prosecutor and declared to be an adverse witness, because he was not giving the answers that were evidently anticipated. Once again, the prosecutor had to attempt impeachment of a witness he had previously called as his own. Additionally, we elicited testimony from two other prosecution witnesses, which was very favorable to Captain Lerro's defense.

What this case has come down to is that the State of Florida has the burden of proof, and it simply has not been satisfied. The prosecutors just haven't met it. There's a problem with the numbers, too. Professor Suarez formulated his opinion based on the numbers he sought to draw from erroneous assumptions, wrongful times, and inaccurate course headings.

There's a funny thing about numbers. I'll just take a second to illustrate that point by way of an entertaining story I once heard. One time Howard Hughes was down in Panama, there was a bomb threat concerning his plane. Panama was in one of its usual revolutions so he asked, "What are the chances of a bomb being on my plane? I want to find out."

Someone called up Lloyd's of London and asked, "What are the chances of a bomb being on Mr. Hughes's plane—it's a Pan American aircraft—flying from Panama to the United States tomorrow afternoon?"

The reply came in a brisk British accent from a statistician at Lloyd's. "We'll put it in our computer, analyze the likelihood, and get back to you." Within a short time, he called back, saying, "Well, it's 32,000 to one." The gentleman from Lloyd's, being very professional and very English, also said, "Now, I can't help but tell you, the chance of two bombs being on the plane are ten million to one."

When informed of the odds, Mr. Hughes said, "Fine, I'll take along a bomb myself. Seems like that way, we'll have a better chance of the plane not blowing up."

It just doesn't work that way. It just doesn't work that way. You can distort numbers and make the figures read any way you want, but eyewitness testimony from people at the scene of the Sunshine Skyway Bridge would be consistent with the local mesoscale that we knew existed in that area as described by the weather experts. The data and information can be unmistakably seen on the computer-generated and colorized pictures of Bill Kowal. The terrible nature of the storm and its extraordinary intensity are also consistent with the number of mesoscale areas that we have now proven to have existed that morning. The prosecution brought you weather reports from Tampa International Airport and the weather station located right here on Kennedy Boulevard. That's not the Sunshine Skyway Bridge, Your Honor. That's six miles from that bridge. Our witnesses, on the other hand, were right there, not miles away.

I have been here in downtown Tampa many days in a dry climate when it was pouring rain, cats and dogs, at the Skyway, and I had to cancel fishing trips. That's exactly what our meteorologist was describing: localized, high pressure intense weather systems that can be consistent with vicious and angry squall lines that we have had the unbelievably good fortune to have captured in photographs of the actual radarscope. The thing that really bothered me the most about the prosecution of this case was the hindsight constantly being used. Having my client here—I wish, in a way, he didn't have to be sitting through all this hindsight, because it makes him further second guess himself and think, "If I had known the wind had changed and goodness, if I had only known that, I would have acted differently and all this tragedy would not have happened." Well, sure, looking back on that fateful day, he might not have gotten out of bed. He would choose to relive that morning and have somebody else bring that ship in that day. But that's not what happened. That's not reality. And judging someone by hindsight should not happen either.

What happened that tragic morning on May 9 is no longer a mystery. The collision between the mighty *Summit Venture* and the once indestructible Sunshine Skyway Bridge is history, unchangeable in all of its deadly effects. What we have seen in the aftermath of that catastrophe was courtroom hindsight. We all listened to our own expert; it wasn't their expert; it was our expert, Dr. Ward, a renowned hydrodynamics authority, who, when he was requested by the prosecutor to make certain computations, said, "I'm going to need a coefficient table." I think he also asked for a computer and calculator. Even with those tools, he said the type of theoretical navigational approach the prosecutor urged would take fifteen minutes, maybe thirty minutes to calculate. At that point, I thought seriously we were going to recess and let him work those figures up.

Captain Lerro did not have fifteen or thirty minutes. This man had fifteen or thirty seconds. He didn't have a coefficient table. He didn't have a computer. He had the extraordinary and all-powerful forces of nature. Captain Lerro did what he was supposed to do. He went on his pilot's knowledge and the proven skills he possessed. To come in and judge that man on the knowledge of hydrodynamicists or sophisticated computer room course recorder expertise is hypocrisy, and it should not be allowed.

Your Honor, there is an awful lot, an awful lot of talk about the fact that this was a very tragic occurrence. I do not think anybody disputes this is a catastrophe that has been of lifetime proportions. It is an event no one will forget and history will record for all time. Captain Lerro would not dispute that. Everyone involved feels badly for the people involved and the lives that were lost.

We didn't come in here with structural integrity reports about the Sunshine Skyway Bridge and raise the issue about why the bridge seemed to so easily collapse. Nor did I bring the notion that better fendering systems, which should have been there but weren't, would have prevented the ship from striking the bridge. That's not a part of this record, though it probably should be. The bridge should never have fallen. There is rampant speculation that the concrete composition of the bridge's piers was grossly flawed. We must now be convinced that the need for protective fenders around the bridge supports was known and ignored. Maybe that is why the state is so zealous in its efforts to focus blame on the pilot in this case. Scrutiny of the bridge and why this mammoth structure crumpled so quickly, the glaring issue of why the structure had no fendering, no protection of any kind…the State of Florida certainly didn't want anyone to focus on those issues. Instead, John Lerro was singled out, prejudged, and targeted as the person to shoulder all of the blame. Looking past the pilot has not been an option.

I am acutely aware that it wasn't our function to find out if that tragic collapse would have occurred absent some other factors. The sole concern in this trial has been the issue of whether or not John Lerro's actions were appropriate that day and whether or not his actions were free from blame; and that is what we have endeavored to prove.

With all respect, Your Honor, I don't envy your task. In closing, I only urge that this man be judged under the principles of fairness that we have come to establish based upon the record made in the trial of this case. The notion that we are not in control of our destinies is true, as much as we hate to admit it. There is such a thing as an Act of God; it simply cannot be denied.

Your Honor, I realize political pressures in this case are intense. It is my fervent hope that you have the courage to rise above it all. We realize that finding a scapegoat in the form of a human being is usually the first reaction to a very, very bad situation. That would not be justice. It is that higher calling we implore you to seek in finding that Captain Lerro should not be found negligent. The charges should be dismissed.

And then I ended the closing argument with a simple "Thank you."

. . . .

The prosecutor took his turn rehashing and restating the original allegations and charges. Talking primarily in generalities, he ignored the specifics of the evidence, and the argument was more rhetoric than substance. Finally, it was over.

"Gentlemen," the judge said, turning to the lawyers, "do you have anything else to present?"

"No, Your Honor," one of the prosecuting attorneys said.

"No, sir," I said in an exhausted voice.

The trial concluded with the graciousness of an experienced judge. As he looked around the courtroom, Judge Bentley said evenly, "I have appreciated your courtesy and the extremely competent and professional manner in which you gentlemen have prepared and presented this case. The efforts and advocacy on behalf of your respective clients have been exceptional and much appreciated. There being nothing further, this trial is adjourned. Thank you."

. . . .

John and I left the crowded courtroom and walked side by side through the throngs of reporters, cameras, and a sea of extended microphones. For the reporters, there would be the standard from the two of us: "No comment." The time for talking was over and I felt remarkably confident that we had put on the best case possible. Every piece of evidence, every witness—both ours and those of the prosecution—had gone our way. John had been brilliant on the witness stand, and all the goals I had set before the trial began had been reached. Now, the terrible wait would begin. I anticipated the judge would take several weeks before rendering a decision. It was a case of a lifetime for everyone—including the judge. The decision was destined to receive widespread attention and scrutiny from virtually everyone and everywhere. The court's ruling would be well thought out and, I prayed, the honest result of our search for the truth.

As if it were scripted, John and I walked out of the courthouse and into a driving rainstorm. The rain had kept the main lobby packed to overflowing with people choosing to stay dry and wait out the weather. John and I had pushed our way through, and then walked three blocks before we ever said a word to each other. The frenzied pace over the past several months was suddenly ending. The deadlines, jam-packed days, and endless nights were all coming to a close. Stunned from really having no place to go and no decisions to make, we found that the feeling of relief was being immediately replaced by the anxiousness of the question, *What now?* The enormity of what we had experienced was fully upon us, and though we walked together under a shared umbrella, we were each alone in our own thoughts.

When we reached the street corner nearest my office building, it was time to go our separate ways. Without any further thought, I extended my umbrella to John, but he immediately pushed it back. Standing there in the downpour of a Florida storm, a tamer but similar version of the one that had caused John so much pain, he looked almost detached as he said, "No, thanks, Steve, the rain won't hurt me...no matter how it turns out, I want you to know how much I appreciate what you have done for me. I'll never forget any of this." There was no handshake. Instead, we warmly embraced each other as the brothers that we had become. In the next moment, he turned and walked away, his shoulders hunched down and his soaking wet coat drawn closely to his chest.

I didn't move for a while. I stared after him long enough to watch his methodical walk into the deluge, and then, within a few more steps, his merger into the eerie darkness of the stormy weather. As I made my way back to the office, suddenly I became very aware I was being shielded from the rain and felt the separation from John even more. I pulled the umbrella down to my side and folded it, all in one motion. I welcomed the immediate wetness and coldness of the rain. I intended to toss the umbrella in a trashcan, but then I noticed an elderly lady at the bus stop in front of the federal courthouse. She had to be in her seventies, and from her appearance, I could tell she had been sitting on the bench for a very long time. Soaked to the bone in bits and pieces of tattered and soiled clothing, she wasn't waiting for a bus I could tell. Like so many of us, in our own way, she was simply waiting for life to give her a break.

I handed the umbrella to her, and then I walked on toward my office—the pelting water stinging my face—as if to share in John's pain for just a little while longer. Together we had experienced so very many emotions, from hopelessness and despair to unbounded spirits and momentary elation. I could not escape the terrible truth that the tragedy and Lerro's internal world of hell and self-conviction would never really end. And deep in my heart, I knew then we would live in each other's lives forever.

In my life, the most desperate times of fear have come from aloneness. I sat in the quietness of my office for over an hour. The last of the law firm's employees had gone home and even the phones were silent. The term "drip dry" certainly didn't apply to me. The only effect of the air conditioning had been the cooling of the pool of water surrounding my soaked pants as I sat motionless on the black leather chair behind my desk.

My mom lived less than ten minutes from the office, but the trial and preparation leading up to it had caused me to miss my twice-weekly visits too many times. My hand reached for the phone. She answered after the second ring.

"Mom," I began earnestly, "I'm sorry I haven't called. I've been overwhelmed with the damned trial and it just took me out. We were—"

"Honey, don't worry about it." Her words stopped me in midsentence. "I know how busy you've been. Your case has been all over the television almost since it started. The lead stories on this evening's news highlighted parts of your closing argument—"

This time I interrupted her. "You know, this crazy superstition you've got that somehow you'll bring me bad luck, you should forget it. Come down and see the real thing for yourself."

"Steven," she called me by my formal name, "how can you complain? Look how well it's worked. As long as we keep winning, I'll stay home and cheer. Besides, I enjoy getting the inside scoop and our rehash of the trial. Our talks help me understand the cases better. And you know our approach makes you come spend time with me!" She laughed warmly and made the moment seem just right. Suddenly, the office didn't seem like the place to be.

I chuckled at her humor. "Okay, okay, enough already. By the way, did you see this morning's *New York Times*?" My mom was an avid reader, often studying in detail the three different newspapers she received each morning.

"No, not yet. Why do you want to know?" she asked.

"Didn't Suzanne talk with you this morning?" I asked, barely containing my excitement.

"No, sweetheart," she answered calmly. "I haven't been home for most of the day. If she did try to call, then I missed it. What's so important?"

"Well, I finally got my mug in the big one! The *New York Times*, Mom! Pop called from D.C. and gave me the heads-up at seven o'clock this morning. Dad said he had already hand-carried a copy of the *Times* to Mrs. Graham's office." My father's work at the *Washington Post* for so many years had resulted in its owner, Katherine Graham, becoming a close, personal friend of my "blue collar" *padre*. Dad had introduced us, and I began my friendship with her at age thirteen. Mrs. Graham's warm and glowing recommendation had been instrumental in my acceptance into law school at Georgetown.

"I'm so very proud of you!" my mother exclaimed, her words reflecting the enormity of love I too often took for granted. Inside, I felt the familiar warmth and sense of well-being. Everything was going to be okay. Hell, she always thought we were going to win...why not? "Why don't you stop by for a drink on your way home?" she continued.

With no hesitation, I knew then I had someplace to go that would

be welcoming and pleasant. "I'll be right over."

And then, her simple words, "Love you." There would be no good-bye. That's how she always ended her conversations with me.

Fifteen minutes later, I knocked on Mom's door. My mother lived in a modest three-bedroom ranch-style house. The house was painted beige and had a neatly groomed lawn. Mom made it a point to plant the most colorful, vibrant flowers of whatever season Florida was enjoying, and even in the dim light, I saw that some of them had not completely closed their petals for the night. The light by the carport stayed on any-time she thought I might come by. On that rainy evening, its brightness radiated through the fine mist of the shower's end.

"Come on in!" I heard the familiar call of her voice. Immediately, I went into the Florida room where she sat waiting. Like many folks, she spent virtually all her waking hours either there, where the big screen television played constantly, or in the kitchen, where some of the best down-home cooking in town often bubbled on the stove. Mom was seated in her usual spot, surrounded by scattered pages of the newspapers of the day. "Missy," as she was nicknamed many years before by her close friends, rose from her favorite chair, gave me a peck on my cheek, and then busied herself making our drinks.

When she came back into the room, we began talking—or I should say, she began talking—for a good twenty minutes. Our discussion was about everything involving the case—questions about the witnesses, theo-ries, and thoughts of all kinds, everything, that is, except my picture in the *Times*. Finally, I could wait no longer. "Mom, my picture in the *Times*...did you forget?"

"No, son," she answered quickly. "I want to see it. Let's have a look." She picked up her reading glasses and the unfolded copy of the newspaper she held directly in front of her. She began to inspect the front page for what seemed like forever.

"Page twenty, Mom," I said to her.

"Oh, sorry, son. You were so excited, I just assumed your picture was on page one." She didn't break a smile as she said the words. She turned quickly to the inside page bearing my photograph. Not until then did we both break out in laughter! Moms sure have a way of keeping egos in check, and could she work it! Boy, oh boy, could she work it.

I will always remember the moment and the laughter, tears, and joy we shared that evening. She made me feel so very happy to see her glowing pride. I knew then, as I should have always known, winning or losing was not nearly as important as giving it everything I had. I had given everything I had to this case, and there was nothing more I could do.

· · · · · · · ·

P ainfully long and agonizing weeks later, the call finally came. Quite appropriately, it was on Christmas Eve, December 24, 1980, that Chief Hearing Officer and Presiding Judge Christopher H. Bentley issued his decision and the text of his ruling that John Lerro acted "reasonably and prudently" in his handling of the *Summit Venture* when it hit the Sunshine Skyway on May 9, 1980. His lengthy and impressively written order held that John was neither incompetent nor negligent at the time of the collision. The evidence, Judge Bentley said, showed that "up to the point of the storm, Lerro had properly performed his duties as a pilot, that he should not have attempted to halt the way of the vessel, and that his only choice was to navigate blindly through the existing weather, which he found himself in through no fault of his own." Judge Bentley further recommended that John's harbor pilot's license be immediately restored and the emergency suspension dissolved. He ordered the reinstatement so John could once again pilot vessels.

On March 3, 1981, the Board of Pilot Commissioners, after lengthy deliberation and a daylong discussion, unanimously voted to adopt the findings of fact and accept the recommendations of Judge Bentley as the final action of the State of Florida in the matter.

We had won, totally and completely. The Sunshine Skyway disaster had officially been declared an Act of God and not one scintilla of fault had been found on John Lerro.

Eleven months after the *Summit Venture* hit the Skyway Bridge, Captain John Eugene Lerro finally returned to sea. He was assigned as the pilot aboard the *New Park Sunlight*, a tugboat pulling an empty barge owned by Gulf Oil out of the waters of Tampa Bay. That was the first time he had piloted a vessel since that fateful morning of May 9, 1980.

I traded my suit in that day for a pair of old jeans and a worn fishing shirt. I rode with John on his eerie maiden voyage of atonement. Early evening was washing over us as we passed under the remaining structure of the sister span of the Skyway. Helicopters hovered overhead and the roadway was crowded with television and radio vans and deployed crews. Dusk, with its pink and powder-blue sky, gave the darkened profile of the remaining bridge span a sort of picture-book beauty. John and I stood on the tugboat's outside steering deck, watching the media circus and exchanging occasional smiles. For a few precious moments, the hell of the past year was forgotten and all seemed right with the world.

Redemption had come at last, if only for a little while.

Epilogue
· · · · · · ·

The world saw the Sunshine Skyway Bridge case as huge, and its impact was much bigger than I realized at the time. People were sending me newspaper headlines and clippings about the case from Beirut, Lebanon, because they knew my grandparents were born there. I also received headlines from Belfast, London, Paris, Calcutta, Sydney, Tokyo, and other cities throughout the world. Childhood friends and long-forgotten classmates from high school, college, and law school emerged by way of notes from faraway places. Old friends called, telling me they were impressed, stunned, or shocked at my newfound fame. Quite a few sent congratulations and praise.

Regardless of the source of the feedback, it was the same—I had won a case that seemed unwinnable. The reaction was often one of disbelief and astonishment. I was a kid, thirty years old, and it was overwhelming. I had become engrossed in the Skyway tragedy because of John Lerro's persona, the enormity of the event, and the fact that a case such as this may happen only once in a lifetime, if at all. Everybody expects a bridge to be there, and nobody expects the pilot aboard the ship not to be at fault when the bridge is struck. People had said to me, "Yeah, yeah, you're going to win this case, all right. What are you going to prove? That the bridge jumped out in front of the ship? You haven't a chance, not a prayer

of winning."

There were very few people who believed that I could win the case. Two of them were my mother and father, Missy and Charlie Yerrid. Although my parents divorced when I was seven years old, they were always together in sharing an unwavering belief in me and everything I did. Frankly, no one else gave John Lerro and me a snowball's chance in hell.

But we did win, and we won on the defense that the tragedy was caused by an Act of God. Blaming God is an altogether different proposition than most. Every person has plans for today, and for today's tomorrows. But an Act of God means that someone or something other than the person has the ultimate say of what is going to happen. I learned just how much people refuse to accept that. *Most people don't want to believe that we are not in control of our own destiny and fate.* To determine that something, some Higher Power, whether it is nature, God, or whatever, has control over whether or not we are going to live or die? That is a hard notion to swallow, much less comprehend and accept.

The case was made more difficult because of the fact that John Lerro was trying to find salvation and vindication for his self-condemned soul. At the same time, as a young, aspiring trial lawyer, I was struggling to believe in the workings of a system of justice in which I had yet to gain total confidence.

In 1980, I thought I was invincible, immortal, and could conquer the world. I thought very little of death, very little of that Higher Power, except as it related to a legal defense. As it turned out, even though John and I won the case and had been victorious, he was never going to overcome the fact that somewhere deep down inside, he would always believe he killed thirty-five people. I came to realize that self-condemnation is absolutely the most severe penalty of all. John convicted his own soul; and for that, there would never be a retrial. His redemption was partial and fleeting.

When John Lerro testified at his trial, he performed as magnificently as an accused can. He was articulate and sincere as he spoke. He opened up his mind and his heart and he spoke the truth. Fascinated, I saw the renewal of fire that had been gone too long from his deep, sad eyes. But it was only for an interval. It was just a brief, small glimmer of an opportunity for him to absolve himself. And then it was closed almost as quickly as it opened by his returning guilt and self-imposed damnation. He was convinced he was responsible for the deaths of those thirty-five people, and that conviction was ever so briefly lifted by the adjudication that he was not guilty. At the time, I simply could not understand his reasoning. I was plenty smart, but over the ensuing years, I have learned intelligence and wisdom are two very different things.

For as long as I live, I will never forget the experience of watching John Lerro testify. Once on the witness stand, he redeemed himself. For those wonderful minutes, John Lerro was the John Lerro of old, the John Lerro I wanted him to be, and the John Lerro he wanted to be. He rose up above all else and really came through. I'm never really sure, even to this day, whether or not he did that for me, for his family, for himself, or maybe for everyone. When he finished testifying and sat down beside me, he asked, "Are you proud of me?" Of course, I couldn't talk, I couldn't answer him. Even now, I get tears in my eyes thinking about that moment. *Yes, John, I was very damned proud of you.*

The case taught me there are always agendas that people bring with them to places where right and wrong are being adjudicated. Agendas are often just like John's condemnation—self-imposed—which means that sometimes it doesn't matter what is really right or wrong. The conclusion has already been reached and an effort is being made simply to justify and find reasons for it. And still, almost as children, there exists a fundamental notion that if we are right, we will win—that despite it all, in the end justice will prevail. In the middle of the trial, I scribbled these thoughts that are as true now as they were then: *To the truth and those who seek it, to justice and those who achieve it, but mostly to the innocent who are often left without both.*

In the Sunshine Skyway Bridge case, I had to convince John Lerro, not in his brain or in his heart, but in the deepest recesses of his soul, that he had done no wrong and could not be blamed for the deaths of those thirty-five people. I also had to convince him that even if he had to do it all over again, the same result would have occurred, no matter what he did or didn't do. It was a monumental task compared to the actual trial of the case.

In defending John Lerro, I often followed my heart. I learned that my most terrible fears were probably ungrounded and unjustified, that right could triumph over might. With very few exceptions I was being told that I was going to lose the case, but there was something within me that told me I wouldn't. I believe that inner determination convinced me that instead of looking for outside endorsement or encouragement, I needed to look inside and I learned that inside my own heart is where the best answers could be found. Before, I had always tended to look to others for validation and approval when the entire time the sources of power, energy, conviction, and courage I sought were all inside my own chest. Everything I needed was right there all the time. It was in my own soul. It was a fundamental, ironic difference: me looking in and finding strength and conviction, John looking in and finding condemnation—but neither of us desiring to look out.

While trying this case, I learned no matter how bad things are or how difficult or desperate situations become, there is a thing called hope; and it is hope, coupled with courage and a determined belief and conviction, that allows us to survive.

In a perfect world, good wins and bad loses. Not always, not in every instance, but most times. There are still massacres of innocent women and children, horrific acts of rape and abuse, random acts of violence, and on and on. There are many different accounts of human conduct that feed the tired belief that there cannot be any overpowering good in life. But I believe there is. There are very few circumstances where good cannot be found, if you look hard enough. That is the whole secret, at least to me.

The trick is not focusing on the bad. It's looking for the good.

Life, as tough as it is, is like a running, ever-changing stream. It has many currents and different flows and directions. Some good, some bad, but not one element or ripple can be isolated and judged to be representative of the whole flow. To me, living is a process of being in the wholeness of the stream, and only then can life be fully experienced and evaluated.

I have come to accept that nothing is a sure thing, whether it's good or bad. I realize I only have today, and I believe each of us has to make the most and best of it, because it is all that is guaranteed. Yesterday is gone forever and tomorrow is only a promise. The only certainty is we're all going to die. The lesson of life is not taught in how we die or when we die; it's taught in how we live. For me, that was the greatest, most valuable lesson in the Skyway Bridge disaster.

. . . .

Even before the *Summit Venture* rammed into the Sunshine Skyway on the morning of May 9, 1980, there had been other maritime incidents involving the enormous bridge. In August of 1970, a nine-thousand-ton freighter ran into the bridge, causing minor damage. Then, in January of 1972, a runaway barge hit the northbound span; it, too, caused only minor damages. Hurricane Agnes swept through the area in June of 1972, eroding portions of the Skyway's causeway. Twenty-three Coast Guard crewmembers of the *U.S.S. Blackthorn* were killed on January 28, 1980, when the buoy tender collided with the mammoth Russian freighter *Capricorn* just west of the Skyway's main ship channel. On February 2, 1980, just days after the *Blackthorn-Capricorn* incident, the freighter *Magic Star* ran aground as it was trying to navigate around the sunken *Blackthorn*. Five days later, the Greek freighter *Thassalini Mana* struck a support beam of the bridge with its loading boom. On February 16 of the same year, the *Jonna Dan*, a 720-foot ship, hit the bridge, knocking loose a ten-foot concrete slab from the center piling of the Skyway. After these accidents occurred, and before the *Summit Venture* hit the Skyway, published reports indicated that the Florida State Highway Department was presented with a plan that developed "bumpers" that could safely absorb a collision with a ship and deflect a

The new Sunshine Skyway Bridge.

ship away from the support piers of the superstructure. The cost for each of the bumpers was a quarter of a million dollars—four would be needed to protect the bridge—but the State of Florida balked at the amount, and no protection of any kind was installed.

After the accident, estimates of repairs to the bridge climbed to $100 million. Rather than "fix" the troubled and inherently flawed structure, officials with the Florida Department of Transportation decided to build a new cable-stayed bridge that would be "much safer" than the old cantilever style. Constructed at a cost of over $300 million, the new state-of-the-art Sunshine Skyway Bridge opened in 1987 to much celebration, with thousands of motorists crossing it the first day.

Special safety features were installed in the new bridge, including a higher rise—more than 180 feet above the water—and bumpers, or "dolphins," as they are called, that would deflect any ships away from the piers of the bridge. The new spans were constructed over a straight section of the shipping channel, rather than in the location of the old bridge, which had required vessels to turn close to making the passage under the main span. As a result, navigation through the channel was easier and the bridge was more extensively protected should something go wrong with a vessel's steering or control. A video camera system was also installed to allow monitoring of the different sections of the bridge, and an emergency warning system was introduced in case of any maritime accidents. The system allows the bridge administration center to initiate a warning and stop traffic. Most significantly, cutting-edge technology was utilized in placing elaborate radar equipment on the main span, which is capable of emitting delineation and honing beacons to approaching vessels under the most severe weather conditions.

All of this comes too late for the thirty-five people who died so tragically on that morning. There were young babies, people in their eighties, and so many in between. A whole litany of personalities and persons were brought together for one final act of life—to die in a very bizarre and unexplainable fashion.

THEIR NAMES ARE: *Wayne Addely of Miami, Florida; Alfonso Blidge of Miami, Florida; Myrtle Brown of St. John's, Newfoundland; Willis L. Brown of St. John's, Newfoundland; John H. Callaway Jr., of Apopka, Florida; Doris Carlson of Pinellas Park, Florida; John Carlson of Pinellas Park, Florida; Leslie Coleman of St. Petersburg, Florida; Charles Collins of Tampa, Florida; Michael J. Curtin of Apollo Beach, Florida, who was the Greyhound bus driver; Lavern Daniels, whose residence was unknown; Sandra Louise Davis of Bordman, Florida; Harry Dietch of St. Petersburg, Florida; Hildred Dietch of St. Petersburg, Florida; Sharon Elaine Dixon of Miami, Florida; Brenda Joyce Green of Miami, Florida; Robert Harding of Glens Falls, New York; Gerda Hedquist of Port Charlotte, Florida; Reginald Hudson of St. John's, Newfoundland; Phyllis Hudson of St. John's, Newfoundland; Louise Johnson of Cataula, Georgia; Yvonne Johnson of Miami, Florida; Horace V. Lemmons of Kings Mountain, North Carolina; Lillian Loucks of Winnipeg, Canada; Louis Lucas of Birmingham, Alabama; Marguerite Mathison of St. Petersburg, Florida; Monisha McGarrah, whose residence was unknown; Wanda McGarrah, whose residence was unknown; Tawanna McClendon of Palmetto, Florida; Ann Pondy of Winnipeg, Canada; James Pryor of Seminole, Florida; Melborn Russell of Chicago, Illinois; Delores Smith of Pennsville, New Jersey; Robert Smith of Pennsville, New Jersey; and Woodrow Triplett of Bainbridge, Georgia.*

These unfortunate souls are gone forever and the majestic golden-beamed superbridge of the new Sunshine Skyway now stands in their honor as a vigilant and solemn guard over the mouth of Tampa Bay. Motorists cross the span, and ships navigate the channel every day underneath the bridge's massive, towering structure, carrying wares and cargo to and from every corner of the earth. More than two decades after the accident, the tragic memories for John Lerro—the once–mighty captain of the *Summit Venture*—were not quite as clear and concise as they were on that tumultuous spring morning so long ago, but they still clouded his mind like a misty fog that refused to melt away. No matter what John was or did before the accident—his triumphs and accomplishments, even his failures—everything was superseded by the fact that on that fateful morning, he piloted the giant ship through the frothing and churning waters of Tampa Bay, toward what would become one of the worst maritime tragedies in the nation's history. Ironically, I suppose, it has become his lasting legacy.

When John was younger, before the tragedy, he had movie-star good looks in a classic sort of Italian way: the long, patrician nose; dark brown, soulful, insightful eyes; and jet-black hair. During the last years of his life he was a broken man, weak and confined to a wheelchair. A twenty-year struggle with the life-draining illness of multiple sclerosis had taken its toll. Frail and very sick with the disease that attacked him a little more than a year after the collision at the Skyway, he became the antithesis of the physically powerful, athletic, and well-muscled seaman he once was.

As John neared death, we saw less of each other and the telephone became our primary link. "Yerrid (or sometimes Counselor)," John would start. "This is Lerro. I'm calling to see what's doin'. Me, I'm…" And the monologue would go on for several minutes, full of information and tidbits about his life. Sometimes, for no reason in particular, he would meticulously recount what happened "that day." Too often his calls centered on graphic descriptions of the Skyway horror and the cars going over the edge of the bridge that he couldn't stop, no matter what he said or did. I think his most troubling memory was always the visual reminder of those people unknowingly going to their deaths as they drove off the broken span. John had total recollection of that image; he could recite every aspect of it in graphic detail. I can't imagine how many times it was played over and over in his mind.

Every couple of months, I would receive late-night voice messages

In November of 2001, my good friend and baseball great Wade Boggs took John on my boat *Justice* for one last trip under the new Skyway Bridge.

from my old, dear friend. Sometimes rambling, sometimes clear and succinct; no matter the tone, they were always welcome. A warm rush of memories never failed to come over me, but inevitably the good feelings were followed by a deep sadness I felt knowing the extent of his pain and suffering—and knowing of that inevitable death that waited so impatiently.

The last time I talked to the man who once steered monstrous freighters and ships through even the slimmest channels and harbors of Tampa Bay, we joked and laughed, and we talked with seriousness. But mostly, we talked as the closest of friends about just exactly what we meant to each other. Typically, John wanted me to tell him what was ahead, how this thing called death worked. I told him what I'd always told him—the truth. I didn't have a damned clue. We laughed again and ended the conversation with assurances that we would talk again soon. I found out later that I had been the last person to talk with John. Minutes after hanging up he had lapsed into a coma. John Lerro died on August 31, 2002. He was fifty-nine years old.

At his funeral, I gave his eulogy. It was one of the hardest things I have ever had to do in my life.

John went to his grave still haunted by the faces that he never saw of those people in the cars, trucks, and the Greyhound bus. His soul was inextricably entwined with those in the plummeting vehicles that he could not save. Maybe now he is in a place to find his peace.

Those who have not brought a child into the world and loved it and planned for it, and then have it suddenly snatched away from them and killed can hardly have an adequate idea of the mental pain and suffering that one undergoes from such a tragedy. No other affliction so tortures and wears down the physical and nervous system. Psychosomatic illness of a serious nature may follow. The emotions may be unstrung, the nerves put on edge, and the end effect may be a period in a rest home, a mental hospital, serious physical derangement, and sometimes death. Damage for mental pain and suffering is one of the late developments in the law and its potentialities are not restricted as they formerly were, because so much has been learned of the evil consequences that flow from mental injury.

■ ■ ■

—Florida Supreme Court Justice Glenn Terrell
(Winner v. Sharpe)

Jessica Bowden, age two.

CHAPTER TWO
An Angel Too Young

On a crisp day in the early part of March, the Florida sun had just begun its daily climb above the horizon. The orange blossoms in the nearby groves had already come alive and sweetened the air, and the vibrant colors of spring stood out against the brown backdrop of the departing winter. Only a few weeks earlier, glittering light frosts had greeted most mornings. While there was still a distinct chill in the air, the day would warm quickly as the sun rose higher and higher. Spring was on its way and life was ready to begin again. But death has no season...and it does not always wait. For two-year-old Jessica Bowden, there would be no more seasons and no more life.

Jessica was born on April 25, 1985, and died on March 7, 1988, just weeks before reaching her third birthday. She was, by far, the youngest person included in the obituaries when her funeral notice appeared in the *Lakeland Ledger.*

A Day of Horror
· · · · · · · ·

On March 7, 1988, Doug was napping in the early afternoon, resting after his midnight shift at Tampa Electric Company, where he worked as a Controls Analyst. The job required that Doug, in his own words, "troubleshoot, install, and repair electronic, pneumatic, and computer process control instrumentation." Usually he worked during the day, but for one week out of every eight, he had to work the night shift.

Jessica was sleeping with Doug in his bed, while Jessica's infant brother, Whitney, dozed in the crib in his own room. Cherie and her five-year-old son, Carl Douglas Bowden III, whom they called Little Carl, were getting ready to go out. Just steps away, no more than twenty feet from the bed where Jessica and her father were sleeping, a contraption called a Johnny Jump-Up was hanging in the archway between the living room and the hallway. The Johnny Jump-Up was a baby exercise device consisting of a canvas seat hanging from two pairs of sturdy nylon straps and a metal spring that allowed the baby to bounce up and down by pushing off the floor. Cherie had bought the exerciser for Whitney at a garage sale for one dollar.

Cherie was frugal, but she never bargained or compromised when it came to her family's welfare. After buying the Johnny Jump-Up at the garage sale, she had gone to the local Wal-Mart, found a new one still in its package, and standing in the aisle, read the directions and warnings to familiarize herself with its use. The instructions specified that the device should be hung from the top of a doorframe with the canvas seat suspended a couple of feet above floor level. Buckles on the straps allowed them to be lengthened or shortened as necessary and then secured so the seat would not slip. The exerciser was intended to help growing infants develop strength, balance, and rhythm as they used leg extensions to push off the floor, and was recommended for babies aged four months up to walking age and weighing no more than twenty-four pounds—just right for Whitney. To fit it properly for Whitney's height and weight, Cherie had adjusted the straps and had also tied a sturdy knot in each strap to bolster the worn buckles.

As her husband and children slept, Cherie prepared to drive into Lakeland from their rural home to run her Saturday errands. She was especially looking forward to her stop at Sears, where she would pick up family portraits that had recently been taken. Ironically, among the group photographs was a separate picture that had been taken of their beautiful girl, Jessica. Before leaving, Cherie quietly opened the door to the bedroom and glanced at her sleeping husband and daughter, and then her eyes moved to the bedside clock. It was nearing two o'clock, time enough to get her errands done and return home to prepare supper well before anyone would wake. Jessica stirred, and partially awakened just long enough to sleepily ask her mother if she could go along, but Cherie decided against it so Jessica could get some more rest. Before she left, Cherie made one last check and noticed that Jessica had already snuggled back up to her father, and was again fast asleep. Satisfied, Cherie took Little Carl's hand and left.

Even after the most intense scrutiny and analysis, we could only speculate as to what probably happened next. Soon after Cherie left for town, Jessica had evidently awakened without disturbing her father. She had climbed down from the bed and begun wandering into the hallway, her eyes eagerly coming to rest on the Johnny Jump-Up that had been left hanging in the archway. Our experts were fairly certain that she must have seen the exerciser as an incredibly inviting toy just waiting to be played with. After all, she had watched many times as her baby brother, Whitney, jumped and bounced around on the exerciser, howling with delight. Maybe it was a desire to have that same fun and joy that had driven her actions. She was too young to realize that her mommy had always, *always* been sitting there on the floor beside the exerciser as Whitney played.

The most likely reconstruction of the terribleness that followed concluded that Jessica had pulled one of the dining room chairs next to the Johnny Jump-Up. Climbing up on the chair, she had taken one final step into the canvas seat of the exerciser. The weight of her small body would have immediately brought the four tough nylon straps tightly together around her throat, catching her head and forming a deadly noose around her neck. Almost certainly, she would have begun gasping and struggling for air. Any efforts to yell and scream would have been rendered nearly impossible by the brutally tight straps across her tiny throat and voice box. She would have engaged in a silent, deadly struggle and fought to pull the nylon away from her neck, but the physical pressure of her body weight and the position of the straps would have stopped her. After a few seconds, there would have been a loss of consciousness followed quickly by strangulation and death. At trial, the medical examiner testified that Jessica likely would have lost consciousness within ten seconds after she became ensnared within the noose, and that she would have been unable to scream to her daddy for help because of the compression on her throat and larynx.

Cherie returned home at four o'clock, and crossed the threshold of the front door with Little Carl trailing along behind her. At trial, Cherie described the grotesque scene as she moved into her living room. "I opened the door and she was hanging by her neck...my baby was hanging by her neck!" At once, she began to shriek for Doug, who recalled his own terror when he was awakened by his wife's screams. He thundered from the bedroom and came headlong upon the terrifying sight of Jessica's head, neck, and body entangled in the straps, with Cherie frantically grasping and tearing at the cords in a desperate effort to free her daughter. With the full power of his muscular frame, Doug Bowden grabbed at his daughter's limp body and pulled on the adjusting straps of the exerciser with all his strength. But the cords had locked in a death grip against the fair and beautiful skin of their victim and he couldn't loosen them.

"Everything was all twisted up around her neck," he recalled in testimony, his eyes closed as he tried to block out the terrible memory. "Her head and neck were in there with that thing all wrapped around her body. I couldn't get my baby out. No matter how much I tried, I couldn't help my little girl." He reddened and choked back tears as he relived his efforts to free her. He spoke of seeing his hands entwined with patches of Jessica's glossy blond hair, matted and wet with vomit and pieces of bloodied scalp that testified to her own violent struggle.

After too many agonizing moments, Doug was finally able to

wrench Jessica loose. During testimony, with tears slipping down his face, he quietly recalled that "she was so cold, so very, very cold." When he was on the witness stand the silence was so complete it seemed as if everyone had stopped breathing. The eyes of two of the female jurors welled with tears as he methodically continued his recounting of the tragedy. He told them how he had laid her on the floor and begun cardiopulmonary resuscitation while Cherie, hysterical and wailing, had rushed to the telephone to call for emergency medical services. This giant of a man described how he had pounded on Jessica's tiny chest and forced his own breath into her lungs but had gotten no response. He recounted how he and Cherie had raced along in their own car behind the ambulance as it rushed Jessica to Lakeland Regional Medical Center, all the time desperately hoping against all odds there was still a chance for their daughter. But it was too late for the little angel. She was pronounced dead shortly after five o'clock that afternoon.

The Clients and the Product Liability Case
· · · · · · ·

Doug and Cherie Bowden came into my office seeking justice against the manufacturer of the Johnny Jump-Up for Jessica's death. They were younger than some of my clients, older than others, and they could have been any young couple you meet on the street, in the mall, at the gas station, anywhere. But they weren't.

After the usual pleasantries associated with an initial client interview, the discussion turned solemn. The enormous tears welling in Cherie's eyes streamed down her face. She had finely honed features and dark chestnut brown hair. She began to speak haltingly, awkwardly. "Our baby is dead, Mr. Yerrid. She was two years old. She looked like an angel, and her blond hair was as fine as silk. And now she's dead. Jessica was her name and she meant the world to us. Can you help us? Can you *please* help us? We don't want any other children to be hurt."

Her eyes widened, but the tears kept coming. Her husband sat silently opposite her, his stare fixed on nothing. He was big and burley, with a full brown beard. He had a soft manner and even from the brief conversation during our introductions, the warmth of his personality and his tenderness had been obvious. He listened to his wife, and looked as if his soul had been torn open.

I listened intently as Cherie recounted the facts surrounding their daughter's death. The Bowdens' youngest son, Whitney, had been the intended user of the Johnny Jump-Up, and Cherie had been there every time he was in it. When young Whitney wasn't using the jumper, it was left hanging in the doorway because Cherie didn't know to take it down: When she had so carefully read the packaging of the exerciser, there had been no warnings about the terrible danger of leaving it in place. Cherie then explained in horrifying detail how she and Doug had found their daughter in the doorway. She graphically described the efforts to free their young baby from the straps of the jumper that were so tightly wrapped around her neck.

I had learned early in my career that there is no greater sorrow than that of parents who have lost a child. It seems to be the greatest form of human suffering. The natural order of life dictates that children bury their parents. But when the sequence is reversed and a child dies before the parents, it strains even the strongest human soul far beyond the breaking point. Cherie and Doug had learned all too well the excruciating anguish of life gone wrong.

Accepting the legal representation of a client is the single most important decision trial lawyers make. Sometimes, it's gut instinct. Other cases require extensive investigation and evaluation by the very best of experts. This one just seemed right. Besides, I needed to take it on because these parents desperately needed help. After carefully weighing all of the factors in Jessica Bowden's death, I took the case.

Without a doubt, the stakes would be high when I sued Spalding & Evenflo Companies, Inc., the manufacturer of the Johnny Jump-Up. The lawsuit would be based on an allegation that her death had been caused by a defective product and had therefore been wrongful. In cases involving a product made by a large corporation, it was typical that the best legal talent would be hired for the defense.

After an extensive factual investigation and consultation with experts in the field of children's toys, we were ready to roll. In August of

1989, Spalding & Evenflo was sued. It had been almost a year and a half since Jessica's death. The lawsuit charged that the Johnny Jump-Up was inherently dangerous because of its design. Specifically, we charged that the support straps were too close to the child's head, and that the manufacturer was aware, or should have been aware, of the risk created. I also asserted that Spalding & Evenflo was negligent for not testing the jumper, and for not adequately warning users of its hazards and that it should be taken down when not in use.

Spalding & Evenflo responded by claiming that the parents were negligent in modifying the jumper by tying a knot in the adjustment straps and by leaving Jessica unsupervised near the suspended exerciser. With the battle lines drawn, we would have to prove that the product was defective in its design and unreasonably dangerous to any children who might use it. In the lawsuit, we also contended that the warning on the Johnny Jump-Up label was inadequate because it failed to warn, in any way, of what we asserted was a known strangulation risk associated with the use of the product.

The Johnny Jump-Up, attached to a doorframe according to the instructions.

Depositions of Spalding & Evenflo's key executives revealed that before Jessica's death previous complaints had been made about entanglement in the straps of the Johnny Jump-Up, even though the corporation repeatedly denied ever receiving any such information. Through discovery of corporate documents maintained by the defendant, we learned that years earlier Sears, Roebuck & Co., had sent a letter to Spalding & Evenflo warning that the design of the exerciser posed a serious problem of a potential "choking situation." The risk of choking presented by the straps, Sears suggested, needed to be addressed and handled properly. The caution from Sears had produced no modifications from the manufacturer and no design changes were implemented for the Johnny Jump-Up to address the risk of entanglement and strangulation.

During the discovery process, a critical piece of evidence came from the defendant's in-house expert. The Evenflo expert testified that there was no risk of strangulation because no danger existed; therefore, there had never been a need for a change in the warning accompanying the exerciser. The toy manufacturer's expert had quickly embraced the singular defense that was asserted so often in these types of cases. He testified that the blanket warning stamped on the product—*Never leave the child unattended*—was enough. Its bold letters had been etched on the canvas seat of the jumper and, he added, on hundreds of other products manufactured by his company for use by children.

Taken to its logical conclusion, a simple warning such as that—*Never leave the child unattended*—could be placed on all baby products and the mantle of responsibility would shift instantly to the parents, regardless of any dangers the product might present. I thought about that fallacy, because no parent, no matter how caring, loving, attentive, or responsible, can "attend" a child every single moment. For the manufacturing industry, it was an ingenious way of providing a defense that would apply in any given case, no matter what the circumstances. Their reasoning was obvious: *If only the parents had watched the child a little more closely, a little more responsibly, none of this would have ever happened.* Spalding & Evenflo was so confident about this defense that no offer to settle the case was made. Zero. We would take the case to trial and let a jury decide.

Two weeks before Christmas, the trial convened. We had gone toe-

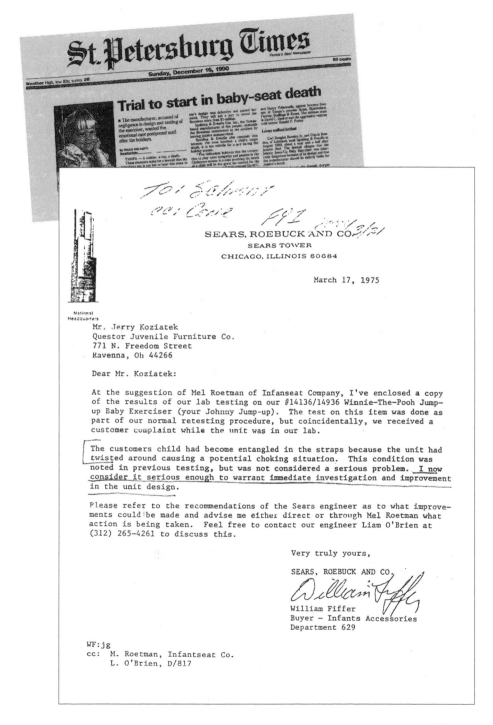

to-toe with the well-monied corporate defendant, and we were still standing. Our confidence ebbed and flowed in an emotional tide of hope and disappointment. Our witnesses were outstanding, and the testimony established a known risk and the horribleness of the death of this innocent victim who had lost her life because of it.

Among the most riveting evidence introduced at trial were letters Cherie had written to Jessica from the time she was born—a compilation of thoughts and reflections that she had planned to give her daughter on her twenty-first birthday.

On January 2, 1988, just over two months before Jessica's death her mother wrote:

> *Hi, Jessica!*
> *Boy, it's getting harder and harder to keep up with all these letters. It seems I'm either feeding someone or cleaning up a mess all day. You went to the doctor two days ago, because you had a bad cold and a fever. You weighed twenty-eight pounds and you're thirty-seven inches tall. You and Little Carl fight like cats and dogs, and you start it most of the time. Your latest thing is to call me an "old girl." You're so close to Daddy, and he loves you so much you can't even imagine it. Daddy wants you to enter a beauty pageant. I'm going to call about one today. You wear a shoe size eight, and you wear a big 3-T or a 4. You have not worn a diaper since January 1st!! You still have a few accidents, but you're doing real good.*
> *I love you!*
> *Mommy*

Another letter from Cherie's precious stack we introduced into evidence dated back to July 28, 1987.

> *Hi, Jess!*
> *OK, you finally hit the terrible twos! Daddy has spoiled you rotten, you sleep in our bed, and you cry when you don't get what you want. I called you a brat, and you said, "I know you are, but what am I?" You are like PeeWee Herman; he's a real goofy guy on TV. Little Carl likes him, too. I have a feeling you're going to be jealous when the new baby gets here.*

*When Carl sits in Daddy's lap, you say, "My Daddy!" and you start
hitting him. You went up to Daddy the other day, kissed him on the leg,
said, "I love you, Daddy," and walked away. You are Daddy's little
"PooPoo."*

> *I love you!*
> *Mommy*
> *P.S. You can count to ten!*

I was overwhelmed by the magnitude of the love these parents had
for their child and I fervently hoped the jurors felt the same way.

On the other hand, the blame heaped on the parents by the defense hung over us all. As each day of trial ended, the constant pressure
of seeking the conviction of the defendant and at the same time the exoneration of these wonderful parents took everyone involved to the
very limits of human endurance. Cherie and Doug had withstood it
all—reliving Jessica's death and the sadness of all that had followed.
Now, as it came time for closing arguments, it was up to me.

On December 21, 1990, I presented my final argument in the case of
*Carl D. Bowden Jr., and Cherie Bowden, as Personal Representatives of the Estate
of Jessica Bowden, Deceased, Versus Spalding & Evenflo Companies, Inc., a Foreign
Corporation.* The place was Courtroom Number One, Hillsborough
County Courthouse, in the Thirteenth Judicial Circuit, in Tampa, Florida.
The judge was the Honorable John N. Gilbert, an older man who was in
every sense typical of what one would expect a judge to look and act like.
In his sixties, he had snow-white hair, an athletic build, and a lively personality. He always wore thick, black-framed glasses, and when he was on
the bench, the dark rims of his glasses perfectly complemented his black
robe. Judge Gilbert had been our referee in the trial, occasionally interrupting the proceeding with evidentiary calls and orderly governance of
the courtroom. But it was a jury trial, and the jury would be the judges of
the facts and would make the ultimate determination as to who was responsible for Jessica Bowden's death.

Perhaps the best, most succinct way to represent this trial is to present the closing argument in its entirety. There is, I believe, no other way
that one can fully and completely understand the sentiment that was rip-

pling through the courtroom on that December day. The final summation provides insight into the events of the trial, as I attempted to wrap up the key points that had been made during those few precious days in the courtroom. To me, summation to the jury is the finest moment of any trial and the highlight of a trial lawyer's professional calling.

Outside the courthouse, it was unusually cold. The sun was bright and shiny in a cloudless, light blue sky. Inside, the courtroom was packed with spectators, a pool television camera that would serve all of the networks was in place, and a roped-off area was swarming with the media, giving notice to all the litigants, as well as the court, that the audience for this case was huge. But for me, the only audience that counted was the jury I was addressing.

■ ■ ■ ■ ■ ■ ■

The Closing Argument

MAY IT PLEASE THE COURT, counsel, ladies and gentlemen of the jury, and most of all, may it please Mr. and Mrs. Bowden. This is a solemn moment. It certainly does not seem a mere four or five days ago that we started this trial. It is a moment that will end soon. And by my own common sense, I can tell you the sun should set tonight; and hopefully, we'll all be here. And I hope, in my deepest hope, that justice by then will finally be achieved. I want to thank you, not only on behalf of the Bowdens, but also I want to thank you on behalf of the defendant, Spalding & Evenflo. Of course, I want to thank you on behalf of all the lawyers for both parties.

And I want to thank everyone who has ever lived and fought and died for the right you are about to exercise. You know, before serving as a juror many people think jury duty is something that simply takes time out of their lives. But, we all know now that being on a jury is much more valuable. A jury trial is the stuff dreams are made of. It is a unique opportunity citizens have in this country, this democracy, to truly come and do justice. Can you imagine anywhere else in this whole world where a defendant corporation like Spalding & Evenflo must be equal with these people? *[I knew that it was important to emphasize the Bowdens as equals to the defendant corporation. I emphasized the point by virtually stopping my summation and motioning first to the defense table and then to the plaintiffs' table where Mr. and Mrs. Ordinary Citizen were seated. I walked around the podium and stood between the jury box and the tables where I pointed. Invariably, each of the jurors' eyes fixed on me, then on the two distinctly different groups of people seated at the counsel tables. I looked into the eyes of each member of the jury and seized the moment to reinforce the undeniable significance of the fact that these parents were representing the two-year-old beautiful little girl whom the jurors had come to know during the testimony of the case. Not one member of the jury spent more than a second or two looking toward the defense table. Instead, I watched their eyes almost collectively fix on the parents. Doug and Cherie had withstood the blame heaped upon them day after day. At this critical point, I was pleased they were looking straight back at the jurors who I hoped had already joined our quest for justice.]* And more importantly, can you ever imagine anywhere in the world where I can come in here on behalf of Mr. and Mrs. Bowden and say, "You're equal. You're no better, no worse. Let's talk and let's do justice."

Because today is Judgment Day. I want to thank you, members of the jury. I want to thank you because it's something very special that will happen today, and I want you to please remember how important it is that you listen; justice is something that is going to happen today. When you walk out of here, and the television camera is flicked off, the bailiff comes and shuts off the lights, and His Honor will go out of this court-room, his patience having been tried a number of times, but his dedica-tion to the law obvious to everyone. The lawyers will pack up their bags, and they'll walk out. We will all have another case. You may or may not sit again as jurors sometime in the future. But you know what won't change? What won't change is the impact that the tragedy in this particularly hor-rible circumstance caused those people sitting there at counsel table. What will never change is that this trial will last the Bowdens a lifetime. And your verdict will be the ultimate determination as to how they remember their lives, both before and after the death of their precious daughter.

The trial and its result will be for all time, as far as the Bowdens are concerned. And your verdict will bring an absolute finality to them. Thankfully, we don't have to take justice in the old manner. There will be no eye for an eye or a tooth for a tooth today.

Do you recall when I asked each of you if you could equate dollars into something that is almost inequitable, to make the impossible possible? *[Again, I stopped. I walked to the front of the jury box and looked directly at Mrs. Sinclair. In her forties, she had hesitated during jury selection and expressed reser-vations about how an appropriate sum of money could ever be calculated to replace such an emotional and subjective loss. In the end, she had promised to do her best, and now I wanted to remind everyone how much that effort would mean.]* Each of you said you could. Now I asked you only this...I want you to listen and listen closely, and I want your decision to be heard as a decision of justice, regardless of who your verdict is for. That is your determination, not mine, not Spalding & Evenflo's, not the Bowdens'—and with all def-erence to the Court—not the judge's, because today everyone who hears about this verdict will know one thing: You were the law. *[The automobile mechanic was staring straight at me. Today, he was as powerful and important as anyone in the country, and from the way he was sitting up, I could tell he was ready for the task].*

You set the standards. Those are the standards we are talking about today, not some standards in Washington, D.C., not some standards in Illinois or Ohio or Mississippi or Wisconsin, but the standards you set by your very conscience, by your very being, the standards you know inside are right. *[I drove this point home to further defuse the parade of hired experts the defense had brought as witnesses. Common sense was the best expert any trial lawyer could ever bring into a courtroom.]*

There is a funny thing about the truth. You remember I talked to you, in voir dire, to speak the truth? *[Voir dire is the process in the trial when potential jurors are questioned and the six-member jury is selected.]* I left it alone, and I didn't make a big production of voir dire because, hopefully, that's all we are about: to speak the truth. When material gains leave, there are very few things—treasures in life, very few treasures remaining. As you go down the path of life, think about it. What's the last thing that you want to see? The face of a loved one. What's the last thing people facing death sometimes ask for? Mama? Daddy? A husband? A wife? A child?

I ask you to perform this awesome task, and I really don't cease to be amazed at a jury's abilities. I asked you to look at this case, and now I ask you to do your duty, fulfill your solemn obligation to equate pain and suffering—a broken heart—with money. And I thought about it. I said to myself, "Oh, boy. You're not asking for much, are you? Just the innermost recesses of these jurors' souls." And then I thought about what the defendant did in this case...*the manufacturer did the exact opposite.* All we are going to do is take us back to where we should have been. You see, it's easy. What they did, they put dollars first, regardless of the fact that dollars equaled pain and suffering, because corporations do not know how to feel pain and suffering, but they sure do know what dollars are. *[I particularly liked the third grade schoolteacher we had impaneled as juror number three. She had been married over thirty years and had two grown children and three grandchildren. As I spoke, I could see her lean forward and imperceptibly nod her head. She was going to be very strong for us. Especially on matters involving a broken heart and the grievous loss of a loved one.]*

Now, we are going to talk about the testimony of their expert.

You know, my daddy one time told me something I'll never forget when we were fishing on the riverbank. Back then, he was the person whom I always went to, to ask questions. It was amazing. I used to ask him, "Dad, why is the sky blue?" He would give me an answer. "Well, why does the sun shine?" He would give me another answer. Sitting on the riverbank, I even asked him one day, "Why does the river go that way instead of that way?" Once again, he gave me the answer.

One night, some boys, two of them, stole my Schwinn Flyer off of the patio. We weren't a family of material wealth, and that bicycle meant the world to me. It was a little dark, and I couldn't quite see who the thieves were. And I went to the second grade the next day, Watts Elementary in Charleston, West Virginia, and I saw the two boys who I thought took my bike.

So, I went up to the two boys the next day and said, "Tell me, did you steal my bicycle?"

They looked at me and said, "We didn't do anything wrong!"

And do you know what I did? Nothing! I went home and asked my daddy again, "What should I do? How do I know when someone is telling the truth?... You're not telling me what to do." He said, "Son, that's one question I can't answer, but I can tell you this: You will know the truth when you see it. And you will know the truth when you hear it. And you will know when the truth is not there."

At that point in the closing argument, the defense counsel objected and requested that we approach the bench for a sidebar conference, which the jury would not hear. After we arrived at the judge's bench and the court reporter had set up her equipment, the defense lawyer began speaking in a too loud voice with his nostrils flaring.

"Your Honor," he said, "Counsel's belief in the truth of any particular witness is not to be argued. That's not proper argument. I object and ask you instruct the jury to disregard Mr. Yerrid's comments."

I turned toward the judge, with a wary eye toward the opposing attorney. "I'm not giving a belief, Your Honor. I would like the record to reflect that I have not mentioned anything about this case. I'm talking about an experience I had with my father, and I am not commenting on the truthfulness of a witness. I am very aware of the rules."

The judge glanced at me over the top of his black-rimmed glasses. "You can't tell the jury you recognize the truth, and tell them who you believe is telling the truth. That's not your job."

"Alright, Your Honor," I conceded, hiding my anger at his ruling. "Thank you." As I turned and walked back to the podium in front of the jury, his last words kept ringing through my head, "that's not my job," that's not my job, that's not my job...I just hoped like hell the job belonged to somebody. I waited for the judge to sustain the objection and instruct the jury to disregard what I had just said, and then I began the closing argument again.

As the judge just made clear, my task in this case is not to find the truth. That is up to you. It was my job that day to find the truth about my Schwinn Flyer. But it is not my job here. I can't tell you which witness to believe in and which one not to believe in, because His Honor, with that correction, just brought to light the exact truth of this courtroom. He runs the courtroom, and he will give you an instruction. And the instruction will be—and I don't recall the number—but the instruction stands out in my mind because it concerns the believability and credibility of witnesses.

This I can tell you. There was a defense witness who sat through this trial and answered, "I don't know," so many times that it says a lot more than the answers that purportedly told you what he did know. The key defense expert testified that he does not get paid for being an expert witness; he merely gets a salary, and part of his job is testifying. If there is a difference there, well, that is something you have to consider.

One of the answers to a question he supposedly didn't know concerned the number of products sold. We do. The defendant sold four million Johnny Jump-Ups...four million Johnny Jump-Ups! The defense brought in another so-called expert from Washington, D.C., who never had been qualified to testify as an expert witness before. They picked that expert and left home the three or four engineers who were involved with this product's design. I can't tell you what they would have said, and neither can the defense attorneys, and neither can the defendant, because we will never know. Ask yourself about a witness's motivation to testify, his or her interest in the outcome, or any bias that may exist. Analyze and consider the expertise of the witness. And you remember I asked the Washington, D.C. expert:

Question: Do you have any experience in engineering? *[Again I left the podium. I walked over to the witness stand and gave the jurors time enough to visualize what I was recalling.]*

Answer: No I don't.

Question: What's your degree? Biology?

Answer: Yes.

[I returned to the front of the jury box and slowly moved along its front row. I made eye contact with each of the jurors and sensed they were with me.] You have to weigh the background of an expert, the credibility, and the qualifications that he or she has. You know, you do it all of your lives. You do it in common sense terms. That's all that's being asked here. But there was something that was constant in the witnesses who were called, in that most were employed and on the payroll of Spalding & Evenflo. Even those defense experts admitted there was a possible danger with this product, which was recognized as early as 1980. The fact that a child tried to get in and could become entangled in the cloth straps, in the opinion of the defendant's key expert, was a known danger prior to the tragedy. But he went on to admit there have never been any tests, never been any inspections, never the dollars that were spent to try this case, never were they spent on testing or a pre-marketing analysis concerning this product before it was sold to the public. And that, folks, brings us back to the board. You see, because my looking at this first lets me hear, "Let's sell these Johnny Jump-Ups! Hey, we don't have to test them because we have got the consuming public! What better guinea pigs than those people? We'll put these products out there and see how it goes. And then, when tragedy strikes, we'll deal with it as it comes because, who knows if tragedy will ever strike? Maybe we'll never be brought before a jury!"

With the manufacturer's records, or better put, their lack of record keeping, who could know how many infants became entangled? But with their own records, we do know the following:

We know plaintiff's Exhibit One—and moved into evidence—we know that on these documents right at the top, right under the Johnny Jump-Ups, the document that wasn't referencing a particular toy or—excuse me—"a piece of furniture," as it was called by the defense; it is specifically labeled Johnny Jump-Ups. "Straps too close to the baby!" "Straps too close to the baby!" *These complaints were documented by their own records kept in a secretary's desk drawer.*

Of course, you listened to the testimony; make your own deductions. If these people who were complaining called from Japan, I assume they had a Japanese interpreter there to tell them, "Oh? Your baby got caught in the straps? Fine. We'll take care of it." If the thing was sold in Mexico, I guess they had someone who spoke Spanish. "Hablamos Espanol, no problem. We'll take care of it. We'll get our people right on it." Well, you know, you didn't have to speak Spanish. You didn't have to speak Japanese. All you had to do in this great country was get an education and be able to read because, you see, folks, this letter from Sears, Roebuck & Co., which is in evidence, says it all.

See what it says in plain English in this letter? "*This problem warrants immediate investigation!* The child can become entangled in the straps, causing a potential choking situation, enough to warrant immediate investigation, improvement in the design." The condition was noticed in previous testing, from Sears, Roebuck, but the defendant takes the position that it was not considered a serious problem. Look at the date: thirteen years before Jessica Bowden's death.

As a result of the experiences I have had trying lawsuits, something just came to my mind. After I looked at that letter, I started looking at the various correspondences that are marked Composite Exhibit 1, and which are dated 1982, and another from 1983: "Straps too close to the child." What happened in those cases? "Straps too close to the child." Look at the numbers, all those Johnny Jump-Ups and all the terrible numbers of complaints out there. Do they have to reach a courtroom with those numbers? Wasn't the risk appreciated? This is what you call *foreseeability.*

It would be great in life if you could tell a two-and-a-half-year-old, "Don't go near that swing! Don't go near that swing! Don't go near that exercise chair because it can kill you!" And have that two-year-old fully appreciate the danger.

You know, no matter how hard we work, and I believe in hard work…no matter how we work, what do we really work for? Americans work for the same thing as Japanese, Mexicans, Africans, Russians, Arabs, and on and on. They work for the treasures of life…the treasures of life! You see, the treasures of life are what you leave behind. That's the hole that will never be filled here for the Bowdens, no matter what you do; so the easiest thing to do is do nothing—except that there be other holes to fill and other straps too close to other children.

I'm not an accident reconstructionist. Each of you must use the evidence to your best abilities, but the apparatus—you can call it a piece of furniture; you can call it a toy; you can call it a piece of garbage. This device was pulled apart by that little girl when she stepped into it and then it became a deadly noose. And then she couldn't pull it apart. Neither could her father. As it tightened its death grip around her neck, she had little time to struggle. And the result was a terrifying five seconds. *Five seconds!* There's no other evidence, no other evidence. Five seconds; that's how long. Five seconds, while Doug Bowden tried to do what he could not; five seconds, while Jessica did whatever she did; five seconds, not two hours.

The defense keeps charging Jessica's mother left the child alone. One of the defense lawyers is going to get up here and say, "What kind of mother would leave her baby for two hours and go to the shopping mall to pick up family pictures? What kind of mother would do that? That kind of mother would—Cherie Bowden."

But it wasn't two hours. It was five seconds. Five seconds! And then death…death. That's five seconds before eternal silence. In five seconds, that's called a flat line. That's the best case scenario. It could be five seconds, maybe even half a minute. An entire minute?

You didn't see the defense lawyers ask a whole lot of questions of the medical examiner, did you? Five seconds when the child was left alone versus the two hours the argument by the defense would have you focus on. That critical and fleeting moment really flies in the face of the defendant's case.

[I turned to look at the defense table for just a moment. I wanted to see their

faces turn red. When I had taken the deposition of the medical examiner it was clear he disliked lawyers—especially plaintiffs' attorneys. At least I was certain he didn't like me. After the first few questions I asked him during his pretrial deposition, the anger and resentment he carried was obvious. He was one of the misinformed doctors who had succumbed to the false propaganda of the insurance industry. Despite the fact insurance companies made more money during the last decade than at any other time in our nation's history, they wanted more. To get more profit, raising premiums for "fat cat" doctors was the easiest and quickest approach. To sell the increases, millions of dollars were spent and continue to be lavished on broad-based media and advertising campaigns that blame medical malpractice lawsuits for rising healthcare costs, and the large premiums are falsely justified as being necessary "pass-throughs."

In truth, there is no tort crisis, nor an explosion of frivolous litigation. The need for tort reform? It doesn't exist. It's all about greed and profit. But try telling that to a brainwashed doctor who works his ass off and gets gouged for huge malpractice premiums. I didn't have the time or the opportunity to explain the real truth of the situation to my very unfriendly medical examiner. I only had time to "handle" him. I used his hostility as my ally, and baited him for the answer I needed. I reflected back on the critical exchange. "Now doctor, you would agree, wouldn't you, that this poor little girl suffered terribly for quite a long time before she died?" I nodded towards him as if to cue his affirmative response. It all worked. "Absolutely not!! Why do you lawyers always seem to make things so dramatic? There would have been very little 'pain and suffering' as you people call it. Within seconds her throat would have been severely constricted and she would have quickly lost consciousness. Death would have been almost immediate." I knew right then that I had an answer for the inevitable "blame the parents" attack I was certain would be the cornerstone of the defense. Best of all, I remembered the smugness of the defense lawyers as the doctor had chided me. It was that contemptuous picture that I remembered so clearly as I looked at the red and worried faces of those same, not so confident, corporate representatives and their team of lawyers. I paused to let the uncomfortableness of a failed defense fully set in.]

How about a simpler scenario? Mother, child, two children, maybe not an only child household, two children, mother. The mother had been working. One of the babies throws up on her. She wants to clean her body. She goes in a room and takes a five-minute shower, a three-minute shower, a thirty-second shower. She keeps the door open in case she hears silence because she knows silence is the worst sound you have when you have a young child, because you know he is into something. The mother is in that shower. That child does the exact same thing young Jessica did. And if that happens, that child is going to be in the exact place that girl is, the exact place.

Jessica is in Oak Lawn Cemetery in a new grave, and every time Doug and Cherie think of their lost child, it wrenches their guts. You know, a broken heart on its worst case can kill you; maybe not physically, but certainly emotionally. These parents have worked hard all their lives for a dream. Is there any doubt that this little girl meant so much to them? That she was their dream?

I'm not going to quantify the damages in this case, because, unlike other cases I have had, I'm not going to be able to give you a dollar figure. I'm not going to be able to give you a monetary amount of damages, because that's what you now must do, if you find either negligence or strict liability. Strict liability means fault without negligence. It means the product is bad, and it should never have left the manufacturing plant.

Was the warning on the Johnny Jump-Up adequate? Was the warning something that would put a parent on notice; say, "Don't leave that thing hanging up." Use your common sense. You don't need an expert to tell you how to do that.

Did they design it properly? No. Where is the spreader bar? The spreader bar was there for the more expensive Johnny Jump-Up "Plus," a more sophisticated, safer product, for the people who had a few extra bucks. For the people who had a few extra dollars, it was there to be able to hold it and keep the straps apart; but for the common folks—the low end, bargain basement consumer—the spreader bar didn't exist.

Regardless, these straps never changed. I'm going to put it to rest real quickly; I just want you to remember what Dr. Benedict, our accident reconstruction expert, said. He said that it wouldn't have made a bit of difference whether or not the bar was there, because the loop on the straps is the same. It would just be the diameter of the loop that would change. The ring would make this a larger loop; but, you see, the buckle that works, it works just like a knot. And the defendants are the ones who said it slipped in their own tests. Do you remember the test we discovered took place in Akron, Ohio? A test that the defense expert can't explain? So, what happened is this case got overwhelming when I looked at that, because I looked at that with the thought of, "How do you undo this equation?"

What you've got to do on damages is, you've got to somehow go back there with the magic that jury room contains and the magic this courtroom holds. Remember during jury selection I asked you about your favorite movie? You may have thought, "What is the lawyer talking about? Favorite movie?" My favorite movie is *Field of Dreams*, and this courtroom is my field. You see, no matter who is here, this is our field of dreams. And the thing about this wonderful field and its beauty and enjoyment is that it's a field that these parents, the Bowdens, will no longer have a ticket to attend after today. You see, the thief of death took the most valuable possession these parents had. Death took the dreams they had for their daughter, and death took their hopes of her future. This accident should not have happened. What Doug and Cherie have never been, they could have become through their child. The lives that they will never have eternally, except through some Divine Intervention, would be carried on by their seed. That's what the wrongdoing took, and it was taken for the most wrongful reason of all: It was taken because of unnecessary fault.

So, when you go back there in the jury room and take this gift that they once had, this loss of their most precious gift that they carry with them every day, you change that equation I talked about earlier. You make it run the other way. That is what I'm going to ask you to do. I want you to equate pain and suffering back into dollars because everyone will be able to understand exactly the language that the defendant corporation speaks every day.

The defendant sold four million of the Johnny Jump-Ups. I asked Mr. and Mrs. Bowden what they thought about this case. They thought of that dollar, that single dollar that Mrs. Bowden paid for the device at a yard sale. Get up and make an issue out of that. I want the defense lawyers to get up and beat on their chests about that, because you know what she did? How about this for a mother? She went to the store and read the packaging just to make sure her baby boy didn't use the exerciser improperly.

And, you see, the defense likes to twist the case around. They would like to say, "Well, you know, she left the baby unattended." Cherie never did, not one time! And is there one piece of evidence that she left her child unattended? Whitney was the intended user of that product—Whitney! She was there every time Whitney used it. And when young Whitney didn't use it, it hung there because Cherie didn't know it posed a deadly risk and needed to be taken down. That's called a latent defect.

Remember the expert testimony of Dr. Benedict? He described the various flaws in products sold as patent or obvious defects, latent defects that are virtually hidden and the various aspects of product use, misuse, and abuse. Hindsight is always so sweet, but what price it has in this case! Do you need an expert to tell you that a two-and-a-half-year-old kid alone for a few moments, a precious few moments, whether it is five seconds, five minutes, or ten hours—do you really need an expert to tell you what your common sense will? A child is going to be attracted to something like this; a child who sees the joy and excitement is going to be attracted to that. And the manufacturer of children's products ought to know that! Certainly, the manufacturer should know that.

Jessica is dead and gone, but not to her parents. She is a memory as strong as the raw emotion that was in this courtroom, a memory that will never be forgotten, a joy now replaced by a sorrow that will tear at the guts of those two people as long as they walk on this earth, as long as the trees grow around her grave.

Now, let's put pain and suffering into dollars. The manufacturer sold four million of the Johnny Jump-Ups. The Bowdens—this is not my obligation—the Bowdens think that if you return a verdict of four million dollars for each one of those exercisers—four million dollars, a dollar for each seat—that might be one way to look at pain and suffering. I thought about that. I got up this morning and read the paper. I saw where a mediocre baseball player was earning eleven million dollars...

"Your Honor!" the defense attorney interrupted again. "This is grossly objectionable! May we approach the bench?"

The judge nodded and motioned us forward.

The following conference was held before His Honor's bench. "If the Court *pleases, we have to move for a mistrial on the basis that it's highly inflammatory. It's improper argument. There are cases that came out exactly on point. I understand Mr. Yerrid may get carried away with this. There are at least two Florida cases in the last several weeks that when an argument was made in which the Court declared a mistrial, I think declared a mistrial, or either the appellate courts reversed. One of them had to do with the argument as to the value of a horse. There had been a horse that sold for, like, ten million dollars, and a lawyer argued that—did you read the paper about the horse that sold for ten million dollars? In this instance, he's talking about a salary, ten-million-dollar salary of a baseball player. And he's got a figure in the jury's minds, and I'm not sure that they will be able to take it out of their minds. In lieu of a mistrial, I would ask the jury be instructed in the strongest possible language to disregard any comments that counsel made concerning sums of money or salaries of other people or anything of that nature."*

Judge Gilbert responded, "I think he's right about salaries. It's not a salary case. I will sustain the objection and instruct the jury. However, the motion for a mistrial is denied."

"Your Honor," I began, "for the record, I was going to leave that. What I am now going to talk about is not with regard to salaries or horses. It's not a salary case. I understand that." My words had an edge to them, but I kept my emotions in check. "May I continue, Your Honor?"

We left the bench and waited for Judge Gilbert to announce his ruling.

"The objection is sustained. Mr. Yerrid, you are not to bring up other people's salaries. We are not to talk about salaries, and the jury is instructed to disregard counsel's last comment," the judge cautioned the jurors with a stern look on his face. "Counsel may now proceed."

I responded with a "thank you, Your Honor" and resumed my summation.

The value of dollars, the value of dollars in today's society is hard to figure. But thankfully, I know that is something you readily understand. When you go back there to the jury room, your only obligation as a citizen of this country and under our laws—and the judge will instruct you—is to require one determination: What is a fair amount of just compensation for the loss suffered? Because that's all any jury can do—a fair amount of money—that the community on whose behalf you will act today, will judge what is adequate for the loss, the pain, and the suffering, the loss of these parents' ability to enjoy life and to forever suffer the death of their child.

You can put it in a thousand different ways, but the point is simple: Everyone needs to find out one day in his or her life, what something so precious is really worth after it is lost. And I asked you this on voir dire: If it's a substantial case, if it's a substantial loss, will you return a substantial verdict, for these people? In your deliberations, you are not limited to the figure requested. That's real important for you to remember. You are not limited to the figure that these defendants may have suggested. And I'm not going to give you a figure on behalf of the plaintiffs, because I don't know how to do that in this case.

I guess the pain and suffering is a constant source of human emotion at any funeral, and this is no exception. But I ask you to consider the following: Jessica Bowden was two. By far, she was one of the youngest persons to appear in any newspaper's obituary column. Her mother clearly pointed that out. As I have said, there's something unnatural about a parent burying a child; there's just something that doesn't square. And if there is fault, and if that death was unnecessary, now is the time to hold people accountable.

You may recall that I suggested some of what would be said in trial would really be "red herrings." Do you know where that term originated? Red herrings are fish—smelt, which have a strong, overwhelming odor. Back in the 1600s, affluent people used to have a couple of little boys out in the fields on foxhunts. And they would take those smelts and they would put them on the bushes. And when those dogs knew one thing, like we know the truth, they knew the scent of a fox, and those dogs would be taken off the trail because of that smelly odor. That is the purpose of a red herring. It doesn't have anything to do with the hunt. It doesn't have anything to do with cunning or the beautiful way a fox can elude the dogs of the hunters, but it has everything to do with half of a truth. It smells like something, but it doesn't smell right, and it is sure to throw off the hunt for the truth.

So does the buckle issue in this case. The buckle issue was inserted in this trial as nothing more than a red herring. The defendant had thirteen years to make this product safe, thirteen years of notice from Sears,

Roebuck. Jessica Bowden's mother—Cherie Bowden—had five seconds. Doug Bowden had no time; he woke from his nap to the screams of his wife.

You know, it's not the funeral picture that's indelibly imprinted on the Bowdens' minds; it's the picture of their baby hanging by a noose like some common criminal at the tender age of two. That picture can never be erased! Three or four more children or a dozen children will never ease that pain. It was a theft; it was a violation.

From time to time, I make it a point to go through the exhibits that the clerk here has been so diligent in his duty organizing, numbering, and entering into evidence for us. I go through pictures, calling certain photographs to your attention. And I will talk about the letters Cherie wrote to Jessica that I read; but, you know, I would be telling a half story, wouldn't I? Do you recall when we went through a pile of documents with one of the experts called to testify, and saying, "Well, you didn't get these, did you?"

"No, I didn't. No, I didn't. No, I didn't. No, I didn't."

"Why not? Why not? Why not?" Why didn't that expert get all of the documents?

Put it all out! The whole truth! A half-truth is nothing more than that.

It's a worse deception of all, because you may believe it. It has a distinct odor, but the smell is not that of the whole truth.

Certainly, when you weigh the ability to perceive things, you have to also weigh the defendant's ability to perceive the danger of a child's product, and what this defendant corporation did as a matter of business. Weigh that against the opportunity Cherie Bowden had to evaluate that product as a matter of common sense, the duties she has, and what she would or wouldn't do as a caring mother.

The first portion of this case concerns the issues of liability, of which there are two portions. First, our claim against the defendant, because it has been—Cherie and Doug, the Bowdens—it's their claim really because, you see, as I said, I'm not going to be here next week with Cherie and Doug.

This is the verdict form. *[In my trial practice, I have always made it a point to blow up on a fairly large set of placards the jury verdict form. I place the verdict before the jury box and walk through each and every sentence. Usually then, right then, I can see the look in the eyes of the jurors who are going to take the case to the next level and sometimes blow the damn roof right off the courthouse. I could see it. The "look" was there.]* The first claim will be: Was the Johnny Jump-Up defective when sold? Not when sold at the garage sale, because that is another red herring. When sold, as in when it left the manufacturer's plant, whether it was defective for, one: having those loops designed the way they were; or two: defective because it didn't have an appropriate warning. You know, to tell somebody, a consumer, that, hey, something bad could happen if you leave this thing hanging up; and following that determination, whether or not either one was the legal cause of the death of Jessica Bowden. On this second portion regarding the issue of placing blame on these parents for the death of their daughter, the defendant has the burden of proof.

No amount of words can change the fact that when that father—Doug Bowden—saw his little tender daughter, his little princess, the heart of his heart, in those straps that were all over her—do you remember that testimony? How long did it take him to get her out of there? One minute? Ten minutes? It must have seemed like forever. How long does the last week of this trial seem? Damn near forever. Compare the amount of time that the defendant had to fix this product compared to the amount of time that one singular plaintiff had to avoid what happened, because there's no comparison there.

When the defense argues that Doug Bowden was negligent and that he falls below the standard of care in the community because he was taking a catnap, having worked all night at Tampa Electric, it will be your decision as to whether or not he walks out of here with the knowledge that he was a negligent parent. On that score, they have to prove the case of the parents' negligence by the greater weight of the evidence. As the plaintiffs, we have to prove the product was bad. To assess any fault against these people, the defense has the burden of proof. They have got to tip the scales. If they don't tip the scales, no comparative negligence can be found. Was there negligence on the part of Spalding & Evenflo Companies, which was a legal cause? That's the other portion of the liability issue that has to be determined by you. In other words, what they didn't do, or what they did do had to have caused this tragedy. There are two separate issues regarding liability. The defective product and its negligent design is one issue; and whether or not the parents were negligent is the other.

Be very careful here. Be very careful here in breaking these two out. Here you decide about the negligence of Cherie and Doug. You, the jury, have to make a determination whether or not those parents were negligent. And the burden of proof is on each party to prove the other side's fault.

I would ask you to do no more and no less for the parents than you would do for that defendant corporation. Think with your hearts and your minds and apply your common sense and your years of experience. Then the jury verdict form requires you to state the negligence of the three culpable parties that are listed here or could be culpable: Spalding & Evenflo Companies, Inc., Cherie Bowden, and Doug Bowden. You can put a hundred percent against that corporation and zero and zero against Doug Bowden and Cherie Bowden, if you think that's just, if you think that's supported by the evidence.

The funeral expenses listed have been stipulated to in open court—I don't know if you recall that—the four thousand dollars, but that is to be awarded only if the verdict is for the plaintiffs. Only give the parents the money they spent burying Jessica, if you find that the defendant corporation was wrong. Or if you find they didn't act negligently, but their product was bad, that's strict liability, and damages are appropriate.

Next, you must determine what is the total amount of any damages sustained by Cherie Bowden. The young lady is twenty-eight years old and she will live—I gave you the mortality tables; you're not bound by them. The judge will give you an instruction; you don't have to do anything other than use common sense. She's twenty-eight years old. How long is she going to live on this earth, unless her life is unnaturally shortened? Doug is thirty-eight. How long is he going to live, unless he suffers a premature death? That's what you look at. You look at the future, because the future for them is not now. The future for them is all the tomorrows that this next day will bring. That's the verdict form.

I want one of the defense lawyers to get up now, whoever gets up, and talk about this dangerous instrumentality and talk about their knife argument. "Well, you would agree, wouldn't you, Dr. Benedict, that a knife, if a mother and parent aren't right there, a kitchen knife is also a dangerous product, under your definition?"

I'm not going to insult anybody's view of this case, and I'm certainly not going to comment on that type of simplistic argument. Known dangers are known to all, especially parents! It's the hidden dangers that will come out and bite you!

There was an old movie on one of the channels this week. It was in the middle of the night. I would like to say it was *Titanic*, but it wasn't; but it was about a boat sinking. A few of the older men were put on lifeboats because of the respect gleaned from their younger companions and what elderly people have gone through and the joys and experiences that they have had in life. The elderly can understand life best because they have lived it. You see, younger people have never had that opportunity. They have never had the joys to remember because that's been taken from them. Do you understand? Old, you have memories. What a terrible and severe injury to be old and be robbed of the memories that should have been but were lost! Anyway, that movie struck home with me because after the old people were put on the lifeboats, men included, they took the women and put them on with the children. And the boats were too heavy, and they took the men off, the old men. The old warriors came off, and then they took the women off. And finally they left only the children on the lifeboats. The children were left on, not out of sympathy; they were left on out of *self-preservation*, because the lives of children represent the essence of the future and the blood of our destiny.

There is a finality there that is avoided with a child. When you walk around the block with a child, it's not around the block you go. It's around the journey of life. You see, when an adult walks around a block, he looks at his watch. He might say, "Well, it should take about eight minutes"; and he walks around. But when he walks around with a child, the child looks at the trees; the child looks at the birds; the child looks at the squirrels; and it becomes a world full of wonders. And to the child, it doesn't matter how long it takes, because for the young child, it is the walk itself that is life's destination.

Well, I have talked probably more than I needed to; maybe I didn't need to come up here at all. I'm sure the Bowdens will be interested to know how the epitaph of this case is written, but certainly no more interested than the rest of us.

Earlier in the case, I showed you two pictures, one of Jessica's birth and one of her grave. I showed you what apparently were the beginning and the end. But I submit to you that grave marker and the tree that seems to stand guard over her burial site is not the end. I submit to you from this day forward, when Cherie and Doug look at the never-ending story of their lives, they'll have another picture in their minds. They will see each of you, and that will be the last photograph of Jessica's final chapter. They will have other notes that will be written, but none more important than the one you will write, which will be the verdict in this case. And that note won't be read by us to you; that note will be read by you to us.

Thank you.

• • • • • • •

There was an immediate relief as the burden of the Bowdens' case, which I had been carrying for two years, had been finally passed on to the jury. I welcomed the warm, rushing wave of exhaustion as I sat down after giving my closing argument. For the first time in days, Doug and Cherie seemed to show some relief as well. I wanted so much for at least some normalcy to return to their lives after the trauma and turmoil of the litigation warfare that had raged for so long. As I watched Cherie, I remembered her testimony during the trial, of how much Doug's life and her own had changed since their daughter's death.

"Doug's and my relationship has been affected," Cherie had begun a day earlier on the witness stand. "I am constantly walking on egg shells around him, because we can't talk about it. I can't say to my husband, 'Do you remember the time Jessica did this?' 'Do you remember the time Jessica crawled in the bed and asked, Daddy, are you my sweetheart?' I can't talk to him about that. He won't even remember the good times. He doesn't want to remember anything or be reminded in any way about the loss of our little girl."

Her words haunting me, I shifted through my notes as I waited for the judge to give the jury their instructions. My hand rested on a letter that Cherie had written just two months after Jessica's death; it was dated May 19, 1988. Cherie's handwriting was shaky.

I think I'm starting to wake up.. It hurts to look at her pictures. I think I am finally realizing she's not coming back. I love Jessica more than anyone does; no one loves anyone more than I love Jessica. I miss her so much it hurts physically, and my heart aches. I wish I could hear her sweet little chipmunk voice again. I know she's okay, but I have to see her…I need to tell her so much.

I love you, Jess!
Mommy

I put the heartwrenching letter aside and stole a glance at Doug, who was as still as stone. He had also testified the previous day about how his and Cherie's lives had changed. "A lot of my ambition, a lot of desires that I used to have, I no longer have," he had said, not looking at the jury. "I go through periods of sorrow, of grief. I just feel sick inside. We haven't had a decent Christmas since Jessica's death. Vacations are ruined. Every time we try to take a vacation, the memories keep coming back. I think that my marriage has suffered. I have a lot of anger in me, and I believe that I take that out a lot of times around the house. And I cry. There's no specific time. It just happens. I get these memories. I can be driving home from work and an ambulance...hearing a siren brings back those bad thoughts. There are certain television shows that I can't watch. There's just an endless list of things that brings back memories of her."

Next, I looked at the judge and jury, hoping that they had all listened carefully with their heads and their hearts to the facts that had been presented during the trial. Jessica was two years, ten months, and thirteen days old when her life was cut short. Judgment Day had come at last, for the defendant corporation, for the grieving and accused parents—and, as always, for me. Each case was always a personal test. Had I done all that I could? Was the very best case possible presented to the jury?

Judge Gilbert had taken about twenty minutes in his monotone, gravelly voice to read the jury instructions, then he had thanked the alternate juror and excused him from further service. The bailiff, clad in the Irish green blazer of the sheriff's office, had led him quietly out of the jury box. The alternate juror had been seated in the jury box during trial in case of sickness or disqualification of one of the six regular members. The look of utter disappointment could always be seen on alternate jurors' faces, as their chance to deliberate and consummate their hard work and inclusion in the trial process was eliminated. Sometimes—in fact, most times—the alternate juror, now severed from the intimate bonds inevitably formed with his fellow jurors, came back into the courtroom and joined the pack of spectators awaiting the outcome of the deliberations. This juror was no exception. A young man in his early thirties, he chose to speak to no one as he found a seat on the wooden bench nearest the jury box. It was there he began the vigil of waiting, just like the rest of us who watched the six jurors file out to the deliberations room.

After retiring to deliberate, the jury more than likely took no more than twenty minutes to settle down and elect a foreperson. That was the necessary first step in the democratic process unique to our great country. If the issue of liability were to be decided against the plaintiffs, it was almost a certainty that it would happen within that first hour or so of deliberations; the defense always prayed for a "quick knock," knowing that a verdict returned within an hour of the jury's retirement most often meant a victory for the defense.

But sixty minutes passed, and the knock did not come. For the Bowdens and me, the most deadly danger zone had been traversed. I had seen the faces of those jurors. They were with us. We just couldn't lose this case—not for this little angel.

With my peripheral vision, I watched the defense attorneys. Their arrogance had begun to erode during the progression of the trial and virtually evaporated during closing arguments. Blank gazes had replaced the somber and serious looks of concern. By the second hour, the signs of the unbelievable emotional toll were beginning to show on everyone as we sat quietly but nervously, our stares fixed on nothing and everything at the same time. My stomach churned nonstop.

As the hours ticked on, most of the crowd that had packed the courtroom during the long days of trial left. The newspaper and television reporters, anxious to beat deadlines, clustered in the hallways, sipping coffee, scribbling last-minute notes, and gossiping softly among themselves. The case had gleaned such widespread attention for one simple reason: It concerned children and their welfare. Additionally, there was a growing sense the verdict could be large. I welcomed the media's presence; the public had a right to know about this case—win or lose. Standing close by the reporters were two lone courthouse guards, the only security needed for the remaining innocence of a relatively crime-free Tampa.

I hated this part: waiting and wondering, more wondering and more waiting. I'm sure waiting for a jury verdict is the aging machine for trial lawyers. There is no feeling quite like it, and minutes can seem like hours and hours and hours. No matter how strong the heart, there just seems to be a limit to the number of these experiences that a trial attorney can survive.

As the December sun fell close to the horizon, long shadows stretched across the now quiet courtroom battlefield. The cleaning crew methodically moved from one empty courtroom to the next, turning off lights and locking the chamber doors one by one. Only the bright lights of Courtroom Number One remained, illuminating the emptiness. The only activity was behind the tightly closed door of the jury room.

At last, at long last, the bailiff came barreling through the door at the back of the courtroom bearing the news that the three knocks had been heard and the jury had reached its verdict. Every muscle in my body tensed as the jury filed back into the courtroom. Their faces yielded nothing. Most of them kept their eyes downcast as they found their assigned seats in the jury box. My God, why weren't they looking over at us? Usually, when they have ruled in your favor, they look, and sometimes even nod and smile, as if to tip off the verdict before the judge takes away the suspense. Cherie, I noted, was trying valiantly not to cry. Hell, if things kept going like this I'd be crying right with her. The foreman first passed the verdict form to the judge. He reviewed the sacred piece of paper, handed it to his bailiff, and then it was given to the clerk of the court. The judge looked directly at the foreman. "Ladies and gentlemen, have you reached your verdict?"

"Yes, we have, Your Honor," the foreman answered in a strong, sure voice. And then, just before the clerk began reading the verdict, several of the jurors looked away from the judge and we made eye contact. Exhilaration rushed all through me. The clerk's words reverberated through the courtroom that had once again filled with people and confirmed what I already knew—we had won! A super-sized adrenalin rush, some warm embraces, and as quickly as it had come, the joy was swept away, and I was flooded with a bone-tired sense of relief. Somewhere after my first few large verdicts, the rush and happiness began to be replaced. Mostly, what I feel now is a profound relief from not having lost.

The defendant had sought to convince the jury that the sole cause of Jessica's death was the negligence of one or both of her parents. This hard approach is always a dangerous and risky defense, which can produce either a total exoneration or a catastrophe. Today, the agenda for the defendant was catastrophic. In Florida, each juror is required to agree on the verdict. In rendering their decision, the jury unanimously found that the Johnny Jump-Up was poorly designed and Spalding & Evenflo should have warned the parents to take the product down when it was not in use. At the conclusion of the evidentiary portion of the trial, the defendant had requested and obtained a special verdict form submitting for jury consideration the issue of whether or not Jessica's death was caused by the negligence of her parents. The jury answered the question simply and succinctly: No.

Because Spalding & Evenflo had opted to blame Jessica's death entirely on Doug and Cherie and had asked the jury to return a verdict exonerating the corporation from any fault, the defense counsel had not even argued the issue of damages. It was a total victory for the Bowdens. The jury's verdict found Spalding & Evenflo liable to the Bowdens for both negligence and strict liability. The assessment of fault said it all. It was an overwhelming vindication: one hundred percent Spalding & Evenflo's negligence, zero negligence on the part of the parents.

The jury awarded Doug and Cherie $3.75 million each—a total of $7.5 million—for the wrongful death of their precious daughter, Jessica.

We had won every issue.

The Verdict's Aftermath
· · · · · · ·

I t was an outstanding result and the verdict exceeded our most optimistic expectations. However, the jury's verdict would not survive.
After losing the case before the jury, Spalding & Evenflo sought a
new trial on the primary ground that the Bowdens had improperly
presented evidence of a post-remedial measure. Ordinarily, the fact that a
defendant has fixed something after an event is not allowed into evidence
as an indication of liability. The public policy of encouraging people to
remedy things that are broken—subsequent remedial measures—makes
such post-incident activities inadmissible in court. The most often used
example in law schools is the person injured on the rotten staircase. After
the stairs break under the weight of someone who gets hurt, the owner
repairs the stairs. Because our society wants dangerous situations correct-
ed, our laws have made any evidence of the stairway repair inadmissible in
any legal proceedings arising from the person's original fall.

Within the course of the discovery in the case, we had learned there
were at least *two versions* of the warnings associated with the same Johnny
Jump-Up product. An expert witness called by the Bowdens had testified
to his opinion that the Johnny Jump-Up was grossly defective because of
the configuration of the straps. He described a design defect that would
endanger any child who stepped up on the unit while holding the straps
with both hands. He said, "The motion is such that they are going to stick
the head in that loop, and when [children] stick their head in that loop
and step off into the seat after doing that, they are going to hang themselves." Of course, the critical question still remained: Why didn't the defendant, knowing the dangers associated with the exerciser, warn parents
to take the contraption down when it wasn't in use? There was an answer—an alarming, chilling answer—and it was pivotal to our case: There
were warnings placed on the packaging of the Johnny Jump-Up to take
the exerciser down when not in use, *but they were indelibly stamped on the*

packaging and instructions for Johnny Jump-Ups sold solely in Canada! The same product sold in the United States did not contain this warning. It was there in black and white or whatever colors Spalding & Evenflo chose, but they were *only* for Canadians who chose to buy the product.

Judge Gilbert did issue a new trial order, and it was primarily based upon a defense motion for mistrial made during the cross-examination of one of Spalding & Evenflo's expert witnesses, when he was asked, "Isn't it a fact, sir, that in Canada, there's a warning, an additional warning, on this Johnny Jump-Up that says you should take it down because a baby can become entangled [in its straps]; isn't that true?"

"I have no idea," was his reply. His condescending and arrogant demeanor had not changed. I clearly remembered his haughtiness, his simmering animosity when he had answered the question during discovery the year before. Ironically, it was that same damn question that ultimately led Judge Gilbert, post-trial, to grant the defense motion for a new trial. The Canadian warning had been placed on the packaging of the product *after* the date Jessica had been killed. Therefore, the defense argued, it was a "subsequent remedial measure" and could not be used as evidence.

On that critical point, in arguing against a new trial we emphasized to the court that the date of the warning was immaterial. We pointed out to the judge that the defendant corporation had strenuously asserted the product posed no risk of strangulation and no such incidents had ever occurred. In light of those circumstances, the defense had justified the inescapable fact that no warning was put on the packaging by asserting that strangulation was not a "foreseeable" danger. The fact that this defendant manufacturer had, on the contrary, warned the hanging product posed a risk—regardless of when—proved conclusively that the danger was not only known, but also appreciated by the defendant. We argued that the warning was not a subsequent remedial measure: It was a written acknowledgment that the product posed a known and appreciated risk.

At the time, the verdict was one of the largest wrongful death judgments in Florida's history. Undoubtedly its sheer enormity had some effect on the presiding judge's decision to rule conservatively on the issue of a new trial. It was also an emotional case with a high public profile.

Whether it was the evidence, the case, the misguided arguments of the defense, or just the overwhelming size of the verdict, seven months after the trial had concluded, Judge Gilbert vacated the jury's decision in its entirety and ordered a new trial. Our only recourse was to appeal the trial judge's decision to a higher court. Our shock and disbelief at the misuse of this evidentiary prohibition concerning remedial measures served to further strengthen our resolve.

On appeal, the defendant corporation continued the nastiness of its attacks and suggested that the trial had been an "emotional circus." One instance, they argued, that was especially illustrative of the atmosphere in which they were forced to defend themselves was the introduction into evidence of the touching letters that Cherie had written to Jessica. "Even the cold record," the defense explained in the brief, "[the letters'] emotional impact is manifest, and the *manner* in which they were published to the jury unduly exacerbated their effect. While reading from the letters, Mrs. Bowden was so overcome with emotion that she could not continue."

During the trial, the defense counsel had objected to Cherie's reading the letters and had asked the court to require that someone else read them. I ended up reading the mother's writings to her baby daughter. Sincere, profound, and from the heart, these pieces of evidence were certainly emotional, but each one spoke the truth. It afforded a clear window to view her suffering and the pain and sorrow raging within her. How in the world can emotion be taken out of a case involving this magnitude of tragedy? It can't. Ever.

The defense also complained to the appeals court that we were making "invidious comparisons" between the Bowdens and the "big corporation" they were up against. Even worse, the defendant argued that I had labeled them a "thief" of Jessica's life in closing argument and had made accusations that they were more interested in money than the safety of their product. The jury, the defendant said of the trial, was entreated by me to "punish the thief" and thereby "send a message" to manufacturers of children's products. The vilifications and nature of attack used on the appeal were unusually mean-spirited. The arguments of defendants that urge a judge to take away multimillion-dollar verdicts are usually very similar: There was "too much emotion" at the trial, or the verdict was the "product of a runaway jury," and on and on and on. Anything to escape taking responsibility or paying money.

Given the poisoning of our society by distorted facts and outright lies, Americans seeking justice face the presumption that big verdicts are flawed, improperly obtained, and should be reduced, if not entirely eliminated. The insurance companies have done a great job of wrongfully convincing too many American people that we have a litigation crisis and our system of justice is out of control.

Millions for defense, but not a dime for compensation: That seems to be the credo of the insurance industry. The defendant's assault was relentless as its appellate brief continued. "The trial court did not abuse its discretion in granting a new trial; indeed plaintiffs' counsel anticipated as much during the trial. The 'circus' atmosphere surrounding the trial, the improper conduct of plaintiffs' counsel, and the relentless emotionalism to which the jury was exposed plainly required a new trial on all issues. By alluding to the supposed fact—which was in truth not a fact at all—that defendant had furnished Canadian parents with a superior warning on the product, plaintiffs' counsel foreclosed any possibility of a fair assessment by the jury of defendant's conduct, and assured that the verdict would be the product of prejudice and rage. In sum, plaintiffs' counsel—in violation of the rules governing lawyer conduct, in violation of a specific ruling of the trial court, and in violation of his own assurances to the trial court that he would 'leave the issue' and not 'risk' the record—deliberately threw a skunk in the jury box and, while the cold record still reeks, this Court, in assessing the trial court's exercise of its discretion, is bound to acknowledge that the trial judge smelled the stench firsthand. Moreover, the record demonstrates a relentless campaign by plaintiffs' counsel to deflect the jury away from the dispassionate and unbiased decision-making process. Among other things, counsel personally vouched for the truth of their clients' cause, personally testified on behalf of their clients during argument, referred to wholly improper, punitive measures of damages after being admonished not to do so, referred pointedly to the economic disparity between the parties, and sought, in a civil case, to criminalize the defendant's conduct. This pattern of behavior apparently stemmed from the disturbing attitude altogether too prevalent among trial lawyers these days—'get the verdict any way you can and worry about it later.' Finally, the record further demonstrates that the trial was supercharged with excessive emotionalism. All of this was successfully calculated to prompt the jury to act from outrage and sympathy and in contravention of the solemn obligations of the jury charge."

In contrast, our approach was directed toward the merits of the evidence. I never really cared for the personal attacks on the attorneys involved in a case, nor was I impressed with the style of nastiness that has come to be known as "hardball litigation." In part, our own appellate briefs read, "The inquiry about the Canadian version of defendant's product was proper for several reasons. It went to impeachment of the defendant's claim that it had made no changes in the warnings for using the Jump-Up in ten years and that there was no difference between the warnings on American and foreign Jump-Ups. Furthermore, defendant created the situation by its lack of candor in discovery. The defense should have produced the Canadian warning rather than deny its existence. In any event, the warning demonstrated the defendant's awareness that strangulation was a foreseeable and known risk of the product."

We further asserted there was no factual basis to find the trial was conducted improperly or with excessive emotionalism. In fact, the record was devoid of any motions for mistrial on the basis of emotion. The jury was never excused because of emotion, nor was any recess taken. The single motion for mistrial based on alleged attorney conduct was summarily denied. In our extensive arguments to get the Bowden verdict restored, we pointed out the trial court recognized that there was no basis for a new trial on these grounds. The substantial evidence against the defendant, a correct application of the law, and a fair reading of the record required the reversal of the new trial order and reinstatement of the jury verdict.

Unfortunately, the new trial order could be reversed and the jury trial reinstated only if the judge had abused his discretion or made a distinct error in the adjudication of the applicable law. Because of this extremely high standard of review, reversals of a trial judge's rulings are rare and occur in little more than ten percent of the cases appealed. Unfortunately, the jurors' unequivocal recognition of the Bowdens' loss was not restored. Without commenting or rendering a written opinion, the appeals court let the new trial order stand. Left with no choice, we would simply have to do it again. My disappointment was replaced by renewed determination and a resolve to once more seek the justice that Jessica's death demanded.

When I met with Doug and Cherie to discuss the impact of the appellate proceedings and the fact that a new trial would be necessary, I was surprised at their acceptance and obvious satisfaction over the final outcome. The Bowdens were genuinely good people. Their goal had never been money. As parents, each sought to establish wrongdoing on the part of the toy manufacturer. More importantly, the exoneration by the jurors of their parental conduct gave Doug and Cherie closure and redemption from the incessant self-blame, as well as the direct accusations of the defendant and its bevy of lawyers.

Shortly after Judge Gilbert scheduled the case for a second trial, I received a handwritten note from Cherie. She explained ever so graciously how much the trial had meant to them. Her profuse expressions of gratitude and kindness brought tears to my eyes. Cherie also shared with me that they had been through enough. She expressed her concerns of the effect a second trial might have on him, on her, and ultimately, upon the entire family. The jury verdict had brought resolution and a peace to the struggle surrounding the tragedy.

She asked me to exert my best efforts to resolve the litigation and avoid a retrial. In a confidential settlement, the entire case was settled and the matter dismissed from the court's docket. While no "guilt" was acknowledged, the terms of the agreement were acceptable to the Bowden family. Presently, Doug and Cherie are doing quite well. None of their six children will ever have to worry about receiving the unconditional love of two great parents.

Epilogue

hen the case of Jessica Bowden was over, I came away having learned many things. I more fully understood that the career of a trial lawyer cannot last very long. Emotionally, the cases just take too much of a toll. I can personally attest to the emotional wear and tear, and the price it unavoid-ably extracts. There just aren't a whole lot of trial lawyers much past fifty that routinely walk into a courtroom.

For me, this case—the wrongful death of an infant—was one of the hardest cases I ever had to try. I simply cannot even fathom the loss of my own son, Gable. Such thoughts are incomprehensible to me. No matter how old a child is, he or she is still that little baby to the parent. Every-thing we ever dreamed of, all our hopes and plans, are represented by our children. One of the biggest fears we face as human beings—death and our own mortality—is counterbalanced by children. A child represents the continuity of life, the potential realization of our unfulfilled dreams, and ultimately a living testament to our own life. It makes the acceptance of our own death so much easier.

As surely as night follows day, we, as parents, expect our children to bury us. Through Jessica Bowden's case, I had a renewed and even deeper appreciation of young children. A child is a real-life miracle. Certainly, Gable has been the greatest miracle that ever happened to me. What I didn't have in my soul before this case was the heartache that comes with losing a child. I shall never forget the actual pain I felt deep inside regard-ing the death of this beautiful little girl. The emotions of the case haunted me to the point where I had difficulty sleeping and eating. The case drove me to the fringes of depression, and I sometimes struggled to keep its darkness away. More than once, I went to bed thinking of this young girl, Jessica, and Doug's description of how he tried to tear that deadly strap away from the throat of his daughter. I felt firsthand his sickness as she lay dead in his arms. It was the worst kind of nightmare because I knew it was real. It was something that happened, and in trying this case, I had relived it in vivid detail, as if the ghoulish experience had been mine.

Jessica's death gave me an appreciation for the value of life and what has been bestowed upon me—the ability to bring life into this world. In the realm of manufacturers and consumers, there is always a fine and sub-tle line between profit and safety. We have been taught these lessons in our industrial history, and we have experienced those teachings in the modern world. In the last few decades, the expansion of product liability litigation has illustrated the necessity of such a demarcation. We have seen it in the

Ford Pinto cases, we have learned through asbestos litigation, and we have had a nationwide view in the courtroom wars involving tobacco. The demand for corporate profit has pushed the envelope of consumer safety and regard for others and the lives of our people to see a new horizon—a horizon where we realize that corporate America is not always concerned with our welfare. What used to be a blind, almost knee-jerk entitlement of trust given to corporate America—that industry is good, companies protect us, and the products they make are safe—has now become a painful realization that sometimes safety is compromised so that money can be made.

In corporate America, pain and suffering don't translate well into the bottom-line concept of dollars. Until big business understands pain and suffering and death in terms to which it can relate—that is, dollars and cents—there can be no real, meaningful change. The loss of a child—no matter how many children a family may have—is a catastrophic and devastating experience. Trial work requires me to tear down the boundaries between myself and my clients. I have come to feel the pain, suffer the loss, and walk the paths of those people I represent. Jessica was a special little treasure, an angel from heaven. Every good parent knows that the most valuable and precious gift of life is the blessing of a child. When a child dies, part of the parent dies also.

This case reaffirmed my view that there remains in our society a fervent belief that our system of justice works. The ancient jury system in its most fundamental form—that of strangers sitting in judgment on the lives of their peers, recording what is right and what is wrong in the form of a jury verdict—is still the best legal process in the world. And the Bowdens truly believed in that justice. Had that jury found them negligent and wrongful in their actions, deciding that they contributed in any way to their baby's death, the Bowdens would have believed a rightful conviction had occurred. When the jury came back and found the Bowdens were totally free from any wrongdoing, I could actually see the physical reaction when each of them sat upright and erect, as though the weight of the terrible burden they had been carrying on their shoulders was lifted. The reaction was not to the large monetary award, which had not yet been read. Their exoneration meant everything. It was never about the money. Absolved from guilt, they were freed to go through the natural grieving process that would ultimately give them the ability to go on with life.

When a young child like Jessica dies, parents' dreams for the future of the child die as well. Those parents will never see their little girl graduate from high school, give her away at a wedding, or share life with her as she becomes a woman. Cherie will never have those mother-daughter talks with Jessica, buy her that first prom dress, or explain to her the wonderful miracle of having a child. The Bowdens will never experience any of that with Jessica. And for the rest of their lives, each will be haunted by the memories of what could have been...but will never be. The salvation they will always have is that their grievous loss will always be tempered by the knowledge that these parents never gave up. They stayed the course and, in the end, made some sense of the unnecessary loss of one of God's youngest angels.

The exercisers have since been redesigned, and more warnings have been posted on the packaging cautioning parents against the dangers that the children may encounter when using the jumpers. Effective in April 1990, Spalding & Evenflo Companies, Inc. incorporated a warning on the instructions of Johnny Jump-Up baby exercisers that reads: *"Always remove baby exerciser from doorway, when not in use, to prevent entanglement in the straps."*

The haunting circumstances of Jessica's death will never be totally erased from Doug and Cherie's minds, but they have managed to go on with their lives, grow stronger as parents and as husband and wife, secure in the knowledge that perhaps—just perhaps—another child's life was saved because of what they did.

· · · · · · · ·

For the Master, this one was almost too easy. Notre Dame's legendary head coach Frank Leahy earned that nickname, in part, due to his unmatched ability to motivate his players. Regardless of circumstance, no matter how talented his team happened to be, no matter how inferior the rest of the world deemed his upcoming opponent to be, Leahy had an uncanny ability to get the most out of his players...The 1949 Irish talent cupboard was typically overstocked. It appeared to nearly everyone that Notre Dame had the means, the motive, and the opportunity to reclaim its accustomed spot atop the college football world...All that stood between Notre Dame and another national championship was a final game at SMU...After three quarters, Notre Dame appeared to be in command, leading 20-7. But SMU's Kyle Rote, capping a brilliant game, scored twice early in the fourth period to tie the score. A Frank Spaniel kick return gave the Irish the ball near midfield. From there, a smash-mouth rushing game...put Notre Dame back in front 27-20. An interception...in the Irish end zone preserved the game, the perfect season, and Notre Dame's third national championship in four seasons... No other team can boast a four-year record to match. Even more, Leahy instilled within his players a love for each other and for Notre Dame that lives on to this day.

■ ■ ■

—Craig Chval, 1999

Frank Spaniel in a classic football pose from his Notre Dame days.

CHAPTER THREE

Fourth and Goal

Toward the end of the deposition on March 9, 1994, Frank Spaniel became tired and frustrated. The last hour of questions and answers had been long, and Frank, weakened by medication and the sheer effort it took to answer the queries, began to look ghostly pale and haggard. His breathing was labored, aided only by willpower and the tube of oxygen flowing into his nostrils. Once topping out at nearly two hundred pounds of muscle and vigor, Frank now weighed 125, only a fraction of the powerful and robust man he had been before. The proof of his former strength lay on his right hand, where he wore a heavy ring: That circle of gold was a National College Football Championship ring from Notre Dame, dated 1949. The team, with Frank as halfback, had been selected by the Associated Press poll of writers as the best in college football in the nation for two of the four years he played. And even at the end of the year 2000, his Notre Dame, which was undefeated in 1946, 1947, 1948, and 1949, was recognized by *Sports Illustrated* as one of the century's greatest teams. Those years were known as the Golden Era of Notre Dame football. Four decades later, Frank still wore the ring, rarely taking it off, as a symbol of the college championship's—and his own—enduring legacy.

The questions—sometimes peppered with objections—came one after the other, in rapid fashion, from the defense attorney and from me. Because he was having great difficulty with his speech, Frank would sometimes supplement his answers using a notepad in his lap, and as the pen moved across the paper, the championship ring glinted even in the dim fluorescent lighting of the stark white hospital room. He was lying on a bed lined with monitors, an intravenous tree supplying liquids, and an oxygen tank with a mask at the ready in case it was needed to help him breathe.

Frank Spaniel was surrounded by lawyers, nurses, a court reporter, and his family. He was dying of throat cancer. Most of his throat and all of his vocal cords had been ravaged by the disease. All that he had been, all that he was, and all that he could ever hope to be, would be brought to summation in those few moments of deposition. Many times the pain that wracked his body showed in Frank's eyes behind his large, wire-frame glasses and through the suppressed grimace on his face. But like the warrior he had always been, he bravely kept going as the questions spilled out of my mouth. "Did you learn you had cancer in your throat?"

Frank nodded and managed a muffled "Yes."

"And how did you feel when you were told that?" I asked him, already knowing the answer. These questions and answers would be for the benefit of a jury, and also for the defense attorney who hovered so closely by.

He paused and chose to write his answer: *Sick.*

"Why did you feel sick, Mr. Spaniel? Take your time, sir. Why were you so upset?"

Again the pen scratched across the paper: *The cancer wasn't found before this.*

Strengthened by Frank's own resolve, I went forward with the questioning. "Did you ever learn that *had* this cancer been found in November of 1990, when you first visited a doctor for your sore throat, your voice box would have been saved, and most likely your cancer could have been cured?"

"Yes," he answered.

"Tell us as best as you can," I started my next question carefully, "what it was like before you got sick, in terms of your life. Just tell what your life was like before the cancer."

Although he was so ill he could barely hold his head up, there was no hesitation in Frank's handwriting as he wrote, *It was a joy. I could taste. I could talk and communicate with my wife, my family, and the people I miss so much. I played golf. I swam. I was a good husband. I hope I was a good father and grandfather.*

My next words were softly spoken. "Mr. Spaniel, what has your life has been like after this cancer was discovered in the spring of 1991 until now, sir?"

He looked directly at me, and then his eyes moved around the roomful of people, each waiting and watching his every move. He gripped the pen, glanced down at the paper for a moment, and began to write in bold strokes. *I can do none of the things that I enjoyed in life. I am living in hell.*

Another question followed. "In the event this deposition is read to the jury when your case comes to trial, is there anything you would like to talk about, or anything you would like to tell the ladies and gentlemen of the jury?"

Frank sighed deeply, and then scrawled, *I hope that what we are doing will prevent things like this from happening to other people.*

There were only two more questions I had of Frank. "What did you love most about life when you were healthy?"

Being able to go out with friends, play golf with my wife, and accomplish something together with a group. A very slight smile crossed his face as he wrote. Perhaps, I thought, a wonderful memory had passed quickly through his mind.

"My last question," I said as I looked directly into his eyes. "Mr. Spaniel, now that your ability to live has been damaged, what do you dislike most about life?"

This time, there was no hint of a smile as he answered, *The pain in everything.*

He laid the pen aside, defeated and drained. Even the defense attorney looked down at the floor, his eyes refusing to meet Frank Spaniel's. The deposition was over.

Everyone involved in the lawsuit expected Frank to be dead by the time the trial commenced. The doctor, the lawyers, even the most loving members of his family expected death to be imminent. In the event he died, the deposition would be used at trial to preserve his testimony. But Frank Spaniel was a fighter. The deposition transcript was never needed.

First Down:
An All-American Start
· · · · · · ·

T he first part of the biography of Frank Spaniel Jr. reads like the American Dream. He came from a family whose ethics were solid Pennsylvania working class, those folks who relished hard work and treated it as a gift and not a chore. Frank was born on May 21, 1928, to Frank Sr. and Stella Spaniel in Vandergrift, a small village in the rolling, rocky hills northeast of Pittsburgh. His father was a blue-collar worker at United Engineering Foundry for forty-five years; his mother stayed at home rearing him and his sister, Eileen, who was ten years his junior.

Frank had been a star from the beginning. He was also a born leader whom people liked and respected. A popular student, he was elected class president during his senior year in high school, and he lettered in four sports. Because of his outstanding talent as a running back, Frank was recruited heavily by a number of large colleges, including the University of Notre Dame. When that school offered him a full four-year scholarship, Frank jumped at the chance to live his dream of being a part of the Fighting Irish. The citizens of Vandergrift hailed the young man as their town hero, and in the fall of 1946, Frank packed his belongings and made the move to South Bend, Indiana. During his college years, from 1946 to 1950, he became a star running back on a spectacular football team that never lost a game.

After he graduated, Frank went to work carrying the football for the NFL's Washington Redskins. He met a beautiful young lady, Kathryn Sebring, during one of his trips back home to Pennsylvania, and the two fell in love at first sight. Frank's career with the Redskins abruptly ended when he was drafted into the army. Prior to leaving for basic training, he asked Kathryn to marry him. They were wed on February 2, 1951. Upon entering the service he was stationed at Fort Benning, Georgia. It was there, in the heart of the hot and sultry South, that Frank and Kathryn began their family. Exactly nine months after their marriage, on November 2, 1951, the couple's first child, Kirk, was born.

In 1953, Frank was honorably discharged from the army, and the young Spaniel family moved back to his hometown, where Frank bought their first home with money saved from his stint in the military. As a civilian, Frank found work as a salesman for the Pittsburgh Plate Glass Company. He and Kathryn soon were blessed with their second child, a beautiful daughter named Debbie. By the late 1950s, Frank had worked his way up to middle management with Allenwood Steel Company in Plymouth Meeting. He was beginning to experience the type of success in the business world that would ensure financial comfort and security. By 1964, Allenwood Steel had become Penco Products, Inc., and Frank had achieved vice-presidency of the entire manufacturing division. Two more daughters, Beth and Mary Kay, completed the family.

Even with all the activities of four growing children, Frank and Kathryn always found time to steal afternoons together to indulge in their mutual passion of golf. The entire family took vacations to places like Doral, Palm Springs, Puerto Rico, and Jamaica, invariably near a golf course. The Spaniels also delighted in watching football games, both college and professional, and regularly returned to Frank's beloved alma mater, Notre Dame. His love for the Fighting Irish was infectious, and the whole family followed the ups and downs of South Bend football. No matter how hard the day, when Frank came home from work he always made it a point to play sports of all types with his son and three daughters. He loved to challenge his children to see who could throw a ball the farthest or who could run the fastest. Sometimes, it was rumored, he let the girls win—a charge he vehemently denied. Through the years, he was an ideal husband, father, and friend.

In 1972, Frank was named president of Penco Products and was given full responsibility for running the company. During the 1970s,

Frank spearheaded a revamping of its marketing and distribution systems. He instituted cost containment programs and modernized the whole company with a major computer installation. Penco's profitability sky-rocketed. Frank was instrumental in the company's fabulous success, as it became a significant player in the country's steel industry.

By 1989, the four Spaniel children—Kirk, Debbie, Beth, and Mary Kay—were grown and had families of their own. Frank had seven grand-children—four grandsons and three granddaughters. Finally, his golden years of retirement and the opportunity for full-time personal enjoy-ment of life had arrived. In 1990, Frank and Kathryn sold their home in Pennsylvania and moved to Fort Myers, a bustling town on the Gold Coast of southern Florida. The couple found an ideal home minutes from the clear, sparkling waters of the Gulf of Mexico overlooking the green grass and white sands of a golf course.

Frank Spaniel was a vibrant sixty-two years old. He rarely sat still for very long and grabbed each day of life with gusto. Quick with a laugh and a smile, Frank often took center stage to entertain his wife, visiting family members, and the close circle of friends they had developed in the golf course community now called home. Days of hard work at the office were replaced with the leisure of gardening, socializing, and spending countless hours with his wife enjoying the fruits of the decades of love they shared. Fortunately, Frank's favorite golf partner was his wife. When he wasn't playing with Kathryn, he was part of a regular foursome of buddies, also retirees who were always ready to hit the links. Frank was a family man and relished his newfound occupation of being around his children and grandchildren, and the woman he adored. Holidays had al-ways been special times, and now every day seemed like one.

And then, because of medical malpractice, the Spaniels' happy lives were shattered.

Second Down:
Thrown for a Loss

• • • • • • •

rank had always been healthy, but in the early summer of 1990, he began experiencing pain and discomfort in his neck and throat that radiated to his right ear and that was aggravated when he swallowed. He also began to experience intermittent hoarseness. There was no dysphasia (a medical term that would become all too familiar to him), which means the impairment of the ability to speak or understand language, nor had Frank suffered any hearing loss. Frank and Kathryn went to see Dr. Richard Wingert, an ear, nose, and throat specialist, to determine exactly what was causing his problems.

On November 9, 1990, Frank gave a history to Dr. Wingert of being a healthy person who was a moderate smoker, perhaps a pack or so of cigarettes a day, and a social drinker. Dr. Wingert's physical examination of Frank revealed the presence of irritated rhinitis—inflammation of the nasal mucous membrane—which he attributed to tobacco smoke, and he also noted reddened mucous membranes. The doctor examined Frank's nasal passages by decongesting, anesthetizing, and viewing the areas with a Michida Fibrelaryngoscope, a rather sophisticated type of endoscope, or internal viewing instrument, used by ear, nose, and throat specialists. Dr. Wingert noted there were no nasal lesions present. Both the nasopharynx (the upper part of the throat lying directly behind the nasal passages and above the soft palate) and the larynx (the structure of muscle and cartilage at the upper end of the trachea containing the vocal cords, otherwise known as the voice box) were normal and clear. At the same time, Dr. Wingert indicated in his office records that the examination was difficult to complete due to a large amount of secretions in Frank's larynx. The diagnosis was simple: probable inflammation causing right throat pain with some pain radiating to the ear. Dr. Wingert prescribed an antibiotic and a steroid and advised Frank to return in ten days for a repeat examination and endoscopic evaluation. The Spaniels left the physician's office feeling relieved there was nothing seriously wrong.

Ten days passed, and Frank was feeling somewhat better when he returned to see Dr. Wingert. Dr. Wingert examined Frank with the scope but still didn't find any nasal lesions. Once again, the doctor noted a questionable accumulation of mucus. He told Frank that while he did not see any actual evidence of cancer, he was worried there might be some abnormal growth of tissue present. Because the actual physical examination had been limited in its capabilities, a CT scan of Frank's neck and pharynx was ordered. Computerized axial tomography, or CT, is a noninvasive imaging technique used by radiologists to help diagnose various disorders inside the body, especially in areas involving soft tissue. The CT scan can reveal things that even the trained eye of a clinical physician using an endoscope cannot see. It combines a series of computer-generated image "slices" to create a three-dimensional view of the area being scanned. The scan ordered for Frank would focus on the muscular and membranous tissues of the cavity leading from the mouth and nasal passages to the sinuses, the larynx, and the esophagus. The scan would be conclusive and the doctor wanted it to rule out the possibility of cancer.

The CT scan was performed at Cape Coral CT Scanner, Inc. Dr. James Walters, a radiologist and shareholder in the firm that owned the corporation, interpreted the scan as "negative." Frank was notified by Dr. Wingert's office on November 29 that the results of his head and neck CT scans were reported as negative for tumor. He was then instructed by Dr. Wingert to return for a "sinus wash."

Still, in early December when he visited Dr. Wingert, Frank expressed concern that his symptoms were persisting. Dr. Wingert reassured him no cancer had been detected by Dr. Walters and everything would be fine. Dr. Wingert's method of treatment, based on that negative CT scan, was to irrigate the sinuses and cleanse the inflamed tissue. The liquid flow from the irrigation was clear and consistent with the original diagnosis of "right maxillary sinusitis, manifest by mucosal edema." As a follow-up, a three-week course of antibiotics was ordered.

As winter and spring passed, Frank's symptoms of sinus and ear pain came and went. Dr. Wingert continued to follow up on Frank, even performing minor sinus surgery that provided some relief. Still, Frank kept having problems and came to accept the intermittent pain in his sinuses as something he just had to live with. By June, despite the periodic treatments for what he believed to be a sinus condition, Frank's symptoms had begun to significantly increase. He had pain and swelling on the right side of his face, including his ears and most of his sinuses. More troubling, he was having a difficult time swallowing and had lost almost thirty pounds. Dr. Wingert's endoscopic examination revealed marked swelling in Frank's throat and Dr. Wingert showed obvious concern when he told his patient that cancer was now suspected. A repeat CT scan was immediately performed, only this time Dr. Robert E. Gerson, not Dr. Walters, read the radiology films. Dr. Gerson confirmed the cancer, and everyone's worst fears were realized.

With the positive results of the CT scan, Frank was immediately admitted to Cape Coral Hospital. More tests revealed that Frank's cancer was not only in his throat, but had spread throughout his throat, up into his sinus cavities, and invaded other regions of his head. Frank and Kathryn were faced with a dreaded disease that was always thought to be a death sentence by those in their generation. After initial fear came the denial, then the anger, and finally the resignation and acceptance of the grim situation confronting them.

Frank and Kathryn found Drs. Richard and Edward Farrior, brilliant father and son surgeons located in Tampa Bay who specialized in cancer of the head and neck, as well as plastic surgery and facial reconstruction. On July 10, 1991, Frank underwent a series of procedures that included a direct laryngoscopy and esophagoscopy, tracheotomy, right modified radical neck dissection, and partial pharyngolaryngectomy. The size and site of the tumor necessitated removing most of the right side of Frank's throat, including his voice box and vocal cords, which meant Frank would no longer be able to speak without the assistance of a mechanical audio device.

During surgery, the doctors cut out tissue samples that were sent to pathology for extensive examination. When the surgeon called Frank's home a few days later, the news was grim. The cancer could not be totally removed, and there was little doubt it had already begun to spread throughout Frank's body.

Disease had been found in his lymph node system. A course of painful radiation treatments was commenced. The family held heart-to-heart discussions of the most tender kind, and Frank was adamant that he would not go down without a fight. Over an almost two-year period, Frank underwent extensive radiation and various other forms of cancer treatment. Radiation to his jaw had required the removal of his teeth. The condition of his throat, or what was left of it, prevented him from eating solid food. The disease, plus his inability to ingest food through his mouth, caused even further and more dramatic weight loss, and this former football star became half the man he had been physically as the disease ravaged him.

By the time Frank and Kathryn came to see me to discuss the possibility of a malpractice suit against Dr. Walters and his radiology group, Frank had lost the ability to speak naturally, taste, play golf, swim, socialize with friends or family, or do almost any of the things he had previously enjoyed. His life of pain medication, liquid meals fed through a tube, and dependence on others was now a nightmare. In the midst of his illness, his daughter Mary Kay was tragically killed in an automobile accident. And then, only months before his visit to my office, his beloved Kathryn was diagnosed with brain cancer. As he and his wife shared the details of their tragedy with me, I saw and felt their pain as their world came apart.

In the year I prepared the case for trial, I grew very close to Frank. During the worst of Kathryn's illness, Frank refrained from taking his own cancer treatments so that he could sit at the bedside of his wife as she lay dying. Frank was that kind of person. He always put others ahead of himself. Somewhere along his journey, he had already learned life's most valuable lesson: Giving was better than getting. Always.

Part of Frank's heart died when Kathryn passed away on March 5, 1994, just four days before Frank's deposition in the hospital and only a month away from the trial. After Kathryn's death, Frank became very, very sick. It was almost as though he had willed himself to stay alive in order to be with his wife until the end. His oldest daughter, Debbie, had taken over the duties of caring for her parents when they could no longer care for each other or themselves. A day in Frank Spaniel's life was directly on the opposite side of the coin from the American Dream he had once lived. I would use Debbie as a key witness at trial to describe Frank's suffering and the ordeal of simply getting through a day...or a night.

Debbie told of the difficult time Frank had putting on his clothes in the morning. Sometimes the task would take him a half hour or even longer. Even then, he would only ask for help if he became too frustrated or too weak to continue. Although Frank had a bedside toilet so he wouldn't have to walk the few steps to the bathroom, he refused to use it. Instead, he insisted on struggling to the bathroom. That task and virtually everything he did required the greatest of efforts. But Frank fought to preserve his dignity and his pride. Home healthcare nurses made regular visits to help him with his medications and bathing, and the compassionate and dedicated hospice workers were always there to provide emotional support. Even near the end, Frank tried to take his own showers and only when he could no longer get out of bed did he submit to being bathed.

Over Frank's vehement objections, Debbie helped him clean his gastronomy tube, which led into his abdomen so that he could get the nutrition he needed. She insisted on doing it because she wanted to spare her father humiliation in front of someone who wasn't family. Frank could have no solid food. He tried to keep up his strength by living on three cans of liquid nutrition a day. It took five hours for one meal to be given through the tube. He received one can early in the day, another during his afternoon nap, and the third while he slept at night. Sometimes, Frank asked for a glass of water, but he would only take a sip or two before shoving the glass aside. When I would meet with Frank and discuss his life and, sometimes, the case, his frustrations and the horribleness of his awful predicament were sometimes acted out in anger and emphasized by large block letters he scrawled with great force across his ever-present notepad.

Frank's medication was also given through his gastronomy tube. Cleaning the tube and giving Frank his medicine took about twenty minutes and had to be done four times a day. After he took his medication, Frank would get fully dressed. It was part of his routine and one of the last vestiges of his once-normal life. He would insist on getting out of his pajamas before he sat down to read the newspaper. He always read the sports section first, and then read every remaining section almost as if he was studying for a test. After at least an hour with his newspaper, he would stay seated on the patio and watch the golfers play through the fairway adjoining his backyard. His friends drove by on their carts and waved to him. Occasionally, on Sundays, some of his golfing buddies would take him for a ten-minute ride on the golf course.

When I first sat down and talked with Debbie at length, she said the thing that bothered her most was seeing her father cry. She told me he cried a lot, and that scared her. The time we spent together created a bond that exceeded the attorney-client relationship. We became friends. Debbie shared her heartache and her feelings, and I learned that it wasn't just Frank who cried. Debbie spent much of her alone time in tears. Always fearful that her father would see her, she would do her best to control her anguish and the emotions that raged just beneath the surface. When Frank slept, she told me how her sobbing was sometimes uncontrollable.

I have always believed that a lawyer must "walk in his clients' shoes." To fully appreciate and comprehend the loss, not just "understand" it, the mind must meld with the heart and the raw emotion of it all must be experienced. Before long, that happened to me and I began to feel the enormity of it all.

Those years after Frank moved to Florida were supposed to be the happiest of his life. After Kathryn's death and the premature death of Mary Kay, Frank's tears came more easily in front of me. Many times we sat together while he would fondly recall some of his favorite memories of his beloved wife and daughter. Whether it was the medication or wishful fantasy, he seemed to become lost in the happy memories and there would be minutes of silence while a slight smile stayed on his face. When I was in Tampa, Debbie would sometimes call me and put Frank on the phone. The conversations were one way, because Frank couldn't use his machine to speak on the phone. I am certainly no Knute Rockne, but on those special phone calls I gave him the best morale-boosting monologue I could muster. Debbie would take the phone and let me know if either my encouragement or my jokes were working. It was a great thrill when she told me I had been able to make him break into a grin…or at least stop crying.

Third Down:
A Case of Medical Malpractice
. . . .

The case, *Frank Spaniel Jr. and Kathryn Spaniel, Plaintiffs, Versus James W. Walters, M.D., and Smith, Hendra & Gerson, M.D., M.D., P.A.*, was filed in the circuit court for Lee County, Florida. My team and I prepared long and hard for this trial and we were ready to prevail in the courtroom. Two people in particular provided invaluable assistance before and during the trial. In medical malpractice cases, I find it very helpful to have a healthcare professional working with me, and I was blessed to have found an extraordinary asset in Wendi Towbin-Dolgin. Wendi is a registered nurse who possesses extensive knowledge of both medicine and hospital protocol. For years, she has assisted me in evaluating potential medical malpractice cases, from the initial interview of the client through the trial itself. She collects and assimilates all the medical records, reviews and analyzes them, prepares medical timelines and reports, and helps evaluate and deal with expert witnesses, who can be so critical to the success of a case. I find one of the greatest benefits she brings is building relationships with the doctors, nurses, and other healthcare providers involved in the care and treatment of our clients. As we began this trial, Wendi was working with me behind the scenes.

Sitting at my side as "second chair" in the courtroom was Lisa Kelley, a bright young lawyer. Lisa had been working diligently for the many months leading up to jury selection and the trial—researching the law, preparing numerous motions, taking some of the depositions, organizing exhibits, and marshalling the witnesses. During the trial, Lisa would be responsible for accessing documents and transcripts, taking notes of key points made during examination and cross-examination and making them available for my use in preparing the final argument, as well as reviewing the key evidentiary points made during the proceedings. Good lawyer that she is, Lisa would also contribute her enthusiasm and energy to keep everyone on our team positive and sharp.

Lisa has gone on to become a successful trial attorney. She now has her own "second chair" to assist her in the courtroom.

At the time of trial, the defendants' final offer to settle the case was a paltry $50,000; our demand was $250,000. It was a modest sum, at least in my view, but it would provide some needed money so Frank's last days would be bearable. We were turned down cold.

Despite Frank's extreme illness and inability to eat, drink, or even speak, he defied the odds and lived long enough to appear at trial. Through sheer will, determination, and courage, he made it through two grueling weeks of courtroom proceedings. He did not miss a day and took breaks only when the jury was also excused.

During the trial when I announced Frank as a witness, the jurors were absolutely on the edge of their seats. In open court, the defense stood up and objected to my bringing him to the stand, citing his inability to speak and presumably to testify. "Your Honor," I said to Circuit Court Judge Lynn Gerald Jr., "with all respect, Mr. Spaniel has indeed lost much of his throat. A portion of his jaw, including his voice box, has been cut out and he can't talk."

"Well, then," the judge began, "how can he testify?"

"Your Honor," I answered as I looked directly at the jury, "he may not be able to talk, but he certainly can write!"

The defense had anticipated I would use Frank's videotaped deposition. In fact, they had assumed we would *have* to use the deposition, because they believed Frank would either be dead or physically incapacitated. Calling him as a witness had been totally unexpected, and the effect of the surprise was obvious on the defense lawyers' faces.

"You may proceed." Judge Gerald seemed anxious to finally hear from Frank himself. His ruling left everyone at the defense table red-faced.

"But, Judge…, " one of the defense attorneys stuttered.

"I have ruled, Counselor. We are going to proceed," the judge stated with finality. Judge Gerald totally controlled the courtroom and he knew the law. When he was growing up, his father had been one of the few judges in the sparsely populated and developing regions of Florida, and the circuit under his sole jurisdiction stretched for several counties. His family was known for integrity and a no-nonsense approach, and his many years on the bench had gained him respect and obedience. "Mr. Spaniel," the judge then turned and said kindly to Frank, "please come forward and take the oath."

With his pad and pen, Frank moved to the witness stand. I would ask him questions, and then he would write down the answers. The trial judge had allowed me to have the clerk of the court read the answers to the jury. She read the responses in a loud, clear, strong voice; in essence, she spoke for Frank Spaniel. The effect was dramatic and overwhelming. On that day, we owned the jury, believe me. Frank was as strong as could be for someone so sick. Soaking wet, he couldn't have weighed 110 pounds. Visually, he was a scary physical remnant of the once-vibrant athlete who had starred as an All-American running back and run Notre Dame into gridiron history. For purposes of the trial, I had put together a two-minute video from the old football film highlights we were able to obtain from Notre Dame to show what Frank had been like before his illness consumed him. The judge happened to be a Notre Dame fan, and I could sense his enjoyment in viewing the video as he considered its admissibility. In the end, he thought the film was too prejudicial, and he would not allow the jury to view it. At the same time, it had surely impressed upon the court the enormity of what had been lost.

Frank's presence on the stand was awesome. Because the cancer had gone into his throat and sinus cavities, and then attacked his head, he was in constant pain that required enormous amounts of pain medication. But on those days in the courtroom, he just lifted himself out of that dying, decaying body and became a strong, powerful presence. I believe his strength came from his belief that he was right. It was a quest for justice, and he seemed to be willing his way through to the end. He knew that the doctor who had misread his CT scan had probably cost him his life. He surely realized he was beyond any hope. But he also knew that by being strong, he might give hope to others in the same situation and, at the same time, prove the wrongness of what had happened. That's a pretty powerful lesson in itself.

I never had any of the careers that Frank had in sports, but he still regarded me as a star in the courtroom. Somewhere during the trial process we became teammates. Finally, there we were, almost at the end of the trial. "We have fourth down and goal, Frank," I had said to him. "We have to go for it. There is only one choice left. We need a touchdown to win."

Frank sort of whispered and mouthed to me, "Yes, I know. It's your turn now. I got us here. I carried the ball far enough, so now it's up to you to punch it over."

With his eyes sparkling, he looked at me and quickly wrote out a note demonstrative of his decisiveness. *We've come this far together, now finish this thing for both of us!!*

. . . .

Fourth Down: The Closing Argument

MAY IT PLEASE THE COURT: Ladies and gentlemen of the jury, counsel, and most of all, may it please you, Mr. Spaniel. This is a time that comes in any trial; it is final summation. Before we say anything else, as an officer of this court, I want to thank each one of you on behalf of Frank Spaniel, the defendant, and on behalf of all of the attorneys in this case, for devoting your time to serve as jurors. You have been asked to have the patience of Job, and now you will be asked to have the wisdom of Solomon.

But the fact is, what you're about to do can only be done in this country, and for that, I think we are all eternally grateful. The time taken out of your lives and your personal commitment to fulfill your civic duty has not gone unnoticed. *[I paused and left the podium to walk in front of the jury box. I slowly passed along the two rows of jurors and I made sure I looked into the eyes of each one. Sometimes, even this early in final summation, I could sense if the juror had committed to our cause. Not one set of eyes broke the contact I was making, and I could actually feel the magnitude of what was coming. I craved the sense of knowing that the journey we had begun separately was now a common path. Right then, I knew the jury had seen the truth and was committed to justice. I completed my slow walk in front of the jury box and returned to the podium.]*

When we talked earlier, the first time I spoke to you during jury selection, I asked if there was anyone here who wouldn't hold a medical provider, a doctor, who we all in our common experiences in life listen to, rely on—is there anyone who would not hold them to the same responsibilities, the same standards of care that you would for any other ordinary person?

I believe all of you answered in the affirmative. The care and the treatment that is being questioned in this case only momentarily had to fall below the acceptable standard of medical treatment. There is no one in this courtroom who will talk about bad doctors. No one in this courtroom will talk about intentional wrongdoing. This case is about a medical mistake, and I will summarize, as best as I can, the evidence supporting our case. It is important that I say everything on behalf of Frank Spaniel and the late Kathryn Spaniel. If I say something that you have already heard, that is why you are sitting there—six collective minds. Someone is undoubtedly saying, "I heard that." On the other hand, if one of you re-members some fact or piece of evidence I fail to bring up, please point those matters out during deliberations, because that collection of abilities is the strength of the jury.

This case has been going on for a while, and who, at some point, didn't say, "That is enough!" We know that sometimes the evidence has been repetitive, and your common sense is not something we underesti-mate. It is not something we don't appreciate. It is just that the burden of proof must be met and, as in every case, is so important that each point be remembered because the result lasts forever. Your verdict doesn't last for a day; it is for all time. Tomorrow, we won't have an opportunity to come back to re-decide this terribly important case.

Frank's family can't come back in twenty years or ten years or three years or next week and say, "Hey! I'm still here!" It is an invaluable oppor-tunity that we have, but it is a one-time opportunity and the burden we have, which is critical to this case, the burden of proof we have, and I have spent some time explaining this in voir dire, is not beyond a reasonable doubt. It is a civil case, and our burden is simply the greater weight of the evidence. When you get the conflicting experts and the testimony of various treating physicians, and citizens like you in the jury box, there is always going to be some doubt. It is a preponderance of the evidence, a greater weight. What is more persuasive? To satisfy our burden of proof, a tipping of the scales of justice, however slight, is all that is required. *[I used my hands with open palms up to illustrate the scales being tipped, and only ever so slightly tipped one hand lower than the other. I wondered if the others in the court-room saw the attractive schoolteacher and the well-seasoned ironworker who was the oldest person on the jury nod their heads.]*

The judge will give you instruction about the credibility of witnesses. Who had the interest in testifying? Who was the impartial person? The treating physicians? The expert witnesses hired? Who really had the bias and motivation? That is for you to determine, not us.

We talked about another interesting thing. I said, if it was a situation where a building burned down and the building was worth ten million dollars, and it was totally destroyed and was found to be wrongfully burned, is there anybody here who would have a problem with the proper amount of damages to compensate for such a loss?

"Well, that was ten million dollars worth of building, and total compensation for that loss is ten million dollars," you might say. During voir dire I believe I used a one-of-a-kind vase sitting on this table as an example of something filled with hopes and dreams that was invaluable. If it was wrongfully broken, how do you determine just compensation? I asked you earlier, "How do you capsulize enjoyment of life and put it into a dollar amount?"

But that is your duty as jurors in this case. You see, one thing that I don't want to ever apologize for is coming up here asking for money, because that is the only way we allow justice to be dispensed. As mighty and powerful as our system of justice is, it is not all-powerful or all-mighty. We cannot say, "Let's go back here to November. Let's go back here, Frank. Let's go back to November. And guess what? This CT scan shows something! We are going to treat you because you have a cancer. We will take you in and do a biopsy, and then locate the cancer and cure it. We will radiate and do whatever modern medicine can do and most likely, you will live."

If we could turn back the hands of time and do that, there is not a person in here who would not have that done. Not one! But we cannot. That is why I'm not ashamed and I'm not apologizing to ask you for full and just compensation in terms of money. That is the only power you have, and it is a great power. By that power and your award of a money verdict, you define what justice is and recognize the significance of the losses that have occurred.

I know you had to hear it when the defense lawyer said, "This is a serious case for my client." There is no doubt about that. It is a serious case for Dr. James Walters. And, you know, sometimes you don't have to say the obvious. But how serious is it for Frank Spaniel?

So, professional people are liable, just like a motorist is liable if he runs a red light. If it is a medical red light, it is called a mistake; it is called negligence, and the standard of care and your common sense applies. I am going to go back to some thoughts that I had early this morning. This is a case that doesn't require anything more than fifty-one percent of proof. It simply requires a conclusion that more likely than not, things would have been different. More likely than not, something should have been seen. Do not be deceived in any way, shape, or form by the argument that is being made in this courtroom that the defendant doctor did everything he could. The defense contends medicine is not a perfect science; he tried the best he could and should somehow be excused from any finding of fault.

Indeed, medicine is a high-risk profession. I am going to be very clear on this, too. It doesn't matter what walk of life you come from, a mistake is a mistake. Some of us, and I won't use me as an example, but let's say some younger people bus tables when working through school. They drop glasses and you hear that crash; that is a mistake. Not intentional, but a mistake. The result of that is there is broken glass, and if you have an understanding employer, he will say, "It is all right. It was an accident. We will get some more glasses."

A radiologist has only one function in the medical care of a patient like Frank Spaniel. It is to accurately and properly read the radiology studies. That is exactly why the CT scan was performed: so the radiologist could look inside Frank Spaniel's head and neck to determine if there was a cancerous tumor. He is not a hospice person. He is not a person who deals with the clinical care and other aspects of treatment taken care of by all those devoted healthcare providers. I heard the testimony of Dr. John A. Arrington, the defense's expert radiologist; he said, "That was something the clinician should have picked up." Was that Dr. Wingert, the board-certified ear, nose, and throat specialist, the Fort Myers doctor who treated him and who was Frank's treating physician? Is that what the defense is asserting? That somehow the treating physician should not have relied on what Dr. Walters, the defendant doctor, told him? Is that Dr. Wingert's fault?

This is a case about a radiologist's failure to diagnose a type of malignant cancer that had a ninety percent chance of a complete cure at the time the diagnosis should have been made. Let's assume it is back in November. You heard all of the cancer reports. You didn't hear cancer experts on the defense side, but you did on our side. Our cancer experts said this cancer was there. It was something that would have been diagnosable seven months before it was diagnosed. It had to have been there in November because of its size when it was finally found. The defense will argue, "Well, it was secretion, it was masked, it was behind some organs, it was a tough area…" and on and on. But how can the defense argue against the plain fact that the cancer was on the CT scan taken by Dr. Walters and he simply missed it? He made a mistake. *[I paused for quite a few moments to reinforce the theme that a medical "mistake" had been made.]*

In November of 1990, Frank Spaniel had a ninety percent chance of cure. I can't get up here and tell you that he would have lived, that there was no chance he would have ever had cancer or that it wouldn't spread. I can't tell you that, but I can tell you that doctors have stated under oath, and it is their testimony as evidence in this case that there was a ninety percent chance of cure in November. More likely than not, he would have been cured of the dreaded disease that grew untreated and is killing him.

You walk that cancer out seven months without treatment, and you know what happens to this chance of cure? We go from ninety percent to less than thirty-five percent. You can use your own judgment when you go back there in the jury room, thirty-five percent with no lymph node involvement. When people listen to cancer situations, they ask, "Did they get it in time? Has it spread? What does the pathology report say?"

I anticipate the defense counsel is going to get up here and argue, "Well, this wasn't a mistake-proof diagnostic tool." Well, I can tell you that Frank Spaniel didn't go get a CT scan for therapeutic reasons; it was specifically done to rule out cancer. From the evidence, it appears that radiologists and radiology in general—mammograms, lung x-rays, those types of things—are pretty accurate diagnostic tools as to whether or not you have something wrong. Listen to the testimony. I think the evidence is there for you to decide whether or not a CT scan is diagnostic and just how "mistake-proof" it may be.

Most likely, the defense lawyer will get up here and spend much time on this anatomical chart that illustrates a person we don't know. We don't know what the chart represents, or whether or not it was a male or female, tall or short, skinny or fat, or if he or she was ugly or pretty. What we do know is that radiologists don't use anatomical charts. Radiologists use x-ray films, CT scans, MRIs, bone scans, and so on. When Dr. William E. Gatlin, a noted radiologist, testified as our expert, did he seem like he knew what he was doing? This expert doctor taught radiology at Harvard University Medical School. But you recall the defense lawyers used this same anatomical chart to cross-examine him, rather than the radiology studies of this case. And even then, I ask you, did he look like he didn't know what he was doing? And what did he say? He pinpointed the exact location of the cancer the defendant doctor missed.

On his side of the case, the defense team wants to talk about what radiologists know about anatomy. They can argue that, but I prefer to tell you what a radiologist should know about radiology. I will tell you what Dr. Walters or any other radiologist ought to know about radiology. The films of Frank Spaniel are right here. *[To illustrate the point I walked to the clerk's desk and picked up the x-ray film. I took the anatomical chart that depicted the muscles, bones, blood vessels, and nerves of a whole human being and placed it to the side. I held up the films and raised my voice.]* This is radiology. A radiologist ought to know what cancer looks like on a CT scan. Period.

Here, in evidence, are the CT scans taken seven months after the first ones. Dr. Gatlin didn't have a problem. It is his territory as a radiologist. What is the significance? I asked him other information on the log, which the defense lawyer put into evidence, and which said, "Pain hypopharynx." Any other information you were looking for? Anything? Like cancer? "No." Not "possibly", or "I can't remember...," but "No."

Which scan do you want to look at during your deliberations? It doesn't matter to me. Folks, when you go back to the jury room, you just apply your common sense and you look at these words. Let me show you. Remember when I wrote them back here? You remember those words. You remember those words, because I asked the doctor, "Is there anything on the CT scan films that indicate Dr. Wingert was concerned about a particular issue?"

And the defense expert said, "No."

I said, "Dr. Arrington, isn't on every single slice..." and he counted them and I can still count and still read, "doesn't each one of the films have written on it the letters, ROCA? Doesn't that stand for 'rule out cancer?" On every single slice, the defendant radiologist was asked to examine the CT film for cancer. And on every single slice where cancer was there and fully visible to a careful radiologist, he missed it.

Folks, that is what this case is about. That is what this lawsuit is about. Because Frank Spaniel ought not to be denied the chance he would have had if acceptable medical care had been rendered. A chance, nothing more. Not a guarantee. Just the ninety percent chance he should have gotten. There is not a guarantee in this courtroom that anybody here will live. The mortality table we have placed in evidence statistically shows that a male Frank's age has a projected life expectancy of 14.9 more years. The projected life spans, put another way, are estimates of death. We all hope everybody lives forever, but the fact is we are all going to die. When a person sees the light of life start to dim a little bit, and the darkness at the end of the tunnel is in sight, he starts to understand how valuable life is. He starts understanding when he gets up in the morning, that he had better thank whomever he believes he should thank for that special day.

I can't say the evidence shows Frank Spaniel would have lived 14.9 more years for certain, but I can say it is reasonable his cancer should have been discovered, most likely would have been cured, and he probably would have lived a longer life. On that fateful day in November, Dr. Wingert, a board-certified ear, nose, and throat doctor, a man who was trying his best to find out what was wrong with Mr. Spaniel, did everything he could. He put an examination scope down Frank's throat not once, but twice, and there is no dispute that his clinical eyes, even with the scope, could not see what modern medicine has brought and developed to "see" even more, the CT scan computer technology.

Dr. Wingert, the clinician, had done everything he could. He sent for a CT scan to be done and a radiologist to look for what he couldn't see. He wanted to make sure there was no cancer and a resolution of this critical issue was the only role and responsibility of the defendant in this case. On the CT scans themselves is the notation: rule out cancer. Frank Spaniel's symptoms of pain in his neck were noted and Dr. Wingert sent him to a radiologist.

Computers are wonderful. I still add on a pad, but I would love to be able to use a computer because they are invaluable tools. This computerized tomography, or CT scan, is a wonderful thing. It was there in 1990. Dr. Wingert knew it. Dr. Farrior knew it. Dr. Walters knew it. And everyone else in the medical community knew it. And you know who else knew it? My football player, Frank Spaniel, because it was the fourth quarter—his fourth quarter of life—that was at stake. Remember, I asked you during jury selection which quarter of life you would pick, the first twenty years, the second twenty years, the third twenty years, or the fourth twenty years. I asked, and you said, "Well, I would pick this or I would pick that." Everybody has his or her own situation. But what about the value and importance of the fourth and final quarter of life?

I want to tell you exactly what happened in November of 1990. One can only imagine how anxious Dr. Wingert, Frank, and Kathryn were as the CT test was being reviewed and analyzed. Did Frank have cancer? When that test came back and the defendant read the CT film as demonstrating a sinus problem --I believe it was labeled "sinusitis," and nothing more, there was total relief and acceptance of those findings. Those symptoms—this is important—those symptoms were exactly consistent with what Frank was experiencing and logically explained what he had wrong with him in November.

When that report came back, and I hope the defense argues this, because they have made some issue that the practitioner didn't have a right to rely on this radiologist. What else did the defendant and his corporation charge that thousand dollars for? You saw the bill. It was a thousand dollars. What did the radiologist do for that fee? You pay the money; you get the service. What did he do for the fee? He read the CT scan and issued a report. Someone said, "Well, maybe Dr. Wingert should have played radiologist. He should have taken off his hat and put on a radiologist's hat, because I bet he took radiology courses in medical school." But that is what radiologists are supposed to do, and that is why Dr. Walters is on trial and not Dr. Wingert.

I guess the defense is going to argue, and I can only anticipate what they will say, "Well, the evidence shows that he should have looked elsewhere." Listen, folks, when the defense lawyer says that, you have to ask yourself only one question: Where is the evidence? How many ear, nose, and throat doctors came in here and said that? None. If Dr. Wingert was supposed to do something that he failed to do, where is the evidence to support that assertion? Where is the medical evidence that he didn't do something he was supposed to do? It has not been presented, because it doesn't exist.

Dr. Wingert then got some improvement with Frank. Remember the issue about the pain? He said, "Look at your office notes."

I said, "Wait a minute. After January, after he had the operation, was there any more pain?"

In November, Frank Spaniel is diagnosed with sinus problems, is treated with antibiotics, has a minor sinus procedure done in January, and then seems to get better. But in late May, early June, when he visits Dr. Wingert for a checkup, he has lost twenty or thirty pounds. We are now seven months from the time of the defendant's interpretation of sinusitis, and Dr. Wingert was concerned about Frank. As he testified during the trial, "We had to look at the weight loss, coupled with the fact that these sinus-like symptoms have now recurred." He looked, and guess what he did? Best evidence in the world—what he did the first time, he did the second time. There is a saying that history repeats itself. The past is a prologue of the future. Isn't that a fact? Dr. Wingert sends Frank to a radiologist group for a repeat scan, but this time he gets Dr. Robert E. Gerson instead of Dr. Walters. This time, the radiologist, Dr. Gerson, finds the cancer that has been there all along. He doesn't mistakenly call it sinusitis. He correctly labels it as cancer. But it is too late for Frank Spaniel.

The bottom line is when this situation arose, Frank Spaniel knew he was in deep, deep trouble. Not like being down when his Notre Dame football team is playing Army, simply a couple of touchdowns in the fourth quarter. No, here we are talking about Big Cancer. It doesn't matter how big and strong his legs were. This was going to be awfully tough. Look at Frank Spaniel. Do you see what that disease can do? Doesn't matter how strong, how rich, how poor, or what color your skin is. [The only African American juror who had been impaneled was elderly. She had been keenly interested in the testimony throughout the trial and I had specifically noted that during jury selection she told us about the lengthy bout of cancer that had taken her father. She didn't have to nod; her face and eyes told me she fully understood the point I was making.] Cancer is going to get you, if you don't get it first, and the key is getting it early. [That early cancer detection can be valuable is common knowledge, and I had made it our central theme, anchoring our strategy to it.]

Now what is the best evidence you have? The only evidence you have with regard to the care and treatment of Dr. Wingert and Dr. Edward Farrior. Dr. Farrior is the ear, nose, and throat surgeon who operated on Frank Spaniel in an effort to save his life. This man graduated near the top of his medical school class, and scored the highest on his board certification exams. Here is a doctor who is on top, one of the best, and he testified that he could not second-guess Dr. Wingert. He believed Dr. Wingert should have been able to rely on the defendant radiologist and rely on his opinion that the cancer was not present on the CT scan. His operation was not successful, and the defense lawyer made sure to point that out. The defense lawyer asked Dr. Farrior, "Well, you operated on the cancer and you didn't do any good, did you?"

"No," Dr. Farrior testified. "Looking at it now, no. But I tried."

You know why he had to try so hard? Because Frank Spaniel presented to him with a twenty-five to thirty-five percent chance of cure. For seven months, that cancer was growing in his throat, for seven months that cancer was spreading, by the time this young Dr. Farrior, gifted as he may have been, got to Frank. He did the best he could and he still could not resect all the margins of tissue containing the deadly disease. He still had to leave some cancer behind.

After the operation, in the hospital waiting room, the question the entire family, including Frank, was asking, "Did you get it all? Did you get all the cancer, Doc?" Bottom line, folks, he didn't get it all. What was left has spread and has come back to kill him. Frank Spaniel has demonstrated time and time again in his life that he is a winner. He is a champion, and he is going to fight until the day he is put in the dirt.

I won't comment on the defense expert, Dr. Arnold S. Blaustein. According to his prognosis, Frank should have been dead long ago. But he is still here. He is sitting here. It doesn't matter what anyone else thought or predicted. Frank is still right here and I'll tell you something. I don't think he is going to live 14.9 more years, the mortality table rate applicable to a normal person. This judge will give you the instruction regarding the use of that mortality table and tell you it is to be used as a guideline, but it is not absolutely binding. I will get to damages in a moment, but I will say this: I don't think it is unreasonable to assume he may not live ten or fifteen years, but he is going to live as long as he can still fight, because that is the type of person Frank Spaniel is.

Normally, we look at a person's track record in life. That is what we do, look and find out what a person has done over life's challenges. You don't judge a person in the first quarter. I know it is the tendency of some parents to judge their child and say, "You're not going to turn out this way or that way." Second quarter…who knows?

When a person hits forty years of age and enters the third quarter of life, it is a revelation. It is then a person might say, "I'm not going to live forever! Now I understand why my parents said all of those things. I want to get all that life has to offer." So, the third quarter brings a greater desire for fulfillment and happiness. That next twenty years is doing that, except you're struggling, working, not being with your family when you want to, and then what happens? You get to age sixty, the fourth quarter, and it is like a sporting event. What a terrible disappointment to leave at the end of the third quarter. It is the last part of the event that is so great; that is when all of the action occurs and the outcome of the entire game is decided. The fourth quarter, the last twenty years, is when everybody's hard work comes to fruition…when you can enjoy the moment. It is when you see the goodness of your life and, hopefully, enjoy its rewards.

I suggest the fourth quarter, as the last season of life, is the most important part. It is not because Frank Spaniel went to Notre Dame; the fourth quarter certainly doesn't belong only to the Fighting Irish. The fourth quarter of life should belong to all of us. Let me tell you what happened in the fourth quarter. In Frank's fourth quarter, he has this to look forward to. He weighs 110 pounds; he can't eat; he can't talk; he can't be with his friends; he can't hold his grandchildren. I have to tell you, that is not the fourth quarter that anybody should want. And I think today you have an opportunity to do some things to address that.

Let's talk about liability a little bit more. It is said life comes in threes. First, Frank found out he had cancer, and then he lost his daughter, and then he lost his wife. It is time right now that he gets justice; that is all I ask, not sympathy. Don't give Frank a minute's sympathy. He has more sympathy from everyone who cares for him than anyone could ask for. There are witnesses who came into the courtroom called "before and after witnesses," and their purpose was to show you what the person was like. They described what Frank was like before he became sick, and then witnesses were called to describe what Frank has been like after the cancer was finally found.

Remember Jerry Groom? Jerry Groom played football with Frank. He was an outstanding NFL player who is a member of the College Football Hall of Fame. He said he didn't recognize Frank when he arrived here to testify. I asked Jerry, "What did you do when you first saw him?" *[I pointed to the vacant witness stand and paused. In those moments I was certain the jurors were visualizing the huge hulk of the former NFL star.]*

He answered, "I cried." If I had to pick a before witness, it would be Jerry Groom, because Jerry Groom could be Frank Spaniel. If I had to pick an after witness, I would pick Jerry Groom, because for the negligence in this case, there was a ninety percent chance, ninety percent chance that Jerry Groom would have been Frank Spaniel's after witness, because without the medical negligence of the defendant, that is the type of life Frank would be living.

There is nothing in life that says you don't break a bone. There is something in life, though, that cries out and says when you break a bone, you go to a doctor and fix it. Let's just give everybody the benefit of the doubt. Let's start by giving the patient the benefit of the doubt. If it is close and the issue is life and death, give the patient the benefit of any doubt. If you are going to err, err on the side of being conservative and assume the worst, because we all know what can happen if you don't. Make sure of the diagnosis when life-threatening cancer is on the table of considerations.

Scout films—number fifty-four in particular—remember that argument that fifty-four is just a slice, not the whole film? The defense's expert, Dr. John Arrington, testified that the abnormality shown was caused by bony osteophyte, not cancer. He was asked, "Dr. Arrington, if a radiologist said that osteophyte had no effect on the appearance of that radiological view, would you agree or disagree?"

His answer was, "I would strongly disagree."

But what about the treating radiologist's testimony? The partner of the defendant doctor who diagnosed the presence of cancer? What did he respond when I asked him, "Dr. Gerson, does that bony osteophyte have any effect on this?"

"No," he testified. "That is not what caused that appearance. It was probably... well, it might have been the movement of the patient, or swelling or breathing or the head tilted. Might have been secretions. But none of those causes pain." Folks, with the pain that was present and the abnormal appearance, it most likely was cancer. We know that for certain now and the defendant probably should have known it then.

Dr. Arrington read the x-ray films blind. In explaining what he meant, he said, "I don't listen to the symptoms of the patient. I read them blind." God bless him, it may be an excellent academic and professional approach. In other words, he had no idea what symptoms Frank Spaniel was experiencing when he rendered his expert interpretation.

But Dr. Gerson, another qualified radiologist, testified, "I read the x-rays, together with the symptoms of the patient. They all have to go together." And both of these physicians came up with dramatically different conclusions.

Then we brought you our expert radiologist, Dr. Gatlin. He is seventy years old, and a learned, very experienced specialist who has been practicing his profession over forty years. He testified that the tumor was right there and demonstrated on that slice of film. The cancer was causing the patient's pain, not some "osteophyte." You notice that however I keep putting these x-rays up on the view box, that something always stays in the same position? That terrible spot the defense identifies as an osteophyte and that we assert is cancer?

Dr. Gatlin says, "It was a mass. That was the thing we were looking for. That is the thing the radiologist needed to look for." It may have been something else, but certainly, cancer should have been at the top of the list. Look where the circle is on the three separate sets of films taken at three separate times. The x-rays were taken at different times, but if I lay one film on top of the other, all of them are identifying the same anatomical area. It comes in threes, doesn't it? One, two, three. And the rule of threes leads us to the horrible conclusion that it was the cancer there all along.

The scout film—common sense. The cancer starts in the red, as I have drawn on the charts. It grows and enlarges as I have drawn in green. One, Dr. Arrington. Two, Dr. Gerson. Three, Dr. Gatlin. You know, maybe baseball has more of an analogy than I thought when I said that in voir dire. Like a baseball game, I indicated we only had to win the burden of proof by one run, that is how I explained the greater weight of the evidence you will decide in this case. It is ironic, though, one, two, three strikes, and Frank was out. In reality, though, Frank Spaniel had one good chance. He didn't have two or three.

It was not just a coincidence the cancer that everyone agrees was present in June was in the same exact place we have circled. The circle drawn on the films got bigger as time went on because this cancer had spread. It was a very large mass by the time it was finally treated. You heard Dr. Farrior say: "I think it was almost three inches when they took it out; it was a very large mass."

Again, it is one, two, three; one, two, three; one, two, three. Dr. Farrior testified if treated earlier, most likely within a reasonable degree of medical probability, that is more likely than not, he would have saved Frank's voice. Frank would have been able to speak and again, more likely than not, the cancer would have been cured.

Dr. Alexander Spiers, the world-renowned cancer expert from Florida's Lee Moffitt Cancer Center, testified as one of our experts. And what did he say? The cancer, if diagnosed earlier, would most probably have been curable. Curable! Simply put, what effect did this delay in diagnosing the cancer create? Frank Spaniel was the odds-on favorite to beat the cancer the first time, and odds-on underdog not to beat the cancer the second time. *[I paused before continuing. During that time, I made eye contact with each juror. Maybe I didn't see nods, but I got that special feeling every damn one of them was with me. Hell, I knew even more the jurors were with Frank and me. I sensed the jury was ready to settle the score.]*

Let me now speak about damages. Remember your sacred promise to follow the law. You do not have the right to talk about what happens to the money if Frank dies tomorrow. The issue to be decided is what is the appropriate compensation for that gentleman, Frank Spaniel, as a result of the loss he has suffered and will sustain in the future. What dollar amount has he lost?

During jury selection, I asked if you would shy away from an amount of money that may be too large—huge, relatively speaking. Of course, that is relatively huge to whom? We hear dollars all over the front page of the newspaper today. Sports section, dollars. You can walk down the street and see the lottery billboards, with all its dollars. Dollars are thrown about everywhere. But in this case, any dollars awarded are to replace something that has been lost.

Here is a document that was put into evidence, and I will be very clear and very quick. These are the medical summaries of the hospital and doctors' bills. The total here is $159,000. There is evidence, however, that if this would not be appropriate to award for all of the past medical expenses because Dr. Wingert said, you will recall, "Frank was still going to need some of that treatment." I think his answer was $20,000 to $30,000. So, in past medicals, you have $159,000; you can make the subtraction: $160,000 less $25,000, so on your past medicals, unless my math is wrong, the amount properly awarded is $135,000.

That is past medicals. Frank didn't work. He came down here to Florida not to work. He came down to retire. So there is no claim for lost earnings in this case. He was going to "work" on the golf course and probably work really hard at that, but he has not sustained any loss of income. No damages are sought, nor should any be awarded in the area of lost earnings, past or future.

As I said earlier, the judge will instruct you that the mortality table that had been read into evidence is a guide, but those life expectancies are not binding on you in this case. Your deliberations are secret. They are confidential to you and to your own heart and soul. Those deliberations belong to each of you. I don't feel comfortable getting up here and saying, "Assume Frank is going to live fifteen years," nor do I feel comfortable saying, "Assume Frank will live one year." It will be your collective judgment as to just how long you believe Frank Spaniel has left and with that remaining life, how much more he will suffer.

Frank is listening. He can hear very well. He listens and he is very smart. Let's just assume for my purposes he has five more years. Five years at $270,000 is something I have calculated here for a total of $1.3 million. If you really assumed a life span of fifteen years, the amount would be four or five million dollars.

There are some things that money cannot buy. There are some things that can never and should never be equated with money. But that will be your sacred duty in just a little while. That is exactly what you have to do as jurors in this case. And on that task, I do not envy any of you in fulfilling that awesome responsibility. I am unsure about the appropriate dollar amount to be awarded in this case.

An old trial judge taught me this—he became my mentor after he left the bench and returned to private practice—he always said, "Don't ask the jury for too much money, because you will scare them away. Don't ask a jury for too little money, because you won't get enough."

I know this as well as I know I'm breathing today. I also know this is a significant case. It is one that will be looked at by you to show in terms of dollars the significance of the loss and the injury and the horror and the anguish and the pain and the unhappiness, an unhappiness that can never be ridden away…never…by anyone on this earth.

So how much is that worth? I can only hope your jury verdict reflects the magnitude of the loss. To have played all your life as a winner and a champion, to have lived all of your life to get to the fourth quarter of life and be deprived of its rewards, its wonder, is a huge loss. I think the fourth quarter is worth as much as every quarter; maybe the quarters of life are million-dollar periods of time increments. Whatever you decide, make us all proud by doing justice.

Thank you.

·······

On April 6, 1994, the jury deliberated less than three hours before finding Dr. Walters negligent in reviewing and interpreting the November 21, 1990, CT scan film. The jury also decided the delay had caused the ravaging disease to spread and had virtually eliminated any opportunity to cure Frank Spaniel. Frank was awarded $900,000 in damages for the seven-month delay in his diagnosis of throat cancer, and Kathryn's estate was awarded $100,000 for her own loss of companionship and marriage partner. As the verdict was read, Frank had tears in his eyes…and so did I. The tears Frank and I shed as we embraced were tears of happiness. We had scored on the final play. To the very end, we carried the ball together. We were a team, a championship team. Together, we had achieved justice against terrible odds and that was really a union of the highest magnitude.

The Appeal
·······

Frank Spaniel would never live to enjoy the fruits of our victory. The defense refused to accept the verdict and took the case to the appellate court. In arguing to overturn the verdict and the trial judge's affirmation of the jury's decision, the legal team representing Dr. Walters and his radiology group contended they should have been permitted at trial to introduce evidence that the cancer they failed to detect was caused by Frank's cigarette smoking and social drinking. Although the Florida rules of evidence prohibit the introduction of evidence that a plaintiff's own conduct caused the medical treatment at issue in a malpractice case, the defendants urged that the rule should not have applied because Frank's smoking and occasional drinking were somehow relevant to their ability to detect his cancer. The defense also claimed that evidence of Frank's conduct should have been admitted because he continued to smoke and drink for several months after a doctor told him not to, and because the "door was opened" to such evi-

Frank Spaniel and his wife, Kathryn.

dence when we introduced evidence concerning his previous active and healthy lifestyle.

The facts and the law stood in the face of all the defendants' arguments. During the trial, the defendants had never contended, much less proved, that the cause of Frank's cancer had anything to do with the defendants' ability to detect its presence. There was also no evidence that Frank's smoking and drinking in the several months after he sought medical treatment—but before his cancer was diagnosed—had made even the slightest difference to the cancer's spread or its deadliness.

We argued these points before the appeals court. We also contended that the evidence of Frank's previous lifestyle was unrelated to the issue of his having been a smoker and social drinker, and so did not "open the door" for impeachment. Further, if the defendants' theory stated the law, then the rule on Florida's books excluding evidence of the plaintiff's own conduct in such cases was meaningless.

The case went all the way up the appellate ladder. The defense wouldn't give Frank a penny during the appeals process, and with his relatively modest financial resources he could not assist many of his relatives, friends, and children in making trips to see him and spend those last hours with him he so desperately wanted. It would have been great if Frank could have enjoyed the verdict recovered in the case, but it was not to happen.

Sadly, near the very end of the weeks and months of the appellate process, Frank Spaniel passed away from complications from the cancer that could have been and should have been treated. Then, a short time after his death, the jury's verdict and the judgment of the trial court were affirmed. There was no opinion given by the appellate court, just a clear-cut, absolute victory.

Epilogue

O ne of my favorite movies has always been *The Wizard of Oz*. All of the things that Cowardly Lion, Tin Man, and Scarecrow wanted—courage, a heart, and a brain—were the things that Frank Spaniel already had. Unlike the wizard, Frank could give these things out like candy, because he had so much of each…especially courage.

I was so impressed by Frank's bravery. He fought like a wildcat to the very end. He wasn't fighting for his life; I believe he could accept its end. Instead, Frank wanted the chance for redemption. He was fighting to make his own personal scoreboard read the right way before the game ended. And that is what he did—he scored the winning touchdown. He was in the game to the end because he knew we were right and the doctors were wrong. Fairness and justness dictated that the final score be right, and like the football player he had been, Frank reached down inside to suit up one more time.

Frank and I were very close. Near his death we became even closer.

Too close, actually. I still have difficulty talking about the case. When I went to Fort Myers to visit Frank for the first time, a kindred spirit ignited between us. I was certain from the first moments of our initial meeting that I would take his remarkable case. When I first met Frank, he could talk. He had lost some weight, but he looked fairly good. I remember that his wife, Kathryn, was extremely nice, quite attractive, and very soft spoken.

Frank was especially proud of his football championship ring that symbolized the glory of his golden years at Notre Dame, yet several times during the course of our time together, he tried to give it to me. Each time I refused, knowing I could never take that precious treasure from his finger. Just before final argument commenced in the courtroom, he had tried once more to give his coveted ring to me. When I refused, he squeezed my hand and tears welled in his eyes. Just before I stood up I whispered to him, "We've got the ball and we're going to win our own championship. Stick around! I need you!" Somehow, this man's man found the strength to survive through it all.

After closing arguments were finished and the jury had gone out to deliberate, Frank and I spent several glorious hours together as we awaited the jury's verdict. We went to a nearby hotel to await the jury's decision because Frank was so tired and ill that he simply couldn't stay in the court-room any longer. I often remember that time with him. There I was with a dying cancer victim as a client, yet we saw each other as champions.

We were all so very proud of him. Even before the jury returned its verdict, I knew absolutely in my heart of hearts that we had won the case. It wasn't a question of whether or not we would win, but a question of when we would win. Frank Spaniel did what he did in that courtroom because even though he knew it was not going to do him any good, he realized his actions might benefit others, and possibly save lives. Frank and I talked often about his hope that as a result of his case future diagnostic studies might be reviewed with more care and scrutiny. He also under-stood that he would never be around to spend whatever money he might win. Instead, his goal was to help his family and the loved ones of others who might be saved from suffering such an unnecessary loss.

Frank found strength and energy enough in those notions to perse-vere. According to all the doctors—both sides—Frank should have been dead a year before the trial. By some miracle, he had lived. When I am feeling down and question my resolve to carry on my work as a trial lawyer, I vividly remember those few hours while we waited at the hotel as the jury deliberated its verdict. He was so terribly weak that he couldn't even get out of his chair without assistance. He wouldn't leave, though. He wouldn't go home. He was going to stay the course and he just wouldn't be broken. Frank Spaniel was going to be there in that courtroom when the jury came back in, no matter what. Amazingly, when the clerk telephoned the hotel to tell us the jury was back, Frank pulled himself up off the chair and walked to the car. He strode into the courtroom without assistance, and the two of us stood side by side.

A great lesson of life I learned from Frank Spaniel was that we should never underestimate the power of the human spirit. Here was a person who didn't have the ability to walk or talk except with extraordinary effort. He had enormous physical burdens, but he was still able to pick himself up and take that witness stand. Although he had to write instead of speak, his delivery was every bit as powerful as if he had been a strong, healthy football star dominating the Notre Dame campus of his youth. As the jurors listened to his riveting testimony, the vision of what he appeared to be began to fade. At first, Frank Spaniel seemed old, he was deathly pale, and his eyes were far back in their darkened sockets. His hair was sparse and patchy. He might have *seemed* like a shriveled-up, elderly man sitting on that witness stand, but nobody saw him that way.

Within a matter of a few minutes, he was the center of everyone's respect and admiration. For those ever so brief moments, Frank returned to what he once was. The pain, the heartache, and the anticipation of death were gone; and I recall fighting back my emotions as I watched him on the stand. It was nothing in particular Frank Spaniel said or did. It was simply the enormity of knowing I was witnessing the greatness of the human spirit. And what a spirit he was...

When Frank passed away, he left some great things for my son, Gable, including a picture of his glory days from the *New York Times*, a drawing that appeared on the front page showing him running the ball. "One day," Frank had written at its bottom, "this will be you, Gable. Stay strong, stay healthy." Frank also gave me a Notre Dame jersey and one of

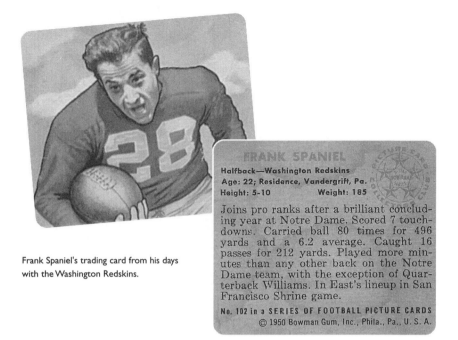

Frank Spaniel's trading card from his days with the Washington Redskins.

FRANK SPANIEL

Halfback—Washington Redskins
Age: 22; Residence, Vandergrift, Pa.
Height: 5-10   Weight: 185

Joins pro ranks after a brilliant concluding year at Notre Dame. Scored 7 touchdowns. Carried ball 80 times for 496 yards and a 6.2 average. Caught 16 passes for 212 yards. Played more minutes than any other back on the Notre Dame team, with the exception of Quarterback Williams. In East's lineup in San Francisco Shrine game.

No. 102 in a SERIES OF FOOTBALL PICTURE CARDS
© 1950 Bowman Gum, Inc., Phila., Pa., U. S. A.

his footballs. I still have his football card from his days in the NFL when he played for the Washington Redskins.

Even now, I keep some photographs of Frank and his beautiful wife, Kathryn, in my personal files at my office. Sometimes, when I need that certain magical strength, I pull the pictures out and remember how very fortunate I am. Frank Spaniel taught me the true meaning of courage— and it's a lesson that has made me a better man.

■ ■ ■ ■ ■ ■ ■

Beware of false prophets, which come to you in sheep's clothing, but inwardly they are ravening wolves...Ye shall know them by their fruits. Do men gather grapes of thorns, or figs of thistles?...Even so every good tree bringeth forth good fruit; but a corrupt tree bringeth forth evil fruit...A good tree cannot bring forth evil fruit, neither can a corrupt tree bring forth good fruit... Every tree that bringeth not forth good fruit is hewn down, and cast into the fire...Wherefore by their fruits ye shall know them.

■ ■ ■

Matthew 7: 15-20

Alexander Scourby and his wife, Lori.

CHAPTER FOUR

The Voice of God

I n a spacious federal courtroom near downtown Orlando, District Court Judge Patricia Fawsett had presided over the trial for the past day and a half. The jury had been selected, sworn, and seated, attorneys for both sides had given opening statements, and now it was time for the trial to begin in earnest with the first introduction of evidence.

"You may call your first witness, Mr. Yerrid," Judge Fawsett directed in a distinct and commanding voice. An attractive woman in her forties, the judge had been in private practice with a large Orlando law firm when she was appointed by President Ronald Reagan to serve a life term on the federal bench in the United States District Court, Middle District of Florida. She was smart, well respected, and knew the Rules of Evidence.

A fair and strong judge like Judge Fawsett was all any trial lawyer could desire. In a basketball or football game, the officials wearing the black-and-white stripes are often referred to as "zebras." Their job is to call penalties and demand fair play. But time-honored tradition dictates that the zebras should never have a hand in deciding the outcome of a game—that must be left to the players. Similarly, in the arena of the courtroom, a lawsuit should never be unfairly determined by the "robes," as trial lawyers often call presiding judges in reference to the black robes they wear in court. The advocates should neither be aided nor hindered in any significant way by the judge. Assuming the rules are not violated, the parties being represented should be the combatants and the lawyers should be the champions of the cause, with the outcome resolved only by the advocacy that prevails.

Judge Fawsett glanced over the courtroom as she waited for me to summon my first witness. My own voice was as strong and sure as the judge's when I announced, "May it please the Court, the plaintiffs call Alexander Scourby."

For one brief moment, a hush fell over the courtroom, and then the thunderous voice of the lead defense attorney echoed loudly and harshly. "Objection, Your Honor! Objection! Mr. Yerrid—and everyone else— knows that Alexander Scourby has been dead for years! This is outrageous, and we strenuously object to this improper conduct before the jury."

Hiding a very slight smile and turning away from the defense attorney's incredulous stare, I looked directly into Judge Fawsett's eyes as I answered the charge. "Your Honor, there is absolutely nothing improper concerning our evidence. This case is all about the voice of Alexander Scourby, and in particular, his narration of the Holy Bible. Mr. Scourby may be dead, but his voice lives on. I have brought audio equipment, and I intend to play short portions of the Scourby narration so the jury may hear firsthand what this case is all about." The judge had met and held my gaze without interrupting, so I continued speaking directly to her. "At this time, I respectfully move the entire Scourby narration of the King James Version of the Holy Bible into evidence as Plaintiff's Exhibit Number One. I ask that we be allowed to publish excerpts of the tapes to the jury by playing approximately two minutes of the seventy-two-hour narration done by the late Alexander Scourby himself."

All of this was taking place in front of the jury, and there was nowhere for the defense's legal team to hide. My move of calling Alexander Scourby, who had passed away several years earlier, as my first witness had been unexpected, and I achieved the desired effect of catching the defense off guard.

Judge Fawsett was deliberate and courteous as she turned to face the defense table. "Given that explanation, does the defense still lodge objection to the jury hearing this evidence?"

Suppressing a sigh, the lead defense lawyer answered in an uneasy tone. "We have no objection to the tapes being admitted, Judge." The opposing side had no choice. Each of the jurors was watching every movement made by the judge, the defense, and me. The looks on their faces were so intent that no one doubted their interest in hearing the renowned Voice of God.

"Very well," Judge Fawsett went on. "The Scourby narration is received into evidence as Exhibit One. Mr. Yerrid, you may proceed."

Before the trial commenced, I had specifically instructed audio technicians I had hired to stand by in the hallway. Usually, the setup of the equipment would be done beforehand in the courtroom, but I did not want to take any chance that my hand would be tipped. The strategy had worked. Even better, there had been no inquiry or objection lodged as to what portion of Scourby's narration the jury was going to hear.

Typically, the defense lawyer's approach to a courtroom war involves a great deal of methodical planning and carefully prepared moves. Flurries of paperwork, avalanches of motions and pleadings, and endless days of grueling depositions are the hallmark of corporate legal defenses. The siege mentality of "going for the capillaries"—which means outspending, outmanning, and outgunning the opposition—could be afforded by those with money and power. The plaintiff's trial lawyer is best served by doing the unexpected, being unpredictable, and striking with full force and quickness. It is an all-out, focused, "go-for-the-jugular" approach that springs more from *instinct* than from learning—or even experience. That is probably where the notion that trial lawyers are born, not made, originated.

Calling a dead man as my first witness carried with it all of those necessary ingredients—unpredictability, surprise, and a no-holds-barred assault—to set the stage for the remainder of the trial. I was familiar with the sound technicians who had helped me stage the attack on the defense, and I knew they were professionals at their craft. They set up the equipment quickly, and within a minute the golden sound of Scourby's voice was filling the courtroom. All of us present—the teams of attorneys and their clients, Judge Fawsett, the jury, and the spectators crowding the gallery—listened attentively to Scourby's deeply inspiring narration of the two passages I had chosen specifically to reinforce the central themes of the case. The jury couldn't help but be impressed.

> *Ecclesiastes 7:1. A good name is better than precious ointment; and the day of death than the day of one's birth.*

Scourby's powerful voice continued:
Matthew 12: 34-37. O generation of vipers, how can ye, being evil, speak good things? For out of the abundance of the heart the mouth speaketh. A good man out of the good treasure of the heart bringeth forth good things: and an evil man out of the evil treasure bringeth forth evil things. But I say unto you, that every idle word that men shall speak, they shall give account thereof in the Day of Judgment. For by thy words thou shalt be justified, and by thy words, thou shalt be condemned.

The whole courtroom sat in silence for a few moments after the tape ended, as if no one could—or even desired to—break the magic spell Scourby's words had cast.

Just who was Alexander Scourby, and what was this case about?

Alexander Scourby
· · · · · · ·

When I first met Lori March Scourby in the mid-1980s, she talked at length about her late husband, Alexander Scourby, to whom she had been married for forty-two years. Lori spoke articulately, and her emerald-green eyes sparkled in rhythm with her words. She wore her hair stylishly short, and its ivory color framed a face that was nearly unlined, with a milk-and-honey complexion. Despite being well into her seventies, she was quite beautiful. No doubt she would have turned heads when she was a young actress living on her own in New York City in the 1940s. That is when she first caught the eye of another young actor who took her breath away. Theirs had been the storybook romance of love at first sight. Alexander Scourby was "beautiful," in Lori's words. She meticulously described the beard he always wore and the handsomeness she adored. But in the end, it had been his wonderful heart that had won her over completely.

After our first meeting, I learned quite a bit about Alexander Scourby. During the four decades of their marriage, both Mr. and Mrs. Scourby had continued their careers in the entertainment business. Although he was in a number of movies, Scourby became internationally renowned for his distinctive voice. Advertisers would often say, "Get me a Scourby voice" if Scourby himself was not available. It was tremendously lyrical and melodious and boomed like thunder rolling across a meadow. Scourby's voice was instantly recognizable to millions. He provided the voice-over for television commercials throughout the 1960s and 1970s, including Eastern Airlines' "The Wings of Man" and the enormously popular and successful series of radio and television spots for Excedrin, Texaco, and Johnson & Johnson. For years, he was the narrator for *National Geographic*, lending his deep, symphonic tones to special nature and educational programs. He appeared in or narrated more than twenty-five movies, and he also made guest appearances on a wide variety of broadcasts.

Lori also had enjoyed a successful and long career, appearing in several feature films and a number of television shows. She became best

The author with the delightful Lori Scourby.

known for her roles in the daytime soap operas *Secret Storm, Guiding Light,* and *One Life to Live.* Lori loved the lights of Broadway, and she appeared in countless plays for more than three decades.

When Alexander Scourby passed away in 1985, he left the legacy of one of the greatest voices in history. During his lifetime, he had become the counterpart to his contemporary, the renowned Orson Welles. Scourby often gave of his talents to serve those less fortunate. He had a special affinity for the blind and physically handicapped. Among the proudest accomplishments of his career were his narrations of more than four hundred so-called Talking Books for the American Foundation for the Blind (AFB), including the Old and New Testaments of the Holy Bible, which he recorded for the AFB in 1954 for the princely sum of one hundred dollars. For those who couldn't see, his words became their vision. After his death, his unique voice was one of his widow's greatest treasures and a lasting legacy of Scourby's willingness to give back the blessings he had received. Now his good works had been taken, and the name of Alexander Scourby was being exploited in the name of God.

The Case
Breach of Contract and Wrongful
Exploitation of Intellectual Property
· · · · · · ·

The Parish of the Air of the Episcopal Radio-TV Foundation, a nonprofit distribution arm of the Episcopal Church based in Atlanta, Georgia, had long admired the AFB narration of the Bible and wanted a newer, higher-quality version to distribute within the community of the Episcopal Church. Organized in the 1940s, the Episcopal Foundation not only provided sound recordings and other materials to the Episcopal Church itself but also made them available on a rental basis to other religious organizations. Alexander Scourby's narrations would be an invaluable asset to its vast library of resources.

On June 12, 1972, Caroline Rakestraw, the executive director of the Episcopal Foundation, contacted Fifi Oscard, Alex and Lori Scourby's talent agent in New York. The Foundation wanted Scourby to narrate the Old

Testament on cassette tape for its nonprofit use. The specific request had originally come about because an elderly woman named Amelia Brown Frazier of Louisville, Kentucky, had begun to lose her ability to see. The Bible was an important and comforting part of Frazier's daily life, and she very much wanted it available to her in one form or another. She sought to have the Bible narrated on tape so she could continue to enjoy the Scriptures in the event she lost her sight completely. A devout Christian, she had given a sizable contribution to the Episcopal Foundation with the express condition that the money be used to record the Bible and make it available to the visually impaired and physically handicapped.

At the time the Episcopal Foundation contacted Fifi Oscard, she had been representing Alexander and Lori for several decades. Through her well-known Oscard Agency, headquartered in the heart of New York City, she had become one of the most highly respected and outstanding agents in the literary and entertainment industry. She was Warren Beatty's and Bernadette Peters's first agent, and maintained a diverse client list that ranged from John Houseman to the crusty and colorful Jack Palance.

Fifi was the Scourbys' exclusive agent and had gradually become one of their closest friends. She had earned her reputation as an agent who got things done and, at the same time, always protected the interests of her clients.

Acting on behalf of her client and friend, Fifi was forced to inform Rakestraw that Scourby *could not* narrate the Old Testament in spite of his strongly expressed personal desires. Scourby was a member of AFTRA, the American Federation of Television and Radio Artists, a union to which virtually all successful entertainers belonged. Because of union rules, Fifi explained, Scourby could not work for the Episcopal Foundation because it was not a signatory to the agreement that the union had executed with various organizations. In addition, AFTRA members were required to pay a percentage of their earnings for each work performed into a fund set aside for indigent, retired, and disabled actors.

But since the tapes were to be nonprofit, Fifi suggested to Rakestraw that AFTRA might grant a waiver of the signatory requirement and the usual welfare and pension fees mandated. She urged Rakestraw to write a letter to Robert Spiro, the chief executive at AFTRA, with whom the

Oscard Agency had a longstanding professional relationship.

The original letter from Rakestraw to Spiro set forth a proposal:

The Parish of the Air
of the Episcopal Radio-TV Foundation, Inc.
Atlanta, Georgia

June 20, 1972

Mr. Robert Spiro
AFTRA
1350 Avenue of the Americas
New York, New York

Dear Mr. Spiro:

Mrs. Fifi Oscard has suggested that I write to you outlining our plans to have Alexander Scourby record the Old Testament.

First, may I say that the Episcopal Radio-TV Foundation is a non-profit organization which is supported entirely by voluntary contributions. The recording of the Old Testament is made possible by a gift to this Foundation. We anticipate no profit from these recordings. They will be utilized primarily by the blind and physically handicapped.

We are quite willing to pay Alexander Scourby for his services and also to pay the pension and welfare involved in the piece of work.

Sincerely,
Caroline Rakestraw
Executive Director

The two sides negotiated and soon worked out some terms. It was specifically understood that the license to the narration would be granted to the Episcopal Foundation for use only by the blind and handicapped and there would be "no profit" made from the recordings. With those conditions in place, AFTRA granted the waiver of its signatory requirement and also excused the pension and welfare payment. The Episcopal Radio-TV Foundation agreed with Scourby and Fifi that the King James Version of the Old Testament would be used. Amelia Brown Frazier's dream would become a reality.

Scourby completed his narration of the Old Testament that year and earned $10,000 for the work. It took over six full weeks to record. Two years later, he was asked by the Episcopal Foundation to narrate the New Testament, which he did. He accepted an even more nominal fee of $5,000, and stayed in the recording studio almost nonstop for over a month. The two works—the Old Testament and the New Testament—would come to be known as the "Episcopal narrations." Everyone understood the money involved was unimportant. Normally, for a morning's work, which would be enough to narrate four or five commercials, Scourby would generate revenues of anywhere from $100,000 to $200,000 a year depending on the number of times the spots aired. For a narration to accompany a film, he typically received a thousand dollars per minute. When he would do a narration for television, like *Twentieth Century* or *National Geographic*, he often earned $20,000 for half a day's work. Thus Scourby, his wife, and his trusted agent saw this as charitable work and a lasting testimony to Scourby's generous spirit.

CBS Evening News anchor Walter Cronkite, a noted Episcopalian, was utilized as a spokesman to promote the tapes through advertisements in the Episcopal Church's publications. The Episcopal narrations soon became extraordinarily popular. As they were distributed throughout the world, over time Scourby became known as the Voice of God.

Nonprofit sales of the Episcopal narrations of the Old and New Testaments went smoothly. But Scourby's earlier narrations done for the AFB began running into a problem in the middle and late 1970s, as cassette tapes began to replace phonograph records. Tape pirates—those who copy recordings without authorization and sell them for personal profit—

began to appear everywhere, and the work of no recording artist was safe from theft. The more popular a recording was, the more pirating activities took place. Probably because of the huge Christian market, Scourby's narrations of the Holy Bible became hot commodities among the profiteers. A few of the larger marketing firms who were selling Scourby's AFB recordings tried to take action against the rampant pirating, filing suit after suit against some of the smaller marauders who were making huge profits on Scourby's narrations. However, the larger marketers were having very little success in stopping the pirates. One reason was that the AFB narrations were not covered by a new copyright law that had been passed in 1974, and they carried no copyright notice.

In 1979, NEVA, Inc., a marketing firm based in Florida, entered into a license agreement with MASC, Inc., Alexander and Lori Scourby's personal corporation, that granted NEVA rights to market and sell the American Foundation for the Blind narration of the 1950s. David Aven, NEVA's founder and president (he came up with the firm's name by spelling his own name backward), was a personable man who had a quick smile and a penchant for laughter. A master at public relations and marketing, he had seen the agreement with Scourby as a great opportunity to commercially market the Bible on tape. Since the Bible had always been a bestseller in book form, he was confident that it could also be a number one bestseller in tape form. His instincts were right: He sold millions of tapes across the country through direct response television campaigns, and millions more through Christian bookstores. But the tape pirates were still a big problem, by some estimates outselling the authorized tapes ten to one.

Because there were so many bootleg distributors of the Scourby narrations, David approached Fifi Oscard and told her that he would like to get an exclusive license agreement. Scourby agreed that NEVA would exclusively market the original AFB version of the Bible. Part of the agreement read: "MASC shall not during the term [of the contract] authorize or permit any person, firm, or corporation other than NEVA to use Scourby's legal or professional name or likeness in connection with the advertising or sale of the phonograph records embodying in whole or in part the King James Version of the Bible, Old and New Testaments. This provision is exclusive of any outstanding agreements MASC or Scourby have with the Episcopal Church, and American Foundation for the Blind, and the American Bible Society." The latter provision was specifically added to protect the older agreement with Caroline Rakestraw and the Episcopal Foundation.

In February of 1985, shortly after the agreements were in place, Alexander Scourby passed away. It was then that the pirates were joined by another predator who sought to exploit the Scourby legacy…this time in the name of God.

R. B. "Jack" Turney of Christian Duplications International (CDI) in Orlando, Florida, had seen the enormous success of the marketing that David Aven and NEVA had conducted for the American Foundation for the Blind narration, and he was aware of the Episcopal narrations as well. Turney traveled to Atlanta and visited Caroline Rakestraw at her office at the Episcopal Foundation. Rakestraw, with her Southern demeanor, was a person of kindness and honesty. Toward the end of their meeting, when Turney told her that he wanted the right to sell the Episcopal narrations in the retail market, Rakestraw responded with an emphatic refusal. The Episcopal narrations, Rakestraw explained to Turney, were bound by an agreement with Alexander Scourby that made it very clear his narrations had been done for the benefit of the blind and handicapped, and for the furtherance of Christian religion. She emphasized that the Episcopal narrations of the Old and New Testaments could not be sold in the commercial market for any monetary gains. Turney thanked Rakestraw for her time, and returned to Florida.

Eventually, Caroline Rakestraw retired from the Episcopal Foundation. Soon after, Turney returned to Atlanta. This time his efforts succeeded. The Episcopal Foundation, under new leadership, granted a license to Turney and Christian Duplications International to sell the Episcopal narrations for profit. Turney and CDI paid the Episcopal Foundation $150,000 for the rights, as well as royalties of ten percent for each narration sold.

For a time, Lori Scourby and Fifi Oscard were unaware that Jack Turney and CDI had begun selling the tapes in the commercial marketplace. When David Aven of NEVA discovered that Turney was selling the

Episcopal narrations nationwide as the "authorized version," he assumed that Turney and CDI had entered into some sort of agreement with Fifi and Lori that altered the nature of Alexander's charitable work specifically recorded for the Episcopal Church. Aven arranged for a meeting with Turney to discuss the matter and specifically address the impact the sale of the Episcopal narrations was having in the commercial marketplace. During their meeting, Turney assured Aven that the necessary agreements and authorizations for the sale of the Episcopal narrations had been obtained and all was well.

Based on those assurances, Aven again focused his efforts on stopping the tape pirates who were wrongfully exploiting and profiting from Scourby's name. He instituted a suit in Texas against nine of the largest distributors who were pirating the American Foundation for the Blind version. Using the state's tape piracy statutes, he won the case and virtually halted the illegal exploitation of the Scourby narrations. At least that is what Aven thought. Encouraged by his success in Texas, he arranged a meeting in New York with Fifi Oscard to advise her of the progress made in protecting the Scourby name. During the discussion, the matter of Jack Turney and the retail sale of the Episcopal narrations came up. Fifi was dumbfounded as she listened to David explain what had gone on during the meeting with Turney. She had no knowledge that the Episcopal Foundation had consented to the commercialization of the Scourby Biblical narrations. She had never heard of Turney or Christian Duplications, and neither she nor the Scourbys had ever consented or agreed to anything other than the original understanding with the Episcopal Foundation. She was shocked and angered when she learned the late Alexander Scourby's work was being exploited, and outraged that narrations intended for the blind and handicapped had been sold by the Episcopal Foundation.

On the instruction of the Oscard Agency and Lori Scourby, again David Aven contacted Jack Turney. Turney was informed that neither he nor CDI had the rights to market the Episcopal Foundation tapes, and these unauthorized sales should be immediately halted. In response, Turney informed Aven that CDI had bought the rights from the Episcopal Foundation. He also told him CDI had purchased full and unrestricted rights to sell the tapes in any manner it chose.

David Aven contacted the Episcopal Foundation and related his understanding of what was occurring. On behalf of the Estate of Alexander Scourby and the Oscard Agency, he expressed clear objection to the commercial exploitation of Scourby's charitable works. He strenuously and emphatically urged the Episcopal Foundation to remedy the situation and preserve the intent of the agreement that had been put into place before Alexander Scourby's death and honored after his passing. The Episcopal Foundation rejected any notion of stopping the commercialization of the Voice of God. Phone calls and correspondence went unreturned as the world marketplace became flooded with commercial sales of Scourby's Episcopal narrations.

The exploitation of Scourby's name increased further when two years after Scourby's death, Christian Duplications International and Turney entered into an agreement with a Texas corporation named International Cassette Corporation (ICC), in which ICC was permitted to sell Scourby's narration in exchange for royalties to be paid to CDI. The ICC deal allowed CDI to make even more profit and furthered the worldwide commercialization of the Episcopal narrations Alexander Scourby had so nobly created. Ironically, the Episcopal narrations were being touted as the "Authorized Alexander Scourby's Latest Narration." The name, voice and legacy Alexander Scourby had created and nurtured were being taken and no action that Aven, Lori, and Fifi attempted had been successful.

By then, David Aven, Lori Scourby, and Fifi Oscard were left with no choice. They needed to go to court against Jack Turney, Christian Duplications International, and the Episcopal Foundation.

The Holy War
• • • • • • •

D avid Aven and I had known each other for several years. He was aggressive and smart, and he had been very successful in the business world. As he sat in my office, I listened closely as he related the facts of this fascinating scenario that had been played out in the mixed world of actors, big business, and organized religion. (I had long been aware that the lines between religion and business were often blurred—if not obliterated—by the modern television saviors. The lucrative lure of money and the growth of televised evangelism had brought scandal to religion.)

I was angered by what I was learning. There was no doubt Alexander Scourby had been a man of high principles and impeccable integrity. Both his voice and his good works were known to me. The matter was worth considering. I would review and analyze the voluminous documents and materials David had brought.

Within a few days, I formulated a clear belief that Scourby's charitable works had been exploited. It was obvious no one had intended that people like Jack Turney benefit from those Episcopal narrations. Nor did I doubt that Scourby had expended enormous effort and countless hours at virtually no profit to make the recordings. Now, with her husband's death, Lori March Scourby carried the responsibility of restoring his name and retrieving the Episcopal narrations from the realm of business profiteering, where millions of dollars were being wrongfully earned.

There wasn't much doubt as to what was right and what was wrong. I agreed to accept the representation. We would file suit, wage war, and restore dignity to the Voice of God.

Chris Knopik, one of my law partners at the time, would co-counsel the case with me. Steve Stein would join our trial team because of his extraordinary knowledge of patent, copyright, and intellectual property law. For years, Steve had specialized in the very complicated areas of intellectual property and the proprietary rights of artists, and in that area he was among the best in the country.

Chris and I often tried complicated cases together. An outstanding lawyer, he had gone to law school at the University of Virginia and then spent two years clerking for Chief Judge Terrell Hodges in central Florida's federal court. I had helped recruit Chris to join Holland & Knight in the early 1980s. We had bonded and stayed in practice together almost fifteen years before he started a law firm of his own. Usually, when we worked a trial together, I would pick the jury and Chris would deliver the opening statement. We would divide the witnesses and the work done during trial, and I would close the case by presenting the final argument. Our skills complemented each other quite well, and the jury verdicts we obtained were invariably outstanding.

Chris rarely questioned my judgment, nor did I second guess him. He knew my talents and was always one of my strongest and most vocal supporters, as I was his. Even though we no longer practice together, we remain friends, and our relationship is built on mutual respect.

It was this talented trial team that would take on Jack Turney and Christian Duplications International on behalf of David Aven, Fifi Oscard, and Lori March Scourby. Officially, the lawsuit was against CDI, Turney, International Cassette Corporation (ICC), and the Episcopal Foundation. We would establish that the trademark "Alexander Scourby" and Scourby's likeness had become uniquely associated with the Biblical narration recorded for the American Foundation for the Blind in the 1950s as authorized by Scourby and commercialized by NEVA, not the Episcopal version that Jack Turney and CDI were marketing throughout the country.

Additionally, we charged that CDI's and ICC's use of the trademark "Authorized Alexander Scourby's Latest Narration" and Scourby's likeness in connection with the sales of the Episcopal narrations constituted a false description and representation and wrongfully designated the Episcopal narrations as approved by Scourby and NEVA. The plaintiffs also contended that Christian Duplications International's conduct violated the law in that they had misrepresented themselves to the public by saying they had been awarded "exclusive production rights" to the Episcopal narrations.

Finally, we alleged that Christian Duplications International's acts violated the Florida Deceptive and Unfair Trade Practices Act. By reason of the agreements between NEVA and MASC, the American Foundation for the Blind, and the estate of Alexander Scourby, NEVA and David Aven were solely authorized to commercially market both the American Foundation for the Blind narration and the Episcopal narrations.

At trial, the defense made the bold assertion that their business and corporations possessed outright ownership of the Episcopal narrations. The defendants, whom I quickly named "the bad guys," took the position that Alexander Scourby was simply a "hired hand" and was paid for the work he had done. The Episcopal Foundation had filed and registered a copyright on "its narration" and urged that the recordings constituted a "work made for hire" by Scourby since he was commissioned by the Episcopal Foundation. One of the defense experts even rendered the brazen opinion that the "Episcopal Foundation was the copyright owner, not Scourby." The Episcopal Foundation adamantly asserted that it owned the concept, not Scourby. According to the defense expert, the "Foundation hired for a fixed amount of money the narrator, and they furnished the recording studio, technical engineers—which account for the quality of the recording—and they paid for the publishing and manufacturing of the work. The only thing the narrator did was come in and read the Bible."

The Episcopal Foundation's boastful claims were not enough in a courtroom. At trial, through witness after witness and document after document, the evidence showed that Alexander Scourby narrated the Holy Bible on tape for *nonprofit and charitable use* by a religious foundation. Our evidence showed that Christian Duplications International began commercially selling those narrations for profit in the commercial marketplace and wrongly used Scourby's name to promote sales of its works, despite the fact that the needed authorization from the Oscard Agency or the Scourbys had never been acquired. During the trial, we clearly established that the defendants generated profit without giving one cent to Scourby during his lifetime, nor did they share their profits with Lori March Scourby, Scourby's estate, or Fifi Oscard after Scourby's death.

The Episcopal Foundation had obtained the rights to distribute these recordings among the blind and handicapped and to sell the recordings throughout the Episcopalian community. The commercial exploitation of Scourby's Voice of God had resulted in millions of dollars in profit. We had several goals at trial. First, stop the illegal sales and distribution of the Episcopal narrations. Second, require the defendants to repay the huge amounts in profits that had been generated by their wrongful actions. Lastly, we demanded the return of the Episcopal narrations to the original and rightful owners—the Estate of Alexander Scourby and his loving wife, Lori.

· · · · · · ·

The Closing Argument

MAY IT PLEASE THE COURT. Ladies and gentlemen of the jury, it has been a long trial. On behalf of everyone, let me assure you that I very much appreciate each of your efforts and the faithful fulfillment of your solemn duty as jurors. I am sure that I am not alone in thanking you for taking time out of your work lives and away from your families. *[I always gave thanks to the men and women of every jury and when I did, I made certain I looked at each one. I also looked and then motioned around the entire courtroom and gestured that everyone gathered was appreciative. Hell, it was the least we could do. In courtrooms across our country Americans are taking time out of their lives and jobs, and time away from their families, to fulfill jury duty. In some states, the juror is paid as little as five dollars a day, and nowhere are jury members paid an amount anywhere near as valuable as the service each is asked to render. I am hopeful that the empowerment, the satisfaction, and the knowledge of being such a fundamental participant in the pursuit of justice are rewards enough. Unfortunately, jury duty is viewed by many as a nuisance and something to be avoided. That notion is a tragedy and a disservice to everything we stand for. A fair trial by a jury of our peers is our basic democratic right. Serving others, dispensing justice, righting wrong, finding truth—to me these are what make our system great. And how I loved being up there looking into the eyes of the jurors who would decide it all!]*

Of course, serving as a juror is also a great privilege. When called as jurors, you have the opportunity so many have died for, the opportunity to sit in judgment about what is right and what is wrong, what is truth and what is not, and what is trust and what is betrayal of trust.

Our jury system is so wonderful because each of you, in your own collective minds, can outthink any one individual. And my words are just that; they are an expression of my singular opinion of what the evidence has shown. If I misspeak, or if I make mistakes, please do not hold that against our clients.

The defense lawyers will soon have an opportunity to tell you what they believe the evidence will show, but I specifically recall that day when Reverend Lewis Schueddig—the "new blood" director of the defendant

Episcopal Radio-TV Foundation—was on the stand. The last question I asked him was, "What does the word 'trust' mean to you?" You heard his response, and it was on that point that the proceedings ended. He was the last witness. *[During cross-examination, he had answered my inquiry with one of his own. In a condescending tone he had replied, "What do you mean by trust?" The flippant response had allowed me to make an invaluable point. If "the Reverend" chose to ask what I meant by trust, he demonstrated either arrogant insincerity or, better for us, a lack of understanding and appreciation for the key issue in the Scourby case. After his response, I had noticed the rolling eyes of two members of the jury and made a mental note. Now, as I continued my summation, I made sure my eye contact with both of them was a bit longer than normal. I will never be sure if I really saw the almost imperceptible nods or simply imagined them, but either way I remember a welcome exhilaration and the renewal of confidence I felt as I continued the closing argument.]*

That issue of trust really signifies the beginning, as well as the end, of the critical issues to be decided in this case. Trust for Lori and Alex Scourby began when they were married, started their careers, and embarked on their journey through life. Each trusted the other to be honest and fair and true, to never give up on life and always believe in its goodness.

And we all know how precious the moments of life are. Yet, I am sure you have become frustrated and tired over the endless hours of objections and lawyer talk that has occurred here. You know, sometimes a person just becomes disillusioned in life. In this case, you have on one hand forty-two years of a marriage full of life, happiness, and trust. You have a man whose heart has to be left to your good judgment and weighed as far as its goodness is concerned; that man is Alexander Scourby. The judge will give you an instruction on credibility of witnesses, motive to testify, interest in the outcome, and bias.

I have entered my fortieth year now, and I have been practicing law for quite some time. I think during my first year of practice, about sixteen years ago, a lawyer said, "You know what happens as you grow older? You are going to learn a lot of things, and one of those things is that a politician will steal your vote. Sometimes the fellow with the only grain elevator in town can slap you on the back and ask you how your family is, all the while shortchanging the crop you have worked for all year by weighing the grain on crooked scales." It is trust, faith, and betrayal in the real world.

So, what is trust and faith in worldwide evangelism? At what price? Where is the line crossed? That is a hard question. Use your common sense, because you do not need a degree in divinity for that task. We learned during your response in jury selection of your accomplishments and academic degrees. And I know education is not a scarcity on the other side of this jury box. It is not a scarcity in your lifestyle. It is not a scarcity where you come from. And there certainly is not a scarcity of common sense in this group, because that is what we all learn as we pass through life. *[In federal court, the jury pool is picked from the Orlando area and the east coast of Florida. Incredibly, we had two engineers employed by NASA at the Cape Kennedy Space Center. I had worked hard to keep them on the jury. I was confident these people would appreciate intellectual property and the "gray matter" of life.]*

As you enter your deliberations, you are finders of the fact. In essence, you are the judges of the facts in this case. What is on the other side of that jury door is very important, because your verdict serves as your rendition of what you think is right and what you think is wrong.

Let's forget the lawyers' fancy jargon used over and over in this courtroom. The search here is simply for the truth. The truth is no stranger. You can almost always tell the truth when you hear it. It is so easy to recognize. And when it comes to you, you realize it is something you knew all along.

This case is about a man's good name, and it certainly concerns his reputation, his voice, and the theft of his life's work. When a person leaves this life, precious little is left behind. The last things that came out of Vietnam were the body bags, the last thing that is put on a person's tomb-stone is a name, and the last thing a person leaves his children is a legacy.

John Keats once wrote, "What weapons has a lion but his heart." You do not need to be a rocket scientist to figure out exactly what is going on here; you merely have to be a human being and use your common sense. *[I wanted to put all the jurors on an equal footing with the NASA engineers and make certain they all knew how much I respected and valued their presence.]*

This case is not about religion. It is about spreading the Word of God to the people of the earth. It is not about worldwide evangelism. It is about taking a person's wonderful voice, his good name, and his noble efforts and using them to benefit the blind and the handicapped. And it is about the exploitation of Alexander Scourby's voice for an unjust profit.

This case is not about the working of a church or a nonprofit corporation. It is about selling the seventy-two hours of Alexander Scourby's narration of the Holy Bible for hundreds of thousands of dollars. When he undertook this worthy effort for a nominal sum of $10,000 for the Old Testament and $5,000 for the New Testament, he thought he was giving his wonderful gift to the blind. Instead, the narration was sold like an ordinary piece of merchandise in places likes Sears, Roebuck & Co., and its catalogues.

I will tell you what this case is about. This case is about the necessity of keeping one's word in the world of business. We are not condemning the Episcopal Radio-TV Foundation. What we are condemning are the methods that were used in this case, to do something that nobody ever intended to be done…to sell Scourby's narration for a profit rather than use it as his intended gift to the blind and handicapped.

Let's go back and review the story this evidence tells. The document marked Exhibit Three, which is in evidence, is the beginning of the involvement of the Scourby voice with these defendants. That is the correspondence between Fifi Oscard and Caroline Rakestraw of the Episcopal Foundation. But that is not really the beginning of the story. The beginning of the story started shortly after 1942 when Alexander Scourby began to narrate over three hundred fifty "talking books" for people who could not see, were illiterate, or for some other reason could not read. He did that because he dedicated part of his life to return some of the money and success he had been fortunate enough to receive. And do you remember when I asked the Episcopal Radio-TV Foundation's representatives about that? Reverend Schueddig said, "Well, Mr. Scourby received ten thousand dollars, maybe even fifteen thousand dollars for doing those narrations. Those are princely sums to a person of my means."

Please. Let's be candid. Alexander Scourby's voice and his name were worth millions, and the defendants knew it. He would have gotten hundreds of thousands of dollars in the real world. The defendants knew he was a celebrity. How many narrations do you think that man would sell? How many narrations do you think ICC's Ollie Moyer would sell? How many narrations do you think Jack Turney would sell? *[This was said as I pointed to the Reverend Schueddig, and then to Ollie Moyer, and then to the entire defense table.]*

Who among all the other countless actors and actresses possessed a voice that would sell like Alexander Scourby? If God spoke, it surely would have been through the wonderfulness of a voice like Alexander Scourby's. The folks now on trial knew what they got in the narration of the Bible by this great voice. It was given for the nominal sum of $10,000 for the Old Testament and $5,000 for the New Testament—this work of seventy-two hours of actual narration—to benefit the blind and handicapped. It was never done to allow these defendants to sell the narrations for profit. It was never intended to allow these defendants to place this holy work in the Sears catalogue and sell it like any other piece of ordinary merchandise. And it will be up to you, the jury, to render a verdict to stop these activities, return Alexander Scourby's master tapes to those who rightfully own them, and assess an appropriate amount of damages to take back the profits that were wrongfully earned.

In the early 1950s, using his brilliant voice, this great man, Alexander Scourby, narrated the Holy Bible, the King James Version, and gave it to the American Foundation for the Blind. As this narration became well known, the Episcopal Radio-TV Foundation learned about the works and believed it would be a good idea, a worthy notion, to have the Episcopal Radio-TV Foundation do the same thing. And so the Episcopal Radio-TV Foundation approached Alexander Scourby's business manager, Fifi Oscard. She owns the nationally known Fifi Oscard Agency in New York City, which represented many, many actors, writers, and other celebrities, including Alexander Scourby.

You recall the testimony has shown that some years back, a little lady who lived in Kentucky was losing her eyesight. Her name was Amelia Brown Frazier. She was fortunate to have a good deal of money. From the correspondence we introduced into evidence, we have learned her intent through her own words. "I am going to let those people who are losing their sight, like me, have this narration. I will give you the money," and she did. She gave the Episcopal Foundation one hundred thousand dollars. But there was a big string. She required them to use her gift for the blind. She wanted to make sure the blind got the benefit of the Bible's narration."

But what happened, as bizarre as this sounds, was that somewhere along the line, the string to the money got cut. The Episcopal Radio-TV Foundation approached the Scourbys and sought to have Alexander Scourby narrate the Old Testament, the King James Version of the Holy Bible. They suggested $10,000 for the task. It was represented the narration was being done for the Episcopal Radio-TV Foundation, a nonprofit organization. The recording was made possible by the gift from Amelia Brown Frazier that required the money to be spent to help the blind.

It was a benevolent type of gift that was distorted and changed into big business when the Episcopal Foundation decided to sell the narration tapes for a large profit to the commercial entities that are the defendants in this lawsuit. We have the documentation in evidence that verifies the tapes were to be utilized primarily by the blind and physically handicapped. There was to be no commercial profit.

In response, the defendants have come forward and argued that the catalogues and other commercial outlets were authorized to sell the narrations. In effect, the defense asserts it was only record stores that could not be used to "market" the Scourby tapes. What is this? It is the bits and pieces, the sleight of hand by using the words and not the meaning: "Will not be available or sold commercially over the counter in record stores throughout the country." When I called Caroline Rakestraw, the Episcopal Radio-TV Foundation's executive director, to the stand, I asked her if that is what it meant, and her response was definitive—it wasn't going to be sold commercially; it was for the blind and handicapped! That is the critical issue, and that was the absolutely clear intention of the parties.

Once again, correspondence we uncovered from the defense's own files is damning. One of the exhibits is a letter from the Episcopal Foundation, which states: "Thank you for your letter of June 23. I can assure you we have no intention of making a recording of the Old Testament available for sale in record stores throughout the country."

Exactly what did Mr. Scourby convey by his graciousness and his wonderful gift? Did he simply retain the rights that these narrations could not be sold in record stores? The defense is going to get up and claim he didn't retain any rights other than those. The defense argument is simple: Where is it written that he retained rights? Seems to me it is kind of like asking somebody over for dinner, a free dinner, out of the goodness of your heart, and then he or she leaving with the silverware. One might say, "I told you that you could eat, but I didn't tell you that you could take the silverware."

The defense didn't ever, ever buy Mr. Scourby's name. They never bought his voice. Through a nominal payment of $10,000 for the Old Testament and $5,000 for the New Testament, they bought the use of his voice for the limited purpose of distributing these master works to the blind and handicapped who could not read the Bible for themselves.

Robert Spiro, the elderly gentleman of AFTRA who was instrumental in spelling out the conveyance on behalf of Alexander Scourby, wrote, "Dear Mrs. Rakestraw: Since your letter of June indicates the Parish of the Air will not offer the recordings for sale in record stores throughout the country..." "Throughout the country"—he could have said, "throughout the world." There was a clear understanding and agreement that they were not going to commercially exploit the recordings. It was David Aven many years before who went and paid royalties and got the agreements necessary to commercially sell and profit from Alexander Scourby's narrations of the Holy Bible.

The end to this tale of exploitation and efforts to get something for nothing stops here—and it stops now with your verdict. Because of the defendants' actions, they cut the string and took it from the charitable work Mrs. Frazier had envisioned when she gave her money for the narration into the world of profit and the commercial stream of commerce.

Your verdict, I humbly suggest, must be decisive on one key issue: Have the plaintiffs, NEVA and the Estate of Alexander Scourby, proved by a preponderance of the evidence that the unauthorized publication and use of Alexander Scourby's name and his narrative work were wrong? *[Framing the issue in terms of right and wrong provided the black-and-white context I believed necessary. Otherwise, the priestly collar of the defendants' rep-*

resentative or the whole concocted notion it was "the Church," the epitome of goodness, would cloud the courtroom. It had to be the good, well-intentioned Scourby versus the wrongdoers.]

I suggest to you the case requires the answer to be yes, because it is clear the plaintiffs never authorized these defendants to use the Scourby name commercially.

Don't be afraid of the difficulty of the complex task of properly deciding this case. You are up to the task. For us, we may go on to the other things in life. But for these parties, this matter will be decided for all time. A simple, straightforward approach may be to award one dollar for every tape the defendants sold. They sold 1.8 million tapes, and I suggest that $1.8 million be the total of damages awarded against those three defendants.

Against the defense lawyer here and Episcopal Radio-TV Foundation, award punitive damages in the amount of one dollar—just send a message. You did wrong. Do not do it again.

To give you an idea concerning the magnitude of the damages, in a year and a half or so of sales, International Cassette Corp., one of the defendant corporations in this case, made $454,512 off the goodness of Alexander Scourby, who did this narration for the Episcopal Radio-TV Foundation to supposedly benefit the blind and handicapped.

This case has to do with profit. I suspected that I might forget some things I probably should have said. But I knew I was not going to forget that power, money, and privilege have now become the new Trinity some people have come to worship. I was not going to forget about the yuppie generation, and I was not going to forget about the value of a good name. I was not going to forget about my father, and I wasn't going to forget about Our Father, who art in Heaven. I wasn't going to forget about the religious overtones of this case. At the same time, I was confident that I would not forget about the profiteers in this case. One principle that must always be remembered very clearly—people should not make money when they break their word. That idea simply cannot be forgotten.

David Aven is not without personal flaws, nor is he a hero. But he is a champion of what is right in this case, and he has taken on the cause of Lori Scourby and Fifi Oscard. You know, all champions are not in shining

armor and riding white horses. They don't all have beautiful ribbons attached to their armor when they go out and joust for what is right.
Sometimes, champions are just ordinary people trying to do the right
thing. But you look inside people, and that is what you have to do in this
case. You have to look inside. And that is where you find the truth. There
is only today. In life, there is no guarantee of tomorrow. And if you walk
out of here, and you have a feeling you did right in deciding your verdict,
that is all we can ever ask.

I know it has been a long trial, but I urge that each of you reach
into your souls and seek out the truth. Look past what people and things
appear to be and determine what reality mandates and justice requires.
When you are in Florida, and you are out in the middle of a field, and
you are squatting down on the ground, and you hear hoof beats, and you
hear and feel a herd of animals coming from behind you...when you look
around—you expect to see horses or cows. You don't expect to see
African zebras. That is what this case is about. The defense has taken
something, with sleight of hand, distorted it, and asked you to see something that simply is not there. How many times did we hear the defense
team say, "Objection! No, we can't read that. Wait, no, we will read this
part, not that part." The whole truth and nothing but the truth, so help
me God...so help me God. The whole, entire truth must and should decide
this case.

I am going to ask you to remember all the things that have happened and use your collective memories. And don't hold what I have or
have not said against my clients. Just do what is right. Take this dead man,
Alexander Scourby, who is still alive through his voice. That is why we
called him by means of his audio narrations as our first witness in this
case. Restore his gripping work of being the "Voice of God" back to his
widow, Lori March Scourby. Restore the ownership and the master tapes
to Mrs. Scourby and give this commercial right and Scourby legacy to
her. I ask that you restore Alexander Scourby's legacy, name, and voice to
the home he envisioned, which is the home of the blind, handicapped,
and nonprofit charitable religious organizations.

Remember, when it comes to damages, the royalties are what we
want back. Let them keep Mrs. Frazier's money, but the many, many

hundreds of thousands of dollars they profiteered and made, we want back.

Recently, I was in New York and visited Rockefeller Square. Chiseled in stone—and I may not remember the exact wording of the plaque, but the message is clear—are words attributed to Nelson Rockefeller that state: "I believe in the worth of an individual and the pursuit of happiness. I believe in the sacredness of a promise, that a man's words should be as good as his bond, and that character, not wealth or power, should be of supreme importance, and that right can and will triumph over might."

It finally comes down to what this case is all about. The defendants, CDI and Jack Turney stole the name and voice of Alexander Scourby and unfairly competed against others. They wrongfully came in and sold products marked "Authorized Alexander Scourby's Latest Narration" in a commercial marketplace.

Yet, David Aven was the only duly licensed and authorized person to commercially sell the Bible narration made by Alexander Scourby. When he found out what the defendants were improperly doing, he came to our courthouse to put a stop to it. He brought a lawsuit. Imagine what it cost to bring these sophisticated corporations through three years of litigation. But he never quit. And here we are. This is his lawsuit now—and Alexander Scourby's lawsuit. It is our lawsuit. Do you think it could come to your consideration if it was frivolous? If it was a frivolous lawsuit, do you think the judge would let it come to you, as jurors?

The defendants have told you that Mr. Aven is going to get ninety-five percent of the rights. That is an outright falsehood. If you find for us, he is going to get the money back that the defendants illegally made. What he is going to get back is the money that he should have made in profits instead of the money being made by the defendants.

We can't show the lost sales of Mr. Aven. We can't show what phone calls were never made or orders that were never placed. To determine what he lost, you simply have to look at what the defendants made. As for the ownership rights to the narration, if we prevail, Lori March Scourby will get those back—all of them. She gets one hundred percent of the rights concerning her great husband's voice.

Remember that the story of this wrong started in the 1970s, when piracy was running rampant. As the Scourbys' agent, Fifi Oscard tried her best to stop it. That is when David Aven came on the scene and started cleaning up the marketplace and properly restoring the rights to where they belonged.

Now, I am going to read to you for Alexander Scourby, since he is not here to read for himself. Fortunately, his words will be listened to by hundreds of thousands of people long after we are gone. These words are from Ecclesiastes in the Old Testament and the Gospel of Matthew in the New Testament, and with them, the late, great narrator certainly earned his reputation as the Voice of God:

> *Ecclesiastes 7:1. A good name is better than precious ointment; and the day of death than the day of one's birth.*

> *Matthew 12:34-37. O generation of vipers, how can ye, being evil, speak good things? For out of the abundance of the heart the mouth speaketh. A good man out of the good treasure of the heart bringeth forth good things: and an evil man out of the evil treasure bringeth forth evil things. But I say unto you, that every idle word that men shall speak, they shall give account thereof in the Day of Judgment. For by thy words thou shalt be justified, and by thy words, thou shalt be condemned.*

The last words you heard me read were from the same passage on that tape we played at the beginning of this trial. There has been an inference that we are somehow seeking a handout for a poor, grieving widow. Don't let them come up with that grieving widow nonsense, because Mrs. Scourby doesn't want your sympathy. She doesn't need it. She is not entitled to it, and the judge will instruct you to disregard that emotion. What she is entitled to is exactly what she said she wants…and that is justice. She was reared as an Episcopalian. She understands what is at stake, and what has been done. She is entitled to justice, and she is entitled to have back in her home that which was stolen.

I am going to ask you to do something that is very hard. Put aside whatever walk of life you come from, whatever your position is now, really put it aside. No matter what your verdict is, just make sure it is the right one. And when you walk out of here, you can tell people that you did your duty. A lot of people have carried our great flag to a lot of places at a huge sacrifice for the very purpose of preserving and allowing our democracy to survive and our jury system to prosper. God be with you in your deliberations.

Thank you.

The Orlando Sentinel

The best newspaper in Florida

Bible narrator's heirs win $1.8 million

Day of Judgment

·······

A fter deliberating over the course of two days, the jury returned a verdict of $1.8 million on behalf of the heirs of Alexander Scourby. Scourby's understanding had been that the tapes would only be used for the blind and handicapped, yet so many others, hoping to capitalize on his name, exploited the tapes solely for the purpose of financial gain. After hearing nearly three weeks' worth of complex testimony, the jury had deliberated for sixteen hours as it decided that Christian Duplications International of Orlando, International Cassette Corp., of Texas, and the Episcopal Radio-TV Foundation of Atlanta did not have the proper authorization or consent to distribute the tapes.

Federal Judge Patricia Fawsett ordered the master tapes of the Scourby narrations returned to their rightful owner, the defendants were prohibited from further distribution of the tapes, and all other copies of the tapes were to be destroyed.

The victory was total and complete. No appeal was filed.

Epilogue

·······

T he lesson of life reiterated time and time again in the Scourby case is as simple as it is ancient: Tell the truth, treat others justly, and have respect for your fellow man. While the notion of goodness dominates the church, I discovered that the sins of hypocrisy and greed sometimes emerge. When our circle of religious faith is broken, it becomes increasingly difficult to place our trust in the church. When that trust is gone, much of what we are taught and cherish about religion becomes suspect. The wonderfulness of Scourby's work should never have been exploited for financial gain. Stopping such a wrong, made me realize there can be hypocrisy in holiness. Today I am willing to question those who purport to be spreading the word of God and I have a better understanding of the age-old phrase, "hucksters of holiness."

The truth remains that Alexander Scourby brought a new quality to the niche of voice-overs and narrations. He was an accomplished actor with a voice that was unique and beautiful. He cared about the blind, the handicapped, and all people. His narrations of the Talking Books and the Holy Bible served as an altruistic work and was his way of giving something back. Scourby had a voice that everybody wanted. It was amazing to discover how many people have heard him at one time or another.

In 1986, the American Foundation for the Blind established the Alexander Scourby Narrator of the Year Awards in memory of Scourby and his contribution, through his Talking Books, to the cause of literacy for blind people. The ceremony features award recipients reading passages from works they have recorded, and the award presenters—visually impaired themselves—speak about the significance of reading in their lives. The awards ceremony is a fitting tribute to Scourby, and Lori has never failed to attend.

■ ■ ■ ■ ■ ■ ■

With the conviction came a store of assurance. He felt a quiet manhood, non-assertive but of sturdy and strong blood. He knew that he would no more quail before his guides wherever they should point. He had been to touch the great death, and found that, after all, it was but the great death. He was a man...So it came to pass that as he trudged from the place of blood and wrath his soul changed. He came from hot plowshares to prospects of clover tranquilly, and it was as if hot plowshares were not. Scars faded as flowers...Yet the youth smiled, for he saw that the world was a world for him, though many discovered it to be made of oaths and walking sticks. He had rid himself of the red sickness of battle. The sultry nightmare was in the past. He had been an animal blistered and sweating in the heat and pain of war. He turned now with a lover's thirst to images of tranquil skies, fresh meadows, cool brooks—an existence of soft and eternal peace... Over the river a golden ray of sun came through the hosts of leaden rain clouds.

■ ■ ■

—Stephen Crane
The Red Badge of Courage

Gary Stakemiller and his family at the newly constructed Marriott World Center, several days before the accident.

CHAPTER FIVE

A Hero's Story

A patchwork quilt, in all its simplicity, is a thing of beauty. Each piece of fabric has its own history, its own story to tell. The small, colorful squares, triangles, and rectangles for a quilt are carefully selected, cut, and handsewn, then stitched together to form a unique blanket or bed covering that will, no doubt, be treasured for generations to come. Parts of the quilt could include a red triangle of cloth from a pretty dress bought especially for Christmas, a checkered square from a flour sack, or a corduroy rectangle that was once a child's overalls. Put aside, perhaps in a barrel or box, these fabric remnants may have been tucked away with an unspoken promise of future value. At the first hint of cold weather, the assorted pieces are pulled out of their hiding place. Useful once again, the cloth of memories will be reassembled and lovingly stitched into a kaleidoscopic masterpiece. There is nothing quite like a patchwork quilt; its allure is pure and comforting. Its history recalls the warmth and security of a family's heritage.

Since both of my parents worked full-time when I was a young boy, I spent many hours in Alum Creek, West Virginia, at the home of my mother's parents, J. K. and Breman Griffith, known simply to me as Pa-Paw and Ma-Maw. I vividly remember my Ma-Maw spending days upon days handstitching quilts of colorful imagination and demonstrating her inner beauty through this remarkable, unique American art. With her high cheekbones and the fair skin of her Irish-English heritage, Ma-Maw was a staunch Baptist who was both giving and kind. Slightly overweight and never without her country apron, she was the master of Southern fried chicken, corn on the cob, the best mashed potatoes in the world, homemade ice cream, and the most elaborate and stunning quilts I have seen to this day. Following his retirement after forty-eight years with C&O Railroad, my Pa-Paw used to glow with pride every time he was going to accompany Ma-Maw to one of her "quilting parties."

The Clients
∎ ∎ ∎ ∎ ∎ ∎ ∎

Gary Vaughn Stakemiller of Auburndale, Florida, was the first human quilt I had ever seen. From his neck down, Gary was handsewn and stapled together with small squares and rectangles of skin that were meshed and fitted one beside the other with bright red line borders that oozed blood and the clear liquid of excreted plasma.

In time, I came to view Gary as a work of art, every bit as marvelous as any quilt Ma-Maw ever crafted. A modest and humble person who possessed an ability to face the most appalling circumstances with equanimity, he carried a hero's resolve to grasp life and never give up, in spite of the tremendous odds and the almost certain death that had confronted him.

At the beginning of 1990, Gary was almost thirty years old. He had worked his way up the ladder of success as an electrical apprentice, then journeyman, until he finally achieved his dream of becoming a master electrician. At a very young age, he had been able to secure a supervisory position with ANECO, one of the largest electrical subcontractors in the United States. Gary was a good-looking man with bright eyes, dark blond hair, and an ever-present smile. His wide shoulders and trim frame testified to his life of hard manual work, and the sinewy muscles in his arms stood out as witness to his power and strength. He was an outdoorsman who, like many growing up in Central Florida's rural areas, enjoyed hunting, fishing, and water sports. Gary Stakemiller was the type of person who fit right in on a construction site.

For all his brawniness, he was a tender and gentle husband to his wife, Pamela Ann, and a loving, physically affectionate father to their children. Pam, dark-haired and full of life, was strikingly pretty. She was the same age as Gary but looked several years younger. The couple had married just before Christmas in 1986. The marriage was the first for Gary and the second for Pam. Pam brought her young daughter, Ashley, to the marriage. Gary raised Ashley as his own; and the couple added two more children, Cameron and Erin Elaine. The family did virtually everything together, and life was good.

Gary Stakemiller's world revolved around his wife, children, and work. He especially liked toiling with his hands. Working alone in his spare time, he had built a large porch onto the family home in Auburndale so everyone could enjoy sitting outside together and watching the magical Florida sunsets. He had also installed a sophisticated sprinkler system in their large yard that kept the well-manicured lawn deep green even in the driest of sweltering summers. Gary and Pam had a passion for flowers, and the two spent countless hours gardening and nurturing the floral landscape each had helped create. The brightly colored flowers and shrubs surrounding the Stakemillers' home were a source of pride. The Florida outdoors was the family's playground, and the young couple often took their children to lakeside parks and beaches, where Gary taught his children to skim-board and water-ski.

A Day in Hell

· · · · · · ·

On a chilly day in January of 1990—one singular defining moment in Gary Stakemiller's life—a catastrophic event was about to occur that would literally tear him apart. Over a year earlier, ANECO had won the contract for a massive electrical installation to power a multimillion-dollar expansion of the Marriott World Center in Orlando. Gary had been handpicked as the job-site superintendent. Critical electrical switchgear and other sophisticated equipment had been purchased from Westinghouse Electric Corporation. The huge main switches that would regulate the vast amounts of power transmitted to the new convention annex had been designed by Westinghouse and delivered as "turn-key equipment," ready to install. Of course, detailed instructions for the installation of the equipment by professional electricians had been provided.

Due to a number of changes and modifications ordered after construction was already under way, overall work on the project had been lagging behind. Marriott had agreed to pay for the substantial amounts of overtime the ANECO employees were required to work, and it was not unusual for the electricians to work seventy and even eighty hours a week. Because of a scheduled visit by then President George Bush (the father), the Marriott project had been placed on the fast track. Completion of the remaining work was frenzied and demanded an around-the-clock construction schedule.

Finally, after numerous delays, the completion of construction neared. But after the huge Westinghouse electrical panels were bolted in to finalize the installation of the power system, there had been a major malfunction. As the government inspectors, ANECO representatives, and Marriott supervisors were in the process of the last walk-through inspection of the hotel facilities before the building was approved for occupancy, the entire electrical system had failed. Westinghouse was immediately notified of the malfunction and it requested that ANECO fix the problem.

Because the World Center had effectively been completed, the entire work force of electrical and assisting personnel had already been moved to another major ANECO project at Orlando International Airport. ANECO radioed the airport worksite, and Gary was immediately summoned to the Marriott. He was among the very best master electricians ANECO had. He was told that time was of the essence. The schedule of the president of the United States would not be changed.

A lot depended on Gary getting the job done—and done quickly. For one thing, the City of Orlando would not grant final approval for the opening of the facility until all systems could be demonstrated to be in working order. And with the president coming, Marriott's public relations department had launched a media blitz touting the scheduled day of the grand opening. Any further delay was simply out of the question.

It took only a few minutes for Gary to make the drive from the airport to the Marriott. After being apprised of the situation, he went as quickly as he could down into the electrical unit room where the large banks of Westinghouse electrical panels and transformers lined the walls. The panels were enormous and imposing to most, but not to Stakemiller. He was proud of the respect he had earned for his abilities and loved his work. He began to troubleshoot the entire system and, after going through the control panel functions, determined there wasn't a problem with either the workmanship or the manual wiring that had been done by the electricians. After checking, rechecking, and checking again, it became clear the electrical malfunction was originating inside the Westinghouse equipment itself.

Gary called ANECO's project manager and asked him to telephone Westinghouse immediately and request factory representatives and repair personnel. The electrical panels would need to be repaired and possibly even replaced by the manufacturer. When it was clear he could do no more, Gary called Pam and told her he was going to wrap things up and then be home in time for dinner.

For a few more minutes, Gary and Scott Granger, another electrician ten years Gary's junior, went through a final check. "We had some dead fronts off the front of the equipment and all of the control wiring," Gary told me when he recalled that day. "We knew it was an inside problem and there was nothing left to do. I was standing in front of the electrical panel. Scott was standing directly behind me. I heard a noise, and then the whole room turned a brilliant white. It was absolutely blinding. There was not even an instant to react."

The next few moments were, at first, a blur in Gary's memories. Much later, he would periodically experience flashbacks, those precious seconds playing out over and over as if in slow motion. Sometimes, late at night, the horrific memories would come in a sudden rush like a bolt of lightning, filling him with a paralyzing fear. Every time it happened, he would break out in a cold sweat and a knotted ache would grip him in the pit of his stomach as he relived the worst experience of his life.

In that one hideous, life-altering millisecond, there had been a tremendous flash—quick, blinding, and all-encompassing—as huge amounts of electricity surged from the main distribution panel.

The whole room instantly became a flaming inferno. Gary had been standing less than two feet from the Westinghouse equipment when it exploded. His body acted as a shield for Scott Granger, the young assistant; only Scott's arms projected beyond Stakemiller's profile. His hands and forearms were badly burned, but miraculously these were the only injuries he suffered.

Taking the full brunt of the searing blast of energy over the entirety of his body, Gary was burned almost beyond recognition in seconds, from the top of his head to his feet. Violently thrown back by the sheer force of the compression, he sailed through the air, carried on the scalding drafts of hot air, as weightless as a rag doll, and smashed into the wall. "I remember hearing the explosion, being blinded by the light, and feeling the flash of the heat." Gary's voice became quiet and low as he practically whispered his recollection of the horrible accident many months later. "A 480-volt, 4,000-amp panel blew up and I happened to be standing in front of it. It didn't really crack or explode; it was just like a *phoom!* Almost as soon as I felt hot wind, I felt my back hit the wall behind me."

When he hit the wall, Gary felt wetness on his clothes, as though his shirt and pants had dampened down on his body. His field of vision cleared, and the flames receded from around him though they still continued to blaze out from what was left of the panel. When he looked at his arms, he felt sick inside. His flesh, skin, and hunks of muscle were dripping off and falling to the floor like massive drizzles of candle wax. A reflex reaction to the explosion had caused him to sharply inhale when the transformer blew. Already he was having difficulty breathing. He would find out later that his lungs—scorched and nearly ruined—had already begun to wither and fail.

Without a mirror, there was no way that he could have known that his dark blond hair, once so thick and healthy, had been burned away His head was bald and the skin was blackened and oozing blood. What he did know, however, was that the electrical room had become a human oven and his life would end if he didn't get out of there. He pulled himself from the floor onto his hands and knees, then painstakingly began to crawl, leaving behind a trail of sooty ash, seared pieces of flesh, and streaks of blood.

After an eternity, he somehow made it out to the hallway. It was then that he realized Scott Granger was missing. Without hesitating, Gary managed to get to his feet and ran back into the inferno to rescue his coworker. Gary was still on fire, and through his own flames and burned eyelids it was hard for him to see anything. He remembered reaching out to find Scott, and then almost immediately ran into him. Together, they backed out of the room and into the safety of the hallway.

Gary, in shock and totally exhausted, hobbled outside and fell down near the curb with Scott to wait for help. With the greatest of efforts, he pulled himself up to a sitting position and stayed as still as he could. His throat was raw and scorched, and he was panting and wheezing for each precious breath of air. Strangely, there was no real pain. The injuries were so severe that several layers of his skin containing most of his nerves had been burned off and stripped away.

Often, burn victims don't realize just how badly they are hurt. Walking, talking, and acting eerily "normal," the most terribly burned people can sometimes carry on conversations from a still-smoldering and charred carcass emitting blackened smoke and traces of steam. But looking into the victim's eyes—lashes, eyebrows, and even eyelids burned away, the whiteness of the eyeballs standing out against the blackened face—is like looking straight into hell.

And so it was with Gary. He was so gravely burned over most of his body that his skin was charcoal-like in appearance and actually emitting smoke. He could hardly breath without wearing himself out. A small crowd of startled hotel guests, construction workers, and security personnel had gathered, and as they stared at the two young men, the reality of what had happened to him began to sink in. Gary Stakemiller felt he was dying.

Sitting on the curbside provided a brief respite from the exhaustion that had overcome his body. His breathing had begun to come under control, despite his injured lungs, and the initial shock of watching his flesh sloughing off his smoldering body had momentarily passed. He was amazed that he felt no pain. In fact, he didn't feel anything at all except a bizarre detachment from what was occurring.

The distant sounds of rescue vehicles could be heard, yet Gary and Scott sat there silent and unmoving, each one trying to figure out, in his own way, exactly what had happened. The flames had burned away most of Gary's shirt and pants, and his underwear, though singed, was the only garment left that was recognizable as clothing. A movement caught Gary's eye, and he noticed someone quickly approaching from the direction of the main portion of the hotel. As the silhouetted figure drew nearer, Gary could see that he was an employee of Marriott. Still fighting for air, he struggled to focus on the dark-suited man who came to a standstill just a few feet away. The man acted as though he, too, would get burned if he got any closer to the two numbed electricians.

"Uh, ummmm," the man stuttered. His face contorted with alarm and disbelief as he looked first at Gary, then at Scott. He finally shifted his gaze from the two men to the small crowd of onlookers, and then over to a stand of palm trees. "Listen," he began again as he already started moving away, "do you mind moving down some and finding a different place to sit? I'm afraid you're going to frighten some of our guests if you stay where you are." Without another word and without looking at Gary or Scott again, the Marriott employee quickly turned and then nearly ran back inside the refuge of the hotel.

Startled by the coldness and detachment of the man's bizarre request, Gary had no time to react further. The loud wails of an ambulance grew nearer and the sweet resonance of the sirens took over his thoughts. Help was on its way and he was still alive. *Pam!* Gary suddenly thought as the brightly lit rescue vehicle slammed to a halt by the curb. *Someone has to call Pam! And the kids! They have to be told!*

"Don't worry," Gary heard a kind voice say from somewhere, he wasn't sure where. "We'll call your wife." He couldn't tell if the voice was male or female, and he didn't remember asking that someone call Pam. Well…it didn't matter. Pam would know he had survived. Then he was inside the ambulance somehow…

How did I get in the ambulance from the curb?

He didn't remember being lifted…

Nothing's right, something's wrong...

Flashes of light, flames, yelling from somewhere...

Scott, where are you?...You okay, buddy?....

Can't talk, can't see...Tired, so tired...

Pam, why aren't you here? Pam, I need you! Will you help me, honey? Pam? Pam?

A sea of blackness swallowed his thoughts and everything went quiet.

The Long Road Home

From the scene of the accident, Gary was transported to Orlando Regional Medical Center, where he was initially treated. He required immediate intubation because of his respiratory difficulties, which eliminated any chance of him even trying to speak. He had suffered third-degree electrical and thermal burns to most of his body, including his front and back, all of his extremities, and most of his head and neck. Like pieces of a patchwork quilt, raw skin still dangled here and there, exposing deeper tissues that oozed a clear, sluggish liquid. If he survived the night then perhaps he could be repaired, sewn and stitched back together. Of course, that was assuming there would be no infection or other complications. At best, he was told by doctors during a few moments of consciousness, he had a ten percent chance of survival. *Ten percent...but only if he survived the night...only if he survived the night...*

It was not until after he was brought into the hospital that the first waves of nausea hit. His insides ached and every one of his muscle fibers felt on fire. Pain began to rack his body and he wanted to scream out but couldn't. He was given heavy doses of morphine, but the medication did little good except for the unconsciousness it sometimes brought. Somehow, through the torturous suffering, the enormous blood loss, and the grisly burns, Gary held on. Pam kept a vigil outside the intensive care unit—no visitors were allowed in. Separated by a hospital wall, Pam fought just as hard as her husband. She cried and prayed, as over and over she heard those haunting words the doctors had spoken: *ten percent chance of living...but only if he survived the night...ten percent chance of living...only if he survived the night...*

When the morning's sun arrived, Gary was still alive. His mind was clouded by morphine, and the suffering was now unending and even more intense. The doctors decided to chance moving him to a specialized burn facility at Tampa General Hospital, which was known nationally and had some of the best burn doctors in the country. Most likely, Gary would not survive the trip from Orlando to Tampa, and even if he did, there remained little hope he would live. Before he could be airlifted to Tampa, however, his condition needed to be stabilized. His lungs were in such bad shape that he had to be kept on a respirator. Through intravenous lines, repeated efforts were made to replace the rapid loss of fluids escaping through the raw areas of exposed flesh.

Again, Gary beat the odds. Stabilized enough to be moved, he arrived by helicopter at Tampa General on Friday, January 26, 1990. The initial medical evaluation was bleak: He was diagnosed as having approximately seventy-five percent burns of the third degree, and thirty-one percent full-thickness burns to his face, trunk, both arms—including wrists and hands—and both legs. He suffered severe pulmonary injury due to inhalation of the fiery air, and both lungs were in acute distress. Gary also had an accumulation of fluid in his eyes, extensive swelling of both ears, and evidence that infection was beginning to set in. His arms and legs were red, raw extensions of exposed flesh and in some places even the bone was visible.

And his face, once so warm and smiling? Gary's facial structures were still in place—nose, cheeks, ears—but the skin was gone and a bloodied red mask was all that remained. Virtually all of his hair and scalp had been burned away.

There were very few places that had not been damaged—the legs below the knees, one small portion of his face and neck, and the area of his genitals, which had been protected by his underwear.

His condition was termed "severely critical," and his prognosis was listed as "extremely poor." Almost from the first day, Gary was being monitored by multiple specialists including pulmonary, infectious disease, ophthalmic, pain management, psychiatric, dietary, rehabilitative medicine, and orthopedic. But the man who was supposed to die...continued to live.

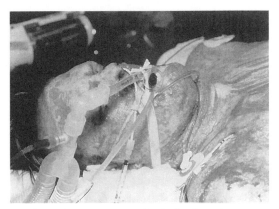

Gary Stakemiller in intensive care shortly after the incident.

Several times, the doctors who were so dedicated to fighting for his life feared the worst. Death appeared to be imminent, but he refused to succumb. The endless rounds of treatment and daily, hourly, and minute-by-minute struggles were a traumatic chronicle of the worst pain and suffering imaginable. Over the next several weeks, Gary's life hung by a thread. His treatment included not only resuscitative care but also the agonizing excision and subsequent grafting of his many burn wounds. Pam was right there through it all.

By the end of March, the whole experience was becoming overwhelming for Pam, who was desperately trying to survive herself and care for their young family. Gary had been their rock, but now it was all up to Pam. Battered by the ordeal of it all, she was physically and emotionally drained.

Just when she didn't think things could get any worse, they did. She learned from coworkers visiting the hospital that Marriott officials were saying that Gary had somehow caused the accident. The blame being placed upon her dying husband made the heartache even greater. There were other problems as well. Even though ANECO was paying the tens and eventually hundreds of thousands of dollars for medical treatment, the weekly income that the family had always relied on for groceries, utilities, and the very basics of life was no longer present.

Gary's stepbrother, Michael Crabb, a staff worker in the Orlando office of the Academy of Florida Trial Lawyers, had recommended that

Pam Stakemiller talk to me. Mike knew a ton of trial lawyers, and I was flattered and honored that I was his personal recommendation. After I spoke with Pam, it was evident to me that something had gone horribly wrong at the Marriott. Interviews with everyone who knew Gary and his abilities contradicted the notion that he had caused the accident. But the drumbeat that he was at fault was being pounded harder than ever by the Marriott executives.

When I began to review the materials and learn about Gary's injuries, I assumed that it might turn out to be a wrongful death case. While Gary fought for his life I met at length with Pam. She was not only pretty on the outside, but also I could tell she had a beautiful heart. Despite the circumstances, the three Stakemiller children, whom Pam often brought to our meetings, were well behaved and demonstrated the results of good parenting. I liked Gary's family so much that I agreed to do something I don't usually do with prospective clients: I went to the hospital to see him.

When I arrived at the burn unit at Tampa General, I was asked put on a mask, gown, and overshoes before entering Gary's room. The ever-present threat of infection was now the most deadly enemy to his survival. It was paramount that Gary be kept isolated and in a sterile environment as much as possible. I couldn't believe what I was seeing. Before Gary opened his eyes, he looked like a piece of burned flesh lying on the bed. His fingers resembled sticks of charcoal, spread apart and being held in place with metallic rods and rubber bands. His body was one huge open sore. It had already been weeks since the accident, and I could not even imagine how he looked that terrible day at the Marriott. After a few moments, Gary opened his eyes, and I saw a strength and determination that changed everything I had observed. When my eyes met his gaze, he became a very real person who needed me.

At first, I did most of the talking. I tried my best to give him confidence and encouragement. I tried to ease his pain. "Don't worry about your family. Everything is being taken care of. Just worry about living. That's enough of a job for you right now. You just have to trust me." The condition of this human being who had been a vital, active young man broke my heart. He kept asking me about what had happened and continued to press me to tell him what he had done or what had gone wrong. He couldn't understand much and he was still in the hazy and muddled world of shock. Everyone in Gary's life was traumatized over all that had occurred, and no explanation seemed to make a great deal of sense.

I saw him several more times. On one occasion he was recovering from his most recent surgery. For the first time in Florida's medical history, the doctors had tried an experimental form of grafting to grow Gary a new "skin."

Delthia Ricks, a staff writer for the *Orlando Sentinel*, wrote an article describing Gary's operations in detail. Ms. Ricks did an exceptional job of reporting on the surgeries, and the article, which appeared on March 15, 1990, read in part:

Swatches of skin cloned in a laboratory have been successfully grafted on the body of an electrician severely burned in Orlando, the first time the rare high-tech procedure has been tried in Florida. The success of the technique at Tampa General Hospital means Florida burn victims no longer must travel out of the state for the treatment...The new tissue was grown from a "starter" medium that uses a patient's healthy skin tissue and a biological cocktail of cells, proteins and nutrients that help trigger growth. It takes about three weeks to grow sheets of healthy skin for grafting. Only 100 burn victims in the country have been treated with the transplant technique, which involves shipping a sample of a patient's healthy skin cells to a Boston laboratory to be grown into swatches of skin, said Dr. Wayne Cruse, medical director of the hospital's Regional Burn Unit. "It is a lifesaving measure for catastrophic burn injuries," Cruse said. Gary Stakemiller, 28, received the skin transplant March 1...So far, Stakemiller's new skin is growing and functioning as it should. "We're encouraged. Things look favorable," Cruse said.

Cultured skin offers a new option for severely burned patients because it makes more healthy tissue available to doctors performing skin grafts, he said. Conventional skin grafting involves taking healthy tissue from an undamaged part of the body and transplanting it to areas destroyed by fire. When burn victims have little healthy tissue left, doctors' only other option is to use donor skin, which runs the risk of rejection. A disadvantage of the transplant technique is that severely burned patients may not survive the three weeks it takes to grow cells into healthy skin tissue. Cruse said doctors removed a tiny patch of undamaged skin from Stakemiller's body and shipped it to BioSurface Technology, a Boston laboratory that specializes in growing sheets of new skin for burn victims. "We'll start with a biopsy from the patient, which is about the size of a postage stamp and that can be increased 10,000 times in three weeks," said Paul Siebert, BioSurface spokeswoman.

The process was patented by a Harvard University doctor and was first attempted experimentally in 1979 at Brigham and Women's Hospital in Boston. It was not until the mid-1980s that the process, medically known as a cultured epithelial autograft, was used successfully at the Shriners Burn Institute in Boston, where many Florida burn patients have been treated...The laboratory uses only the dermis, or underlying layer of skin, to grow sheets of the tissue in culture dishes. Once it is ready for grafting, it is cut into pieces about the size of a playing card and shipped to the hospital. The cost for each piece, Siebert said, ranges between $300 and $350. Doctors use about 120 pieces, which are surgically stapled to the patient, to perform the average graft. Fifty to 80 percent of the skin takes after it becomes nourished by blood vessels. About 10 percent of the skin on Stakemiller's body has been replaced with cloned skin. He also had some conventional skin grafts.

Cruse left open the possibility of future cosmetic grafts for Stakemiller, whose skin cells are being kept in a Boston "skin bank" at the laboratory where the samples are grown. In addition to the operation involving the cloned tissue, Stakemiller underwent surgical removal of charred skin and two grafts using skin from his left leg and his arms. Doctors are monitoring him for signs of infection, a critical problem for people who have suffered severe burns. Stakemiller, who is in serious condition, uttered his first words Monday after seven operations and weeks of silence in the burn unit...his wife, Pam, said he is just beginning to realize what happened to him. "This young man has gone through a lot," Cruse said. "His courage and the support of his family have helped him get through this."

On April 12, 1990, some three and a half months after Gary was first burned, he was transferred to the Rehabilitation Unit at Tampa General. He began an intense program of occupational, speech, and physical therapy. It wasn't until April 26, exactly four months after he was initially admitted to Tampa General, that he was transferred back to the burn unit to undergo his last scheduled surgery prior to discharge. He continued with his therapies while recovering from surgery until he left the hospital for the last time on May 22, 1990, when he went home to his wife and children and a life that had so utterly and completely changed.

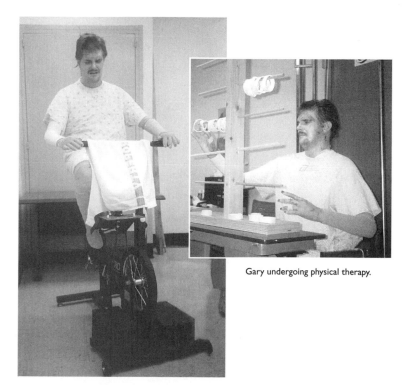

Gary undergoing physical therapy.

The Case
· · · · · · ·

M any months later, a lawsuit for personal injury, *not* death, was filed and we embarked on our efforts to obtain justice. We asserted that the tragedy had been caused by defective equipment, while the defense vigorously blamed the entire incident on Gary. In preparation for trial, the attorneys for all of the parties involved agreed that Gary needed to be completely evaluated. This was done in October of 1990. He was diagnosed as one hundred percent disabled and entirely dependent upon others for support in order to live. He was unable to perform the simplest of tasks around the house; opening and closing his own dresser drawers, gaining access to his medicine cabinet, bending, sitting, even walking, were painful activities because of the stiffness and weakness of the skin on the joints of his fingers, elbows, and knees. He was unable to grip objects. The simple act of twisting off a bottle cap was impossible; so was the turning of a doorknob, the opening of a car door—the list was long. Awful and long.

The evaluation also demonstrated that Gary's role as a father had been greatly impaired. If the children hugged or tried to physically interact in any way with him, the huge areas of stitched scar tissue would rip open and stream blood. Intimacy with Pam was very difficult, not just because of his handicaps, but also because of self-consciousness about his appearance. Depression set in as he realized the severity of his situation.

Terrible things happen to burn victims with skin injuries of this magnitude. Gary could not take direct sun, and he had lost the ability to perspire. He no longer could enjoy the outdoors he so loved. Playing baseball, fishing, jet-skiing, boating, even taking long walks with Pam and the children were now memories. From an active participant in life, he was relegated to being only an observer. The rugged life he relished so very much was gone forever.

The medical aspects of the evaluation were numerous. His back itched constantly because of its extreme dryness. He could tolerate sitting in a chair for only twenty to thirty minutes at a time and he had to wear a specially fitted full-body suit to guard against further injuries to his delicate skin. Even a slight bump would rend and tear the thin areas of scar tissue. The suit, which he initially had to wear twenty-three hours a day, was hot and constricting. It also rubbed against his elbows and the tops of his feet and would continually wear any areas of healthy skin raw.

The evaluation demonstrated that Gary had severely limited range of motion in his right arm, with minimal grip and strength in his right hand and wrist. His elbow had calcified, and he had less than ten degrees of bend in it. Since Gary was right-handed, he would have to relearn life as a southpaw. He experienced joint stiffness and muscle weakness in both legs. His leg injuries and the severity of the muscle weakness and stiffness in his joints made it a certainty that he would never be able to run again.

The Stakemiller evaluation concluded by detailing the non-physical injuries Gary and his family had sustained. He was experiencing frequent nightmares about the day of the accident, often getting up from bed and sitting in the living room for entire nights just to avoid dreaming. Prior to the accident, Gary had no history of emotional difficulties. Post-accident bouts with severe depression and anxiety necessitated extensive psychiatric and psychological counseling. Even with the therapy, he often became angry and irritable with his wife and children. He had begun to withdraw from his family and become more distant and isolated. His level of motivation decreased significantly as the frustration of trying so hard at virtually everything took its toll. Pam also sought help and recounted with awful sadness that Gary was no longer the kind, gentle, and loving husband she had married. In an emotional outburst with her psychiatrist, she stated tearfully, "All I want is my husband back, and all the children want is their father back."

That was part of the challenge. More than anything, I wanted to help the Stakemiller family in their desperate efforts to put their lives back together. With each visit or telephone conversation, I tried to assure Gary that everything would be all right, that Pam and I would take care of things. I realized it would be difficult, if not impossible, for Gary to accept that his life would once again have meaning. His hardworking commitment to his family had been filled with love and limitless hopes and dreams for the future. The accident had shattered those dreams.

And then, Gary hit rock bottom. Under the maddening spell of his injuries, pain, and mental torment, he snapped. The rage and violent outbursts against Pam and the children drove them away. Pam blamed her husband's bizarre and frightening behavior on the severe pain he experienced and the strong medications he took just to function. She made excuses, but most often she and the children would simply stay away and avoid the man they all loved and missed so very much.

During these difficult times, I was much more a counselor than an attorney. I had lengthy talks with both Pam and Gary about the ongoing destruction of their family's life. Pam came to visit me on several occasions and cried her eyes out as she described her once-gracious husband's downward spiral into an emotional abyss that, unless something dramatic occurred, would consume him and the entire family. To add to the heartache, there were also well-founded concerns about the possibility of Gary committing suicide.

Sometimes, Pam would escape from the house—from Gary's festering anger, disturbing bitterness, and venomous remarks—to find a pay phone and call Cindy Heilman, my assistant. Too often, Pam could do nothing but cry into the telephone for several minutes. Pam always told Cindy that it helped her feel just a little bit better to have someone with whom to cry.

Cindy has worked for me for many years. She has become invaluable to my law practice and in my life. Cindy and I share an enormously strong bond of respect, friendship, and trust. She is attractive inside and out, with fine blond hair, blue eyes, and translucent skin. She truly cares for the people we represent, and she has a heart full of love and understanding. Clients invariably bond with her almost instantly. Cindy was everything Pam needed in a friend—someone who would listen.

The seams of the Stakemiller marriage were ripping apart. His children lived in fear of their father. Then something happened. I prefer to believe it was a miracle. All of a sudden, Gary seemed to realize what he was doing to himself and his family. It was as if he finally understood that he would have to rally against the dark emotions haunting him day in and day out, or he would surely lose everything. Gary saw that he needed to muster all that he had left and find enough courage to face his demons and fight for his spiritual life. He became determined to gain back his self-esteem and the pride that had been gone for so long.

Death and dying no longer dominated his thoughts. Instead, he focused on his newfound energy and outlook on life. Gary became revitalized. Miraculously, he learned to walk without assistance. He worked through the pain and increased the mobility of his arms and legs. His anger, though still present, went from a full boil down to a slight simmer, and resentment faded as each day brought new challenges. A warm appreciation for life and its wonders started to fill him again with contentment and happiness. With a determined spirit, Gary began to overcome his anxiety, and he learned to look forward to each new day. We talked often of his progress and I conveyed my astonishment at how far he had come. Pam had her husband back, and the children had their daddy once again.

For Pam and the kids, Gary's resolve renewed a sense of hope in each of them. Certainly, the healing process—both emotional and physical—would take time, but for the Stakemiller family, every second would be worth the wait. For Pam, for Ashley, Cameron, and Erin, and for himself, the road to recovery would be trying and exhausting, but the light at the end of the tunnel was near...and it was bright.

The Settlement
. . . .

While Gary recovered, my law firm was hard at work preparing the lawsuit, taking depositions, procuring documents, and making extensive efforts to discover everything about the case. I did as much as I could to encourage the Stakemillers to keep fighting and hold fast to a belief that we could prevail.

Despite all the claims from the defense that the "accident" was caused by human error, the more we learned about the facts, the clearer it became that neither Gary Stakemiller nor Scott Granger had been at fault. I retained two of the top experts in the country on electrical engineering in general and the intricacies of this type of electrical equipment in particular. I also hired a master electrician to track and retrack everything the electricians had done.

Our experts were unanimous in determining that Gary had not

caused the accident. Neither he nor Scott Granger had had anything to do with what happened. We felt strongly that the origin of the electrical catastrophe was inside the Westinghouse panel itself, but we needed to prove it.

Our investigation led us to the Westinghouse "troubleshooter" who had been dispatched to the scene immediately after the fire. His name was Hector Gonzalez, and he lived in Texas. Since the accident, he had left Westinghouse and accepted a new position with El Paso Electrical Products, a high-end electrical contracting company. Hector Gonzalez was the person who knew the Westinghouse equipment best and who had also made the hands-on inspection and repair to the equipment after its failure. His observations and opinions would be critical evidence. Since he was no longer an employee of the defendant corporation, I could contact him directly and discuss what he believed had happened. What he had seen and what he knew gave us the best chance of discovering what had caused this tragedy.

My first contact with Hector Gonzalez would be by phone. Whenever I prepare for a telephone call of such magnitude, I get butterflies in my gut. A flood of questions rushes through my head. At the same time, I'm both eager to find out the truth and fearful that it might prove my theories wrong. Would this person even talk to me? If he did, were there issues that might affect his opinion one way or the other? If he had been fired from Westinghouse, would he attempt to use me to get back at the company? If he had left for a better job, maybe he was still so loyal to Westinghouse that he would refuse to be critical. In the final analysis, it was simple: Whatever he had to say I had to assume would be the truth. As for the rest of it, we just needed to let the chips fall where they may.

I had two Texas telephone numbers for Hector Gonzalez. I dialed his home number and he answered on the second ring. I had found Hector. We briefly exchanged pleasantries and I went straight to the purpose of my call: I needed to meet with him and personally discuss the accident at the Marriott World Center. I explained my role as the attorney for Gary Stakemiller and the situation of the lawsuit, the catastrophic injuries suffered, and the need to know what had really happened. I asked for no more than the opportunity to talk with him. He seemed to understand the importance of my request. Hector Gonzalez's manner was kind and courteous. I could sense his goodness and concern even over the telephone. We agreed to sit down and talk, and I told him I would call the next morning to arrange the logistics.

I always make it a practice to meet face-to-face with a potentially important witness. The easier method of a telephone interview is rarely, if ever, as effective. Within twenty-four hours, accompanied by an electrical engineer and my investigator, David Ross, I was on my way to El Paso. We arranged to meet Hector Gonzalez in a hotel conference room near the airport. David had investigated many of my cases and he was reliable and thorough, and I considered him to be the best.

When Hector came to talk to us about the accident, the first thing I learned made my stomach roll over: *He had already spoken with Westinghouse and given them a statement.* The defense had already conducted a taped telephone interview with him, and he had given them an account of the accident. They had found him before we did.

Well, I could not change that. I went forward with my interview of Hector. I found that he was a gifted and quick-thinking electrician who had routinely been called in by Westinghouse to troubleshoot catastrophic situations and forensically determine what had gone wrong. The incident involving Gary Stakemiller had been no different. Hector, with his bright brown eyes and short black hair, answered my questions in a direct, matter-of-fact manner. I liked him from the start.

Hector's high level of intelligence was apparent. I learned that he had graduated as valedictorian of his high school in Canutillo, Texas. He had then gone into the navy, where he was selected for the elite nuclear submarine program. While in training, he attended San Diego City College and because of his performance received a full scholarship to the University of Texas in Austin. He graduated from UT with a degree in electrical engineering and power systems. During his senior year, the navy sent him to Officer Candidate School in Newport, Rhode Island, and he received his commission. He eventually headed up the electrical and nuclear weapons division for the USS *Canopus*, considered one of the best-equipped and most technologically advanced nuclear submarines in the world.

After completing his military service, Hector had gotten tremendous experience in the private sector. He worked for Rockwell International, taught electrical engineering at Mexico State University, and held an impressive position with General Electric before accepting employment at Westinghouse. He was hired as a power engineer with Westinghouse Engineering Services, and they also used his expertise in power systems. He particularly excelled at any system that utilized low-, medium-, or high-voltage switchgears or transformers. Originally based in El Paso, he held the position of resident electrical engineer and supported the company in Texas, New Mexico, Arizona, and Mexico. In 1989, Hector was transferred to Tampa. He was named field engineer for several projects that were going on in Florida at that time, and specialized in troubleshooting.

When Hector and his wife's fifth child arrived, they decided to return home to Texas to rear their family. That is where Hector found the position as electrical engineer and salesman for El Paso Electrical Products, which he said in later testimony dealt almost exclusively with Westinghouse products. According to Hector it was "Westinghouse. They just changed the name, but they are a hundred percent Westinghouse."

After filling me in on his background and the circumstances surrounding his involvement in the incident at Marriott, he told me that Westinghouse first notified him of the accident late Sunday afternoon. Since the accident had occurred a couple of days before, Hector was instructed to travel to Orlando immediately. I realized that since the manufacturer had called him in to repair the destroyed equipment, the information Hector possessed could be of tremendous importance. As his narrative unfolded, I was captivated. Never could I have imagined discovering a witness with such an eye-opening and startling account of the kind of first-hand evidence that is so very critical in a product liability case, especially one that caused such grievous personal injuries.

I learned that when Hector arrived on the scene, he had found representatives from both ANECO and Marriott waiting for him. Hector explained to me that he had had three prior experiences with ground fault relay systems failing—much like this accident. In those incidents, there had been significant damage to the equipment, but fortunately only minor injuries had been sustained by those involved. Each time, he had found the cause to be system failure *within the Westinghouse equipment itself.* And those accidents were "just like this one," he offered.

I had found the witness of a lifetime who held the critical evidence that could virtually win the Stakemiller case. I would rely on his integrity, honesty, and willingness to come forward and tell the truth on the record, despite the possible consequences to himself.

Again and again, we had asked ourselves what had happened. Now, with Hector's information we were solving the mystery that had first plagued Gary and then the entire legal team. We were exhilarated by our new witness—this session was the trial lawyer's version of "being in the zone." Every aspect, every answer, seemed to be going our way. Proof and testimony this dynamic on the issue of liability, coupled with the extent of Gary's terrible injuries, made settlement more likely and dramatically reduced the chances we would have to endure the ordeal of a traumatic trial. As the meeting went on and I learned more and more about the equipment failure, I felt better and better about Gary's case; but then, without warning, my soaring emotions stalled as I suddenly remembered what Hector had said at the beginning of our meeting: He had *already* talked to Westinghouse and they had recorded his statement over the telephone.

There were two possibilities concerning his recorded statement with the defense lawyers. One, that he had given a generalized statement that was not in depth, so Westinghouse might feel they had nothing to worry about. Or two, that he had indicated the same things over the phone he had been relating to me, and somehow Westinghouse hoped I wouldn't find him.

In my opinion, the defense team had already made one mistake by failing to conduct a personal, face-to-face interview with Hector Gonzalez immediately after the accident. It seemed unlikely that the talent-laden and high-powered group of defense lawyers would have made another. If Hector Gonzalez had given them the same account we were getting, there would have been a massive follow-up and a series of actions to mitigate the adverse nature of his potentially devastating testimony.

What in the hell had he told them? I wondered over and over. As our conference in the El Paso meeting room was winding down, I reluctantly brought up the telephone interview. "Hector, you mentioned Westinghouse had interviewed you over the telephone a couple of months back. Do you remember what was said? Do you remember what you told them?" The all too familiar wrenching feeling deep inside my gut had returned with a vengeance.

Hector Gonzalez appeared totally unconcerned about whatever answers he had given to the defense. "Mr. Yerrid, the interview wasn't very long. And, as I recall, the telephone call came just as I was walking out the door on my way to work. I remember they asked me about a Florida project that was one of many I'd had over the last couple of years. I told them what I could, and I answered their questions, but we didn't get into any specifics or go into any of the detail we have talked about here today."

Usually when a statement of a witness is recorded or transcribed, a copy is made available to the witness. It is not only a courtesy, but also serves to "cement" the transcript's accuracy. If the declarant receives a copy and says or does nothing to revise, modify, or correct its content, that goes a long way to halt any future attempt by the declarant to change, contest, or refute what had been originally said. I needed to know if Hector had a copy.

I took my shot and asked quickly, "Hector, did the lawyers send you a copy of the statement you gave?" My body tensed as I waited for his answer.

He thought for a moment, and then answered, "Yes. Yes, I think so. But since that time, my family and I have moved and I would have to look for it in our packed boxes. I'm not really sure I still have it."

"Hector," I started with a touch of authority in my voice, "that transcript of your statement is really important. In fact, it's critical. If it differs from what you have said today, you can expect the defense lawyers to confront you with it, if and when you testify in this case." I held nothing back. He was entitled to know every aspect of my concerns.

"When I get home, I'll unpack the three boxes that have all my business papers in them. I'll do my best to find the interview and give you a call." Hector's answer brimmed with sincerity, and that made me feel better. I was confident he would find his written statement, but worried as hell about what it might say.

With nothing left to be done at that point but wait for his call, I thanked the soft-spoken gentleman, fully realizing he might well be the person whose testimony would determine the outcome of the case.

We arrived at the El Paso airport for our return trip to Tampa only to find that our flight had been closed out. We stood helplessly at the gate and watched through the window as the plane was pushed out from the terminal's jetway. Ten hours and two standby flights later, we finally were on our way back to Tampa. I should have been dead tired, but the anxiety of carrying the burden of the Stakemiller family kept my eyes "wide shut" and my mind racing about all the possibilities ahead.

Fortunately, I did not stay in limbo long. My secretary interrupted an office conference the next afternoon to tell me Hector Gonzalez was on the phone and wanted to talk with me. *He had found the statement!* It was brief and to the point, he said, and he could read it to me over the telephone if I had the time. Or, he went on, he could drop a copy in the mail. I didn't care how long it took to read it on the phone, I had to know then what it said and I sure as hell couldn't wait. I clamped down on my emotions as I asked him to read it.

Hector took about five minutes to read the entire interview. The Westinghouse lawyers had put forth their questions in a gentle yet leading manner that contained not the slightest hint of concern. In essence, many of the questions had been simply answered "yes" or "no" by Hector, and he had more or less agreed that he could not recall finding anything wrong with the equipment. He had also agreed that most accidents of this nature were caused by a worker's error, and that most likely the electricians at the job site had caused this incident as well. He had specifically stated that he could not recall any of the particulars concerning this incident, and he had expressed a willingness to meet with the Westinghouse representatives to go over the specifics. The lawyers had concluded the interview by telling Hector that he would be contacted, and a meeting would be arranged in the near future. When he finished reading, I was direct and to the point. "Hector, you obviously told them there was nothing wrong with the equipment, that it was a case of human error. That's not what you told me at our meeting in El Paso. What's going on here?"

There was not the slightest bit of hesitation before he answered. "When we met in El Paso, you brought the documents, the incident reports, the repair billings, and the job descriptions. You also showed me the many photographs taken at the accident site of the equipment and the area itself. I am absolutely certain of everything we discussed, that there was equipment failure, and every detail of what I told you is accurate. When I received the telephone call from the other lawyers, I had none of those things. I simply confused what they were talking about with another similar accident. I'll be glad to clarify that it was my mistake, but there is not one doubt about what happened in this case. None."

Every concern I had lived with and anguished about evaporated. Whether we won or lost the case, I knew Hector Gonzalez was honest and truthful. And in the end, a just and truthful cause is all a trial lawyer can ever hope to bring to the court of justice. I explained to Hector the importance of his testimony to the fair outcome of the case and to the Stakemillers. He told me he understood and would make himself available whenever he was needed.

Before we hung up, I told him the obvious. If he came forward with this type of incriminating testimony against Westinghouse, he could expect a very difficult time and his subcontract work could be jeopardized. He ended our telephone conversation by telling me that was his problem, not mine. I recall him saying something about the fact that the truth was all that mattered, regardless of the consequences, but by then, I thought I was already dreaming...

Meanwhile, the pretrial discovery and related work on the case had reached a frenzied pace. But all that really mattered was Hector. I had decided to gamble and would bring him to Orlando for the trial. Once the pretrial discovery in the case was completed, I would just have to wait for the time when, or if, the Gonzalez card would be played. As it turned out, I didn't have to wait long.

Less than two weeks after my visit to El Paso and Hector's phone call to me about his recorded statement, he telephoned again. The Westinghouse lawyers had tracked him down. They requested that Hector travel to Florida the following week. He would be flown first class into Orlando to meet with the defense team and confer with them regarding the lawsuit that had been filed. He was informed that he would be needed from Tuesday through all of Friday. Of course, Westinghouse would pay a top rate for his time and expenses. Thanking Hector, I told him I would call right back.

I immediately had Cindy call opposing counsel with a request that several depositions be set. Among the names on the list was Hector's. Cindy was told that while several of the individuals we wanted to depose were available, others were not. Unfortunately, it was explained, Hector

Gonzalez had been summoned to Norway on Westinghouse business and probably would not be available, even for trial.

Knowing that Hector was not in Norway, I picked the name of one of the engineers, Damian Davis, who was said to be available, and I noticed the deposition for the following Monday morning at ten o'clock in Orlando. ("Noticed" is a lawyer's way of saying that a time and date had been scheduled and all parties informed.) Within an hour, the deposition time was cleared on every lawyer's calendar. I then called Hector back and asked if he could fly to Orlando early Monday morning instead of later in the day on the flight the defense team had arranged. He said he had cleared the whole week, so taking an earlier flight would not be a problem. I told him we would schedule his deposition for Monday at ten o'clock in a conference room in the same hotel where Westinghouse had booked him. I assured Hector we would also pay for his time on Monday and any extra expenses. The airplane ticket was already paid for—compliments of Westinghouse.

I waited until Friday before contacting the defense lawyers and amending the notice of deposition set for ten o'clock on Monday morning. I made the call myself. I told them the scheduled deponent—Damian Davis—was being canceled, but the time and place were still on. In the place of Mr. Davis, we would be taking the deposition of Hector Gonzalez. I explained that Hector Gonzalez had been found to be available after all and wasn't in Norway as the defense team had led us to believe. Since the deposition schedule had already been cleared on everyone's calendar, we intended to proceed. I explained that because he evidently traveled so much, it was necessary to take his testimony when we could, and indeed it was extremely fortunate that we had this opportunity.

There was shock, followed by a loud objection, and then outrage from the defense lawyers. I chose not to respond to the flood of angry words. Nor did it matter what was being said. Everything was on the line for Gary Stakemiller, so the deposition would go forward as scheduled, I stated, and I strongly suggested everyone show up. Either way, we were proceeding.

Rather than paraphrase or give a secondhand account of what transpired that unforgettable Monday, I will let the following excerpts from the actual deposition testimony tell the story.

· · · · · · ·

In the Circuit Court of the Ninth Judicial Circuit of the State of Florida in and for Orange County

Sworn Deposition of Hector Valenzuela Gonzalez

Place: Howard Johnson, 304 West Colonial Drive, Orlando, Florida

Date and Time: November 18, 1991 at 1:25 p.m.

With appearances by:

C. Steven Yerrid, Esquire, Tampa, Florida

Joseph H. Varner III, Esquire, Tampa, Florida

J. Thomas Cardwell, Esquire, Orlando, Florida

Virginia B. Townes, Esquire, Orlando, Florida

Alan J. Landerman, Esquire, Orlando, Florida

Clara Margaret H. Groover, Esquire, Orlando, Florida

David Ross, Investigator, Tampa, Florida

Paul E. Pritzker, Engineer, Massachusetts

Defense Attorney Thomas Cardwell: Before we get under way with this deposition, I would like to note an objection to its being taken at this time. Mr. Gonzalez was originally noticed for his deposition, as I understand, by the plaintiff's counsel, for the 10th of January. We had arranged for Mr. Gonzalez to come down, have an opportunity to look at the equipment, and talk with him; he is a former employee of Westinghouse. We were advised in mid-, or the end of last week, that Mr. Gonzalez's firm had been retained by the plaintiff's counsel, and that he had been assigned a mission of coming down here and giving testimony this Monday morning. By virtue of having changed the date of his deposition, and by having hired him and brought him down here for the purpose of this deposition, we have not had an opportunity to visit with him, as we would have liked to have had the opportunity beforehand as a former employee. I recognize the right of counsel to take this—to notice this deposition as he sees fit. I would like the record to reflect that I do object to it, and note that there may come a time later on in this litigation when we will seek to re-depose Mr. Gonzalez after having had some further opportunity, perhaps, to confer with him. So, I wanted to say this on the record at the very front end so there are no later surprises about that.

Yerrid: It always is good to start with a clear record, so let me correct defense counsel, with all respect, on a couple of gross misstatements that he made. First of all, I have not retained Mr. Gonzalez's firm. What occurred was, I was told by the defense lawyers that Mr. Gonzalez was in Norway, or some such thing, overseas, and I have no reason to doubt the accuracy of that. I was in contact with Mr. Gonzalez—our office was, I should say—because of the courtesy of Virginia Townes [who also represents Westinghouse]. I believe Ms. Townes either gave us the address or the telephone number, probably both. And the January 10th date for Hector Gonzalez was arrived at after some discussion with the lawyers in this case, but it was impossible for them to agree on it because of scheduling conflicts.

Damian Davis's deposition was set this morning. And up until this moment in time, which is now twenty minutes until two, I never received any objection, even though notice of this deposition went out last week. I never received any objection to its taking. I would point out, although I am sure Mr. Cardwell has, maybe through an oversight, not mentioned that this is not a surprise to him. I learned from Mr. Gonzalez that he was going to be in the state of Florida on business. When I inquired further, Mr. Cardwell's office, in fact, and Westinghouse, had pre-arranged a visit with Mr. Gonzalez to the state, compliments of Westinghouse's payroll, for four days, Tuesday, Wednesday, Thursday, and Friday of this week.

Because we represent the aggrieved parties to this case—well, you can shake your head and say it's not true, but let me just say this: I believe Mr. Gonzalez was coming down here to talk to Westinghouse. That was never told to me in the conversations with your office. Secondly, because we are not operating with the financial resources of Westinghouse, I could see no prejudice to having his deposition taken today since he was coming to the state anyway.

We agreed to pay for his airfare and whatever time, as we do any witness, whatever time was expended in giving us the courtesy of performing a duty, as a citizen, of testifying under oath. And the last point I wanted to make was, it seems odd that such an objection would come from the defense lawyers of Westinghouse when they took it upon themselves to call this individual in El Paso, fully brief him, at least to their minds, and elicit some type of telephone interview that ultimately was reduced to some type of statement. However inadequate that may have been, this is hardly a surprise witness, and it's hardly an opportunity for them to object, simply because we are saving the time and expense by taking his deposition. Frankly, I think they don't want us to take his deposition, because I hope they are not going to like what he says, but that's for another day.

Cardwell: Well, let me conclude this by first correcting the idea that he was brought down on Westinghouse payroll. He wasn't. And, as I have explained for the record, and there really isn't any sense in getting in a big argument over—

Yerrid: Sure. Okay.

Cardwell: We believe that the conduct of plaintiff's counsel in this has effectively deprived us of the ability to talk to this witness in a manner of which we would have chosen. And we think that if this is to our prejudice in the presentation of our case, like any lawyer attempting to represent the best interests of his client and see that they have full justice in this court of law, we will re-notice and take it again, should the need to do so arise in our judgment. Now that we have each made our self-serving statements on the record here—

Yerrid: Wait, wait, wait. No. Hold it, hold it. You said something that I may have a problem with, because I am pretty accurate. What conduct are you inferring that I did, that would have precluded or in any way hindered your ability to talk with Mr. Gonzalez? What conduct does that relate to? Because I know of no such admonishment from my office to Mr. Gonzalez. In fact, I believe you have been in telephone communication the last several days. What have I done to stop you from talking to your own ex-employee?

Cardwell: I think, as I explained in the earlier statement—and certainly I want to be totally above-board with you, Mr. Yerrid, as I am sure you are with me—that we had, in fact, asked Mr. Gonzalez to come down here to be able to look at this equipment, to be able to refresh his recollection in anticipation of his deposition being taken in January, which is when we thought it was being taken. And Mr. Gonzalez told me, and we can ask him this on the record, that it would have been helpful for him to actually see it so that he could give his best testimony. By virtue of you having noticed his deposition for the Monday morning immediately beforehand, with his getting into town, he has been precluded, and we have been precluded, of this opportunity. That is my complaint. I have no other complaint about your contacting him, talking to him, or whatever else you are obviously entitled to do; and like good and effective counsel, you have.

Yerrid: Right. I just...I took that wrong. I thought maybe you felt that I had admonished him not to talk to you, or that I, in any way, tried to inhibit your access to him, because I haven't done that.

Cardwell: No.

Yerrid: He can correct me if—

Cardwell: No.

Yerrid: If anybody thinks that, that is just not the way it was. Okay. He's sworn in, right? State your name, for the record, please.

Gonzalez: My name is Hector Valenzuela Gonzalez.

Yerrid: And Mr. Gonzalez, you understand you are appearing here today because I knew that you were going to be in the state tomorrow at the request of the defense lawyers?

Gonzalez: Exactly.

Yerrid: And you gave us the courtesy of coming here today to give your testimony under oath?

Gonzalez: Yes, I did.

Yerrid: And other than the fact that I agree to compensate you for whatever time was expended or lost due to me, that would be yesterday evening, today, have I made any promises to you of any kind whatsoever?

Gonzalez: No, sir. You haven't.

Yerrid: You understand the purpose of your presence here today is to give sworn testimony under oath with all parties present?

Gonzalez: Yes, it's my understanding, sir.

. . .

Yerrid: When were you first notified that a problem had occurred at the Marriott Trade Center in Orlando, Florida, involving Westinghouse equipment…and what were your instructions? What were you notified with regard to the equipment at the Marriott Center?

Gonzalez: It was on a Sunday…I received a digital page first. I have one of those pagers that has messages on it…I was on my way from Bradenton, Florida, down to Tampa to go home. And I received this page, and it says, "Go to Orlando, Florida. Report to the Marriott Trade Center immediately. There has been an accident."

. . .

Yerrid: You spent several days there?

Gonzalez: Four days.

. . .

Yerrid: What was your diagnosis of the problem that presented itself there, Mr. Gonzalez?

Gonzalez: At that time, or right now?

Yerrid: At that time.

Gonzalez: At that time, my diagnosis was [that] there had been an accident, a blowout. Something had happened, had been a fault of some sort induced on the system—how it was induced, I had no idea—and that there had been an explosion. The explosion caused the fire, the fire caused the sprinkler system to come on, and the sprinkler system caused damage.

Yerrid: Is it routine or is it customary when something occurs sufficient such as this, the equipment is something that's not usually blamed? Is that…do you look for other reasons, other than equipment failure?

Gonzalez: My first instinct is to…when somebody says there is an accident, I know there are people involved. My first instinct is somebody fell on [the busbar, a conducting bar that carries heavy currents to supply several electric circuits] or somebody did something while [the busbar] was hot. That would be…that's my first instinct.

. . .

Yerrid: And had you had prior experience with those ground fault relays failing in new equipment?

Gonzalez: Yes, three instances before this one. This would have been the fourth one at that time.

Yerrid: When those ground fault relays failed in the other three instances, were there any results such as damaged equipment, or anything such as...?

Gonzalez: There were injuries. There were injuries and damage to the equipment. I got there after the fact, like this time, exactly.

Yerrid: Fire?

Gonzalez: There would be explosions, people getting hurt, and fire and smoke damage.

Yerrid: And those have all taken place in Florida while you were working for Westinghouse?

Gonzalez: They were in Florida and Arizona. And it would be from southern Georgia, all the way down to Miami.

Yerrid: And those particular instances would have involved Westinghouse equipment?

Gonzalez: Exactly. Only Westinghouse.

∎ ∎ ∎

Yerrid: In light of that, did it surprise you when you arrived and saw this scene that you saw out here at the Marriott World Center?

Gonzalez: I wasn't surprised, no.

∎ ∎ ∎

Yerrid: Was there anything unique about the equipment? And I'm talking about in terms of the characteristics, the functioning. Anything unique about the equipment that was used out in Arizona as opposed to the equipment in Florida? Or, was it all Westinghouse uniform type of equipment?

Gonzalez: It was all uniform Westinghouse equipment.

Yerrid: Okay.

Gonzalez: But I noticed this one had things missing, and they weren't missing because of the fire because one section was complete, and it was exactly the same one as the section that was melted down. It had terminal boards missing.

∎ ∎ ∎

Yerrid: Did you notice that this equipment was not the same? That it was lacking in some respects?

Gonzalez: Yes, I did. The section that was complete, and even the section that was shipped in new to replace the other section, the new section that was shipped in new to replace the burned out section, the melted down section, even that section was incomplete. There were wires missing, where I had to go in there and physically put in wires that should have been done in the factory.

Yerrid: That's a point I want to clarify. Are these wires you are talking about that were missing, the sections you determined were incomplete, are these the wires and the sections that would be field completed or field created, or are these things that would normally be done at the factory?

Gonzalez: This should be done at the factory. It shouldn't be done in the field.

. . .

Yerrid: Is the purpose able to be accomplished if the ground fault relay is wired in the manner depicted in Exhibit One?

Gonzalez: No, not according to this wiring. It's missing two wires.

Yerrid: And assuming this wiring was put into place, and a fault occurred, what would you expect to happen?

Gonzalez: The fault would keep on going.

Yerrid: And if the equipment was being energized, and electricity and power were going into the system, would that ground fault relay, as wired under Plaintiff's Exhibit One diagram, disrupt the current?

Gonzalez: If the current was energized, if the ground fault relay was triggered, and assuming it was wired exactly like this, then the fault would continue. Whatever that fault was, it would continue.

Yerrid: What would that mean to a person like Gary Stakemiller or his coworker, who were in the room working on the equipment, and a fault occurred? What would this type of wiring mean?

Gonzalez: The system would not protect them…but, if it's wired incorrectly or incomplete, as this one is incomplete, the equipment in that room was incomplete, then it would not protect them.

. . .

Yerrid: Why was that necessary, Mr. Gonzalez, to redesign what had been done at the factory?

Gonzalez: Because it was not checked at the factory. We call it quality control. That quality control was not at the factory.

• • •

Yerrid: And the last day [of the repairs], did you work on [the system] while it was energized, Mr. Gonzalez?

Gonzalez: The last few hours, I had to, yeah. That's the only way to check a ground fault. You have to actually do it when it's running, when it's hot.

Yerrid: Is that kind of like taking the pulse of someone? It's better to take it while he is alive, as opposed to when he is dead?

Gonzalez: Exactly.

• • •

Yerrid: You had to work on the system while it was energized, as I understand from your last answer, to check the ground fault relays?

Gonzalez: You have to give a dynamic test before you can…you have two types, static and dynamic. Static, you can do it when it's dead. There's no power. Dynamic, the system is energized. You don't want to interrupt, or you do want to interrupt the power flow. Either way, it's called dynamic. And I did the dynamics and could prove to the county inspector that it was doing its work, doing its job.

Yerrid: Was it your understanding that Mr. Stakemiller and Mr. Granger had worked on this equipment while it was energized?

Gonzalez: Yes. That was my understanding.

Yerrid: With your background and expertise in your position at Westinghouse, do you find that something that troubles you, the fact that they worked on this equipment that was energized?

Gonzalez: No. That's pretty standard.

• • •

Yerrid: For whatever reason, had the ground fault been functioning on that particular day when these two young men were in that switch room, what, in your opinion, would the effect have been on this incident?

Gonzalez: I can tell you what would have happened if that system had been working and there had been a fault. No matter how that fault was induced, if there had been a fault and that system had been working, within four to six cycles, the current would have been shut off. That means there might have been an arc, there might have been a flash, but there would not have been fire, because there was no source for the fire. That would not have happened.

Yerrid: Would there have been an explosion?

Gonzalez: No. Negative. There would not have been an explosion.

■ ■ ■

[After more questioning, Hector Gonzalez then stated that he resigned from working full-time with Westinghouse in August of 1990.]

Yerrid: And since that time, were you contacted by the defense attorneys with regard to this case?

Gonzalez: Yes, I was. A few months ago.

Yerrid: And was that done by telephone?

Gonzalez: By telephone. Yes, it was.

Yerrid: And where were you? Were you at your home or your office?

Gonzalez: I was in my office.

Yerrid: And were you asked about this particular incident? Your opinion about certain things?

Gonzalez: Yes, I was.

Yerrid: Were you supplied with any photographs, or were you supplied with any materials?

Gonzalez: No, just a copy of the February 2 engineering report.

Yerrid: What about the schematics or the diagrams or the photographs, the documentation, or any of the materials surrounding this case?

Gonzalez: No. I wasn't supplied with any of that.

■ ■ ■

Yerrid: And since that time, have you had an opportunity to review the photographs taken at this particular scene, the documents concerning this particular occurrence, and any and all materials that you felt were appropriate?

Gonzalez: Yes, I have.

■ ■ ■

Yerrid: Did I, or did people from my office, elect to show you photographs of the scene?

Gonzalez: Yes, sir. I asked for them.

Yerrid: Now that you have had access to the photographs, the documents and data, do you believe, sitting here today, as you have testified, that you have a more accurate recollection of what occurred and the events that transpired of this entire tragedy at the Marriott Trade Center than you would have had when you made the statement to these defense lawyers back in June in the telephone conversation you had?

Gonzalez: Yes, I do.

. . .

Yerrid: I understand you are going to be in Orlando for the next couple of days.

Gonzalez: Yes, sir.

Yerrid: What business are you going to have here in Orlando?

Gonzalez: Originally, it was planned for Virginia Townes and Thomas Cardwell, for their law firm, but they called me Friday and canceled that. It is just that I already canceled all my jobs in San Diego for those three days.

Yerrid: I'm not sure what you meant, three days. Did the defense lawyers have you scheduled to talk with them for three days?

Gonzalez: Yes. Tuesday, Wednesday, and Thursday, and I was going to fly back Friday.

. . .

Yerrid: Did Westinghouse have a full test of the system, in your opinion, before it was delivered to the site out at the Marriott?

Gonzalez: No. They didn't.

Yerrid: And how do you arrive at that?

Gonzalez: By the missing wires, just by missing wires—wires that were missing that told me that nobody had really looked at it or given it any kind of quality inspection.

Yerrid: Would that have been something that would have been obvious if an inspection had been made?

Gonzalez: Exactly. It would have been a complete unit, and it wasn't complete.

. . .

Yerrid: Now, we have mentioned that, I believe in your testimony, sir, that you have left the full-time employment with Westinghouse. Is that correct?

Gonzalez: That's correct.

. . .

Yerrid: Other than the work that was to be done this week, either at

Westinghouse, the request of Westinghouse, or the request of Westinghouse defense lawyers in this case, the two people sitting here at the table, are you, from time to time, engaged by Westinghouse to perform other activities?

Gonzalez: Yes, I am. I have a contract with Westinghouse that is a yearly contract. It's updated every January. And I'm an international electrical engineer for Westinghouse. So, I've done work in Norway and South America, and I'll probably do some work, before the end of the year, in Kuwait.

Yerrid: Do you think that the work you may do in Kuwait may be jeopardized by the fact that you have sat here and given your testimony under oath?

Gonzalez: I couldn't tell at this point.

[Now the time came for cross-examination by Thomas Cardwell, attorney for Westinghouse.]

Cardwell: Mr. Gonzalez, my name is Tom Cardwell. I am the counsel representing Westinghouse in this case. And we have had occasion to speak prior to your being here over the phone, have we not?

Gonzalez: Yes, sir. We have.

Cardwell: Now, is Mr. Yerrid paying you for your trip down here?

Gonzalez: He is going to be charged for two days, and then probably your office will be charged for the remaining two days.

Cardwell: Now, how did the arrangements come to be made for Mr. Yerrid to pay for you being down here?

Gonzalez: Originally, I was scheduled to be down here for your firm for three days: the 18th, 19th, and 20th. And Mr. Yerrid found out that I was going to be here during that time, so he asked me if I could take a deposition on the 18th.

■ ■ ■

Cardwell: How much are you being paid by Mr. Yerrid to be down here?

Gonzalez: The engineering rates are really constant. For regular days, regular straight time is $125 an hour, overtime is $167 an hour, and Saturday, Sunday, and holidays, it's $218 an hour.

Cardwell: All right. Now, how many hours on behalf of the plaintiff, Mr. Yerrid, have you put in, in this matter, prior to your testimony here today?

Gonzalez: Four hours. [The plaintiffs] went to see me in El Paso for four hours, and I was presented with these pictures that we have here. Exhibit Number Six, and also Exhibit Numbers Four and Five were presented to me for four hours in El Paso, Texas.

Cardwell: And since you have been here, have you met with counsel prior to testifying here?

Gonzalez: No. I have not.

· · ·

Cardwell: Do you recall indicating to me that you did not feel that you would be prepared to testify here on Monday?

Gonzalez: Exactly.

Cardwell: Do you remember telling me that you felt that your recollection would not be clear here on Monday?

Gonzalez: Exactly.

Cardwell: Has anything happened between the time that you spoke with me last week and being here, that makes you feel any more comfortable about testifying?

Gonzalez: Just for clarification, on this report here, and these drawings here, I did not have these drawings in front of me, Exhibit Four, Exhibit One, and Exhibit Two. And they presented—I asked them if they could show them to me...

Cardwell: Other than that, have they done anything else to clarify and to help you understand this better?

Gonzalez: Not at all. They did do one thing: They showed me the blown-up pictures of this, which I did not know existed. They showed me some blow-ups.

· · ·

Cardwell: Are you up to speed with everything you need to know to testify currently about this event?

Gonzalez: With everything in front of me, I am.

· · ·

Cardwell: Now, would the panel boards work at all with these wires missing?

Gonzalez: They would work, but they wouldn't trip on a fault. The ground fault would not work.

■ ■ ■

Cardwell: If the plaintiff, Mr. Stakemiller, had opened these, visually would the absence of these wires have been apparent to him?

Gonzalez: It would not have been apparent to anybody outside of a Westinghouse engineer or a factory-trained person.

■ ■ ■

Cardwell: Now, what is the effect, again, of the failure or the absence of these wires to be connected in there?

Gonzalez: Then you have no ground fault protection. In effect, you have no ground fault protection at all.

Cardwell: Does this mean that the first time that there is any fault at all, that the system will do what?

Gonzalez: It will take the fault...the first time any fault occurred on this system, it would not see it; the ground fault electronics would not see it. There would be no protection. It would just keep on happening until the electric power took the building down.

Cardwell: And what do you mean, the electric power?

Gonzalez: Until fuses blew on the main transformer. They have fuses in the main transformer feeding the whole building. Then when those fuses got overloaded and overheated and blew, that's when the current would stop...the system would keep on functioning like nothing was there, and never see a fault. It could be burning it and never see it.

Cardwell: There could be something burning and it would never see it?

Gonzalez: Exactly. It could go on for days. It could go on for years and never see it until something outside of that building turned it off.

■ ■ ■

Cardwell: Were the wires that you believed to be missing the ones that interconnected the ground fault relays?

Gonzalez: They were.

■ ■ ■

Cardwell: You testified earlier that you were aware of certain accidents that had occurred with respect to panel boards?

Gonzalez: Yes, I was.

Cardwell: Were you aware, during the time that you were working in Florida, of any specific incident with respect to damaged property or injury to a person as a result of a panel board?

Gonzalez: Of three in particular.

■ ■ ■

Cardwell: With respect to the three that you have testified that you had knowledge of, do you believe there were injuries associated with them?

Gonzalez: Just like this one, I walked into a place, and I see blood. I don't have to be...you don't have to be very smart to figure out that somebody got hurt just before you walk in. That's the same...I walked into three other ones just like it.

Cardwell: Do you know where they were?

Gonzalez: In Florida.

■ ■ ■

Cardwell: When you spoke with me previously, Mr. Gonzalez, you indicated that when you looked at the equipment in there, you thought you saw a spot where a screwdriver had touched a busbar.

Gonzalez: That's right. I told you that exactly.

Cardwell: Is that correct?

Gonzalez: Yes.

Cardwell: Is that still your belief?

Gonzalez: After looking at the pictures, no. I had that job...I am...I am probably more than seventy-five percent sure now that I had that job confused with another job around the same time. Because when I looked at the busbar, they were not the ones I was picturing when I was talking to you on the phone.

■ ■ ■

Cardwell: And are you absolutely positive, as we sit here today, that contrary to what you told me before, that you saw no evidence that there was a piece of foreign metal, perhaps from a screwdriver, touching the busbar?

Gonzalez: Assuming that Exhibit Six is the equipment that I worked on, then I am about ninety percent sure.

Cardwell: Now, did your assurance on this come by virtue of your conversation with the plaintiff's counsel and his representatives?

Gonzalez: Negative. No. It didn't. It came from looking at the busbars...
[The plaintiff's attorneys] interviewed me for four hours, and they wanted to know how much I knew about the case. And just for four hours, that's

about as deep as I got. [They] showed me the pictures.

Cardwell: All right. And that was at your office or at your house?

Gonzalez: It was at the Radisson Inn at the airport in El Paso, Texas.

. . .

Cardwell: Is your company treating you as giving expert testimony here?

Gonzalez: Exactly.

Cardwell: Have you been required by your company to be here?

Gonzalez: Yes, I have.

Cardwell: Did they tell you that being here was a part of your job?

Gonzalez: Yes, they did.

. . .

Cardwell: Tell me the name of your company again.

Gonzalez: El Paso Electrical Products.

Cardwell: El Paso Electrical Products. At the present time, sir, does it have any interaction or any business dealings with Westinghouse?

Gonzalez: They are Westinghouse. They just changed the name, but they are a hundred percent Westinghouse, except for the name.

Cardwell: And so when they instructed you to come to Florida, are you clear on whether they were instructing you to come because some injured folks...the attorney for some injured folks has asked you to come, or were you being instructed because Westinghouse had called?

Gonzalez: I would say it was irrelevant who had called. Just somebody needed me on a job, and that's the way they looked at it.

. . .

Cardwell: In fact, did you find it uncomfortable here knowing that your company, El Paso...what's the name of it?

Gonzalez: Electrical Products.

Cardwell: Is so closely affiliated with Westinghouse? Do you find that to be troublesome here in giving your testimony?

Gonzalez: Well, I do.

Cardwell: And do you believe it could have some effect on your particular situation? Your work situation?

Gonzalez: It could have an effect, but it wouldn't bother me anyway.

[I then began redirect examination.]

Yerrid: Why wouldn't it bother you, Mr. Gonzalez? Why would it not bother you to the point where you would fly down here to Orlando, Florida, have two defense lawyers from Westinghouse sit here at the table, and have your sworn testimony elicited? Why would that not bother you, that it could have some effect on you?

Gonzalez: I have enough confidence in myself where I could get another job tomorrow. I don't need Westinghouse or General Electric.

• • •

Yerrid: How powerful was this equipment in terms of the amount of sheer energy that was being put into that shed from Florida Power's generators? How powerful is that equipment?

Gonzalez: You had a potential of fourteen megawatts. You could dump fourteen megawatts into that system. That's a lot of power. You can drop almost what a turbine uses…you could dump a lot of energy in that place. It would blow eventually, but it could handle it. Lightning could hit, and it could handle it. Just a few million volts, and it would blow.

• • •

Yerrid: In a world not involving monetary considerations, but only with regard to safety and good engineering practice—do you understand what I'm asking you, sir? In accordance with good engineering practice, do you believe equipment generating fourteen megawatts' worth of capacity, do you believe, in that type of equipment, that a start-up inspection is essential?

[Hector didn't answer, so I continued.]

Yerrid: Are you familiar with good engineering practices as a qualified electrician?

Gonzalez: Yes, I am.

Yerrid: Are you familiar with good engineering practices as a qualified engineer?

Gonzalez: Yes, I am.

Yerrid: Does a failure to do a start-up inspection on this type of equipment, in your judgment, deviate from the accepted standard of care?

Gonzalez: It should have had a start-up by a factory-trained person.

Yerrid: Are you a qualified practicing engineer at the present time, as we sit here at this deposition?

Gonzalez: Yes, I am.

Yerrid: And you worked on Westinghouse equipment, you are familiar with this operation, and certainly had some responsibility in the field operations Westinghouse employed from 1989, 1990, 1991, here in the State of Florida?

Gonzalez: Yes, I am.

Yerrid: Do you know what good engineering practice constitutes?

Gonzalez: Yes, I do.

Yerrid: In your judgment, would the failure to do a start-up inspection of the equipment that was installed at the Marriott Trade Center constitute a deviation from the accepted standard of care in accordance with good engineering practices?

Gonzalez: Yes. They deviated from standard practices.

• • •

Yerrid: Who was responsible for the deviation? In your judgment, who should have done that start-up inspection?

Gonzalez: Westinghouse Engineering Services should have done the start-up.

• • •

Yerrid: Mr. Gonzalez, you heard the defense lawyer object that they didn't have enough time and they really weren't prepared, and those things, with regard to participating in your deposition today?

Gonzalez: I heard them, yes.

Yerrid: And you have heard me ask you about your opinions and various things with regard to this case, yes?

Gonzalez: Yes.

Yerrid: Did you hear anything as far as them not being prepared to take your statement when they called you back in June and asked you what happened and what your opinion was, and things such as that? Did they ever mention to you that they were not prepared to do something like that?

Gonzalez: No, they didn't.

• • •

Yerrid: How many photographs did Westinghouse or its lawyers show you before your statement was taken in June?

Gonzalez: None.

Yerrid: How many photographs did the lawyers, the defense lawyers from

Westinghouse, or Westinghouse itself, show you before your deposition here today?

Gonzalez: None.

Yerrid: Did you ever refuse to talk to the lawyers from Westinghouse, or refuse to comply with any request Westinghouse made of you in preparing for this case or testimony in this case?

Gonzalez: Not at all.

[And now defense lawyer Cardwell had the chance to cross-examine again.]

Cardwell: With respect to the pictures that we have here, there's been some testimony previously about the fact that you have stated on the record that in a conversation with me, you indicated that you thought you had seen some specks or some imprint, which led you to believe that this accident was caused by a contact between a foreign metal object, presumably of someone working in there, and the energized equipment, is that correct?

Gonzalez: That's correct.

Cardwell: And you have subsequently testified that your view on this has changed.

Gonzalez: Yes, it has.

Cardwell: And you have testified that it had changed as a result of looking at the pictures that you have in front of you, is that correct?

Gonzalez: That's correct.

Yerrid: I want to object. He also testified it changed because he was confusing this accident with another accident.

. . .

Cardwell: Would it have helped you even further if you had actually seen the equipment itself?

Gonzalez: That would clear up the other ten percent of this. I mentioned before eighty-eight percent. I'm eighty-eight percent sure right now. If I could talk to the electricians who were on site and clear up a few points, and if I could see the equipment, then I would say I would be real close to a hundred percent sure.

. . .

Yerrid: I've got a better idea, Mr. Gonzalez. So that the judge is not under any misimpression, would you be available to stay tomorrow and go look at that equipment, if Westinghouse made it available to you to confirm that ten percent, so that you could be one hundred percent certain?

Gonzalez: I am available until after Wednesday for you all.

Yerrid: Then let me offer that opportunity on the record. Can we send Mr. Gonzalez out to look at—

Virginia Townes (co-counsel for defendant Westinghouse): It has to be arranged a week in advance.

Yerrid: My understanding was that he was coming down for that purpose, as of Friday of last week.

Townes: When we were told you had hired him as your expert, we did not feel it was appropriate for us to step on your expert relationship. That's why we canceled—

Yerrid: I hired him as a witness who was a former employee—

Townes: He told us he was hired as an expert witness.

■ ■ ■

Yerrid: Are you saying that we can't get access to the equipment, even through stipulation of all the lawyers in this case?

Townes: That's not the problem. The problem is you have to go through Pinkerton. They have to set up an appointment to get the equipment moved out of the storage cell into an area where it can be viewed with Father & Sons [storage company], and I have to get a check or get cash to pay for that. And that's just not something I can arrange for tomorrow. I had it arranged when we were told by Mr. Gonzalez that he had been hired as your expert. We felt it was unethical for us to enter into any kind of arrangement with him.

Yerrid: Why didn't you call me? I would have told you differently.

Townes: Because I think I am correct as to what the ethics of the situation required. I didn't want to—

Yerrid: I think he probably didn't know what an expert is.

■ ■ ■

Yerrid: Mr. Gonzalez…with regard to you coming here today and answering the questions that you have answered today, do you feel that you were prepared to give me the responses that you gave me here under oath?

Gonzalez: Yes. I do.

. . . .

After Hector Gonzalez's testimony, which was clearly devastating to the defense, I suggested to the Westinghouse and Marriott lawyers, and the representatives of the other related companies I sued on Gary's behalf, that we convene a meeting for the purpose of discussing settlement. I suggested the damages would be large and there seemed to be plenty enough fault to go around.

I also played a trump card. I advised them all that there would not be any sort of settlement if Gary were put through a deposition; instead, we would, without a doubt, take the case to a jury verdict. He had been through enough in my opinion, and the case was already laid out. The defense had a choice: Take the opportunity to discuss settlement or insist on taking his deposition and guarantee a trial.

For the defendants it was simply too big a risk. Everyone agreed to a settlement conference, and it would be held without taking Gary's deposition. Most cases involving electrical accidents are work-related, which usually means that the worker did something wrong. Human error is traditionally the best defense in a product liability case. I knew how badly the defense wanted to take Gary's deposition. In view of the Gonzalez testimony, it was their only chance of avoiding liability. Conceding the opportunity and agreeing to talk settlement was a hell of a good sign.

The initial settlement conference convened in a room filled with clients, lawyers, corporate representatives from Westinghouse and Marriott, claims analysts, economic experts, and structured settlement specialists. As the first of what would turn out to be two settlement sessions got under way, I proceeded by assuming liability was established. By passing the issue of fault, I focused solely on damages in an intentional move to pressure the defendants. I began my presentation on damages simply. "I thought it would be helpful if the injuries this young man suffered were brought to you first hand...without explanation, without comment, and with frightening accuracy." I played selected portions of the video created by the medical school that chronicled the course of his many surgeries. It was short but devastatingly dramatic.

That was probably the beginning of my infatuation with the use of videos and animated recreations to really get a point across. When we're young, we learn that a picture is worth a thousand words. But in the real world, we like to talk, especially lawyers. We don't like to listen. Videos, on the other hand, don't make us talk or listen, nor do they make us choose between the two. In a case like this, the pictures and videos were overwhelming. To conclude the presentation, I showed a several-minute video I had prepared, entitled "A Day in the Life of Gary Stakemiller." It depicted what he faced and dealt with on a daily basis, in terms of the adaptations to his home, his lifestyle, how he now functioned —in effect, a too real experience of walking in Gary's shoes for a day.

The final settlement meeting was in Lakeland, Florida, which is halfway between Orlando, where the Westinghouse lawyers were based, and Tampa, where my law office was located. In view of Hector Gonzalez's statement, Dr. Cruse's videos of the skin graft surgeries, the "Day in the Life of Gary Stakemiller" video, *and* the damning evidence assembled through the many depositions that had been taken in the case, I was confident it was over. It was. The entire case was settled for an undisclosed, confidential amount. In addition to the money, I also imposed one other condition: I agreed to take the settlement being offered but *only* if I received a letter of apology from Marriott for their employee's conduct in telling Gary to get off the sidewalk where he was sitting just after he was burned. I also insisted that the letter be written on behalf of the entire Marriott corporation.

I emphasized that the settlement was not only about money. It was important to Gary and me that Marriott apologize for the unacceptable actions of their employee on the day of the accident. I demanded the apology because Gary was entitled to it and I knew that the money alone could never make what happened acceptable. At first, I sensed the defense lawyers thought I was showboating, that when the money got right, I would surely drop the demand that Marriott apologize. They were wrong. Finally convinced that the written apology was a "deal breaker" and that it was as important as the huge sums of money being discussed, we received the letter of apology—and a very nice settlement check.

Epilogue

· · · · · · ·

Gary Stakemiller had given me a great deal of strength. He had shown me by example just how much could be accomplished with a courageous effort and a spirit of never giving up. Certainly both he and Pam were entitled to the same commitment from their trial lawyer. From the beginning, I had decided that on the legal side we just could not give up until we prevailed.

I also learned from the Stakemiller case that even in the most hideous of circumstances, there still can be beauty. Sometimes during my visits to see Gary lying on that hospital bed, he would move and parts of his skin would stay on the sheet. And do you know what I came to see? Not the ugliness of a horribly damaged human being but, instead, the awesome sight of raw courage. It was really beautiful in a horrific way. As much as I wanted to look away, I couldn't. Instead, I learned to look at his eyes, because the eyes were the life that was still left in an otherwise destroyed body. And in Gary Stakemiller's eyes, I saw sheer determination set deep inside that reflected the grit and courage of the man who refused to die.

During our struggles, I harbored great doubts as to whether Gary could actually come back—mentally, spiritually, and physically—from his devastating injuries. With his disfiguring burns and excruciating pain, he seemingly had nothing to live for. In fact, death might have been the easiest way out. But Gary wouldn't give up. He wouldn't quit on himself or the people around him. But could he survive? Would he believe in me? Even though he had been burned beyond recognition and on the outside appeared as a seared remnant of what he had once been, it was up to me to look further, seek the truth, and find what really remained intact.

Before it was over, I was reminded once again of what is really important in life. Gratitude. Like many people, I constantly have to be reminded of how fortunate I am. It's something I have to work on all the time: not taking things for granted and truly appreciating the moment. Too often, I find myself saying, "I have to do this, I have to do that."

At some point, I began to realize that Gary was doing what I needed to do. He was lying there thinking about what is really important in life, and I was running around going nowhere. I was logging a lot of miles and wasting meaningful time, and I wasn't getting any closer to happiness. But this kid, in his own crippled way, showed me a fresh outlook: a new approach of looking inside as opposed to looking outside for the happiness and goodness of life.

Of course, I was pleased about the case and the outcome, but mostly I was blessed to learn so much from Gary. I was not the teacher in his case. Sure, I may have taught Gary that the judicial system works, but I already knew that could happen. That's the only reason I continue to do what I do. But he taught me that it doesn't matter what the system does or what others may choose to do; you can control your own happiness by staying inside of yourself and being grateful for the wonders of life so often taken for granted or simply overlooked.

Gary and his family are doing wonderfully today. Physically, Gary has healed well, although he still has some health problems. He continues to make his family's home in Florida, where the climate is mild and the seasons not so hostile. Unfortunately, one of his permanent handicaps is the scar tissue and his inability to sweat. He is not able to perspire because all of his sweat glands have been destroyed. He has regained some ability to play with his children, though. And thankfully, he can run his air conditioner all day long because he will never have to worry about paying his electric bill…or any other bills, for that matter.

The Stakemillers have built their dream home on a beautiful piece of land surrounded by Florida's wilderness. Gary and Pam are still happily married. Pam stuck by Gary and, in her own way, matched the courage he had demonstrated. The children have their dad back, and everyone has gone on with their life. The entire family is doing splendidly.

The year after the case was over, I invited Gary and Pam to our law firm's Christmas luncheon. I wondered what kind of gift I could come up with. He could pretty much afford to buy whatever he wanted. I was determined to get him a special present. A friend of mine owns a trophy shop, and I had him make a beautiful award adorned by a large, gold championship cup and had it entitled "Champion of Courage." The wording I had inscribed read: *To a man who is a champion to all who know him and love him and all who will meet and have the pleasure of knowing him. To a courageous champion who overcame adversity and fought death for the lives of his family and those he loves. To a champion who defined courage and never gave up.*

I waited until the end of the luncheon to present Gary with his trophy. He started crying, and everyone was so very moved. But then what did the kid do? He pulled out a Christmas gift for me from under the table: a gold Rolex watch, with my initials etched on the back.

When the case was over, I used to laugh with Gary, telling him, "You know, now I need two things, some business cards to give to ambulance drivers and a gold Rolex."

He would jokingly reply, "You don't need the cards, but you would probably look good in one of those gold Rolexes."

So, there I was at lunch thinking that I couldn't possibly learn much more from this remarkable young man. And what does he do? He gives me a totally materialistic present, but he made it into one from the heart. He knew that I always joked about having a fancy Rolex, but he also knew that I might not buy one. I probably would never bring myself to do it, coming from where I came from. So Gary had done it for me. I started crying, too.

More than anything, I wanted to help the Stakemillers piece their lives back together. I was able to accomplish my goal, and I came away from the case with a much richer soul. His life, once a patchwork quilt collection of tatters and pieces, is good and whole again, and stands as a marvelous testament to the beauty of the human spirit. Together, the family and the justice we obtained formed a genuine piece of the law's extraordinary art.

■ ■ ■ ■ ■ ■ ■

For I dipped into the future,
far as human eye could see,
Saw the Vision of the world,
and all the wonder that would be…

■ ■ ■

—Alfred, Lord Tennyson
"Locksley Hall"

CHAPTER SIX

Not Us

The August day had been hot and humid, typical for subtropical St. Petersburg, Florida, during the summer. The thick, steamy air, stirred only by occasional breezes flowing in from the Gulf of Mexico, was saturated with moisture, and the intensity of the heat hadn't diminished when the sun went down. Being outside was like being in a steam room with clothes on.

Around nine o'clock that muggy evening in 1985, Kenneth Hansen made his way from the Payless Shoe Store he managed to the Barnett Bank of Pinellas County to make a cash deposit from the day's sales. Payless was a bargain shoe store located in the Central Plaza Shopping Center. The shop was on busy Central Avenue just across from Barnett Bank. Making the deposit was part of Hansen's daily routine, and for matters of safety, he purposefully selected a different time each day to go to the depository. About ninety percent of the time, he would go while it was still daylight. The other deposits he made at night, always staggering the hour so that it wouldn't be possible for anyone to know precisely when he would arrive at the bank.

Hansen and his fellow employee, Eugene Sils, drove the five hundred feet of the busy road to make the deposit. Company policy stipulated that two employees should make the cash deposit in the crime-ridden neighborhood where the store was located. It was also standard procedure to drive, because it was considered safer than walking to the bank with cash for even that short distance.

The branch office was one of Barnett Bank's busiest and prettiest. No cost had been spared in landscaping the plush grounds surrounding its location. Subtle illumination of the exotic shrubbery dimly lit the area surrounding the building's white brick walls, and the overall effect gave the bank the *Architectural Digest* look that it wanted. After Hansen parked the car in the lot at the back, he began briskly walking the twenty-five or so steps to the outside night depository. As he approached the bank, he experienced the same sense of nervousness he usually felt about the numerous large trees, bushes, and shrubbery—some of it twelve feet tall—that surrounded the bank. Always careful when he carried cash, Hansen glanced around in the darkness but saw nothing to alarm him. He knew the area was a customary hangout for vagrants, who slept, loitered, and drank in and around the darkness of the bushes, but on that night he didn't see anyone at all. Except for Sils, who stayed in the car, Hansen was utterly alone—no security guards, no video cameras, no emergency telephones or alarms—just like every other time when he made his evening deposits.

The next few seconds rushed by in a blur for Ken Hansen. But the fear that filled him seared the terror deep into his being. Later, when he recalled what happened, the memories were sharp and clear. Just before he was going to toss the cash-filled bag into the depository, he heard the rustling of leaves. Suddenly, a large, burly figure vaulted out of the bushes and sprinted toward him, as quick and sure-footed as a starving leopard after its prey. There had been no time to react—and certainly no chance to flee. In a startlingly brief instant, Hansen realized what was happening: He was being robbed!

Instinctively, he turned and tried to run to the car where Sils still sat, too shocked and frightened to move as the terrifying scene played out before him. Surprisingly, Hansen almost made it. He was only a couple of steps from the safety of the automobile when another man, almost as big and brawny as the first, appeared and blocked his escape. Trying to sidestep the second attacker, Hansen tripped and fell to the ground, helpless against the two figures that closed in upon him. During the next few seconds, the two large men just stood there, as if they were contemplating their next move. Then both sprang into action. The bank bag was ripped from Hansen's right hand, and he felt the savage pounding of fists. Along with the blows, a heavy object that felt something like a baseball bat crashed against his left side, both legs, and his left arm. Initially, Hansen tried to fight back, but it was no use. The violence of the assault was overpowering. He curled up into a ball and took the assault without further resistance.

Maybe that is what saved him. The beating finally stopped and he could hear the two men running away. He heard the car door open as his terrified partner got out to help. Hansen—bloodied, bruised, and sore— slowly dragged himself to his feet. Without wasting any more time, Sils half-carried Hansen to the car, gunned the engine, and sped toward the closest hospital with his passenger moaning in pain.

Three days later, Hansen was released from the hospital. He had suffered some nasty bruising, a few cuts, cracked ribs, and a badly broken arm. Still, he had been lucky. In the meantime, the police investigation into the robbery turned up nothing. Within a week of the attack, Hansen went to Barnett Bank on two separate occasions to complain about what had occurred and to ask why something like this had to happen. He had specifically complained to the bank officers about the dense shrubbery and inadequate lighting around the night depository, even pointing out that a "small army" could hide behind the expansiveness of the bushes. When nothing was done by the bank to alleviate the problem, Hansen went back to the bank a third time. He wasn't *complaining*, he later said, he was *pleading* with Barnett that something needed to be done. He urged that corrective measures be taken immediately, before the same thing happened to someone else.

The day after his last visit, a representative from Barnett's insurance company, the Reliance Insurance Corporation, contacted Hansen. In return for a release of any and all claims against the bank and for his injuries, he would be paid a thousand dollars. The insurance adjuster insisted that its insured, Barnett Bank, could not be held responsible for the acts of criminals, especially since the incident had occurred outside the bank building. He pointed out that was a job for the police and not the bank. Besides, the adjuster reasoned, Hansen's arm was healing well, and the police would be following up on the matter. He soothingly assured Hansen that taking the money would be the best thing for everyone concerned. Most importantly, he assured Hansen that remedial actions would be taken to prevent this sort of thing from happening in the future. After much thought, Hansen decided to take the money and move on with his life.

Shortly after the attack, a Barnett security officer had prepared an incident report and circulated it to his superiors, as well as to the claims department of the Reliance Insurance Company. For reasons that could never be explained, neither the report nor any notice of the incident was ever given to the bank's manager or its operations officer. Nothing further was done.

For the next two months, Hansen continued working at Payless before he quit the job and left town. During that time, he never saw any corrective measures taken. The bushes weren't cut back or removed, the lighting around the bank remained as dim as ever, and no security guards or surveillance cameras were posted or installed. More troubling, vagrants still used the area as a gathering spot to drink and sleep.

While he was still at Payless, Hansen made sure all deposits were made before dark. He continued to be very troubled by the nagging feeling that someday there would be another victim.

Just a few months later, history repeated itself. Except this time, the victim would not be forgotten.

Déjà vu
· · · · · · ·

On a cool February evening in 1986, just six months after the savage attack on Kenneth Hansen, a young man named Anthony "Tony" Verran was working for Plitt Southern's Plaza Movie Theater, in the same shopping area as the Payless store. Just twenty-four years old, Tony had moved to St. Petersburg from Daytona Beach a few months earlier. He was an economics major at nearby Eckerd

College, a small, church-related liberal arts college, where he was at the top of his class, maintaining an impressive 3.9 grade average.

Born in Elizabethton, Tennessee, in 1962 to Harley and Vonda Verran, Tony graduated from University High School in Johnson City in May of 1980. After high school, he was offered several athletic scholarships because of his skills on the tennis court. Tony was anxious to further his education and pursue his tennis career, but the Verran family had fallen on hard times. His father, who had been a hard-working businessman all of his adult life, was having great difficulty keeping his pest control business afloat. Worse, Harley Verran's health had begun to deteriorate. As the only son, Tony made a decision that required little thought: He would hold off on college, turn down the scholarships, and put his hopes and dreams aside—at least for a while.

Tony stayed home to help his parents and took a job as a desk clerk at the Buffalo Mountain Inn in Unicoi, Tennessee, in the heart of the Smoky Mountains. When his father's business improved and his health gradually returned over the next couple of years, Tony felt it was time to move on with his own life once again. He relocated to Florida and took a management trainee position with Plitt Southern Theaters in South Daytona Beach. He longed to further his education and quickly accepted an opportunity to transfer to Plitt Southern's Plaza Movie Theater in St. Petersburg in May of 1984 so he could enroll at nearby Eckerd College in August of that same year.

On the night of February 26, 1986, Tony was responsible for closing the movie theater after the late feature. The last show usually ended around midnight, and it was company policy that two employees of the theater take the day's receipts in a bank-provided moneybag to the night depository at Barnett Bank—the same bank where Kenneth Hansen had been attacked a few months before. Under no circumstances was the money to stay overnight at the theater. Whoever took the money to the bank always drove; no one ever walked alone at that time of night in that neighborhood, even though the theater and the bank were not far from each other.

Tony never liked making the late night deposits; none of the employees did. He was keenly aware of the dense foliage around the night depository and its dim lighting. He knew the neighborhood, and he knew only too well its high incidence of crime. He was also aware of the attack on Kenneth Hansen a few months earlier. Tony had made sure to alert everyone who worked at the theater of the incident. He cautioned all of the employees about the need to be extra careful when making the deposits. Most often, he simply chose to carry the money himself, rather than ask others to take the risk.

On the night of February 26, after the theater closed, Della Hudson, one of the younger employees, was the only person available to accompany Tony to make the night drop. Around one o'clock in the morning, the two climbed into Della's car, with Tony sitting in the passenger seat holding the moneybag containing $630. Della drove across 31st Street, a busy thoroughfare even at that time of the early morning. The distance was a little more than a block across First Avenue and into the Barnett Bank parking lot.

The passenger side headlight of Della's car was out of alignment, so it didn't shine straight ahead. "Normally, the lights would be shining straight ahead, but on Della's car, one of the lights was pointed to the right, high and askew so it was shining over the top of those bushes," Tony later testified in his deposition recalling the events of that night. "I was making a joke that we were lucky her car's twisted headlight illuminated the bushes so we could see if any bad guys were hiding back there." Ironically, he remarked to Della as they pulled up to the depository, "No wonder this was such a good place for a robbery. It looks like a jungle!" Della recalled Tony's exact words during her own testimony. She related how the two had actually been laughing about her headlights being cockeyed.

After Della parked, she pulled the keys out of the ignition. The key to the night depository was on her key ring. Tony and Della continued to make nervous small talk as they hurriedly walked across the parking lot and up the walkway leading to the night depository. The shine of Della's car lights against the large plants created tall, dark shadows against the backdrop of the bank's brick wall. They arrived at the same time side by side, with Tony carrying the moneybag. Della reached forward, unlocked the box, and pulled it open. Tony said he then "just threw the bag in—not out of fear, but just to get rid of the money and be through with it for the night. The bag was already in the air and the box was closing when I heard someone yell something like, 'da, da, da, money!' *Money* was the only word I could distinguish."

When he heard the voice, Tony sensed a movement to his left and heard the crackling sound of branches and twigs breaking as someone or something emerged from the tall bushes. As he turned, a man with a gun suddenly appeared. "There was a perception of someone going by," he recalled of that chilling moment. "I turned around and stepped over toward Della. She was sort of behind me, to the right, against the wall next to where the night deposit was located." At the instant he turned around to see what was going on, he felt something that he first thought was gravel hitting his right eye. Then, in the next second, he realized what had actually happened. "I was shot. I felt the air from the blast, I felt the gunpowder burn as it hit my eye, and I felt the thud of the impact. I dropped to my knees and grabbed my eye. Della ended up behind me with her back against the wall with her hands up in the air. She was just screaming and screaming. I realized I had been shot, but I didn't know how badly. Then the guy looked at me—a big man with his eyes staring right at me. He was just standing there with the gun. I was sure I was a dead man. Then, as suddenly as he had appeared he was gone. He ran away into the darkness and cover of the bushes."

Even though he was in extreme pain, in shock over being shot, and blinded in one eye, Tony could recall his assailant. He would later be able to give an excellent description to the police of the fleeting, blood-soaked images in his mind: *black male...closely cropped hair...my height, about six feet tall, maybe just a bit shorter...eighteen to twenty-two years old...blue sweater...tan shorts...*

As the assailant ran off, Tony reported to the police investigators, "someone else ran by me. Until that point, I didn't know there were two of them. I don't know whether he stopped in front of me, the other guy, or whether he came running around the building, but when he ran by, he bumped my right shoulder and arm and almost knocked me down. I was holding my eye when he ran by. All I saw was that he was hooded and had on a yellow sweater. That was all I saw of the second one."

After both assailants disappeared into the darkness of the foliage, Della became hysterical. She just stood there with her hands up in the air, alternately gasping for breath and screaming at the top of her lungs. When she began to regain some composure, she looked at Tony's bleeding face. "Oh, my God!" she began shrieking as her hysteria took hold again. "You've...been...shot!"

"Come on, Della, we've got to get out of here," Tony responded in a low voice but with urgency. By now, blood was pouring down his face and onto his clothes and dripping onto the ground. Della was still screaming, but he knew he had to calm her down enough so that she could get him to a hospital. He grabbed at her arm and said, "I need to get to a hospital. You need to get me help...and fast!"

Tony and Della scrambled back to her car. "I was looking around, scared those guys were going to come back," he recalled. "They didn't get the money, and that is why I thought they would come back for us. My eye was swollen, really huge, and I could feel it. I knew something was terribly wrong with my face. I knew I had been shot in the head, but I didn't know how bad. Everything was numb and my head was filled with a loud ringing."

As Della drove, Tony kept his eye covered with his hand, but it wasn't enough to stop the blood that was now gushing all over him and onto the car seat. He remembered that his eye "felt as if a grapefruit were coming out of my head. I couldn't open whatever was left of my eye. I knew we were near a hospital, but neither of us could recall either its name or location. I was afraid I would pass out, and I felt nauseous. I knew I was losing a lot of blood, because with my good eye I saw blood all over my arms, hands, shorts, everything. I felt the warm liquid of my own blood everywhere. I was getting dizzy, and for the first time I realized I might be dying."

Just down the street, Della zipped her car into a Hess gas station. She ran inside, asked directions to the nearest hospital, and then ran back to Tony, who had stayed in the car. As she pulled out of the gas station, she started screaming again, which Tony clearly recalled. "She forgot the directions within a block of leaving the gas station. She was freaking out." Tony asked Della to pull into the parking lot at an all-night Subway sandwich shop. It was clear that Della could no longer drive. Someone from the sandwich shop dialed 911.

"The ambulance got there almost immediately. Within a minute or two, I was being taken to Bayfront Medical Center. By the time we arrived at the hospital, my head had cleared some and I was coherent. I talked to people in the emergency room and was able to tell them what had happened. I was trying to stay calm, but I was scared. I knew I had lost my eye, and I was worried what the bullet had done to the inside of my head."

In the few minutes Tony and Della waited in the trauma unit for a physician, the hospital staff asked Tony several questions. One nurse asked him who his next of kin was, because he would have to have immediate surgery. Frightened and lightheaded, Tony was guided to a phone, where a call was placed to his parents in Johnson City, Tennessee. Unable to get through, he contacted his sister, Pamela, who also lived in Johnson City. He rapidly explained the events of the evening, and asked her to find their parents as soon as possible. But his sister also panicked when he told her he had been shot. She began screaming into the telephone, totally hysterical. Tony tried to comfort her, just as he had done with Della. Then he again began to fully realize his own situation: *Am I going to die? Will I see my mother and father again? Will I have brain damage? Should I leave my family any final messages in case I die? My God! Things have been going so well for me! How could this have happened to me? Why me? What did I do to deserve this? I have done so well but I have so much left to do! This is not fair! It just is not fair! Why me? Why?*

After a few anxious moments, his sister seemed to calm down. Pamela promised Tony that somehow, some way, she would find their parents. No matter what, she assured Tony that they all would be with him as soon as possible.

Within a couple of hours of arriving at the hospital, Tony underwent major surgery to repair the extensive damage in and around his right eye. Because Tony's assailant had been an inch or two shorter than he was, the bullet had traveled upward, shattered on his cheekbone, partially fragmented, and entered his eye at an angle. There was massive trauma to his eye, the socket and the surrounding area. The doctor told him later

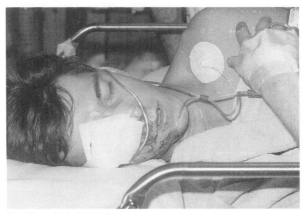

Tony Verran in the hospital.

that the bullet had come within a few millimeters of striking vital portions of his brain. It was a miracle he hadn't been killed instantly. In the surgery, the grotesquely swollen tissue surrounding the collapsed eye had been probed and most of the metal fragments and bone chips removed.

When Tony awoke from the surgery, the focus of his remaining eye rested upon Peter Hammerschmidt, a distinguished professor of economics who was also the dean of students at Eckerd College. Della had summoned Dr. Hammerschmidt, and the worried dean had immediately driven to the hospital. Before Tony could utter a word, he lapsed back into a darkness of unconsciousness. The next time he awoke, his mother and father were in the room with him. Just as his mother took his hand and began squeezing it, Tony spoke for the first time. "Don't worry, Mom. I am going to be all right. I won't leave you."

A few days after the surgery, the doctors explained to Tony that he was no longer in danger of dying from his wounds. There was massive damage in his right eye, and its blindness was a certainty. Some bullet fragments remained lodged in his head but, miraculously, there had been no brain damage.

When Tony was discharged from the hospital, Dr. Hammerschmidt and his wife, Jody, invited him to live at their home while he recuperated. Jody became Tony's nurse, and Peter became his personal tutor so that he wouldn't fall behind in his studies. Tony's attitude and determination were fueled by the warm support the Hammerschmidts provided.

The first day Tony was left alone at the Hammerschmidts' home, the doorbell rang, and he jumped at the sound. He made his way slowly to the door, still dizzy and disoriented from his adjustment to life with one eye. He opened the door to a tall, middle-aged man. "Mr. Verran? I'm from the bank's insurance company. I'm here to talk to you about settling your case. May I come in?"

The two men sat on the sofa and the adjuster continued in a matter-of-fact tone, "We want to give you $10,000 to settle your case. I have the check and all of the papers with me. If you are ready to sign a release we can resolve this matter right now."

Tony was taken aback at the suggestion of a settlement and surprised at the direction of the conversation. He had not been asked one word about his injuries or his condition. He answered in a soft voice, "But I don't know how I am going to be. I don't have an attorney yet and I can't deal with all these papers right now. I'll probably be seeing a lawyer next week, and I'll be happy to talk with you once I have spoken to someone."

The man raised his voice and his calm demeanor changed markedly. "I can't talk to you once you talk to an attorney. If you want this money, you had better sign now. Otherwise, you might be sorry and end up with nothing."

Tony had heard enough. He was not going to be pushed. He politely told the man that he didn't want to talk to him anymore and asked him to leave. For the first time, he knew with certainty he would need a lawyer.

The next week, Peter Hammerschmidt brought Tony Verran to my office. Peter and I had known each other for several years. He knew of my reputation as a trial lawyer who specialized in catastrophic cases and he wanted Tony to meet with me.

Peter and the young man sat before me, and Tony explained the events of the night he was shot. I studied Tony as he spoke. His remaining eye shone green in one light and brown in another. He related the facts of the incident concisely and he showed no emotion. I was impressed by his intelligence and self-control. Despite his grotesque injury, he was a good-looking kid, and he carried himself well. He was also respectful and sincere. I liked him. More importantly, I knew he needed my help.

I asked him a multitude of questions, and he answered each firmly and with no hesitation in his voice. I specifically avoided any mention of his treatment or the effects of his blindness. Tony explained the uneasiness he had often felt as he went to Barnett Bank's depository each night and he seemed to be blaming himself for what had happened. He wondered aloud about what he could have—what he should have—done differently. Then he told me about everything that he had gone through since the injury—the surgeries, hospitalizations, pain, and even his deepest fears. We had crossed the first hurdle: He trusted me.

During that first meeting, Tony wore a patch to cover what remained of his shattered eye. When I asked that he remove it, the young man before me paused only a moment before baring the gruesome injury to me. As I studied the damage to his eye, I felt my anger begin to rise as he told me of another man who had been brutally attacked at the same location just a few months earlier. Astoundingly, even though they knew of that incident, Barnett Bank had chosen to do nothing to clear the foliage or illuminate the area where Kenneth Hansen's attackers had been hiding. Tony slid the patch back over his eye and in a strong, sure voice explained to me that he would have to live with his injury and a fear of total blindness for the rest of his life. However, that did not mean he would accept what had happened.

"The bank shouldn't be allowed to get away with allowing such a situation to exist, Mr. Yerrid," Tony said as he looked intently at me. "By choosing to do nothing, every single customer is exposed to the risk that something terrible might happen. If I—we—don't do something, the bank will get away with it, and more people will get hurt or even killed. The bank knew there was a problem, yet they did nothing. Now, look at me. We have got to do our best to see it doesn't happen to anyone else."

The young man stood up and moved closer to my desk. "Mr. Yerrid," he began to speak again, slowly at first, and then the words came out in a rush. "My eye hurts all the time. It stings and waters and sometimes closes up entirely. I have been getting migraine headaches since I was shot, and sometimes they last a full day and night. I never had migraines before. My blind eye tracks more slowly than my good eye, and as you can see, it has begun to turn outward, as if I am always looking to the side. The headaches and constant flashbacks of that bullet hitting my eye keep me from sleeping at night. When I sneeze or somehow happen to jerk my head, there is pressure on my temples, almost like something is smashing against my head, and I feel as if my head is going to explode. I know I look strange, Mr. Yerrid, and I feel ugly when people stare at me. I always have to explain what happened, and I hate doing that. I even shy away from meeting new people, and that's something I used to love.

"What will happen to me if something should go wrong with my other eye? I couldn't take that—I just couldn't. And no matter what I do or how careful I am, there is always that chance. I don't have any money, except for student loans, and my parents really can't afford to help me out much. They have done plenty already. I can't work full time because of my eye—and because of my studies—and I don't know how I'm going to live. Are you going to be able to help me? Do I have a case?"

I had wanted to help Tony from the first few minutes of our meeting. He was a bright, young college student who didn't have two cents to his name, and there was no doubt in my mind that what had happened was just plain wrong. "Tony," I began as I stood up and held out my hand, "there will be a tremendous amount of work here, and there is always the possibility that we will lose the case. Are you ready for that? Can you keep up your faith, work with me—no matter what it takes—and go the distance?"

"Yes, sir, Mr. Yerrid." He took my outstretched hand and answered in a soft voice tinged with determination. "I can."

In the weeks and months after our first meeting as we prepared for trial, Tony Verran's condition worsened. The gunshot wound had opened up a large area outside of the eyeball itself, and the force of the bullet had removed almost all of the internal parts of the eye. As a result of the damage, Tony had developed a cataract. The clouding over of the natural lens of his eye made his appearance even more startling and the deadness of his eye more prominent than ever.

Doctors continually advised Tony to have what was left of his right eye removed. They feared that the blind eye might have adverse effects on his remaining vision. There was always the risk of sympathetic ophthalmia, a condition in which inflammation in an injured eye transfers to the uninjured eye. I learned, and Tony was told, that sympathetic ophthalmia could sometimes show up years after the injury. Also, the injured eyeball had collapsed and shrunk because there was less fluid in it to maintain an outward pressure, and this could lead to further complications. There was a permanent risk that scar tissue inside the eye could someday cause blood vessels to rupture and bleed, with additional disastrous consequences.

We also learned from the doctors that, as Tony had already noticed, a blind eye can "drift" either inward or outward. This is because the brain needs signals from both eyes in order to keep them in proper alignment; if one eye is "dead," like Tony's was, the brain doesn't get the feedback it needs to keep the eyes pointed in the same direction. Tony didn't need any such explanation—all he had to do was look in the mirror.

Despite all of the risks involved, Tony decided not to have his eye removed. He told me that he just didn't want to lose any more of himself than he already had.

The Trial
· · · · · · ·

The case of *Anthony Wayne Verran Versus Barnett Bank of Pinellas County* was styled as a premises liability case and was based on the somewhat novel theory—at least back then—that the bank was liable for third-party criminal assaults at its night depository and automated teller machine (ATM) facility. The bank, in keeping with the posture of the entire banking industry, took the position that the police, not the bank, had the responsibility for attacks on customers that occurred outside the actual bank building. The bank also raised the defense of comparative negligence, suggesting that reasonable people should not go into places to make deposits at night, even though the bank offered the twenty-four-hour night depository service as a way to make money from its customers.

In recent years, premises liability cases have become an accepted part of our legal world. At the time of Tony's case, however, things were much different. These cases have since made businesses aware of their duty to protect their customers and have forced the abandonment of the notion that it is totally up to the police department to protect the public.

The trial began in February of 1988, two years after the attack on

Tony Verran. One of those things that can never be predicted happened during *voir dire*. In my questioning during the process to pick the jury, I learned that a potential juror had only one eye. Without a doubt, I knew that the bank's lawyers would use a peremptory challenge (one where no reason needs to be given in order to remove the juror) and strike him from the jury panel. Before that could be done, I asked the juror a question that provided the opportunity for a profoundly simple response. "Does having one eye impact your life?"

"Oh, sure," the gentleman answered. "You never get over having one eye."

That was invaluable "testimony" for us, before the first witness had even been called to the stand.

I was fairly confident that our first impression had been a good one. The bank must have thought so, too. After the jury was selected, the defense lawyers decided it was time to make an offer: They proposed $200,000 to settle the case. It was a lot of money for a young man from Tennessee. Such a sum would get Tony through college and law school, pay off the mortgage on his parents' home, and buy him a new car. I felt we had the momentum going our way. But because the amount offered was so significant to a person in Tony's position, I stayed silent and told him it would be his decision and his decision alone. I would recommend neither for nor against the settlement offer.

I was proud of Tony when he quickly informed me that he wanted to turn the money down. I could sense the concern running through the defense team when we declined the bank's offer. It was clear to me the defense realized it had already been hurt. Skilled advocates, the defense team had done their best to downplay our theory of the case, but from the look of the jurors and the reactions sometimes flashing across their faces, it was apparent they liked what we were saying.

The trial itself was draining and hotly contested. Certainly our confidence ebbed and flowed, but at the close of each day, it was becoming increasingly clear that our legal theories were beginning to take hold in the jurors' minds. We were doing a good job of establishing the evidence necessary to prove Tony's case. A key theme I reiterated time and again focused on the inescapable fact that this type of incident was foreseeable by the bank, which had a duty to protect Tony Verran and other innocent customers from criminal attacks by third parties.

The legal theories were based on several key points. First was the bank's invitation to the public to deposit money and other valuable items in the depository at any hour of the day or night. The bank's location in a high crime area where substantial violent criminal activity had occurred prior to the attack on Tony was also a significant factor. To visually demonstrate the extent of crime, we used police crime grids of an area within four blocks of the bank to show where numerous robberies, rapes, and violent attacks had occurred within a very short span of time. Included among the crimes was a murder at a nearby Walgreen's. Everyone in the area was well aware of this criminal activity, and Barnett Bank of course had specific knowledge of the assault on Ken Hansen at their own depository.

Through the testimony of the bank's own employees, we demonstrated its knowledge of undesirable persons sleeping, drinking, and using drugs in the foliage immediately adjacent to the night depository. In the months before the attacks on Hansen and Verran, there had been a marked increase in crimes occurring at other bank automated teller machines and depositories in the vicinity. Through premises liability and security experts, we established that the threat of such criminal acts was becoming a known and considered factor in the banking industry.

There could be little doubt that the overgrown bushes, trees, and shrubbery around the night depository had created a haven that invited criminal conduct. By emphasizing aesthetics rather than security, Barnett had breached its duty to exercise reasonable care.

As the case unfolded, the mounting evidence began to support an additional charge that the bank had acted with reckless disregard and with conscious indifference to the safety of the public and its customers by ignoring known criminal incidents and dangerous conditions that had been specifically brought to its attention.

During trial, the evidence established that the bank, even though it was given the opportunity, had chosen not to relocate its facilities so as to provide drive-up access to the night depository. We proved that no security procedures, patrols, equipment, personnel, or any other measures were in place for those customers using the outside ATM or night depository.

Even though appropriate technology was available, we showed that the bank elected not to install any surveillance or video camera equipment, alarm systems, or emergency telephones. At the time, the argument that banks "didn't do these sorts of things" was largely true. However, we emphasized the need for doing what was right, not necessarily what everyone else was doing. Now, of course, those security precautions are the norm, not the exception.

Finally, punitive damages—those directed toward punishing the bank for what had happened to Tony—had to be considered. The elements of negligence necessary to sustain an award of punitive damages require showing that the conduct of the company was of a gross and flagrant nature and evidenced a reckless disregard of human life or of the safety of persons exposed to its dangerous effect. The law provides that a reckless indifference to the rights of others is equivalent to an *intentional* violation, and Florida courts have viewed punitive damages as a vehicle to vindicate wrongs arising from such behavior and the most satisfactory way to correct institutionally bad conduct in areas not covered by criminal law. The other important goal of punitive damages is to deter others from acting in the same manner. In essence, it is a civics lesson taught in our own courtrooms.

I argued that the outrageous facts in this case constituted the exact type of conduct contemplated by Florida law as sufficient to sustain a claim for punitive damages. Despite the high crime area and prior knowledge both of the security problems with the outdoor premises and of the attack on Hansen, the bank chose to do absolutely nothing. It didn't cut back the foliage, install adequate lighting, or employ more stringent security procedures. I argued that conscious and reckless indifference to the security problems surrounding the outdoor premises constituted an entire want of care, that Tony should be allowed to claim for punitive damages, and that this element should be rightfully considered by the jury.

We were sitting in the courtroom of Judge Thomas E. Penick Jr., who was a trial judge in the Sixth Judicial Circuit, one of Florida's most conservative. I watched the judge listen closely to the proffer of proof supporting punitive damages. I could tell that he was concerned—and quite disturbed—by the conduct of the bank. He also appeared unmoved by the defense lawyers' arguments that the bank's conduct did not rise to the level of the outrageous behavior necessary to allow us the opportunity to add punitive damages to Tony's case. The tension on both sides mounted as the arguments wore on. A brief recess was taken as everyone waited for Judge Penick's decision.

When Judge Penick resumed his seat, he spoke slowly and deliberately. "The court is very concerned about the evidence shown in this record. However, because of the severity of the relief being sought and the very high standard of the proof required, at this time I will not grant the plaintiff's motion to add punitive damages. At the same time, I believe the evidence that exists may preclude me from denying it. I will therefore take the matter under advisement and render a ruling later in these proceedings after more evidence has been heard."

The case would go forward on the issues of liability and compensatory damages—at least for a while. The fact that the risk to the bank of extraordinary punitive damages still existed was putting even more pressure on the bank and its defense team to settle.

One of the bank's senior officers testified that ATMs and night depositories served to keep the bank open for business twenty-four hours a day, seven days a week. Under cross-examination, he reluctantly acknowledged that he considered the large amount of high foliage at the bank "unusual." He was also forced to admit that he had never seen another bank branch with this extent of overgrown foliage in his twenty years in the business.

In an apparent effort to explain away his individual responsibility, the bank's senior officer unexpectedly volunteered that Barnett's president had personally insisted on the dense landscaping and foliage, in part because of the beautification award that the bank had won from the City of St. Petersburg some years earlier. I felt relief when he was pressed to admit that banks should probably focus more on security than beautification. By the end of his examination, he was worn down. His testimony concluded with his admission that he wouldn't want to walk through such foliage nor would he expect his customers to do it. Before I was finished cross-examining him, I was able to elicit his agreement that a safety award might be more important than any award for aesthetics.

The bank's hired expert, identified as a professional security consultant, testified that banks should maintain night depositories because in his view customers "needed them." Because a consumer could deposit valuables during the day, he reasoned that the risk of making an after-hours deposit was left up to the judgment of the customer. His testimony was pointedly in support of the industry. "The burden is on the consumer to bring his deposit to the bank in a safe environment." It was only under exhaustive cross-examination that he finally conceded that the bank also possessed some degree of duty to take all reasonably available steps to make night depositories as safe as possible. Ultimately, he admitted that the use of any night depository invariably involves risk, but that the bank should make efforts to minimize that risk.

In a trial with good, experienced attorneys the ability to adapt and react to changing circumstances is critical. With the evidence going so totally against the bank, its legal team decided to admit liability in the middle of trial and try the Verran case solely on the issue of damages.

Obviously, the defense had considered that a continuing refusal by the bank to accept at least some responsibility for its actions might have a significant effect on the amount of money the jury would consider awarding. If the "not us" position was maintained, there was a very real risk that the defense would lose any credibility it would otherwise have had to contest the amount of damages. It was simple. If the jury didn't believe the defense on the issue of liability, they might also carry that disbelief over when they assessed damages. At the end of the day, the most compelling issue in any case is credibility.

Additionally, by avoiding the presentation of incriminating evidence that would undoubtedly stir up anger about the bank's conduct, the defense would probably be able to minimize, if not totally eliminate, any desire on the jury's part to punish the defendant. If successful, the bank's defense team would focus the jury's attention solely on money—hard dollars and cents. How much, in terms of money, is the loss of one eye worth?

The case would now go to the jury on damages alone. The evidence put forward by the defense was direct and simple. The loss of one eye was unfortunate and tragic, but Tony had not lost his vision. He had not been blinded, and despite the trauma of the event and the relatively modest medical bills incurred, the defense emphasized, he had fared well in overcoming his injuries. Tony had finished out the school semester in which he was shot, only dropping one class out of five and ending up with straight A's. Further, it was pointed out that he had graduated first in his class at Eckerd College with a perfect 4.0 grade point average. He seemed to be doing quite well. In fact, the defense lawyers repeatedly emphasized he was doing as well with one eye as he had done with two.

Our damages case centered on Tony. His testimony was sincere and believable. Since the assault, his good eye was often strained if he used it too long. Headaches were constant due to the extra effort of one eye trying to do the work of two. Instead of studying for two straight hours, Tony would read for fifteen minutes, take a fifteen-minute break, and so on, to reduce the strain and pain. His stellar academic performance and outstanding grades were the result of more than double the effort.

I had asked Tony to testify as if he were conversing with friends in his own living room—to be relaxed and candid. Holding nothing back, he did just that, and I could see the jury liked him and what he had to say. Rather than making his disfigurement an uncomfortable focal point by having him take off the lightly tinted glasses he now wore almost all the time to hide his injuries, I used photographs to show how badly he had been hurt. I believe the jury appreciated the low-key manner in which we handled the issue; and, at least for Tony, it was the right way to go. Still, I knew we needed more emphasis on his one-eyed vision.

I had retained Dr. Frank Mendelblatt, the chief of ophthalmology at nearby University of South Florida Medical School, as our expert for trial. When I first went to meet with him in his office, he had shown me a device he used to simulate one-eyed vision: an apparatus that resembled an odd-looking pair of glasses. I put them on and was immediately as-tounded: They precisely simulated what it must be like to have sight in only one eye. I really had no idea of the magnitude of the impairment until I had personally experienced it. I knew right away that this would be an extremely persuasive tool at trial, and I asked Dr. Mendelblatt to bring a boxful of the "one-eyed glasses" with him to court.

Dr. Mendelblatt' s impeccable credentials, along with the clarity of his explanations, made him an outstanding witness. On the stand, he first described the various limitations of having vision in only one eye. Then I asked the judge if the jurors could be provided with the devices Dr.

Mendelblatt had brought along. Of course the defense lawyers loudly and strenuously objected. But it did no good. The judge not only overruled the objection and instructed the bailiff to pass them out to the jury—*he also asked for a pair himself.*

After the rest of the evidence was presented, the stage was set. It was time for summation.

· · · · · · ·

The Closing Argument

LADIES AND GENTLEMEN OF THE JURY, I think it would be appropriate at this time to thank you on behalf of everyone involved in this case. It is coming to a conclusion and I believe I speak for the defense counsel; their client, Barnett Bank; and I certainly know I speak for my client, Tony Verran, and the Court in expressing our deepest appreciation for taking time out of your lives to serve as jurors. You, the jury, have made our system work; and your duties as jurors, as I have mentioned earlier, are solemn.

I now ask you to listen for a while longer. I should not take much more of your time. Please listen closely, because it is the only time that you will ever hear the story of Tony Verran. And I want to thank you on behalf of everybody, not just the plaintiff in this case. This time, I thank you for listening.

In the opening statement, I talked to you about the evidence and the respective burdens of proof. I am sure each of you recalls the blind lady of justice as she holds the scales of truth. I talked to you about the issue of liability and the issue of damages. The issue of liability is no longer before you. That issue has now been resolved in favor of Tony Verran. We are here to determine one thing: the amount of monetary compensation that will address the terrible loss that has been suffered. I reminded you that at the beginning of this case damages were going to be extremely difficult. I asked each of you if you could promise in dollar terms "a price tag" for the suffering that has occurred—because that is what this system does. It is the best we have come up with.

Of course, these are the types of things that are the most difficult in the world to equate into dollars: the anguish of human pain and suffering, of loss and disfigurement, and the loss of enjoyment of life itself. I will go through each aspect of those damages in the next few minutes.

During your selection as jurors, I asked if you would be able to follow the law as the judge instructs you, and each of you said you would. I asked if you would disregard your own station in life, and I requested that you listen to all of the evidence and each witness with regard to the duty—the solemn duty you swore to do to uphold as jurors—and you each said you would do that.

Days, weeks, and many months have now elapsed since the tragic occurrence involving Tony changed his life. Today, the burden, which I have had since this young man came into my office, sat down, told me what occurred, and asked me to prove his case in court, will shift to you. That burden has been with me, and it has been a heavy one. Let me suggest to you that I may not have done all that I should have done. I may have stumbled. Soon, however, the weight of this case shifts to you, the jury, and it will be your burden to decide the justice of this case.

I fully anticipate that Barnett Bank will argue the issue of damages as vigorously as it once contested liability. I fully anticipate to hear the words real dollars, hard working dollars, but I want you to never forget that when you leave here today, you will leave behind this case for all time. Those words, those little catchwords, those little lawyer words, hard dollars, you are going to hear the defense use them, and you should think about that in a real dollars sense.

This case is about a lot of money. It is going to be a lot of money. I do not know if I can even suggest a figure to you. I am going to try. But I want you to understand that next week these lawyers and those lawyers will be in another courtroom; and if I am correct, you'll be back—hopefully healthy—in your lives and this will be another case in our system of justice that has been decided. The court reporter will be transcribing another trial. And another, probably more able, lawyer will be up here talking to a different jury. The bailiff who has worked so hard will have other duties involving other people and other cases. The clerk and His Honor—certainly a judge who has shown the patience of Job and the wisdom of Solomon—will have another case. But Tony's case will never be heard again. This is his one day in court, and I want you not to forget that your verdict will influence him for the rest of his life—and that responsibility I am happy to give to you. Hopefully, this case and your verdict will be something you can look back on years from now and you can know that you did justice and can be proud.

Do not let sympathy play a role in this. The judge will so instruct you, and I suggest to you that it is not so difficult to put sympathy aside. This is a place of justice, not sympathy; and deciding the case in that manner is no more difficult than speaking the truth. I suggest you apply your common sense and do what each one of these witnesses in this case has tried to do—your very best—and if you do that, Tony Verran will walk out of here and live the rest of his life happily and at peace with everything that has happened.

The reason there are six of you, and with all deference to the alternate juror, who will be excused shortly, the reason there are six of you is because of the group's collective strength and wisdom. I know you are going to hear words such as windfall, and you are going to hear those defense words of hard-earned, real dollars. I wrote that down many times. The defense lawyer mentioned those catchwords three times in his opening statement as this trial got under way.

What I really couldn't figure out is how to get you to understand what has really been lost here, because it is no secret that this young man, Tony Verran, is something special. What I am worried about is not being able to show you in real terms how special he is and have you come back with a verdict that is less than adequate. Someone may mistakenly say, "Well, this amount of money will make him feel better. He'll be all right." That is a sympathy verdict, and I am telling you we do not want your sympathy because Tony has had enough sympathy to last a lifetime. What I would like for you to do is think about this example that I thought of just a few moments ago. I wrote it down on this torn piece of paper. Let us just take this example:

A person goes into a jewelry store, and the salesperson says to him or her, "Look, we have this diamond that is perfect. It is really the best we have, the best of the best, and this is how much it is worth." Then the customer is shown another diamond, which looks almost identical to the first diamond. It is about the same size, except it is flawed, but no one can see how flawed. A person cannot really tell how flawed that diamond is by just looking at it. You see, it looks fine and perfect, but it is not. It is just how it appears; it is simply the image that is being projected.

Here, it looks like Tony has not really lost a lot: He can still ski, he can still play tennis, and he can do a lot of things. He is not a cripple, but that, of course, is not our obligation to prove the extent of such a loss, nor is it your duty to talk about whether or not he is a cripple. What is your unmistakable duty in this case is to award a fair and adequate amount of damages in dollar terms that Barnett Bank can understand very well for the loss that occurred. And the judge will make it easier by giving you the applicable law. And if you follow the law, this task, the awesome task of sitting in judgment of another person, can be discharged to the satisfaction of everyone. When that happens, this community will know that once again, the system of justice was tried; and once again, the system of justice prevailed. We talked about runaway verdicts; we talked about other cases; we talked about all of that during jury selection. I suggest this to you: Judge this case on its own merits, because that is what Tony is going to live with for the rest of his life, and these are the elements of damages and considerations you must apply.

The amount of damages to be awarded is your decision. This figure I wrote down on the chalkboard—2035—has to do with the losses sustained in this case. I will explain its meaning to you later. There are two categories of damages. These are all the elements, past damages. It is amazing to review the extent of this terrible and needless tragedy. And for the two years of the past damages, these are the things that you have to look at. Take your time when you deliberate. I will go through them with you now so that it may be easier to follow the verdict form.

Pain and suffering: I will try to remember, as best as I can, but that is why there are so many of you and so few of me, to use your collective memories to recall what you heard from the witness stand. Tony's girlfriend, Melissa Horton, talked about the fact that Tony really keeps things to himself, keeps his emotions inside. There have been pictures showing dried blood on the pavement at the scene of the shooting. I brought you other pictures, which are in evidence regarding this case. But I am not able to show you pictures of pain and suffering, only the results. It is not something that can be photographed. Tony described his headaches as "gravel inside his head, exploding gravel," or something like that. I do not know how you place a price tag on that type of day in, day out pain and suffering. I just cannot.

One category of damages for your consideration is labeled "past damages." We know that Tony was not right for a few months after this accident. He went to work in June, and I think the defense pointed out that he was "okay" in May, according to the defense who acts much like the jewelry salesperson. The diamond was fine. Look at Tony: He is as good as new, no flaws. The patch is off. He doesn't look so bad. Past damages? How do you put a figure in there? Maybe the bank's lawyer will come up and suggest a figure. They are very good when it comes to money.

Another element of damages is "disfigurement." Tony doesn't look bad to me, but I imagine that is because I know him, and I see what he is like inside. I do not know what disfigurement would be like to live with, maybe like a mask that can't be taken off, causing other people looking at you, wondering which eye to look into. I do not know for the last two years the laughter, sometimes directed as jokes by well-meaning people and sometimes as barbs thrown by malicious people. The pain that comes from disfigurement really doesn't flow well into words or money.

But what about mental anguish? How do you put a dollar figure on that? The loss of capacity for the enjoyment of life is another element of damages for you to consider; and frankly, that really bothers me the most. I mean, I do not know how you, as jurors, can sit there and put a dollar figure on someone's inability to enjoy life. I really do not. And I admire your task ahead of you, because once it is completed, you will have satisfaction in it.

Medical expenses are also a proper award of damages and in that regard, I can help you. Those expenses I can fill in and do so gladly: $8,748.39. And that goes up through August 6, 1987.

The lost earnings: I do not recall specifically what the definitive figure was. I think that Tony said that between February and, I believe, June, he lost something like a thousand to fifteen hundred dollars. So, let us say a thousand dollars. I think it was a thousand, though it might have been fifteen hundred. I can only suggest this to you: I ran some computations about the hours, days, and all of that. I do not recall how many hours there are in two years, but I can tell you every one of them Tony has lived have been filled. Every waking hour he has experienced contains some pain, some anguish, and some suffering—some hours contain more of that than others.

Certainly, despite his brilliance and excellence, there is surely some knowledge that he is not what he was, and that there is some loss of capacity for the enjoyment of life. I do not know what that is worth, but it must be a fair amount that fully compensates for such a tragic loss. I think these aspects are what make life worth living, and I ask that you use your best judgment and return a fair and just verdict on the two years of past damages.

Remarkably, Tony's words describing that past were, "I thought I was going to die. I was so afraid. I was sick to my stomach. I asked the first person in the hospital if I had lost my eye, and I asked the doctors if I going to see again. There has never been a day when I haven't thought about the loss of my vision and the threat of blindness."

You are going to hear from the defense on that score. They will be quick to say Tony hasn't lost his vision. That is true, but the thought and fear were there then and continue to be experienced every single day by this young, brave man.

One of the witnesses talked about the road that I wanted to travel. He unknowingly said something that really helped me out. He said that Tony had lost his "spare tire." And I realized this was all about the road of life that every person must travel. This road of life has been pretty well defined for Tony over the past two years, pretty well defined. Tony traveled that road *without a spare tire* and now he is here. He *can* see. If I dropped my notes on the floor, you can bet that Tony Verran is going to pick them up and help me. That is all he has done for his entire life, from high school when he started working after graduation, to when he turned down the scholarships all the way through his college graduation. He chose to go to work. All he has ever done is be dependable and helpful.

Tony didn't come in here and ask for your sympathy. He asked you for justice, and this case demands it, just *screams* for the need to give justice. So, let me suggest to you that thankfully, that spare tire was not needed for the first two years following the loss of his eye. But still, I do not know what you would put in terms of a figure for the two years of hell he has gone through.

Today, in this sacred house of truth, let us talk about future damages. Let us talk about future pain and suffering. Let us talk about future disability.

Let us talk about permanent disfigurement, continued mental anguish, and loss of capacity for life. Let us talk about it in terms we can all understand—47.5 years, the projected length of his life expectancy. That makes Tony about seventy-three when he goes to his grave.

I was watching Willard Scott on the *Today* show when I got up this morning. He keeps showing more and more pictures every morning of people living to be a hundred. I hope that everyone lives to be a hundred, but I do not think that is going to happen; so, accepting that fact and accepting that the normal age limit is all we can project into the future, I suggest to you that based upon the evidence admitted before you, that 47.5 years from now Tony will leave this life and pass on. But it is the *quality* of that life that really demands your attention. Forty-seven and a half years, what do you put on these figures? Forty-seven and a half years amount to approximately 416,100 hours. And I say, "Well, how do I put that in terms of pain and suffering? How much is a migraine headache three times a month worth to Tony Verran?" I can't tell you. I do not know. Well, what is the minimum wage? I asked Tony because he has worked at minimum wage for a long time. He said, "$3.35 an hour." Three dollars and thirty-five cents an hour, let us just say three dollars. All right, three dollars times 416,100 hours is what? Do I need to fill that in? Minimum wage, and that is excluding my hope that he goes on to get a Ph.D., or takes my job as a lawyer. I hope he comes into court and shows what a one-eyed person can do. And I hope nothing happens to him along the way.

But what is the loss he undeniably suffered worth? I invite the defense to come up and say any amount is too much. Some of you, as jurors, put a fair figure in there and others still may look at it and say, "Boy! That is a lot of money!" But I remind you, this is Tony's only opportunity to receive compensatory damages for the rest of his life, because in fifteen years, twenty years from now, he can't come back and say, "Wait a minute! Wait a minute! I deserve more money." And I want you to assume just for the moment that Tony doesn't go blind. That is an assumption I do not have a right to make. And I will not ask you to assume that for purposes of your verdict.

Pain and suffering, future disability, I do not know what Tony will be disabled from doing. Just use your own judgment. I do not know how much that is worth, those activities he would have once enjoyed and has now lost. I really can't put a price tag on disfigurement for 47.5 years; I do not know what he does for his blind, dead eye. Does he have the eye taken out? In effect, that would be the second time. That is the irony of this. That is the terrible beauty of a nightmare. You know, on the one hand, it captivates your imagination as you sleep, and on the other, it scares you. Well, I suggest this is what this young man has gotten now. He has two choices: Leave it in and be disfigured or take it out and be disfigured.

Negligence in this case is not an issue. We are talking about damages. A penetrating eye wound is the leading cause of sympathetic ophthalmia to the good eye, and the second cause that may jeopardize the good eye is further surgical procedures. So, now, he has the choice of taking another chance. Sure, let us take the eye out and see if anything happens because, look, if he makes it through the first three months or six months or a year, and then after forty years, he doesn't have to worry about it. The defense lawyers are going to say, "Well, he doesn't really look that bad, and if he does look that bad, he could get a false eye." I will leave it for the defense to make that awful argument.

Mental anguish? I simply can't put a price there. How worried do you think Tony is every day? How much is that worth? I do not know. I think we are talking seven figures, one million dollars. I have said that for a long time. But you jurors are going to say it now, and it will have the force and effect of the law: *seven figures in this case.* I feel good about that.

Loss of capacity for the enjoyment of life: Again, over 47.5 years, it is overwhelming. I cannot fathom that. It is beyond my comprehension. But once again, I am not the one sitting there at the table; it is the client. I am the lawyer, and I will move on to another case. What is that total? Your verdict form is going to include those elements we talked about, and it is going to basically ask you one question: How much is this case worth? That is the only question that is really going to be asked.

Remember Dr. Peter Hammerschmidt, the economist who was also Tony's professor? His quick but generalized approach used the cost of a house as an example. A house that cost $50,000 in 1966 costs $160,000 in 1986. I have been to enough movie shows to be shocked about the cost of things. When my wife and I went to a movie the other day, it cost $9.00 for each of us to get in. I know twenty years ago, I could get into a movie a lot cheaper. I do not know what the defense wants to say as far as damages and all that, but let me tell you what the judge will instruct you. It is, as a matter of law, your responsibility to follow those instructions. The court's guidance makes it easy. Future damages have to be reduced to present value, those anticipated values, and those dollars of the future, you should reduce in your award and that process was explained by the economist who testified in this case.

Let me just run through it very quickly, for the future effect of those dollars today is only limited in reducing to these elements, and I will fill these in for you, future lost earnings. We *haven't* proved Tony is going to lose any future income. In fact, we have proved that this young man is going to try his guts out to make it. This is how much I want you to award for loss of future earnings or earning capacity: zero. Tony is going to work until he is sixty-five, and he is going to work if he has to crawl there. As for any career as a tennis professional? I doubt if he would have ever been Arthur Ashe or Stan Smith or any of those great tennis players. He was just a kid on the college tennis team. But he was the first person on the practice court, and he was the last one to leave. He was, and is, a young man who always gives everything his best shot. Future lost earnings? We ask for nothing.

Future medical expenses? Other than routine and periodic eye examinations, there probably won't be any. I doubt Tony will ever risk having his eye removed, and so we ask for nothing in the way of damages.

Now, I suppose it is time to explain that number of "2035" that I wrote on the chalkboard at the beginning of my final argument. That number represents the year 2035. That will be the year, if Tony lives his full life, in which he will die at a ripe old age in his late seventies. And every day from now until then, he will live with the verdict and pronouncement of judgment you are about to render.

I think a jury award of one million dollars is adequate. I added some things together trying to put in my own mind what I would value this case at, if I were sitting as a juror, which I am not. That figure is totally, totally my opinion. It includes the past and the future. It includes everything. That is not evidence, but that is a number that I can live with.

In summation, the truth as I learned it, as I was growing up, from my father, is very easy to recognize when you see it. It is very easy to understand when it is told to you, and when you touch it, you know what it feels like. You know, the truth is absolutely wonderful, and if the truth prevails here, you'll return a large verdict against the Barnett Bank in favor of Tony Verran, not because of any other reason than you are doing your duty. And I think that is all we can ask.

It may be the hardest thing you may ever have to do: to sit in judgment of people. But you have to do it. I want to leave you with this one thought. Please do not be restricted and do not be afraid. Do not be restricted by the number that I gave you, because if you think it is too high, reduce it; and if you think it is too low, increase it. Do not be afraid. Just do what is right.

Thank you.

An Eye Toward the Future

· · · · · · ·

We had done well in the trial, and I felt the evidence was clear, if the jury wanted to seize it. Most of the time when the court made a ruling, it seemed to go our way, though Judge Penick was very fair to both sides. His demeanor and presence ensured the proceedings had been orderly and without incident. The jury had been allowed to view the case without disruption or excessive breaks in the flow of witnesses and documents that made up the evidence. The jurors had been riveted to the case from the first moments of the trial.

The defense never made any real headway against our case or our theory that the bank had a problem, knew the facts, and decided to gamble that another incident like the one that happened to Kenneth Hansen wouldn't happen again...and they had lost. Tragically, Tony had lost, too. The bank's defensive theory was vague and suggested nothing more than the idea that, "Well, crime happens. It is the responsibility of the police, and the banking industry cannot be liable for what occurred outside banks or in their parking lots after hours." Now, the verdict was in the hands of the jury.

After the closing arguments were given and the jurors retired, the judge retired to chambers and the clerk, court reporter, and bailiff left the courtroom to take a break while the jury began its deliberations. There had been a large number of spectators, but after summations they had gone. The bank's representatives and the insurance adjuster stayed behind huddled with the defense lawyers. The settlement offer was increased to $300,000. Once again, I declined to advise Tony as to whether or not he should accept it; and once again, no advice was needed. He turned the offer down.

As the settlement drama was playing out, the jury remained behind closed doors in deliberations. After two hours, the jurors knocked three times on the door of the jury room, signifying a verdict had been reached. Everyone returned to the courtroom and the tension could actually be felt in the air. The lead defense lawyer, a seasoned and well-respected courtroom adversary, immediately motioned to me, indicating he wished to talk one last time. I stood up and asked Judge Penick for a five-minute recess before the jury was called back into the courtroom to deliver its verdict. He consented and instructed the bailiff to inform the jurors they would be summoned in a few minutes' time.

I could see the look of frustration in the lawyers' eyes as I stood by the defense table and it was explained that a substantial offer would be made if an understanding could be reached that my client would be willing to accept such an amount. In trial practice, the drill that was being played out is called "fishing." It goes something like this: The defense asks, "If we offer x-amount of dollars, will your client accept?" Young, inexperienced lawyers sometimes fall victim to the ploy. If the answer is yes, more than occasionally the defense team comes back and says something to the effect of, "Well, we couldn't get x-amount of dollars, but we do have y-amount of dollars." The y-amount is always a lesser sum. "Will your client accept our settlement offer?"

I don't "fish" in courtrooms or in my law practice. I fish only on my boat. My response in Tony's case was direct and to the point. "I don't discuss settlement offers until an amount is offered. What are you saying? We don't have time for games. Make a definitive offer or let's get on with the jury verdict."

Before anyone else could respond, the senior trial lawyer said in an even monotone, "Five hundred thousand dollars...and we'll call it a day."

I looked at him thoughtfully, hiding a slight smile, before I replied, "I'll need a minute or two to discuss this with Tony." Then I walked slowly back to our long, dark-wooded counsel table. It had been cleared off, and the only thing remaining on its worn surface was the blank verdict form. It had become my habit to fill the form in as the jury's verdict was read. At that point, it was still very, very blank. "Tony," I began as I turned to face him, "they have offered $500,000."

For the first time, I could see hesitation and even a little confusion in Tony's face. "That's a tremendous amount of money, Steve. I mean, it could turn a lot of things around for me," he said thoughtfully. Then he hesitated for just a second before asking quietly, "And it's tax-free, right?"

That was certainly a question an economics major might ask, I thought as I answered him, "Yes and yes. It's a helluva lot of money, and because it's compensatory damages for your pain, suffering, and disfigurement, there would be no taxation. So, what do you want me to tell them?" I made sure my voice was soft, but direct.

The young man nervously glanced around the courtroom, and then back at me, "Steve, what do you think? What should I do?"

My voice remained low. "Tony, I have told you twice before, this is your decision, not mine. I know how much an amount of money like that can mean to you, and I realize it's an awful lot to risk. But you have to decide this one for yourself."

"I know, Steve, I know," Tony said humbly, looking down at the blank verdict form. "I have trusted you from the beginning, and I trust you now. But I really would appreciate knowing what you think. Please."

I could stay silent no more. "Tony, we have sweated blood to get the case this far. I think the trial has gone extremely well. I believe the jury is with us. Mostly, I can't imagine not letting these jurors decide this case, as opposed to the bank. You need to trust the jury. If you can do that, and if you are prepared to live with that decision for the rest of your life, what are we waiting around for?"

His smile stretched from ear to ear, lighting his face with confidence. "You're right. What are we waiting for."

I stood up and addressed the small group clustered at the defense table. "Gentlemen? Mr. Verran thanks you for your offer. He has decided to decline it." I didn't wait for a reaction before turning to the judge. "Your Honor, we are ready to accept the jury verdict. If it please the Court, we ask the jury be returned."

"Very well, Counsel." Judge Penick's words were deliberate and formal. "Bring the jury in, Mr. Bailiff."

Although we felt the trial had gone our way, I had learned early in my career that a verdict is never certain until it is rendered. Tony had told me just moments before that the verdict would be the most important thing that had ever happened in his life. He also told me we needed to win, because he wanted the case to have an impact on society. For two years after the attack, he had keenly observed many banks in the area in which he lived. Many had overgrown bushes and tall foliage. More than a few had inadequate lighting around their night depositories. Nothing had really changed since he had been attacked, even with the publicity the case had received. We both knew that a jury verdict in the case was absolutely essential if any meaningful changes were to occur. Hopefully, our successful efforts would save lives.

With the jurors sitting patiently in their seats, and after a quick review and inspection of the verdict form by the judge, the clerk began reading the jury's decision. I could sense the verdict as soon as the jurors began filing into the courtroom. Tony and I both held our breath. We also held each other's hands under the table in anticipation of the moment.

The clerk's words confirmed that we had won. The jury awarded Tony one million dollars, plus the $8,748.39 for the medical bills he had sustained. Every penny. Judge Penick graciously thanked the jurors for their invaluable service, complimented the lawyers and adjourned the proceedings. I embraced Tony with a bear hug, and we both nearly squeezed the air out of each other. I was so very proud of him. Hell, he had a better "vision" of life than most two-eyed people.

I walked across the courtroom to the defense table and shook each of the lawyers' hands. I commended their professionalism and the integrity they had demonstrated in representing the interests of their client. In most cases, I make it a practice to show such respect. I believe in taking the high road whenever possible. Of course, in those cases I try against attorneys who refuse to play fairly or otherwise act unprofessionally, I don't even acknowledge their presence, let alone extend my hand.

It is a special moment when a jury verdict is rendered in a courtroom. Every real trial lawyer knows the absolute truth at times like these—there is always a winner and there is always a loser. In these battles of life, there are no ties.

Although Tony and I embraced each other in the thrill of victory, we knew it was bittersweet. Tony's sight in his right eye would never be restored. He could never recapture what had been lost. But we also knew the case was significant because the bank had been held liable for a substantial judgment as the result of a third-party criminal act. The use of automated teller machines and night depositories had become widespread, and it was our position that banks should be obligated to provide proper security measures and precautions to protect the safety of all customers using a bank's outdoor facilities after hours.

The verdict was front-page news in the morning newspapers. A couple of hours after the papers came out, I received a telephone call I will never forget. A man named Larry—of Larry's Landscaping, or something like that—was calling me from St. Petersburg. He told me he had called simply to thank me. I assumed he had an interest in consumer issues, bank safety, or some other profound aspect of the case. I was wrong. As Larry explained, he was calling to thank me for the business he had just received. It seemed that shortly after his landscaping office opened, the holding company that was responsible for all of the twenty-six Barnett Bank branches located in Pinellas County had put in a work order for all bushes and foliage to be cut to eighteen inches around every single one of their ATMs and night depositories. I was filled with satisfaction as I realized once again that people can make a real difference…and I was happy for Larry, too. I half expected "Ed the Electrician" to telephone, too. I learned later that all the lighting around the various ATMs and night depositories had been inspected, repaired, replaced and—in Barnett and most of the other competing banks—enhanced.

Epilogue
· · · · · · ·

There are so many things we take for granted, like running water, electricity, and telephone service, but when they are temporarily taken from us during an outage, we suddenly become aware of the value and comfort that normalcy provides. We have other gadgets, machinery, and conveniences that we also take for granted—just like our public utilities—although there was a time when we didn't have these luxuries, including automated teller machines and night depositories. Frequently, I wonder how in the world we ever got along without the little conveniences that make our lives so much easier.

One of playwright and author George Bernard Shaw's most oft-quoted remarks perhaps best describes my view of a visionary: "Some people see the way things are and ask, Why? I see the way things might be

Robbery victim awarded $1-million

By PAUL L. McGORRIAN
Times Staff Writer

CLEARWATER — A jury awarded $1-million Thursday to a man who was shot and blinded in one eye while making a night deposit at Barnett Bank in St. Petersburg two years ago.

Anthony Verran blamed the bank for his injury because the night drop was in a high-crime area, was poorly lit and was shrouded by overgrown shrubbery.

Moments before the verdict was read — after the jury had deliberated for more than an hour — the insurer for Barnett

Bank of Pinellas County offered to settle the case for $500,000.

But Verran, a 26 year-old senior majoring in economics at Eckerd College, turned down the offer because he said he thought he deserved more compensation for his injuries.

"It feels right and just," he said of the jury's award. "I think it's fair."

On Feb. 20, 1986, Verran was working part-time for the Plaza Theatres on First Avenue S in St. Petersburg when he and the theater's assistant manager took the night's earnings and deposited them

at Barnett Bank's night drop at 3100 Central Ave.

Verran was assaulted by two men who jumped out from behind nearby bushes, and one of them shot Verran in the face. He spent four days in the hospital and is permanently blind in his right eye. Attorneys said it's possible — though not likely — that he could lose sight in his left eye, too.

His companion was not seriously injured.

Please see **ROBBERY** 8-B

and ask, Why not?" I vividly recall the eulogy of Bobby Kennedy by his brother, Ted. Using the same phraseology, he changed the wording ever so slightly, and in my view, created a sentiment I fully embrace: "Some people see the way things are and ask, Why? I *dream* things that never were and ask, Why not?"

Too often, the terrible truth is that change doesn't take place until a harsh reality illuminates the problem. Tony Verran never intended for his savage blinding to be the source of enlightenment that was needed to revamp the manner in which the banking industry did business—it just turned out that way.

Over the past few decades, citizens have increasingly called for greater protection from criminal activity. That protection should be provided at all reasonable cost by putting people first—not profits, aesthetics, or convenience. What happened to Tony confirmed my conclusion that a tragic price seemingly must be paid to compel corporate America to make the changes necessary for our public good. Tony's case was one of tough issues and even tougher decisions, and to address the societal questions that were raised it was impossible to compromise with the bank. There simply was no middle ground. But now, in large part because of the verdict in Tony Verran's case and others like it, appropriate landscaping and adequate lighting around ATMs and night depositories have become the standard in the banking industry. Security precautions have taken precedence over aesthetic considerations, and video cameras and surveillance equipment—once perceived as unneeded and out of the ordinary—are commonplace.

Post-Trial

· · · · · · ·

A fter the verdict, the defense had moved for a new trial, citing a variety of grounds, none of which I believed had the legal or factual merit necessary to set aside the decision of the jury. In response, I moved to renew our earlier motion to allow a trial on punitive damages. Mindful that Judge Penick had taken the matter under advisement, I argued that the subsequent evidence introduced during the trial had demonstrated a reckless, willful, and wanton disregard of safety to others. I urged the trial judge to allow us to go forward with a jury trial to consider monetary damages that would both punish the defendant and deter others from behaving in this fashion. I urged the court to consider the overwhelming nature of the evidence the trial had produced and to rule favorably on the motion he was still considering.

Judge Penick was a retired high-ranking military officer who knew right from wrong through instinct and through decades of hands-on experience. He was a conservative trial judge who had been on the bench for many years. Still, I was optimistic. Clearly, he had been bothered by the bank's conduct and the evidence in the case. His rulings on the post-trial motions were swift and decisive. Barnett Bank's motion for a new trial was denied. Our motion for a new trial on punitive damages was granted. It was an overwhelming victory.

Confronted with this catastrophic development, the bank and its defense team would, I knew, be reeling. It was time to make a move. My proposition was simple: If the bank would pay every dollar of the jury's verdict—the entire one million dollars—we would file for a dismissal of the case and walk away. I added another term to the deal. Since banks were so fond of deadlines for customers, I gave one to the defendant. The money had to be paid by hand delivery of an actual check to my office within seventy-two hours. The deadline would be five o'clock on the upcoming Friday. No extensions.

That Thursday, I received a telephone call from one of the lead defense lawyers advising me that Barnett Bank had accepted the offer. I was assured the money would be paid on time. The next afternoon at 4:50, ten minutes before my deadline, a courier arrived at the law firm with the million-dollar check.

Tony Verran became very interested in the law and its wonderful ability to help people. After earning his bachelor's degree at Eckerd College, he enrolled in law school at Emory University in Atlanta, Georgia. While there he earned his Juris Doctorate and Master of Business Administration, graduating with highest honors.

Currently, Tony lives in California and is married to a beautiful young woman named Karen. Recently, the couple had their first child. He enjoys success as a lawyer and entrepreneur. Tony is active in charity work and continues to help the underprivileged and handicapped. He opened a pro-bono law firm and provides free legal services to the poor. Tony and I share other things in common. He tells me that whenever he passes an ATM or night depository, he smiles. So do I.

■ ■ ■ ■ ■ ■ ■

Tallahassee, Florida
December 27, 1967

Dearest Uncle Bob,
Every year at this time, I remember that I should write
you, but each year I manage to let time pass without
doing it. The other day, our pastor used an illustration
of how children always write Santa Claus what they
want and flood the post office with letters before
Christmas, but when a letter to Santa Claus came to
the attention of the post office in February, they were
surprised to find a thank you note in a child's handwriting. This reminded me that like most children, I
had not thanked Santa Claus. I want to take this
opportunity to say thank you for all the many times
you were Santa Claus to four little girls. I know words
have a way of sounding empty, but from my heart I
want to say thank you for all the things you did to
make me happy for so many years. I know I can't
repay you, but in some way, I may make another child
happy. We went down to see mother Saturday…she
showed me the picture of you and your family. Your
wife and little girl are beautiful…I do hope that you
will come down to Florida soon and come to see us. We
would like to see you. Thank you again.

With Love,
Martha Jane (McReynolds) Johnson

Bob Smith dancing with Alma (left) and his daughter, Deborah, at Deborah's wedding.

CHAPTER SEVEN

A Deadly Cure

Long before daylight, in the very early hours of October 5, 1994, an elderly gentleman named Robert "Bob" Smith lay quietly on a single bed at Sabal Palms Nursing Home in Largo, Florida. For weeks on end, he hadn't been able to speak or stand, and he could only move when someone turned him from one side to the other in an effort to prevent bedsores. Every few moments, his eyes slightly opened almost as if he was watching the ethereal figures of nurses moving around him. The nurses must have seemed like shadowy apparitions in his fading mind as they checked his pulse, blood pressure, and respiration rate, all of which were rapidly beginning to shut down. A staunch Southern Baptist who had once served as a deacon in his church, Bob was nearing the end of his time.

As she had been since the day they met, Alma was right by his side. In the awful coldness of the stark white hospital where her beloved husband would meet his death, she recalled when it had all started. Alma and Bob had their first date in 1965. She had been pretty then—at least that's what she was often told. She had the classic features of a North Carolina-born Southern belle: high, finely honed cheekbones, dark hair, beautiful brown eyes that were wide and innocent, and skin that glowed with the freshness of youth.

The night of their first date, Bob had come roaring up to her house in a spiffy four-door Lincoln Continental. From the moment they met, it had been love at first sight. Alma, who had grown up on a North Carolina farm, was a young widow, and Bob's first wife had died in an automobile accident the same year Alma lost her husband. The pains and heartaches each had experienced healed into a wonderful happiness and a shared love that blossomed. Although Bob was seventeen years older than Alma, age had made no difference.

Alma was momentarily pulled back from her memories when a nurse came silently into the room, picked up his arm to take his pulse, and attentively watched the seconds tick off as Bob drifted further away. The nurse seemed intent on minimizing her presence and gently smiled at Alma as she left the room. Alma was sure she had made the right choice in becoming Bob's partner. Marrying him had been the best decision of her life. She could not bear the thought of a life without him.

Bob Smith had grown up in Chattahoochee, a tiny speck of a town in Florida's panhandle. Born on October 21, 1910, he was one of nine children and was extremely close to his brothers and sister. He and his siblings spent many long, lazy summer days fishing with cane poles, skipping rocks across ponds, and climbing the massive, ancient oaks that dotted North Florida's landscape. Bob's mother died when he was only sixteen years old. The torment of cancer had racked her body unmercifully until she cried out in pain and begged for her life to end. He stayed with her through the whole ordeal, holding her hand and touching her face until she took her last breath. On those few occasions when he talked to Alma about it, tears always welled in his eyes.

Shortly after his mother's death, Bob joined the navy, eventually serving in the cool blue Pacific on the exotic island of Guam. While he was there he got the news that his father had been in a dreadful accident in Apalachicola, where he was working with the railroad. A crane had been moving a boxcar when the cable on the crane somehow slipped. The boxcar had come crashing down and his father had taken the full brunt of the massive impact.

For almost six weeks, Bob's dad fought for his life in the hospital, his injuries so extensive and critical that it was a miracle he survived at all. Bob had told Alma of the sickness in the pit of his stomach that stayed with him as he traveled the seemingly endless miles to the Apalachicola hospital where his father lay dying. Now, as he lay in his own hospital bed, Alma recalled Bob's description of the time he had kneeled by the bedside of his own father. When he arrived his dad had turned his head and looked at him, softly whispering, "I knew my Bobby would come." Two hours later, his father closed his eyes for the last time. Sitting alone with the man she loved so much, Alma wondered how much time her Bob had left.

Bob's breath started coming in deep rasps, and she tenderly wiped a cold cloth across his forehead again and again. As he struggled for air, she felt strangely helpless. She thought about just how far in life her wonderful Bob had gone. Overcoming his poor upbringing, the agonizing deaths of his mother and father, the unfortunate death of his first wife, and even the Great Depression, Bob Smith had been very successful. During their most sensitive talks Bob confessed that he had succeeded beyond his wildest dreams, especially in finding the love of his life in Alma.

In his prime, he had been a large, robust man, more than six feet tall and a muscular 220 pounds. Aging had given him pure white hair. His face had few lines and full, rounded cheeks and often glowed with a friendly smile. His hazel eyes radiated wisdom, kindness, and a gentle warmth. He was a man who was instantly likable. Very little of the hard work and challenges he had been through during his lifetime showed on his softened features.

Bob had always had a natural ability with people, and success had evolved into a career pattern. He had gotten his start in Atlanta, Georgia, in banking and gradually moved into the commercial marketplace. Before his retirement in 1968, he made it all the way up the ladder, one rung at a time, to the position of President of the Pepsi-Cola Bottling Company. The couple of years he had spent "seeing the world" and fulfilling his wartime service with the navy had been his only break from a lifetime of fifteen-hour workdays in the business world. Alma had always thought him a perfectionist, and many was the time he had nearly driven her crazy with his penchant for getting the details "just right."

The marriage gave Bob and Alma a gorgeous daughter, Deborah. Debbie was born with the brown eyes and dark hair of her mother. He had been fifty-seven years old and Alma forty when Debbie was born. Their daughter brought freshness and renewed youth to each of them. Debbie was their only child, and Bob had worshipped her for over thirty years.

As he became sicker, he had voiced repeated concern at the thought of leaving his "little girl." Who would protect her and take care of her? Alma thought of Debbie's sweetness and caring since her father had become sick over the last few months. She and Alma had been his voice when he could no longer speak and his legs when he could no longer walk. Both his wife and daughter had been much stronger, mentally and emotionally, than either would have ever imagined.

When their daughter was growing up, Bob and Alma had secretly worried whether Debbie had inherited her father's strength and determination, but her actions over the past few months had taken that concern away.

Sometimes when Debbie gave him baths and fed him, he would attempt to smile at her as she spoke softly to him. Most times, however, the smiles just couldn't force their way onto the frozen mask that used to be his face. Alma recalled how hard Debbie had been crying the day before when she left the hospital room. Alma was sure he had wanted to tell his daughter how much she meant to him, but no words would come.

Debbie's son, Stephen, had been the apple of Bob's eye since the day he was born. Bob adored his young grandson and treated him just like his own child. When Debbie's first marriage failed and she began working two jobs to help make ends meet, Stephen had moved in with them. Bob had taken his grandson with him everywhere he went and the two became inseparable. Stephen's presence had made Bob and Alma's marriage even closer and made them feel like young parents again. Many evenings, Alma read Bible stories to Stephen while Bob, always close by, listened and watched his grandson learn about Adam and Eve, Noah's Ark, and the goodness of life.

The memories faded and an unwelcome awareness of Bob's surroundings returned. For a moment, Bob seemed to summon what strength he had left; his eyes flickered open and he made a slight guttural sound as if he was trying to call out. Almost as quickly his eyelids closed and he fell silent again except for the short gasps of breath that now seemed so difficult. She knew it wouldn't be long now. She would go home for a few hours of sleep and return before sunup.

Her face streaked with tears, she held his hand, then leaned down across the bed and kissed him delicately on the lips. "Good night, my sweet husband," she softly whispered. "If I don't see you in the morning, I'll see you in heaven. I love you." As Alma went to the door, she glanced back at him, her dark brown eyes filled with love and sorrow.

Just before three o'clock in the morning, his breathing—so hard and labored—began to shorten and come in soft wisps. The attending nurse lifted his left hand and wrapped her warm fingers around his wrist, then placed a stethoscope against his chest. She shook her head, saying in a low, quiet voice, "It won't be long now. His pulse is almost gone. There's nothing more we can do for him."

Another nurse moved quickly to the bedside telephone. "I'm going to call his wife and tell her to get here as fast as she can."

"Tell her there's no need to hurry," the first nurse said in a low voice as she felt for some sign of a pulse. "His heart has stopped. He's gone."

The two nurses gently pulled a sheet over Bob's head, turned off the light, and quietly closed the door.

Comfort Measures

· · · · · · ·

Bob Smith's story is one of intense heartache and pain. His rendezvous with death began in early March of 1994. Bob was eighty-three years old and in good health. He and Alma had driven to Durham, North Carolina, from their home in Belleair, Florida, to attend a funeral. Alma's sister, Elizabeth Cooke, had just lost her husband, Bryant, and the Smiths had decided to make the journey in order to comfort Elizabeth and to help her with the arrangements.

The day after the funeral, Bob awoke with what he termed "fuzzy vision" in his right eye. He had had cataract surgery several years before, but the fuzziness seemed nothing like that. He became concerned enough that he decided to seek medical treatment while they were still in Durham. "Bob was well during Bryant's funeral," Alma later told me in interviews as we prepared for trial. "He had driven all the way to North Carolina from our home in Belleair. Everything was fine until he woke up the next day and was having difficulty seeing out of his right eye."

The next day, Bob drove to the North Carolina Eye and Ear Hospital, where Alma's sister had arranged an appointment. Other than the problem with his right eye, he had no symptoms. Bob told the doctor that he had previously had cataract surgery, and explained that the diabetes he had had for several years was under control. He also told the ophthalmologist about his prostrate cancer, which had been diagnosed and treated in 1989. It had been in remission ever since.

Two doctors examined Bob, and both came to the conclusion that he most likely had suffered a small cerebral stroke in an area of the brain consistent with his symptoms of blurred vision. The doctors offered to treat Bob with stroke medications there and then, but also gave him the option of returning to Florida and seeking care from his family physician. Well enough to travel, Bob decided to return home.

During the examination in North Carolina, one of the doctors raised the remote possibility that Bob's prostate cancer had recurred and perhaps metastasized. Metastasis, in Bob's case, would have meant that the cancer in his prostate gland had returned and spread to other parts of his body through the bloodstream or the lymph node system. The doctors assured him that metastasis of prostate cancer to the brain was extremely rare, and it was an almost certainty that Bob had suffered a small stroke. As a precaution, Bob was advised to have his physicians in Florida consider both possibilities.

Before the couple left North Carolina for Florida, with Alma at the wheel because of Bob's obscured eyesight, he called Debbie to let her know they were coming home. "Daddy told me that the doctor had examined him," Debbie said in deposition testimony prior to trial. "He said the doctor thought he had suffered a mild stroke. The day my parents came home, Daddy was still having some difficulty seeing out of his right eye, but by the next day, his vision had gotten back to normal. Although he looked and seemed fine, we all agreed he should be checked out by his doctors."

First, Bob visited St. Luke's Eye Clinic in Largo, where he had had his cataract surgery several years before. He brought with him the medical records from the North Carolina Eye and Ear Hospital. After he was examined and the records reviewed, the doctor agreed with the diagnosis that Bob, indeed, had experienced a small stroke.

On March 16, Bob sought further treatment with Dr. Granger Benson, who practiced at the Diagnostic Clinic in Largo. Dr. Benson had found the initial prostate cancer in 1989. Because Bob felt that Dr. Benson had saved his life before, he wanted his opinion concerning the stroke that had been diagnosed. Bob was told that short of a biopsy, the most reliable way to detect active prostate cancer was a prostate-specific antigen (PSA) test. The patient's blood would be drawn and measured for an antigen, or type of protein, produced by prostate gland cells at high levels in the presence of cancer. Dr. Benson immediately ordered the PSA analysis for Bob. The level was very low, a result consistent with complete remission and an absence of any active prostate cancer.

On March 25, to complete the diagnostic workup, an MRI was also done. MRI, or magnetic resonance imaging, creates an image of internal tissues and is especially good with soft tissues such as those of the brain, which don't show up well in x-rays. Dr. Linton Herbert of the Largo Diagnostic Clinic interpreted the radiological studies. Dr. Herbert was a graduate of Harvard Medical School and specialized in the field of radiology. Through his deposition testimony, we later discovered he had not been specially trained in the reading of MRIs, and that he basically learned how to read them through seminars and correspondence courses. According to Dr. Herbert's interpretation of the MRI, Bob had "two masses. The appearance strongly suggests metastatic tumor." Fancy talk for the deadly message that he believed Bob Smith had two cancerous tumors in his brain. Dr. Herbert also said the tumors were incurable.

Bob's treating physicians were informed of Dr. Herbert's interpretation of the MRI study. When the diagnosis was explained to him, Bob was devastated. Debbie remembered the shock and despair in his voice when he told her. When her father called, he was crying as he explained how the doctors had told him he had malignant brain tumors and were calling in a cancer specialist.

Bob was admitted to HCA Medical Center on March 31. For the first time, he saw Dr. David Longacre, an oncologist who examined him and read his medical history. In our preparation for trial, reviewing voluminous medical treatises and consulting several of the best cancer specialists in the world, we learned that the spread (or metastasis) of prostate cancer to the brain is an extremely rare, almost unheard-of occurrence. More troubling, we also learned that Dr. Longacre was not specifically familiar with the spread of this type of cancer to the brain. Nonetheless, Dr. Longacre determined that Bob most likely had brain metastases and recommended that he consult with a radiation oncologist. No biopsies of the suspected brain tumors were ever ordered or performed.

With the diagnoses of Dr. Herbert and Dr. Longacre seemingly confirming each other, Bob Smith agreed to see Dr. Michael Gauwitz, a specialist in radiation oncology, for consideration of palliative whole brain radiation therapy. The term "palliative" means the treatment was intended to ease the pain and allow the patient to more easily tolerate the symptoms of the disease and die in a more comfortable and less anguished manner. Whole brain radiation is not designed to cure the underlying disease, and its administration is an almost certain sign the cancer has been diagnosed as terminal. There is virtually no hope and no chance of living for any substantial period of time once the entire brain has been exposed to radiation.

From the start, Dr. Gauwitz had access to all of Bob's medical records, diagnostic reports, and test results, as well as the opinions of the other physicians who had been involved in his case. Additionally, he was able to personally conduct a complete medical examination. Significantly, Dr. Gauwitz also had a number of diagnostic tools available to further confirm and corroborate the existence of the "brain tumors." It was clear that he could also have ordered a biopsy to be sure of the deadly diagnosis.

Instead, Dr. Gauwitz concurred with the diagnosis of Dr. Longacre and Dr. Herbert that Bob Smith had incurable brain cancer. The immediate treatment of choice, according to Dr. Gauwitz, was palliative whole brain radiation therapy, and he was quite anxious about starting the treatments as soon as possible.

Both Alma and Debbie recommended to Bob that he get a second opinion, around the time the radiation treatments were to start, but everything happened so fast: The radiation treatments started almost immediately after the diagnosis.

"It was boom, bam, boom, all within a span of three days," Debbie had explained to me in our initial conversations. "My mother and I both suggested to my father, 'We need to slow down a minute. Let's stop and look at this thing.' But Daddy kept telling us, 'No, Dr. Longacre is in a big hurry. He told me that you have to treat these things right away and that we can't fool around. He and Dr. Gauwitz told me that we have to start radiation treatments immediately, and I have to trust them.'"

The whole brain radiation therapy began on April 5, which was Good Friday. Debbie again talked to Dr. Longacre about the idea of getting a second opinion to ascertain if the MRIs might be showing a stroke—which had been the most probable diagnosis at the outset—rather than cancerous lesions, but the physician told her that he was certain that Bob had malignant brain tumors.

Bob immediately underwent three weeks of whole brain radiation. It was commenced, administered, and completed by Dr. Gauwitz. Toward the end of the three weeks of daily radiation, Bob started suffering bouts of nausea. He began to lose the strength in his legs and had trouble walking or climbing stairs. The family also noticed that he was having difficulty concentrating on even simple things. When Bob complained of his problems, he was told his symptoms were temporary and probably due to an interaction of the radiation with his diabetes medication. He told Alma that he thought the radiation had done something to his mind, because he was unable to think clearly.

In startling detail, Alma later recalled those days during and after the radiation when something terribly wrong emerged. Following the radiation treatments, Bob's condition worsened. He needed a cane to walk. His appetite became virtually nonexistent. On the rare occasions he ate, he could not keep the food down. Then his hair began falling out.

Bob became very emotional, and his family saw him cry for hours at a time. At night, he would awaken and complain that he was seeing and hearing strange things. Bob's downhill slide got worse, and Alma became very frightened.

One day late in the spring, Bob was at home sitting at his desk and trying to work on his checkbook. Debbie recounted the incident in her testimony. "All of a sudden, Daddy began yelling, 'There is something trying to get out of my brain! This radiation has done something to my brain! I can't think! There is something trying to get out of my head! My skull is going to explode!' I tried to calm him and tell him everything was going to be okay, but then he looked at me funny and called me 'Mama.' I said, 'No, Daddy, it's me, Deborah.' Then he said, 'Mama, it's been so long. I missed you so much.'"

With the beginning of summer, there were more frequent visits to the doctors and hospitals as Bob grew sicker and weaker with each day. He became delusional and hallucinated. At times, he became profoundly agitated and would yell and scream loudly at everyone around him. Other times, he would sit quietly in a daze or emit occasional groans of pain.

By the middle of the summer, Alma could no longer care for Bob on her own. Her husband's deteriorating health required his placement in a critical care facility. Dr. Stuart Sinoff had been called in for a consultation. A graduate of Georgetown Medical School, he was a board-certified specialist in neurology with an outstanding reputation. He interviewed and examined Bob and also meticulously reviewed his records and the imaging studies.

Dr. Sinoff was greatly disturbed by what he learned. He read and reread the voluminous medical records and realized that something was terribly wrong. He felt certain that Bob did not have prostate carcinoma that had spread to the central nervous system and that, tragically, there had never been cancer in his brain. When Dr. Benson—Bob's original prostate cancer doctor—received the results of the MRI and spoke with Dr. Sinoff, he realized that Bob had been diagnosed and treated for a brain cancer that did not exist. While the family was in the intensive care unit, Dr. Benson explained that a "terrible mistake" had been made. Bob had suffered a slight stroke, and the drastic radiation treatments had been unnecessary.

Then the doctors revealed the most devastating news: Irreversible damage had been done. Bob's continual fever meant his hypothalamus, the body's temperature regulator located deep within the brain, had been severely damaged by the radiation treatments and his body could no longer control its own temperature. Dr. Sinoff told the family that the twelve whole brain radiation treatments had badly damaged the lining of the blood vessels in the brain, causing them to disintegrate and become, in Dr. Sinoff's words, "very, very sick." As the radiation damage fully set in, Bob would become much sicker, and he would suffer a very bad death. Everything possible would be done to ease his pain, but there would be no cure, and death was a certainty.

In August, one of the most knowledgeable and senior neurologists in Florida's medical community, Dr. Thomas Harrison, was called in to help. By this time, and in the weeks leading into September, Bob was lapsing in and out of consciousness. For two and three days at a time, he would be in a coma-like state, and then suddenly he would awaken, lucid and talkative, acting almost as if all was normal. It was a horribly cruel and confusing time for Alma, and her life vacillated between hope and heartache. For the first time since she was a young widow, she began to cry herself to sleep.

At the end of September, Bob was admitted to the hospital for the last time. He had become quadriparetic, meaning he had weakness and rigidity in all four limbs. He also suffered from severe encephalopathy— his brain was so weakened and diseased that it functioned only sporadically and, most often, at a very minimal level. Amazingly, he still had moments of consciousness and could even speak, though in an almost muted manner. Dr. Harrison sadly concluded that Bob's death was imminent. He would die within days, if not hours. There was nothing that could be done, and the doctor ordered that "comfort measures" be given.

By the beginning of October, Bob was in Sabal Palms Nursing Home. Completely bedridden, he lay curled up in a fetal position most of the time. He was no longer able to speak coherently, and he communicated with his family only through eye movements, facial gestures, and occasional grunts. He wasn't able to hold anything with his hands, which were permanently frozen and clawed. A feeding tube had been placed in his stomach. Bob kept trying to speak, but nothing logical or understandable would come out. He continued to suffer, and through it all, his loyal and loving wife, daughter, and grandson prayed for a miracle. It did not come.

On October 5, 1994, Bob Smith's suffering finally ended.

The Quest for Redemption—
A Case of Medical Malpractice
∎ ∎ ∎ ∎ ∎ ∎ ∎

When Alma and Debbie came to my office to see me about taking the case, I knew immediately Alma would become my client. She looked much younger than her seventy-plus years, and with her graceful North Carolina accent, she showed the class of a true lady. But her soft demeanor was filled with despondency and sadness. Bob had been eighty-three years old—or, as Alma reminded me, "eighty-three years young"—when he passed away. She and Debbie had spoken with several attorneys before me, but they had all refused to take the case because of his age—and hers as well.

Under Florida law governing medical negligence litigation, Alma would be limited in her damages to funeral expenses, medical bills, and her own pain and suffering. If she died, the case would die with her. Legally, no damages could be sought on behalf of Bob for the horror and agony he endured before his death. Any lawyer's reluctance to accept a case that was so difficult, on both the issues of liability and damages, was understandable. Hell, it was just good sense.

For Alma, the case was not about money. Bob had been very successful and his family was financially sound. Her goal was simple. She wanted to vindicate her husband's death and do her best to help prevent it from happening to someone else. I listened to Bob Smith's family describe his colorful and long life, and then his awful death. Both mother and daughter began to weep as they described the horror of the radiation sickness, the agony of his death, and the devastating effect of his loss on their lives.

After a few moments, I began speaking slowly and methodically, allowing a calmness to settle in. "I have reviewed the volumes of medical records you sent to me before our conference. I have already had medical experts review the case. Bringing a lawsuit against a doctor is an extremely difficult process. We have to convince a jury that an unacceptable mistake was made in caring for the patient. It won't be easy, and the odds are usually against the plaintiff in a case like this—especially given your husband's age. But I am honored you came to me, and I have decided to take your case. I'll do everything I can to help you. What happened to Bob should never have happened. We're going to try to set things straight and make it right."

During the first of the meetings with Alma and Debbie, I brought in my colleague, Ralph Gonzalez, to help me with the case. Ralph joined my firm in 1995. With his Harvard education, intelligence, and warmth, Ralph became a tremendous asset to our law practice. He was initially hired to work with me in a mammoth case involving the State of Florida against America's tobacco companies (see chapter eight) and to become involved in the area of medical malpractice litigation. Throughout the tobacco case, he had proved to be hardworking and loyal. His attention to detail, insight, and legal expertise were invaluable.

Even though Ralph is a dedicated family man, he always gave wholeheartedly of himself to benefit our clients and the firm. He worked tirelessly on the tobacco case and traveled with me virtually nonstop back and forth to West Palm Beach, where Florida's lawsuit had been filed. His understanding wife, Cindy, never once complained about raising their four beautiful children virtually on her own during this spell.

Ralph wanted to help Alma as much as I did. We filed the wrongful death lawsuit in 1996. In essence, it charged that the medical standard of care had been violated by misdiagnosis and radical treatment of a brain cancer that did not exist. The whole brain radiation used as a palliative treatment had caused Bob Smith horrific suffering and a premature death.

Because of the complexity of the case and the number of doctors involved, the preparation of the lawsuit was grueling and time-consuming, lasting more than three years. The trial itself, in the spring of 2000, was combative; the testimony of Alma and Debbie was the only source of human warmth. By and large the case had been a battle of experts and conflicting opinions about extremely complicated medical issues. My summation to the jury needed to be thorough but simple and very clear.

. . . .

The Closing Argument

GOOD MORNING, LADIES AND GENTLEMEN. This is the opportunity I have to summarize the evidence in this case before you begin your deliberations. When we talked in voir dire, we exchanged information about each other, and we learned a little bit about what the case involved. Then we talked, in the opening statement, about what we thought the picture on the puzzle box would portray after all the pieces of the evidence produced in the trial had been put together.

It is with great relief that the burden the lawyers and the parties in this case have carried for the last three and a half years will finally be given to you in just a very short period of time. As the jury in this case, we will all trust in your judgment, wisdom, and sense of justice.

On behalf of everyone involved, I wish to thank you for your time and patience. For over two hundred years, this same process has gone on in courtrooms across America. You recall that during jury selection, some potential jurors expressed the view that maybe professional regulation and regulators should take the place of a jury trial. That maybe we should have fellow medical professionals deal with the conduct of doctors and determine what, if any, penalties or consequences are appropriate. But that is not what our system of justice is all about. Our democracy is founded upon a citizen's right to trial by jury. It is on that fundamental right that we have all come together this day.

When I begin to discuss the evidence, what I believe the evidence has shown, and what has been demonstrated in this trial, remember that you—the jury—are six collective minds and memories, not one. If I forget, misstate, or don't remember something exactly right, each of you, individually, has the opportunity to say, "Wait! That's not how I remember it. No, that's not the way it happened. I was there."

In addition to the notion that maybe somebody other than the jury system should judge the parties' conduct and what should and should not have been done, there was another notion mentioned during jury selection. You may recall it—that doctors—and all people—are entitled to make mistakes. Who could argue with that concept? I will be very candid with you. No one. But the conduct of the defendants will not be judged by other doctors or bureaucrats. It will be up to you, the jury, to determine if the defendants have deviated from an acceptable standard of medical care. At the end of this trial, I anticipate the defense will say to you, and on the verdict form, there will be two other people who you should blame in addition to Dr. Gauwitz and the corporation that employs him.

Don't be surprised. Their names will be Dr. Longacre and Dr. Herbert. What has been shown is that Dr. Longacre, who is an oncologist, was called in, made a decision, and said, "I believe this could be a stroke, but it also could be cancer. And since Robert Smith had prostate cancer back in the late 1980s, he may be having a recurrence. We had better work this patient up."

Dr. Herbert, you recall, was the radiologist who read and interpreted the MRIs as showing that Bob Smith had several cancerous brain tumors. He received his medical education at Harvard, and when he was called to the witness stand, what did he say? "Well," he testified, "I never saw the patient. And my role in the case was that I was the radiologist. That is what I do for a living. I read films. I don't treat the actual patient."

Radiologists and neuroradiologists are the doctors who read and interpret films; that is what they do every day. That is the responsibility they are charged with and that is what patients expect. They perform the MRI procedure that Dr. Herbert went to great lengths to talk about.

The defense will say that Dr. Herbert made a mistake. I agree with them. The evidence shows that he misread the radiology films of Bob Smith. But here is where the rubber hits the road, as the old saying goes. The defense will argue that Dr. Gauwitz was entitled to rely on Dr. Herbert. And since Dr. Herbert said the MRI scans showed metastatic cancer, multiple areas of cancer, Dr. Gauwitz had a right to rely on the radiologist and radiate Bob Smith for a brain cancer he did not have. The defense argues that Dr. Herbert was culpable and Dr. Gauwitz did nothing wrong.

What about the other doctor the defense will blame? Dr. Longacre is the oncologist, a cancer specialist. He knows about cancer. That is his specialty. Dr. Longacre opined that at the end of March, Bob Smith probably had a stroke, but he may have had a recurrence of cancer. Ultimately, he finally concluded it was indeed cancer and not a stroke. As a matter of fact, you heard Dr. Longacre's testimony during the trial. He still believes Bob Smith had cancer.

Late last night in preparing to talk with you here today, it came to me the best way to illustrate to you the difference between a mistake and standard of care. In a lawsuit, you have to show there was an error or a wrongdoing. Then there is a second part that is required. And I am going to tell you how subtly this second part has been brought out by the defense. That is the part called causation. The negligence or wrongdoing must have caused the harm.

The defense argues, "We didn't do anything wrong. Even if we did, it didn't cause the result experienced by the patient. In other words, the old man was going to die anyway, and he died of stroke or cancer or whatever; therefore, even if we did make a mistake, we're not responsible for his death."

What the evidence shows is that Dr. Longacre and Dr. Herbert, on their worst day, let's just assume, made a mistake. Neither of them was dealing with the full world of informational facts. And that is why I emphasized that point during the trial. You may recall that I asked, "What is a radiation oncologist? Was he just a person who, in fact, just saw films, or was the defendant the one doctor who knew more and had more information than any other healthcare provider rendering care to Bob Smith?"

The one person who knew more than any doctor caring for Bob Smith was Dr. Gauwitz. Dr. Longacre testified, "That is why I called in a radiation oncologist." The defendant is the man with the radiation gun and his finger on the trigger. It was his obligation to look at the entire picture and treat the patient. Do you remember when we went through that? He had all the facts from all the specialists, and he alone could look at the entire clinical picture, all of the radiological studies, and examine the patient himself. He could have ordered more tests and did not have to proceed unless he was absolutely, positively certain.

And the defense will say, "Well, he really didn't look at the entire clinical picture. He just looked at Dr. Herbert's report, and he just looked at Dr. Longacre's diagnosis."

Dr. Herbert's report and Dr. Longacre's initial impression was that Bob Smith had cancer. Dr. Herbert's report has at the top of the document that has been placed into evidence for your consideration, "Admitting for MRI to the brain, CVA." That is my red circle drawn around the CVA: It stands for cerebral vascular accident—in essence, a minor stroke.

The defense will get up and say, "Look what it says here, 'rule out metastatic disease.'"

Yes, it does say that. When you have a patient who has problems, you have to rule out all of the possibilities. Someone comes in with a headache, and the doctor has to say, "Well, it's possible he could have simply had a bad night last night. Or he could have some children yelling at him all day. Or he could have an aneurysm, a little bubble in a blood vessel that burst. He could have a malignant brain tumor." And on and on.

Then the defense will argue that Dr. Gauwitz had every reason to suspect that Bob Smith had a recurring metastatic disease. Ladies and gentlemen of the jury, here is where the defense and the defendant run into problems.

You can't have it both ways. Harry Truman, our former president, coined the phrase, "The buck stops here." Where it all stops in this case is when this clinician does a full clinical evaluation. That is the person with whom and where responsibility ultimately rests. And that person is the defendant, Dr. Gauwitz.

Do you remember when I asked those questions of the defendant? "Did you talk to Mr. Smith?" I inquired.

"Well," said Dr. Gauwitz, "I talked to Mr. Smith, and I examined him. And there is a consultation report that is in evidence."

"And did you look at the films?" I asked him.

He answered, "Oh, certainly. I looked at the films."

For the very first time, now, in the year 2000, the defense in this case has come up with the theory that the MRIs showed there were multiple lesions. You must have heard that: multiple lesions all over Bob Smith's brain. Not just two brain tumors, but multiple ones! These various defense witnesses who have been hired to testify during this trial are now coming forward to talk about all these "multiple" sites of cancer that were never seen while the patient was being treated back in 1994. Remember, with regard to the testimony that is given, you are allowed to judge the demeanor and credibility of witnesses and any interest the witnesses may have in the outcome of the case.

I want you to understand what we did as part of putting this puzzle box together, so that the significance of what has occurred can, I hope, be made clear. You may recollect that we called those "tumors" the upper lesion and the lower lesion. The defendant doctor said, "Well, this, to me, was an infarct from the stroke, but I didn't know about this. I believed, and I still believe, it was metastatic disease." And the defendant states that if it was metastatic disease, he had to do something to halt this thing from, as one of the defense experts said, "smashing the brain stem," as the tumor grew inside Bob Smith's skull and began to enlarge.

But where are all these terrible symptoms? The compression of the brain tissue and any signs whatsoever of this growing mass smashing its way into Bob Smith's brain? Do I need to spend any time with you talking about symptoms? What symptoms do you think this man had? I mean, forget what the defense is reading in the records and all this litany of tragedy…that this man could barely move, that he was medicated beyond any comprehension, that he had all kinds of diseases, lung cancer, and on and on.

Is this the same person you heard about from his family and his physicians? Is it? Really, is this the same person? Charles Dickens wrote *A Tale of Two Cities*. And I'm telling you, this is a tale about two very different men. Can you doubt that Alma Smith describes a very different man than the old, infirm, and ready-to-die person who the defense would have you believe was Bob Smith?

The Bob Smith who Alma tells you about was vibrant, played golf, and did chores, both in the house and outside in the yard. What was her motivation? What do you think her motivation has been for the past four years of this litigation? To hire some fancy-pants lawyer to come in here, big and successful, and say, "Oh, give her a lot of money so I can get a big fee?" Is that her motivation? So that she can get money? You have to ask yourself, "Why did she bring this case? And why did Steve Yerrid take it?" Ask yourself those questions. When you ask yourself those questions, follow that up, and ask, "Why has she steadfastly stayed the course for four long, agonizing years?" *[I paused. The argument had been going on for several minutes, and I had seen the nods and ever so slight affirmations on most of the jurors' faces. All except one. Juror number two, seated front row center, wasn't listening. I hated seeing that. Instead of focusing on me, feeling the argument and riding the current of emotion, he was staring straight ahead. Detached? Heard enough? Tired? Maybe he had already made up his mind. Maybe he was already there and was just waiting for the opportunity to render his verdict. I would press on and center some attention his way to get a better read. I left the podium in front of the jury and walked over to the stacked boxes behind our counsel table.]*

These are the depositions of just Alma Smith and her daughter, Debbie Bowman. Look how thick they are. Do you know how many hours they were deposed by the defense lawyers? Over two full days. But Alma never faltered, and she is here in the courtroom. And for what? In the Supreme Court, in the highest court in the land, above the entrance to the building we have these words etched in stone: Equal Justice Under Law. And justice should and must be dispensed equally and fairly, regardless of who you are or how old you are. Alma Smith has the burden of proof, to prove that the defendants were negligent—and it has been satisfied.

Let me tie that in. We talked about Bob Smith's symptoms. At best, they were as follows: He drove up to North Carolina with his wife. He was a healthy man leading a full and active life. While there, he experienced some blurred vision in his right eye.

As I said, you, the jury, need to weigh and consider the credibility and believability of witnesses and any interest in the outcome. Dr. Caukins, the high-priced expert the defense brought in and made a great fanfare about, didn't even know what was wrong with the gentleman. I specifically asked Dr. Caukins what problems Bob Smith initially experienced, and he replied, "Well, his eyes."

"Which eye?" I asked.

Amazingly, he answered, "Both eyes."

More questions quickly followed. "Had Mr. Smith's vision returned to baseline? Did it return to normal before they ever started treating him with this whole brain radiation?"

Dr. Caukins answered, "I'm not really sure."

Not sure? Not sure? Just use your collective minds. Bob Smith's symptoms consisted, I would suggest from the evidence, of only one complaint—the vision in only his right eye was blurred for a short period of time before returning to normal. I have shown you the history and physical examination results of Bob Smith by Dr. Granger Benson. Dr. Benson said, in his history of present illness written on March 31, "[Robert Smith's] visual symptoms in his right eye then had gradually improved to the point where he is barely aware of any visual loss at the time of my examination."

What other symptoms did Bob have? None. Based on this single, minor symptom and the fact that he had prostate cancer five years before, the defendant chose to initiate whole brain radiation—the deadly consequences of which were irreversible.

You do remember when I asked the clerk of court, who has been very patient with us all, "Could I have that document?" She handed me a portion of the medical records introduced into evidence. Right after Dr. Gauwitz suspected this recurrent prostate cancer, the doctors in fact did what was suggested. They did the workup and blood tests necessary to detect whether or not there was recurrent prostate cancer. Additionally, other tests and a bone scan were performed. All the testing was *negative*. There were no symptoms; and that is because there was no brain cancer. Bob Smith had suffered a minor stroke, not a recurrence of his prostate disease. But Dr. Gauwitz still chose to pull the trigger of whole brain radiation that was inappropriate and deadly. It wasn't a cure. It was a death sentence.

The defense experts repeatedly testified there was no evidence concerning the long-term effects of radiation. The reason, by the way, you don't see a lot of studies concerning the long-term effects of whole brain radiation is because most people die within months after receiving this type of treatment. By the time a patient is treated in this manner, he or she is either close to death or suffering an incurable disease. The doctors use whole brain radiation for palliative reasons, not to cure, but to make the patient more comfortable as he or she dies. I don't need to belabor it. I can't point that out to you any better than Dr. Caukins did. The defense's own radiation oncology expert, when she testified on direct, said, "I have been involved with approximately two thousand patients who have received whole brain radiation."

"Really?" I asked. "You testified this treatment is not fatal, so let's discuss your group of patients—the two thousand. What were the long-term effects? What happened to them?" Specifically, I asked her, "Doctor, how many of these patients had long-term consequences?"

She answered, "The only patient I had who lived to even see something that would be considered 'long term' was one, and I don't know if he had metastatic disease all over his body or what."

"So," I asked, "that would be 1,999 out of two thousand very sick patients who died shortly after receiving whole brain radiation?"

And I think you will recall she was forced to admit those terrible numbers were true. You get the point. Surviving whole brain radiation is a rare bird, indeed.

Let's turn to the health of Bob Smith before he received the whole brain radiation. That is why I called Dr. Kilgore as our first witness to discuss Bob's health and describe his physical condition. What was the point of the plaintiff's case in bringing him in? To prove that the gentleman was not whatever the defense was doing to try to portray him to be. He wasn't some sick, diseased old man on death's doorstep. Bob Smith was vibrant, active, and relatively healthy for an eighty-three-year-old man.

Within days of this terrible misdiagnosis and the absolutely wrongful decision to administer whole brain radiation, Bob Smith was seeing Dr. Kilgore, an orthopedic surgeon, so he could have knee replacements to improve his golf game and help him walk and climb stairs better. One thing we don't have to teach jurors in this country is common sense. Does this sound like a broken-down, sick, elderly man who was falling apart and dying?

And if this man was so sick and feeble and cancer-ridden, how are Bob's knee replacements explained? Dr. Kilgore's logic was inescapable. "I saw him and agreed to schedule surgery for his knee replacements the same day he was getting this diagnosis of recurrent cancer. He was in good health; otherwise, I would not have agreed to replace his knees."

But that was a big point made by the defense at every opportunity. And I want it to be very clear that up to the very day the defendant doctor commenced these deadly radiation treatments, Bob Smith was still active around the house, and the services he provided to his wife, Alma, were valuable and real. In making its case, the defense knows that loss of household services are damages that will be awarded, should you return a verdict in favor of the plaintiff.

Do we ever say that Mr. Smith mowed the yard? That seemed to be a big thing with the defense. You have all of these household services we proved that he performed, but what about mowing the grass? No, the eighty-three-year-old man didn't get out and mow the grass, but he did a lot of other things.

So, what's the point of all of that? What type of life did Bob Smith lead before he received his deadly cure? The point is that Dr. Kilgore gave you an illustration when he related to you the story of a ninety-three-year-old patient he once treated who wanted knee replacements. Dr. Kilgore said something to the effect, "You know, sir, you are ninety-three. Why are you doing this?" And the elderly patient pointed out that it is not the *quantity* of life, but the *quality* of life that is important. He didn't really care how long he lived. What was important to him was how *well* he lived.

That is not a bad goal for all of us. Even doctors cannot tell us when we are going to die. How dare the defense get up and argue Bob Smith was already on "borrowed time?" Doctors aren't the people who are in charge of when you die—no one on this earth is. If everyone lived out his or her life according to the life expectancy tables created by the doctors, then everybody at Columbine High School in Colorado would still be alive. The victims of the Alfred Murrah Federal Office Building in Oklahoma City, Oklahoma, would still be living. And Willard Scott would be a real short segment on the *Today* show because he wouldn't have any pictures to show of people having their one hundredth birthdays. Because according to these doctors we are all dead and no one lives to be one hundred years old. Their so-called "medical opinions" are disputed and shown to be wrong in our everyday experiences. The defense is not in a position to assert Bob Smith was at the end of his life and, as a result, argue the actions of the defendant had no effect in shortening it.

I suggest the evidence proves there was wrongdoing, not only the mistake variety, because nobody is perfect, but that the conduct in this case was not just a mistake, but in fact, also a deviation from the accepted standard of medical care. *[He still wasn't looking. Juror number two had tuned out. I could see that clearly now. What the hell had I done? Leaving him on the jury had seemed a good idea. He was in his mid-fifties, a former merchant marine seaman with a tanned and weathered face. He'd been around. I was comfortable he could relate to a man like Bob Smith. Certainly, he could understand the wrong and the torment of Alma. But he wasn't buying our case and even appeared to be getting hostile.*

There's nothing worse for a trial lawyer than losing a jury. I have heard stories of all kinds. Jurors falling asleep, shaking their heads in disbelief, rolling their eyes—but this wasn't a story. This was real, and I was in trouble. I could keep trying to turn him, but at the same time, I decided to redouble my efforts on the other five jury members. I had not lost the jury, I had lost one juror. I still could do this; besides, I didn't have the option of giving up. Could I get him back? If not, would he have influence over the rest and kill our chances of success? My thoughts raced and then I pulled back. There was no sense thinking this trash. I needed to continue my all-out assault on the defense.]

All of this conclusive proof establishing negligence and liability allows you to focus on the issue of damages. The reality is Mr. Smith was a vibrant man. Mrs. Smith, an elderly lady who certainly doesn't look her age, came in and talked to you about the type of career that Bob Smith had. We did not need to parade a bunch of witnesses into this courtroom to talk about his military record or recount what he did as an executive at Pepsi-Cola, one of the largest corporations in America. Bob Smith's life and his accomplishments were simply and quickly established. There was no need to elaborate.

The defense cautions against giving us sympathy. Do not do that. Mrs. Smith has already had all the sympathy in the world. The judge is going to instruct you on this, and I am going to tell you, we don't want sympathy. Mrs. Smith has had enough sympathy to last a lifetime and two more. We want justice, which is far different from sympathy. Far different.

The defense is accusatory in saying, "The plaintiff is using hindsight." They argue, "All these tests came back negative after the radiation was commenced, but how was Dr. Gauwitz to know he didn't have cancer at the time he began the treatments? You have to place Dr. Gauwitz back there in the circumstances existing on April 1, 1994. Not now, after we know the test results." That is exactly the point. Why didn't he wait for all the tests to come back? What was the rush? Why in the world did the defendant doctor administer this deadly treatment before he knew everything he possibly could learn?

The defense would have you believe there were signs that Bob Smith had cancer. Do you remember the rectal bleeding part? It was inferred that at the time the decision to radiate was made, the medical history showed there was rectal bleeding. That symptom, certainly, would be consistent with the recurrence of prostate cancer. But when I went into detail, I asked Dr. Longacre if Mr. Smith had bled rectally in 1994. He said, no, not in his examination, but that was his history. He did bleed rectally. It is in the records, of course, but the rectal bleeding occurred *in 1989, not 1994!* Back five years earlier, when he was having that active issue with his prostate and getting treated for it, he did pass some blood through his rectum. That is an accurate history then, and it is an accurate history now. If Mr. Smith were here, he would tell you the same thing. But he is not here, and we know from the medical records there was no rectal bleeding at the time his non-existing recurrence of prostate cancer was misdiagnosed.

Use your common sense. The way the defense presented the rectal bleeding, it appeared to be at the time Dr. Gauwitz saw him, he may have been experiencing some type of gastrointestinal bleeding. Somehow, that might show he had recurrent prostate cancer. We had to specifically point out there was no rectal bleeding in 1994. None.

I also brought out the point that Dr. Gauwitz did not wait for the results of the bone scan. What is the common theme you heard? That with prostate cancer, 99.9 percent of the time, it metastasizes to the bone. Like ants are drawn to honey, prostate cancer is drawn to bone. Most probably, ants would not go to salt, and in this case, the prostate cancer most probably would not go to the tissue of Bob Smith's brain. Prostate cancer loves bone. If you assume it is active and metastatic, that is where it always goes…to the bone. And a bone scan is the test used to determine if there is a spread of prostate cancer. Yet Dr. Gauwitz, the defendant doctor, didn't wait for the results of the bone scan, and he made the decision to immediately initiate whole brain radiation. As we proved by the medical records, when the bone scan results came back, less than three days after he began whole brain radiation, they were negative. No bone cancer.

The truth is, ladies and gentlemen, at the time the defendant ordered Mr. Smith to be radiated, there was no urgency. There were no symptoms. In fact, I made certain testimony was elicited that the first time the defendant saw Bob Smith was at four o'clock in the afternoon, and he almost began the deadly radiation treatment that very day.

When I introduced the defendant Dr. Gauwitz's consultation report, which the defense did not want to show you, it stated, "I decided to immediately initiate radiation." The buck does stop there. And it does stop!

When was this pre-radiation conference that Dr. Gauwitz had with his employer, Dr. Allen Tralins? Was it that afternoon? Supposedly, they met in the hospital; sometime after Dr. Gauwitz decided to radiate, these two radiation oncologists met in the conference room. What do you think occurred? Do you think they got out all of the films and went through this case presentation and Dr. Gauwitz said something like, "Oh, by the way. I have this old guy. You saw him several years back when he had some prostate cancer, and I think he has a recurrence. I'm told he has a recurrence. I'm going to give him whole brain radiation, because he is not long for this world, anyway." *[I had little choice. In a case like this, it was all or nothing. Our theory required the jury to accept or reject the argument of a failure to use caution and that it was the immediate radiation treatment that had caused Bob Smith's death. There was no middle ground.]*

Use your common sense. I wasn't in the room. But you heard the physician sitting there at counsel table. You heard him testify as to what happened. Again, it is about credibility and believability of witnesses. *[I turned and looked directly at the defendant. The jurors focused their attention on him as well. The courtroom was air-conditioned, but he sure looked like he was sweating.]* I submit to you that the evidence is that this gentleman did not wait for a bone scan. He did not wait for the results of the colonoscopy exam. He wasn't concerned about any rectal bleeding, because there was none. No, the inescapable fact is that the defendant doctor made the bad decision to administer whole brain radiation, and that decision was wrong. This is a case about the consequences of that wrongful decision and that negligent course of medical treatment that resulted in Bob

Smith's horrible demise.

Of course, the defendants can't use an elevated PSA to bolster the claim of active cancer in this instance because there was none. The medical evidence in this case and your own common sense tell you that the best indicator of recurrent prostate cancer is an elevated PSA. But Bob Smith simply did not fit this diagnostic picture, either. He didn't have an elevated PSA. So, what was the basis of deciding to administer this drastic measure to cure a cancer that wasn't there?

How many times did I ask him, "Where was the cancer? Where was the cancer?" This last defense witness was good about explaining something I can't figure out. Where was the cancer? He said it was microscopic and existed in the form of millions and millions of cells so small as to be un-detectable. He used an example that in China, there are a billion people, kind of like cancer cells. They're so small the tests can't detect them. That was the inference.

What did he mean when he said tests that could not detect these tiny, microscopic cancer cells? Could it be that doctor was talking about things he has no expertise in? That is for you to decide. MRIs, CT scans, who reads those? Who interprets them? The radiological experts of this world, the experts and neuroradiologists who we brought before you as witnesses on our side of the case to interpret those diagnostic tests and to reach the inescapable conclusion there simply were no cancer cells there.

The difference in those witnesses testifying in this case is extreme and obvious. There are the treating physicians who unanimously found no cancer as Bob Smith was cared for when he was dying in 1994. Then, there are the so-called "experts" getting paid to appear here at trial in the year 2000. Again, those people were not treating physicians and appeared in this courtroom as retained "experts" in the vigorous defense of this lawsuit.

The glaring fact is obvious. The defendant didn't wait for the results even for the barest minimum of time before giving Bob Smith this deadly radiation. I would submit this to you—if Dr. Gauwitz had waited as long as you have been sitting in this jury box, we wouldn't be here today; and in all likelihood, Bob Smith would still be alive.

Two weeks of this trial seems like a long time. You can imagine three and a half years and what those were like. Three and a half years of litigation. Yet, if Dr. Gauwitz had waited just two weeks to initiate the whole brain radiation therapy...

The questions you need to ask yourself are these: One, was radiation therapy appropriate? I suggest the answer to that is no. Two, even if it was questionable and this palliative treatment was going to make Mr. Smith's life more comfortable, why in the world did the radiation have to begin right away? What was going on that made it so urgent?

You may recall I asked Dr. Gauwitz that. I asked, "Why? Why did you decide to do it right away? You know, once you do it, you can't take it back." And he testified something along the lines that the dosage of radiation he administered really wouldn't adversely affect Bob Smith, that it wouldn't really hurt him.

And there is a DeVita's book, which is one of the authoritative texts on cancer, right here. That book, *DeVita's Cancer: Principles and Practice of Oncology,* alludes to the long-term effects of radiation. The defense is going to get up and say, "Too soon. You can't really determine the adverse effects of radiation for at least two years." Actually I think Dr. Tralins, the president of the defendant corporation, testified that the long-term effects of the whole brain radiation would not show up for at least six months, but Mr. Smith didn't live that long.

To illustrate the point about statistics and how good they are, I used the prostate example. Do you remember that? If Mr. Smith did indeed have recurrent cancer, it would take thirty months for him to die; I think their cancer expert said two and one half to three years. Under his statistical analysis, Mr. Smith would have been dead a long time before he ever got to the defendant. So statistics, when they serve the right purpose, are used...well, he should have been dead anyway, because he had recurrent cancer. The defense used statistics. When it doesn't serve the defendants, they ignore the statistics. The point being that this recurrent prostate cancer, of cancer in the brain, which is what they were talking about, is so, so remote.

Remember, I told you about the other defenses. They are traditional arguments in medical malpractice cases. The defense asserts, "We didn't do anything wrong, and even if we did, it didn't hurt the patient. Even if we hurt the patient, he was already suffering from other problems and was going to die anyway."

Let me address this latter point of the radiation not hurting Mr. Smith. I want you to utilize and again rely on your common sense. The radiation, the lead vests that we see, even as non-doctors, and being required to go out of the room when radiation is administered, show us in simplistic terms that radiation is bad.

Our country has taken radiation and its usage to new heights, this great nation of ours. We light our cities at night through nuclear power plants. We keep our people warm, and we do it through atomic energy. But we can also use nuclear energy tragically, as we did in Hiroshima, Japan. What does Hiroshima have to do with anything? Why am I bringing that up? To show the effects, as best as I can, of whole brain radiation. And do you know why I bring that up? Because Dr. Gauwitz said, even ten times the dosage he administered would not hurt Mr. Smith. Ten times. That is thirty-six grays, thirty-six hundred rads. When I asked our expert radiation oncologist what thirty-six thousand rads would do, which is ten times the dosage he received, and she said that it would make Mr. Smith's flesh fall off. It would toast him. It would burn him up. In her opinion, she said it would be worse than the injuries inflicted on those poor people exposed to the radiation at Hiroshima.

What we are talking about is the application of this amount of radiation on an eighty-three-year-old man. The judge will give you an instruction. He will say that if you have an existing malady—it's called an "eggshell skull" type of scenario—and you heard me repeatedly say that as a lawyer, you take the plaintiff as you find him. You take the people as you find them. As a matter of law, that is your solemn duty. That is your solemn obligation.

You take Bob Smith the way he presented. What was he like in 1994? He was an eighty-three-year-old man who had some "old wires," some old nerves, in his brain, as well as old blood vessels. Was he ready to die? His treating family physician, Dr. Whiting, didn't think so. Dr. Whiting was the second witness called in this case. He was Bob's primary care physician for almost twenty years. He thought Bob was going to live into his late eighties and maybe into his nineties. Dr. Whiting said, "In 1994, Bob Smith's physical health was good. He had some problems, but inferentially, everybody who gets that age has some problems, but I thought he would make it into his nineties."

Let me give you a little bit of comfort there. I talked to you about economic damages when I was picking you as the jury, and I talked to you about non-economic damages. The smaller elements in this case consist of the economic damages. That is why we called an expert economist. Let me just give you some comfort. For purposes of those economic forecasts that are in evidence, we're going to assume Bob Smith would have been dead today, by the year 2000. In other words, he would have lived to eighty-nine years of age.

The thrust of this case is not so much how long Bob Smith would have lived, but instead what Alma Smith goes through, what is in her mind, what her life was like, and what her life expectancy may be. She is not dead today, and every single day she lives, she suffers with the emotional pain caused by the wrongful death of her husband. According to the mortality tables, she will live another twelve years, and she will, I submit, continue to suffer during that time ahead.

If Alma Smith had passed on in the last four years, there wouldn't be a lawsuit. She is bringing an action on her own behalf and as the representative of Bob Smith. The judge will tell you the elements of damages; the elements of damages that we produced on the witness stand for you to at least consider, and for which Alma Smith is entitled to compensation. But for four years, she has stayed the course of litigation, and the validity of her case has lived through her.

When you put out of your mind your station in life, and when you give total compensation for the element of damages with no notion about who we are going to make rich, remember that all the money in the world won't bring Bob Smith back or take away Alma's anguish. You may recall our discussions during jury selection about that concept, and I hope you do. But as a matter of law, just and full monetary compensation must be awarded.

It is this system that is so very important, ladies and gentlemen. It is the system of this great country that is important. When we talk about damages, and someone starts getting into that mindset that money should not be awarded because it won't bring him back, then stop your deliberations and say, "Wait a minute! That is not what we are supposed to consider. That is not the law." *[I wanted to give the other five jurors as much ammunition as I could. From the angry look on good old number two, it would be needed.]*

Make no mistake. Whatever I have said about our burdens up to this point is nothing compared to the duty you have as jurors in this case. Never, in the rest of your lives, although some of you have been jurors before, but certainly rarely in your lives will you have the power that you will have in just a few short moments. Relatively speaking, this power is overwhelming.

With all respect to Judge Gerard O'Brien, he is the judge of the law. He wears a black robe, but just as surely as his black robe is on his back, that figurative black robe will also be affixed to your backs, because you will be the sole and absolute judges of the facts. And that decision will, for all time, determine what justice is, and it will be announced through your verdict form.

Your collective decision will demonstrate the loss and the extent to which Alma Smith has suffered as a result of that loss. It is true that money damages will not bring Bob Smith back; it will absolutely not bring him back. However, compensatory damages should and must represent the full and complete loss, to put it in a positive way, full and complete loss of what Mrs. Smith has suffered and will continue to suffer in the future.

You may recall me asking, "How do you diagnose a broken heart?" I don't know. I'm not a doctor. But I think some objective things demonstrate this type of pain, such as Alma Smith not sleeping and saying, "I don't feel complete," or "I have lost my soulmate."

Do you remember Harry Smith? Bob's younger brother who, because of their large age difference, he treated like a son? We didn't bring Harry in to give him damages. Harry is not entitled to recover damages in a case such as this. Bob and Alma Smith's one blessed daughter, Deborah, also testified. Again, we didn't bring her in to make you feel that she deserves something. No claim is being made on her behalf. The grandson who has been sitting here, Stephen, and Scott, the son-in-law. They were brought here to testify and relate to you what has occurred to Alma, not to elicit your sympathy nor get money for themselves.

Not only do we have an asymptomatic man who was given whole brain radiation, made sick, and then died because of it, but also we have had suffering of the highest magnitude. Not only in him, but also in Alma Smith, his true love, his real true love. Marriages are not perfect, and I know there are not supposed to always be storybook endings. But sometimes there can be. And true love…the bond of love between people can be quite amazing. And the bond I'm talking about is simple—when Bob Smith suffered, he suffered no more than the suffering endured by Alma Smith, who loved him so much that her suffering may actually be more than his. Does that make sense? I hope so.

This man didn't deserve palliative treatment to make him feel better; and worse, the whole brain radiation used to deal with brain cancer he didn't have was absolutely destined to kill him. Do you want to read about the human suffering? The medical records in this case are a four-month diary of suffering of the highest order. Do you want to read what Bob Smith went through? And what Alma Smith went through—and continues to go through today? It is all right there. *[I held up the black bound notebook of medical records introduced into evidence that read like pages from hell.]*

Not only does Alma have to suffer what she saw and the memories she should have had that are being lost, but also she has to suffer with the terrible fact that a wrong has been committed, and her husband has been needlessly and wrongfully taken from her. Of course, the defense argues he may have died the next day. Ladies and gentlemen, he may have died in May of 1994. A car may have struck him. He could have had a fatal heart attack. He may have been hit by lightning. And the defense would still be heard to say, "Well, he was going to die of old age." That may have happened; that may have happened. Nobody is promised tomorrow, nobody. But Mrs. Smith has, in addition to that suffering, hurt, and a broken heart, that terrible memory of knowing her husband was taken in such a terrible way. It didn't have to happen. It was the "cure" that killed him, not the disease of cancer.

One can only imagine how Alma Smith felt when she sat down with Dr. Harrison and Dr. Sinoff, the treating neurologists who were called in to determine why Bob Smith was dying. One record here describes, "This is a large, white male, lying on the emergency room stretcher with marked psychomotor retardation." He was so frail and sick with radiation that he couldn't even hold up his head. Do you remember Debbie talking about squeezing his hand, and then in response, the blinking of his eyes? Did he understand what was going on? Mrs. Smith said that she sometimes didn't think so, but there were times when the doctors themselves recorded their discussions with him. There were times when he knew exactly what was going on.

You have to ask yourself one question: Who was in the best position in the whole wide world to determine what was wrong with Mr. Smith? The doctors who were hired for this trial to render their opinions or the treating physicians who cared and exerted their best efforts to give him medical care?

Dr. Harrison, one of the senior, most qualified neurologists in his specialized field, was asked if he had any discussions with Dr. Gauwitz in the case. "Yes," he answered. "Dr. Gauwitz came up to me in the hospital and asked, 'What have you done to me? You have written this report. What have you done to me?'" That is Dr. Harrison's report, wherein it says leukoencephalopathy due to radiation exposure was killing Bob Smith, not some imagined brain cancer.

Again, please remember, this radiation was administered to a person who was eighty-three years old. It is not a thirty-year-old. There is no doubt that this cerebral vascular condition of this gentleman was more affected by this dosage of radiation than a younger person would have been. His aged blood vessels and the network of nerves in his brain simply could not withstand this radiation, which was exacerbated by his advanced age. *[I was counting on the health and vigor of the youngest juror to drive this point home.]*

The judge is going to give you the instruction that if a person has an underlying disease process, and you find that another act—in this case, the whole brain radiation—accelerated or made more grave the underlying disease process, then the tortfeasor, as the wrongdoer, is responsible for the entire scope of the resulting damages. It is called the concurrent causation instruction. In layman's terms it may be called the "straw that broke the camel's back" instruction—and you are going to get that from Judge

O'Brien. It must be followed as a matter of law and in fulfillment of your sacred duties as jurors.

Next, we turn to the issue of biopsy. Again, credibility is an underlying test that escapes no one. You will determine the issue of credibility. According to the defendant, the Smiths refused the biopsy. From Dr. Gauwitz's own mouth, he testified that a biopsy was explained to the Smiths, and they refused it. According to the defendant, he sat down and talked to Bob and Alma Smith, and both decided that the biopsy was too risky. There are a couple of problems with that. One, Alma is alive, and you heard her testimony. She said no such discussion ever took place and a biopsy was not performed because one was never offered nor even discussed. Two, Dr. Gauwitz would not be the doctor to have that discussion in the first place.

Do you remember what Dr. Rosa said as the defendant's specialist in neurosurgery? It was the defense's own expert witness who testified that when a patient is discussing having a biopsy done, a neurosurgeon would do the consult, *not* a radiation oncologist such as the defendant.

According to Dr. Rosa, the neurosurgeon would explain to the patient the biopsy procedure, and the patient would then sign a consent form. Well, that was not done. No consent was ever signed. More importantly, not one entry was ever made that the Smiths were offered, much less refused, a biopsy. Some might say, "Mr. Yerrid, that's awful stringent to keep records. Records aren't that important..." But I submit there is an old saying in the keeping of medical records: If it isn't written, it didn't happen. *[This was my best play to get juror number two back. When I had asked the potential jury panel about their ideas concerning record keeping, the old salt had used that phrase. I looked directly at him and he had a slight smile...amusement? contempt? I didn't like it and a sick feeling crept into my gut. But I continued to get good vibes from the other five, and I was bolstered by their reaction.]*

Surely, if an event like that happened wherein a patient refused a critical diagnostic test such as a biopsy—and you can use your common sense—certainly if an event like that happened, it would have been recorded in the medical charts. And before we use this whole brain radiation, which, no doubt about it, is going to kill you. It's going to make you a little more comfortable—not that Bob Smith needed comfort—before it kills you, you should feel a little better. It should make your passing a little easier. But before we do that, to make sure, because we can't take the radiation back once it is given, we want to do a biopsy. Given all that is at stake and the patient still refuses this all-important biopsy, don't you think the doctor would put that in the record somewhere? Probably in very large letters—"Patient refuses biopsy against medical advice."

Finally, the defense argues Bob Smith signed a consent form and in doing so, agreed to accept the radiation treatment and any of its consequences. The defense lawyers showed you this, a huge, blown-up placard of the printed boiler plate consent form with Bob Smith's signature on it. *[I had picked up one of the many expensive demonstrative exhibits from the stack beside the defense lawyer's table. I enjoyed using the other side's weapons against them and the move invariably agitated my adversaries.]* He signed the consent, so he participated in the decision to radiate his whole brain. And then the defense read its language to you. It was read to you, as if Robert Smith were hearing it. Does that writing look remotely clear?

What had happened was that they, the defendants, had the consent form executed in an attempt to cover their liability. And the man signed it. When do you think he signed it? It is dated. And why do you think he signed it? The conversation leading up to his signature probably went something like this, "Mr. Smith, you have metastatic disease. Your brain has cancer. You have metastatic disease from whatever they said—prostate cancer, colon cancer, lung cancer, or from somewhere else. We're going to try to catch it right now. We're going to stop it. We're going to do it with this whole brain radiation."

Or do you really suppose he signed it after they said, "Now, Mr. Smith, let me tell you something. This whole brain radiation is going to kill you. It's going to really burn up your brain. But hopefully, it's going to get that cancer stopped so that you can have a few good months of life before you die. Now, we're not really sure that you have metastatic cancer, because we don't have all the test results in. But given the fact that you and Alma won't agree to a biopsy, and the fact that we really don't need all these tests, and the fact that we believe it has to be done immediately, you need to sign it so that we can give you a deadly dosage of whole brain radiation."

Or, most logically, do you think the most likely scenario was when the patient went in to talk to the defendants, he said, "What should we do? I'm having this problem. It is kind of resolved and my eye is okay, and I'm feeling pretty good, but I want to make sure I'm around to watch my grandson graduate from high school. What do you think we ought to do?"

"Well," they might have said, "we ought to do whole brain radiation. All you have to do is sign this consent form. And if you sign it, then we can do the procedure. We can do it today. You'll be done in two and a half weeks."

I suggest the terrible parts, the downside of this radical treatment, were never discussed. Otherwise, why wouldn't a gentleman as smart as Bob Smith have stopped everything, required diagnostic tests to confirm cancer, and gotten all of the information possible about whether or not he did or did not have cancer *before* receiving whole brain radiation? What difference would a few days make? Using common sense…isn't that the most likely scenario?

Certainly there can be risks, complications, and side effects whenever somebody undergoes radiation treatments. Doctors cannot disclose every possible risk, but what about the fact that if this whole brain radiation is done, death is a certainty? Shouldn't the defendant have really said to Bob Smith something like, "We really haven't been able to rule out that it's just a meningioma or some other harmless condition. We haven't been able to rule that out, but we'll go ahead and treat you for metastatic cancer anyway, even though it may be benign. We're not going to wait for the tests. We're going to go ahead and treat you. Sign here, and here, and here. And hurry! Hurry! You had better sign quickly!"

Dr. Harvey Greenberg, one of our experts, is a nationally known and eminently qualified expert in the field of radiation oncology. His title is Director of Radiation Therapy at Lee Moffitt Cancer Center, one of the top cancer facilities in the world. His opinion was clear that radiation to the brain without cancer is misuse. Whole brain radiation, in any dosage, was not appropriate and absolutely unnecessary. As to the so-called "minimal" effect of this whole brain radiation, Dr. Greenberg testified it was the radiation that killed Bob Smith, not some imagined brain cancer.

Something happened to the man. We know something happened that caused him to die. What was it? Why do you think he died? The defense would have you believe Bob Smith had brain cancer. On what basis?

Dr. Harrison, the treating neurologist, did not believe there was any metastatic disease in Bob Smith's body, not in his brain, not anywhere. Dr. Sinoff, the neurologist with Georgetown credentials, said there was no metastatic disease, nothing even in the MRIs.

And what were the horrible results of the suffering endured? We have introduced into evidence several documents. These are the instructions this family was given from hospice during Bob's final weeks. And I must warn you, if you do not want to read about the horrific, graphic details contained in the hospice medical records, do not read them. They talk about all the things that this family had to do for this gentleman and what they had to go through. It is detailed and gruesome. Everything you can imagine is there. If you want to read what the hospice people saw with their own eyes, these dedicated hospice people, it is all there. If you want to read about the actual impact, the crying spells, the most tragic consequences of human misery, if you want to read that, it has been put in evidence, and you can go back and read it as long as you want. The hospice records highlight all you need to know about the damage and the magnitude of the loss suffered in this case. There has to be an accountability. There has to be a taking of responsibility for the suffering and unnecessary death that occurred in this case.

Do you recall Milu McNay, the elderly lady who testified about the breakfast meetings she had with Bob on a regular basis? *[Again, five jurors nodded heads and acknowledged my argument was being followed. Juror number two was immobile and cold as stone. I ignored what I saw.]* She talked to you about all the things that Mr. Smith was going through after he learned that he was going to die and the things he shared with her about not being there for his wife, his daughter, and for his surrogate son, Stephen. Bob Smith was the cornerstone, the patriarch, the protector, the wise advisor, and the loving senior partner in that family unit. What is left now?

What is that story we learned about as kids? You play with fire, you are going to get burned. Ready, shoot, aim. That is how I will just summarize the treatment given Bob Smith. Ready, shoot, aim. Instead of marking their targets, avoiding "friendly fire," and making sure about what was being done before doing it, the defendants acted in a wrong and irreversible fashion. It can't be undone. *[I now began to focus my attention on the other two male jurors I knew were critical. The oldest juror was retired military. The youngest of the jurors was a handsome, athletic-looking man with short blond hair. He had shown keen interest in the proceedings throughout the trial. In voir dire, I had learned he was the manager of a Chili's restaurant and a part-time college student. One of the two, preferably both, would have to neutralize and then turn around juror number two.]*

It doesn't take anybody who spent time in a war conflict to figure this one out: calling in napalm on your own positions. Hopelessly outnumbered and overrun, in real trouble, you call in the napalm. Why do you do that? To kill everything and everyone in the hope that something good lives through it. And that is what the defendants did to Bob Smith. They said he had cancerous tumors in his brain, so they called in the napalm, except there was no enemy there. There was no cancer to radiate and no disease to kill. And, inexcusably, they didn't wait to look. They ordered this deadly strike without looking and without warning and under conditions that absolutely did not require such quick, drastic measures.

Lastly, I want to talk to you about Alma Smith and what she both saw and felt her husband going through. You should remember the significance of the mortality tables. The tables are something that you need to look at in order to calculate the life expectancy of Alma Smith. I think it is about six years that she has had so far in past suffering, and then, for twelve more years, she will suffer heartache, assuming she lives to her normal life expectancy. If you find liability and causation, you then must decide the amount of damages that are to be awarded to Mrs. Smith for the wrongful death of her husband.

This chart I have placed into evidence summarizes the economic losses Alma suffered. It includes the funeral costs, medical bills, and the value of lost services. Every dollar should be awarded. That is simply what I think. I think that is fairness. I think that is justice. And I hope that will be your verdict.

As I told you when the case began, your verdict that concludes this case will be in the form of money. I realize that arriving at a dollar amount is an extremely difficult task. What is fair compensation? What does money mean? Our world has gotten just crazy about money. But you need to understand, even though it is expressed in terms of money, that is not what this case is about. Your verdict is about judging the loss. And I hope you understand that the only way you can signify the depth of the value and the magnitude of the loss to Mrs. Smith is through your verdict, through a monetary amount.

In the end, the tragedy of this case has become a proven reality. All of the radiology demonstrated diffused bilateral white matter destruction of the brain; in other words, the awful damage caused by the whole brain radiation burned up and gradually disintegrated the once-marvelous mind of Bob Smith. The unnecessary radiation to the whole of his brain wiped out his ability to think, to talk, to remember, to function, and finally, to live. Worst of all, as I have said repeatedly, he received radiation treatment for a cancer that wasn't there.

There was absolutely no evidence of metastasis anywhere in Mr. Smith's body. That was the testimony not only of our experts, but also, in the end, the defendants' own experts as well. And why was the radiation administered so quickly? Why didn't the defendants wait and verify the existence of the suspected cancer? The symptoms weren't there. Dr. Gauwitz himself finally admitted there was no urgency to radiate Mr. Smith. The bone scan was a greater determiner of metastatic cancer. Yet, the radiation was started even before those test results were obtained. No evidence of prostate cancer was anywhere else in the body. Not one single diagnostic test came back positive. There were no symptoms. Still, Bob Smith was given radiation.

The defense is going to get up and talk about the dosage. In other words, admitting that radiation was given, it will be argued Bob Smith was given a "normal" amount, not something that was lethal. On that point, I hope the defense gets up and uses that DeVita's oncology book sitting right there on their own table. It says anything more than 2.5 grays of radiation should not be used unless you really want to risk some severe consequences, or unless the patient is going to die really quickly, and the sole objective is to make the patient as comfortable as possible in the final stages of the dying process.

And no matter who did what, and make no mistake, the defense is going to get up and talk about mistakes by other physicians, but in the end, there was only one doctor who pulled that trigger. And tragically, there was only one physician who had all the information, one doctor who called in the napalm, which in this case was whole brain radiation. At the end of this trial, you will judge the conduct of that physician—and he is Dr. Gauwitz. Even after he commenced the whole brain radiation, why didn't he stop the treatments when the test results came back negative? Why did he do the whole twelve doses of radiation? At some point, shouldn't someone have said, "Goodness! We could be wrong! These tests—the bone scans, the gastrointestinal test results, the blood work—are coming back negative, and no cancer is being found. Whatever we are doing, let's stop." If stopped at any time during the weeks of treatment, whatever the dosage would have been, it would have been less than the 3,600 rads administered through the full course of the twelve radiation treatments Bob endured.

The only thing that means anything in the world is how you live it. That is life. And the only thing that is going to matter when you leave here, regardless of what your verdict may be, is that you do what you think justice demands. When you leave this courtroom, it is important that you feel good about what you have done. You must be able to forever believe you dispensed true justice in this case.

Five years from now, if you are fortunate enough to be alive, be able to look back and say, "We really did right." It is important that you listen to everything the defense has to say. I want you to have no doubt you did justice here, because, you see, in the end, that is all that matters.

Thank you.

PORTIONS OF THE CLOSING ARGUMENT
OF DEFENSE COUNSEL
·······

Mr. Yerrid told you that this case is like *A Tale of Two Cities*, a Dickensian story that is fiction. This case is not like *A Tale of Two Cities* at all. It's not fiction; it's fact.

Mr. Yerrid has made a big point about the case, that this case has been pending for three and a half to four years. Ladies and gentlemen of the jury, for three and a half to four years, Dr. Michael Gauwitz and Dr. Allen Tralins, through South Florida Regional Cancer Center, have been accused of killing Robert Smith.

This is not a case of fiction. This is not a Dickensian tale. If anything were to be called as an analogy as to the type of case this is, this is a case where the plaintiffs would have you believe in the story of the *Emperor's New Clothes*. If you look at the *Emperor's New Clothes*, if you look past what everybody in the town was called upon to believe, and look at the facts of this case, what you will see is that this gentleman, Mr. Smith, at the age of eighty-three, passed away because it was his time.

How do we know this? We know it directly from evidence that the plaintiffs prepared. This board that the plaintiffs prepared, they called your attention down here to tell you about Mr. Smith's condition when he was dying, that he was a large white male in the emergency room, on a stretcher.

It also highlighted—which they didn't talk to you about—this language from the medical reports. "There was no discrete, single event which heralded these changes. They have occurred gradually."

What occurred gradually? What occurred gradually was the debilitation and death of a man who was healthy, of a man who did have a full, rich, fulfilling, and prosperous life, but a man whose time had come because of his hypertension, because of his abnormal EKG, because of his degenerative joint disease, because of his hiatal hernia, because of his chest pain, because of his diverticulosis, because of his transient disequilibrium, because of his carcinoma of the prostate, because he couldn't walk—his joints were degenerating to the extent that if he fell down, he couldn't get up, and he couldn't walk up and down stairs—because of his diabetes, because of his chronic obstructive pulmonary disease—"COPD" in those records—because of his coronary artery disease, because of the multiple strokes that he suffered before he ever saw Dr. Michael Gauwitz. The facts of this case cry out, and the evidence cries out as to what really happened.

Mr. Smith got into his car with his wife to go to North Carolina to attend a funeral. And it was a solemn event. And if things had turned out the way he hoped, he would have driven home, but he didn't. He drove up there, and maybe at that point in time, at eighty-three years of age, with all the problems he had, the trip was a little too much for him, because when he got there, he suffered some sudden loss of vision in his right eye. That is what his doctor said; and he had the vision loss. Additionally, the doctor in North Carolina said it may be a stroke, and it may be brain metastasis from a recurrence of the prostate cancer he had in 1989.

Mrs. Smith had to drive him back; she drove him home. At that point, Mr. Smith's health deteriorated. The doctors looked at the films and looked at the reports. It's very interesting that the only thing that the plaintiffs have focused on is two lesions out of six. They didn't talk about the other four. The plaintiffs didn't talk about the other four. They just sort of ignored those other four lesions, like they didn't exist. But Robert Smith had multiple brain metastasis, along with a stroke. That is what the records showed he had when he was referred to Dr. Gauwitz and South Florida Regional Cancer Consultants for care and treatment for that problem. He had a number of brain tumors in his head.

There is not a single piece of evidence from that witness stand that one week into the treatments, those half treatments caused Mr. Smith to end up in a wheelchair or a walker and begin his spiral down toward the end of his life. It could not have happened.

The undisputed evidence—and I say it's undisputed because this evidence came from Dr. Harvey Greenberg, whom the plaintiffs called as one of their key expert witnesses—showed that 150,000 people are treated every year for brain metastasis by radiation therapists. If radiation therapy killed, as if it had some nuclear bomb "Hiroshima type" effect, 150,000 people a year, there is no way that would be an approved proper treatment for brain metastasis. It just wouldn't happen.

The other defense lawyer has told you to use your common sense.

I wrote down exactly what Dr. Greenberg, the plaintiff's expert, said. Question, I had asked him, "Do you tell them that they may die from whole brain radiation in the same quantities administered by Dr. Gauwitz in this case?" I asked Dr. Greenberg that question, and his answer was no. The plaintiff's expert does not tell the patients he sees at Lee Moffitt Cancer Center that they can die from this radiation.

Yet, Mr. Yerrid has told you whole brain radiation will "kill you." They radiated Bob Smith and learned he would die because of it.

Not a single physician on that witness stand, plaintiff's or defense's, ever told you that whole brain radiation kills people. It doesn't do that. People may die because of the disease process, but not by use of an accepted and approved procedure.

Their expert, Dr. Greenberg, was asked about the type of radiation that was given and whether or not it was appropriate. And what did he say? He said that he had absolutely no criticism whatsoever of the amount of the dosage or the procedures or the quantity or accuracy of the delivery of the radiation that were given.

That is what he testified to as the first witness in this case on behalf of the plaintiff. So, Dr. Greenberg acknowledged that the treatment that Dr. Gauwitz gave not only wouldn't cause any problem, the type of problem that they alleged, but that it was an appropriate treatment.

Dr. Gauwitz performed the procedure in accordance with the standard of care, exactly as the plaintiff's expert witness does. Dr. Greenberg also acknowledged—and this is really the heart of the issue, and it was the first day of trial—that what plaintiff's claim in this case, that the radiation treatment killed Mr. Smith, that Dr. Gauwitz and South Florida and Dr. Tralins killed Mr. Smith by giving him the radiation. He admitted that he had no idea whether it did or whether it didn't. He couldn't give an answer, because I asked him. I asked him specifically, "Doctor, there is no way that you would be able to know one way or the other whether or not the radiation treatment that [Mr. Smith] received accelerated his death. Isn't that correct?"

And Dr. Greenberg replied, "Not without an autopsy."

So what you are being asked to believe in this case and accept as truth, not as fiction, is that the administration of radiation, which was designed to provide this patient with a better quality of life, was so lethal that it killed the patient, under circumstances where the expert called by the plaintiff herself acknowledges that is not the case.

Now, the plaintiff has also suggested that Dr. Recht was a defense expert; and therefore, what Dr. Recht had to say was inappropriate supports their position. Well, you may recall that when Dr. Recht's deposition testimony was read to you, we got up and read the remaining portion of the testimony. Dr. Recht was specifically asked—and this is, again, in the plaintiff's case, as the plaintiff's witness, even though he was admittedly hired by the defense, didn't come down and testify because we had Dr. Caukins testify, who is local—"Was it a deviation below the standard of care for Dr. Gauwitz to initiate radiation therapy, for failing to recognize that the larger lesion was a meningioma?"

Answer: "No."

Question: "And is the reason that it was not a deviation below the standard of care because there is sufficient doubt about what the other lesions looked like, that it was appropriate for him to rely on a radiologist?"

And Dr. Recht testified, "The other lesions were not clear-cut, benign lesions that a radiation oncologist would have been able, himself or herself, to define as clearly benign." So that relying on the judgment of the diagnostic radiologist for those other lesions, the ones inside the brain matter, was appropriate. It was also the fact that other physicians involved in the patient's care also have believed that these were representative of metastasis rather than benign disease. Dr. Recht, called by the plaintiffs, testified consistently with Dr. Greenberg, the plaintiff's expert, that they rely on the opinion of a diagnostic radiologist, just as Dr. Michael Gauwitz did, and that was appropriate and within the standard of care.

Let me turn for a moment to some of the other comments that Mr. Yerrid made during the course of his argument. First of all, he told you—and I wrote this down—that Dr. Tralins and Dr. Gauwitz cannot read and interpret films. Well, folks, if that is the case, why in the world is Dr. Gauwitz a defendant in this case? Because the only negligence that they can charge him with is that he did not override the two radiologists' reports that said Mr. Smith had metastatic tumors in his brain. I would submit to you that if Dr. Gauwitz made the decision to ignore a medical oncologist, an internal medicine doctor, Dr. Benson, Dr. Longacre—who's a medical oncologist—Dr. Bartone, Dr. Herbert, and said, "I'm not going to treat the patient, Mr. Smith would have died anyway from the strokes that he had." Then we would be in this courtroom, and he would be sued for not having given the treatments, based on the same interpretation. *A Tale of Two Cities* has indeed been presented to you.

Mr. Yerrid has also told us that this case is based on a lot of red herrings and white flies in the case. Well, red herrings, quite frankly, and white flies have no business in the courtroom. The facts are what have business in the courtroom. And as the triers of fact, as the judges of the facts, you, the jury, need to discard the red herrings and the white flies and the speckled masses and the speculation, and the comparison of different slices of films, to arrive at a conclusion that is not logical, does not follow common sense, and that does not comport with the medical evidence of the case.

A few other points. As the other defense lawyer told you, we don't feel anything but sympathy for Mrs. Smith or her family. I do not think you can look at the family and look at the photographs and pictures that Mr. Yerrid has brought into the courtroom and not feel sympathy. And you can look at this, and you can say that Bob Smith was a man who was blessed with a full and complete life. He was fortunate enough to have a daughter when he was older, fortunate enough to survive her marriage and dance with her at her wedding, fortunate enough to have a grandchild when he was basically sort of great-grandfather age, and bring that child up in his home. He's fortunate enough to have been able to live under circumstances where the average life expectancy of recurrent cancer is two and one half to three years, and live well beyond that. He's fortunate enough to have been able to have his health strong and vigorous enough that he could fight off, for a long period of time, the illnesses that would have affected and led to the demise of other people, because he was a strong, healthy guy. He's fortunate enough to have been surrounded by loving friends and family and to have that family with him up until his last days.

But ladies and gentlemen of the jury, Dr. Michael Gauwitz did not kill Bob Smith. Bob Smith died of natural causes due to the progression of the aging process that was clearly evident in the radiology films that all of you saw, well before Michael Gauwitz ever saw Bob Smith.

Mr. Yerrid showed you a board regarding non-economic pain and suffering and damages. Ladies and gentlemen, there are no numbers written on here, and that is exactly the way it should be left because, although Mrs. Smith did lose her husband, she lost him in the ordinary way of life, in the way that happens to all of us.

And compensating her for past and future non-economic damages by blaming the process of life and the ending of that process of life and the ending of that process on a physician, who did his very best to prolong Mr. Smith's life, is not the way the justice that we seek here in the courtroom works. We ask you to give us that justice, and return a verdict for the defense.

MY REBUTTAL

First, let's set the record straight: This is not a murder trial. Nobody said the defendant killed anyone. The plaintiff is not held to that standard of proof, nor should she be. The proof required in this case is not beyond a reasonable doubt. Do you remember we talked about that in jury selection? Specifically, we pointed out the difference between a criminal case and a civil case such as this one.

The burden that must be satisfied to prove our case is the greater weight of the evidence. The judge will instruct you, as a matter of law, that all the plaintiffs need to do is tip those scales ever so slightly. We don't need to prove that the defendants killed Bob Smith. In fact, let me be very clear: We don't even need to prove that the radiation was the only cause of Mr. Smith's death. That is why you will receive a jury instruction entitled "concurrent causation." That jury instruction, as well as all the others, will be sent with you to the jury room for your use during deliberations. The instructions are not very long, but read them carefully, and you will see that the law to be applied is all laid out. Nothing fancy about being a lawyer. You, the jury, will be able to figure it out. *[I needed to immediately refute the notion the defense lawyer had laid out. It is very difficult to win a medical negligence case. It is virtually impossible to "convict" a doctor of intentional wrongdoing. Understandably, there is a belief physicians intend to help and render care. Many people will accept the notion that sometimes inexcusable mistakes are made. I had to transform this case back to that simple proposition.]*

Now, this verdict form I am using is mine. It is a little marked up. When you retire to deliberate, you will get a fresh four-page verdict form that is filled with blanks. I just wanted to point out to you these dollar figures I have penned in are called "economic damages." Here, we are talking about the amount of any loss because of the decedent's services, debt from medical bills, and funeral costs. Our economist didn't include anything like loss of consortium or anything that might cause you some confusion or difficulty in arriving at an amount of damages for economic loss.

From the date of Bob Smith's death in October 1994 to the present, that number is $249,000. I have written the figure on my verdict form, and I suggest you may do the same on yours.

You may remember when I asked Alma Smith how she was doing at the present time. She answered, "Fine."

"Where are you living?" I asked.

"I'm living in my home, the home Bob and I lived in," she replied.

"What's going to happen after this case is over, or in the future?" I inquired.

"Oh," she said, "I'm going to continue to live in my home."

Remember when I said that this verdict is for all time? So, if she does, in fact, need extra support or services, that is the way you need to look at it as future damages. Suppose you remove her beloved sister, Elizabeth, who has temporarily moved in to help her out. If you remove her, what would her loss of services be, if you believe payment for those activities would be required? That is the number I have suggested in order to allow Alma to pay for those assisting care services, if she needs them in the future.

The defense argues you should not award any money for economic damages because Mr. Smith would have died in 1994 from old age and not from anything to do with medical negligence. What else are they going to say?

Of course, we have reduced the dollar amount of economic damages we are seeking in order to be fair. For example, if you have $100,000 now, and you invest it, you would get more than $100,000 over the next four years. I think $100,000 would probably be reduced to present values of $84,000 or $85,000 now. So, if you invest it, and some of you have backgrounds in finance, so I'm sure you can follow my muddled thought process, the resulting amount will be right around $100,000. It is that process the jury instruction is referencing when it requires you to reduce any economic damages awarded to present value.

When Dr. Tralins, who appeared as one of the defense witnesses, was being questioned, he made it a point to explain the tests could have been negative, and yet Bob still may have had brain cancer. He explained that scenario could occur, because ten percent of the time cancer doesn't even show up on these tests. That is just exactly the type of thing I am talking about, that the defense takes the exception to the rule and seeks exoneration. Please remember, overwhelming all of this is the inescapable fact that 99.9 percent of the time, prostate cancer does not metastasize to the brain.

The greater weight of the evidence...even if you took what they said, that ten percent, there's a ten percent chance Mr. Smith—because we don't know, you don't know unless an autopsy had been performed—ten percent chance that Mr. Smith somehow had this cancer and nobody knew about it and no tests showed it. To take it another way, in all fairness, there is a ninety percent chance that he did not have cancer. That is our worst day, even under their best-case scenario. We only need fifty-one percent probability to prove this case. That, ladies and gentlemen, is exactly what the greater weight of the evidence means.

The defense then contends that even if there was negligence, it was the fault of Dr. Longacre and Dr. Herbert, not Dr. Gauwitz. And exactly why are these other two doctors on the verdict form? I could have sat down and not explained this to you, but you need to know the answer. It is money. It is about being responsible for paying less damages in the event you render a verdict in favor of the plaintiff. If you put on the verdict form, Was Dr. Herbert negligent? And you check yes. Was Dr. Longacre negligent? And you check yes. Well, after that, on your verdict form, it will have the percentages of neglect you affix to each one. This is really important. So, if you, for example, find Dr. Herbert ten percent negligent and Dr. Longacre ten percent negligent, and then Dr. Gauwitz eighty percent negligent, what happens is, by the reduction of that twenty percent, Dr. Gauwitz is then only responsible for eighty percent of your verdict in terms of any damages awarded.

In essence, any percentage points of fault you affix to other people means less percentage points of responsibility for Dr. Gauwitz. That equates into liability, and that equates into a reduction of any money awarded. And that is precisely why the other two doctors are on the verdict form.

As for the testimony of doctors, how can anything be clearer than the testimony of Dr. Greenberg, a world-renowned expert who is the head of radiation oncology at one of the best cancer treatment centers in the country? There are a lot of people floating around who are legends in their own minds. Certainly, you have heard the self-accolades of the parade of experts the defense has brought before you. I will simply rest on the record concerning the credentials of Dr. Greenberg and the Lee Moffitt Cancer Center. No, contrary to what the defense lawyer has argued, they don't radiate patients like this. They don't have any history or statistics of it, because, thank goodness, they can't come up with any instances where they gave whole brain radiation to a man who didn't have metastatic disease in his head. Most importantly, there was not one bit of hesitation when Dr. Greenberg testified that the defendant Dr. Gauwitz deviated from an acceptable standard of care.

You expect physicians to be right. Not perfect, for sure, but right in the sense that the proper treatment is given under circumstances where a mistake should not occur. Not perfection, simply good judgment. That is the standard. And one hopes that when they are wrong, the mistake is promptly admitted.

Yet, even if there was negligence, the defendant's lawyer argues, there should be no liability. "This case is about causation," the defense says. "In essence, even if he made a mistake, so what? It was not Dr. Gauwitz who caused this tragedy. He was simply carrying through and relying upon the mistakes of others."

Indeed, it is the plaintiff's burden to prove causation. Did the negligence cause what happened? You only need to use your common sense. That person sitting there, Dr. Gauwitz, is the one with the radiation gun. And the last wrongful thing that happened in this case occurred when he pulled the trigger and radiated the brain of Bob Smith.

When a physician is directing that deadly radiation beam, don't you think he has to be precise and know exactly where it is going? What was this defendant's target?

Let me wrap up by addressing the issue of whether or not a biopsy should have been performed. Apparently, giving up on their initial argument that a biopsy was offered but refused, the defense has asserted that a biopsy was not necessary, that it was too risky. And maybe I am mistaken, but I thought that was the very subject I questioned Dr. Rosa, the defendant's neurosurgeon expert, about. I asked him to tell us the risks of biopsy. He testified the risk of complications from the biopsy was five to ten percent. Then I read to you his deposition that was taken before trial. At that time, he said there is a five percent chance—a five percent risk, not even a ten percent danger. So, even if you give him the benefit of the doubt, five or ten percent does not mean it is likely bad things are going to happen. Forget the glass being half full or half empty. We have a ninety to ninety-five percent chance Mr. Smith's biopsy was going to go uneventfully and that this "misidentified cancer" would have been discovered to be nothing. If that simple biopsy procedure had been performed, there never would have been any whole brain radiation.

This is a case about failing to exercise good care and prudence. There are a lot of stories we have heard about what intellect does and what the intellect is after it has been affected by what we call wisdom. Intellect tells you this is a problem we have to address. Wisdom tells us how to do it. Where was the urgency? Why not wait for the test results? Why not do a biopsy and make sure before any radiation was given?

I'm not going to talk about the defendant's motivations as to why doctors do the things they do. But let me just say they used all their professional services and they billed accordingly. The defense wants to say Mr. Smith died, just kind of sailed off into the sunset. If they have their way, that is exactly what the end of the story will be.

But this case will not end that way because it is not a story of fiction. Charles Dickens wasn't talking about fiction when he wrote *A Tale of Two Cities*. He was talking about life. He used fiction to illustrate what life teaches us all. What life teaches us all is that right is right.

The defense argues it was a team approach. I submit to you that was not the way a team should work. On a team, you use everything that you have, all the pieces of information and logic; and just like when I hope you go back to the jury room, all of you use each other's brain and your wisdom and your heart and your collective common sense. That is the team approach. But if one person is wrong, let's have some responsibility. If that causes a bad result, let's have some responsibility.

I was going to read some entries from the medical records that vividly describe the demise of Bob Smith as he gradually wound down. But I will not take that time. It is there for you in evidence. Once again, I will elect not to read all these terrible accounts of what the family went through and the tragic way Bob's life ended. But I will say this: The gist of what I got from the defense lawyers was that Bob's passing was just a part of the cycle of life. I just hope that isn't so. And I hope you remember what Dr. Harrison, the experienced consulting neurologist, said when he came in here and testified about what he wrote and told one of Bob's treating physicians, words to the effect of, "Dr. Sinoff, we have the answer to your question as to what is wrong. This patient has a bad, bad situation. He is dying of radiation sickness. We are going to give him hospice care because his condition is hopeless. Mr. Smith will never make it, and he is going to die because of the radiation that was given to him, on top of the already underlying problem of his old age."

This case does cry out. It cries out for justice. Do your best. We can ask for no more.

Thank you.

An Endless Night

· · · · · · ·

When the jury went into deliberations, the trial had been steadily marching on for nearly two weeks. In the final analysis, the medical complexity of the case had been simplified. A delightful, kind, caring, loving gentleman who had a true zest for life was dead. The jury would determine why. The wait in the courtroom grew…one hour, and then two, three, and on and on. The jury had gone behind closed doors at nearly one o'clock on the afternoon of April 21, 2000. It was Good Friday, and I realized the terrible irony that it was on a Good Friday six years earlier that Bob Smith had commenced the radiation treatments that would take his life.

At almost seven o'clock in the evening—after nearly four years of preparations—the unimaginable happened: The jury delivered a note to the court advising that they were deadlocked. I strongly believe a trial lawyer has certain natural instincts—feelings and beliefs that seem to bubble up to the surface in the form of a hunch. My gut had told me that juror number two was trouble. Now that seemed to be a certainty.

Judge O'Brien responded to the jurors with a note of his own that contained firm instructions. "No juror, from mere pride of opinion hastily formed or expressed, should refuse to agree. Yet, no juror, simply for the purpose of terminating the case, should acquiesce in a conclusion that is contrary to his or her own conscientiously held view of the evidence.…You should listen to each other's views, you should talk over your differences of opinion…in a spirit of fairness and candor and, if possible, resolve your differences…and come to a common conclusion so that a verdict may be reached and this case may be disposed of."

We had depended on the members of the jury to arrive at a verdict. That simply had not happened. I felt one holdout juror saw Robert Smith as an elderly man whose time to die had come and there had been no medical negligence. Worse, perhaps I was wrong. Maybe only one juror felt we had proven our case and was the only thing between us and a verdict for the defense. From the jurors' eyes, and the way each had looked at me, I could sense they had been with me in closing argument—that is, all except juror number two. Could I have been that wrong? How in the world would we ever be able to handle a defeat of this magnitude? What about Alma? For now, the questions would remain unanswered. We could only wait.

The evening hours wore on, stretching into eight, nine, ten, and eleven o'clock. As the time neared midnight, the jury once again sent a note; this time, the word "hopeless" was used. It read, "Your Honor, we are hopelessly deadlocked and unable to reach a unanimous verdict."

The age and experience of the trial judge somehow told him to give it one more try. Judge O'Brien called the jury back into the courtroom and advised them that after thirty more minutes, the jury would be excused for the weekend and fresh deliberations would commence on the following Monday morning. The jury's walk into the courtroom confirmed my earlier fears and my gut instincts. They had been engaged in a war of wills. The look of fatigue and disappointment was apparent. I knew at once it was five against one. Body movements and eye contact confirmed my suspicion.

The other five jurors had disengaged from juror number two. He seemed to be sitting alone among his fellow jurors, who leaned away from him even as they all sat together in the jury box. He refused to look our way and instead focused his attention on the defense table. To my utter amazement, I actually saw him shrug his shoulders and mouth the words "I'm trying" to the defendant doctor. The other five looked first at Judge O'Brien and, after a time, focused intently on Alma. I made eye contact and instantly felt their support and allegiance. We had a holdout juror who seemed determined to stop any verdict against the defense. Fueled by a break and food, the six jurors obediently moved again to the jury room for more deliberations.

Just a few minutes passed when the twice-deadlocked jury sent word that they were close to a verdict. The time was nearing one o'clock in the morning. They requested another ten minutes to ascertain whether or not an agreement could be reached. Finally, after over eleven hours of deliberations, the news came that the jury had reached a decision. The door to the jury room opened quietly and the jurors came out in single file. The handsome, athletic-looking young man who managed the Chili's restaurant—he had been elected jury foreman—held the verdict in his hand. Now he would manage the solemn duty of conveying the jury's decision to the court and the litigants.

As word spread that the jury had finally reached a verdict, even at this hour, more and more people began appearing. Family, friends, members of the various legal teams, and even some spectators filed in and the bench seats filled. Watching the case had become personal to some of the gallery. The strain of the evening's tension was apparent on everyone's face. The formal and well-established protocol unfolded as the bailiff retrieved the verdict from the jury foreman and delivered it to Judge O'Brien. The judge closely examined the jury verdict form and seemed to read it twice. "You may publish the verdict," he said as he solemnly handed it to the court's clerk. We all stood as she began reading the jury's decision. Her voice, tired from the long day, quickly picked up pace as her words reverberated in the courtroom:

We, the jury, return the following verdict. One, was there negligence on the part of the defendant Michael Gauwitz, M.D., which was a legal cause of death of Robert B. Smith? Yes.

Two, was there negligence on the part of M. Linton Herbert, M.D., which was a legal cause of the death of Robert B. Smith? Yes.

Three, was there negligence on the part of David Longacre, M.D., which was a legal cause of the death of Robert B. Smith? Yes.

Four, state the percentage of any negligence, which was a legal cause of Robert B. Smith's death that you charge to Michael Gauwitz, M.D., and South Florida Regional Cancer Consultants One, Inc. Thirty-three and a third percent.

M. Linton Herbert, M.D. Thirty-three and a third percent.

David Longacre, M.D. Thirty-three and a third percent.

One, what is the amount of any medical or funeral expenses resulting from Robert B. Smith's injury and death charged to the estate or paid by someone other than the survivors? Zero.

Two, what is the amount of any medical or funeral expenses paid by Alma B. Smith, the survivor? $171,659.86.

Three, what is the amount of any loss by Alma B. Smith of the decedent's support and service (A) from the date of death to the present? *$78,000.00.* (B) In the future? Zero. What is the number of years over which these future damages are intended to provide compensation? Zero. (C) What is the present value of those future damages entered above? Zero. What is the total amount of economic damages? *$249,659.86.*

Four, what is the amount of any damage sustained by Alma B. Smith in the loss of her husband's companionship and protection and in pain and suffering as a result of Robert B. Smith's injury and death? (A) In the past? Zero. (B) In the future? Zero. What is the total amount of non-economic damages? Zero.

The total damages of the estate of Robert B. Smith and his survivor, Alma B. Smith? *$249,659.86.*

So say we all.

It was 1:30 in the morning as we sat silent and stunned—and still awaiting the justice we had sought for so very long.

We had won, but the verdict was terribly flawed. *Zero for pain and suffering?* Zero for pain and suffering! I was shocked. No way could the jury find liability, conclude that medical negligence caused Bob Smith's unnecessary death, and at the same time fail to compensate the widow for the horrendous suffering so clearly established throughout the entirety of the evidentiary record. Deep down, I knew what had happened. The holdout made the others reduce the amount of the award in return for his agreement to a plaintiff's verdict. It was that, or a hung jury and mistrial. If a mistrial was declared, Alma would get nothing and be forced to go through another trial maybe a year away, providing she lived that long. In the end, I knew the other jurors had no choice.

After the jury had left the room, I asked the trial judge for immediate consideration of an "additur," given the finding of negligence and the overwhelming case that was presented by us on non-economic damages. There was simply no way that "zero" damages for Alma's pain and suffering was acceptable under the law. A motion for additur, in essence, means that the jury didn't properly evaluate the issue of damages, and that their award was way out of line and "shocking" to the court's conscience.

In order for the judge to intervene, however, he had to find the verdict was grossly disparate from what it should have been. Under those unique and rare circumstances, the law allows the presiding judge to step in and right the wrong of the inadequate award. Most times, judges are called on to step in and reduce an award because it is too much and considered excessive. The McDonald's coffee spill case is a good example. A very large verdict was rendered by a jury to a lady who had just bought a cup of hot coffee from McDonald's and then spilled it in her own lap, which caused burns and blisters. She sued the fast food chain, contending the coffee was too hot, and won, but the large jury verdict was sliced in half by the trial judge as being excessive and "contrary" to the evidence.

Here, we had the exact opposite happen. The jury had given nothing for the value of the pain and suffering endured by Alma Smith. The motion for additur asked the judge to supplement the jury verdict by awarding non-economic damages for the pain, torment, and agony Alma experienced in her husband's suffering, and for the non-economic damages she would continue to suffer until her death. The jury, in my opinion, shocked the conscience of the court when it failed to award any non-economic damages whatsoever. I argued the verdict was terribly inconsistent with the jury's findings of negligence, and that the jurors could not find negligence and award economic damages of $249,659.86 and, at the same time, say that Alma was entitled to "zero" for pain and suffering in the past and in the future.

After several days, we were notified that the judge would hear our motion for additur. It was the first time it had ever happened in all my years of practicing law. Now the lawyers for both sides would argue as to whether or not the judge should award additional damages, and if so, how much.

Both sides filed voluminous briefs, and oral argument was scheduled. The hearing began with Judge O'Brien expressing his agreement with the jury on the verdict of economic damages for medical expenses, funeral costs, and lost support. He continued in his findings by observing, "I thought that the use of the word 'kill' during closing argument was unusually strong, but it was non-equivocating. I wondered how the jury would react to it, especially in view of the fact the jury had before it a man who had complex medical problems…but the question was put to the jury, 'Was the death of Robert B. Smith the result of the negligent act by these three doctors?' The jury answered the question bluntly as given, 'Yes.'"

We argued for almost three hours over the amount of damages the court should award through the additur process. Very rarely have I advocated more forcefully or passionately. In the middle of my argument, one of the defense lawyers objected by stating, "I object, Judge. Mr. Yerrid is doing nothing more than making a jury argument." Of course, that was exactly what I was doing, and it was perfectly proper. The judge, in effect, had become the sole juror with regard to making a determination of the non-economic aspects of the jury's verdict based upon the evidence that he had heard at trial. As a one-person jury, his decision as to the amount of damages would be based upon the testimony, the ages of both Bob and Alma, and all of the considerations that were available to the original jurors, including final argument.

There is a school of thought among some attorneys that judges can best set appropriate damage amounts because they are less likely than a jury to be reversed on appeal. In our modern society, a fairly popular notion seems to have evolved that judges are better than juries. Somewhere along the line, many Americans seem to have lost respect for the jury system upon which our country was founded. As for me, I think a trial by jury is the best thing our democracy ever created. But in this case, on the issue of damages the jury had failed us. Now, it was up to the judge.

As the hearing moved forward, the judge, well into his seventies, white-haired and solemn, continued with his findings. "All during the course of the testimony on the plaintiff's side, the death was shown not to be sudden, not quick and painless. From the time of April of 1994, when the administration of radiation was given to the total brain of Robert Smith until the time of his death in October, the testimony was that he was in agony....That is a long period of death passage, you might say. It did not proceed quickly. This wasn't a death itself that was painless, sudden, but was a death that was slow and both agonizing to the victim, Robert Smith, as well as to the wife and his daughter, both of whom were always present in the hospital on a daily basis trying to nurse him, care for him, doing the duties of a nurse such as caring for his body by cleaning him, turning him so he wouldn't get bedsores, listening to his obvious agony, and trying to feed him and keep him properly cleaned."

The judge stopped for a moment, took a deep breath as if visualizing the last hours of Bob Smith's life, and continued, "Now, there's testimony to that effect, and when you think in terms of somebody's death going on agonizingly in your presence over a period of weeks and months, from April until October, it's impossible in my mind to concede how the jury could both answer the question affirmatively that the death did result from the doctors; and listening to all the testimony about what his death was like, how they could remove the wife from feeling the suffering herself, the emotional feelings that she must have had under the circumstances after twenty-eight years of marriage, kind of escapes my reasoning process. I don't think the court has much of a choice under the statute [but] to grant the motion of additur. [The statute] states, 'Whether it appears that the trier of fact [the jury] ignored the evidence in reaching a verdict or misconceived the merit to the case relating to the amounts of damages recoverable.' I think that happened in this situation. Somehow they misconceived the merits of the case from the standpoint of pain and suffering, and I think that definitely applies here for reasons I have already given."

To emphasize the basis of his authority, the trial judge picked up a volume of the Florida statutes and began reading word for word, "Where the amount awarded bears a reasonable relation to the amount of damages proved and injuries suffered." As he put the text down, he had an almost pained expression on his face, and then he took another short pause before he began speaking again. "I don't think that the damages for pain and suffering are consistent with the injury suffered. To put in a zero for the injuries suffered is contradictory to all the testimony. The plaintiffs had sufficient evidence to support medical testimony that is—and I think the treating physician himself testified at the trial—that the death was brought about by radiation, and that the suffering they were witnessing was brought about by the radiation. That is the basis of the lawsuit getting started. Post-radiation treatment analysis by the treating physician more or less confirms, I think, what the family was wondering during this period of time, seeing the degeneration take place in the decedent. If this wasn't the fallout of the radiation, doctors merely confirmed it. It's a logical conclusion that even lay people can make."

With a quick glance at the defense lawyer, and then Alma, and then me, Judge O'Brien kept speaking in an even voice. "And since it was shown there is no medical proof that Mr. Smith's prostate cancer had metastasized to the brain, which would have justified the application of the radiation as a normal medical procedure and the amount of radiation that was given, that is the dosage, if it had been proven to the jury that he had metastasized to the prostate cancer to the brain, they might very well have gone along with the defense that Dr. Gauwitz's actions were permissible, and found that he was not acting outside the scope of medical treatment to render the radiation that was rendered here. So, I'm in a position where I don't think I have any choice but to grant the additur. It would be a miscarriage of justice not to grant additur for all the reasons I have given...and I don't wish to have it be thought that this jury was greedy themselves, negligent, or not carrying out their duties, but for some reason or another, the message never got through to them that before they left the jury room, they had to consider pain and suffering. It might be the defense did not make a big issue out of that, by way of challenging Alma Smith's testimony or her daughter's testimony or of the brother, Harry Smith, in his testimony. It seemed that the defense was very discreet in the sense of not trying to embarrass the family members to having them consent to having over-described the pain and suffering."

Alma Smith endured six months of watching her husband suffer and die, and then she endured six years of her own tremendous pain and suffering after his death. The judge's decision to grant the motion of additur was just under the law and amply supported by the barometer of whether or not it was a correct or incorrect use of the court's inherent power. I was so very proud of this courageous, compassionate judge and his valiant actions to deliver total justice.

The judge not only took notes during the trial itself, but he also observed the intent, demeanor, and credibility of the witnesses. He looked at the evidence, just as any of the jurors had. I had seen him move on more than a dozen occasions from the bench to the side observation point where he could, with the jury, see the demonstrations and actual physical presentation of the evidence—even though he couldn't have known that he himself would become, in effect, a juror. At long last, Judge O'Brien looked at me and asked the question I had anticipated for so long. "Mr. Yerrid, how much do you believe I should award...what would be fair, in your opinion?"

Invariably, in litigation, when a plaintiff's lawyer submits or suggests an amount of money, it is always subject to criticism. I was willing to take that on. Gazing directly into Judge O'Brien's eyes, I answered, "If it please the Court, I believe two million dollars should be added to the jury's verdict." I went to great lengths in detailing the significance of what Alma Smith had sustained in pain and suffering because of the loss of her husband and his companionship, wisdom, and the love he had provided in their long marriage. To me, there are no greater losses than those of the heart. In a marriage as strong and faithful as the Smiths', there comes with it an unbelievable sense of oneness. I don't know that the phrase "soulmates" is appropriate, but I can tell you the undisputed evidence was that Alma and Bob Smith had an absolute loving and total devotion to each other. As an arbiter of both the law and the facts, Judge O'Brien would be telling Alma what the loss she had sustained was worth in terms of monetary compensation under the law.

It was obvious Judge O'Brien had read the materials and reviewed the case law. Additionally, he had given both sides unlimited time to argue. He was ready to rule. His voice was strong and sure as his words closed the hearing. "I have studied the arguments in light of the records in this case, Mr. Yerrid...I'm not going to grant non-economic damages in that amount. And I am not going to go higher than that amount; however, in view of the fact the decedent in this case died prematurely and while he was already of advanced age, I don't think that being at an advanced age means you should die either sooner to what nature calls for at the hands of your medical assistants, and least of all, you should not have to die an agonizing death.

"One of the things that struck me about this man's death, as described, is the fact that it was testified that his limbs became stiff and distended, that his arms went straight out. He couldn't bend them; his legs went straight out. He could not bend them or walk to do anything like that, and his limbs quivered and were distended. I think that his death was very tragic and very unfortunate, and it's difficult to assess monetarily how to arrive at compensation for the surviving widow.

"I am convinced that if she had her druthers, she would waive any compensation in favor of her husband continuing to live. There is absolutely no way the court can measure the impact of his death upon her life and her survivability. The fact that she had suffered depression and has also needed the care of her sister who did move down here, according to the record to help live with her, help her out.

"Grief is a natural for surviving loved one. Grief is to be expected and it's to be welcomed, because grief is nature's way of both compensating and giving the survivor an opportunity to cut the strings, so to speak. Grief is healthy and normal, but nobody wishes that on anybody else. Grief brings along severe depression. I think Mrs. Smith has already entered into the depression mode, according to her doctors…I think one million dollars is not unreasonable, not too high and not too low… The motion for additur is granted. The court awards for non-economic damages a total award…of one million dollars."

Several days later, the case settled and no appeal was filed.

Epilogue
· · · · · · ·

I n proportion as a man's backbone weakens, his wishbone seems to develop. Things in our body, whether muscle or bone, develop by usage, and if we use the wishbone all the time, it will develop into huge proportion. Bob Smith is one young man who, I can say without fear of contradiction, never uses his wishbone, for he has no use for it. I have watched him at his work in the Printing Department at the Trust Company of Georgia Building, and his attitude is always the same—"I WILL" instead of "I WISH." When he is bowling, that backbone of his does double duty, and if you had seen him on March 25th when he simply jumped into the play-off between the Interior and the Bookkeeping departments and wrecked things right and left, you would readily have seen that Bob Smith has eliminated entirely from his make-up such a thing as a wishbone. The writer has never seen a more perfect type of a strong, well-balanced, cool, steady and all 'round fair player without any put-on or show. That's Bob Smith, champion duckpin bowler of the First National Bank & Trust Company of Georgia. One who loves his work as he does his play. Bob's motto is "Never use your wishbone—Bring

*your backbone into play—As one is a "will-o'-the-wisp"—And the other is
with you to stay.*

These words were written about Bob in May of 1932 by George W.
Bosman for *The Teller*, the newsletter of First National Bank & Trust
Company of Georgia. Bob Smith had lived a very good life that was laden
with both professional and personal accomplishments. He had spent many
wonderful years with his lovely Alma, reared a fine daughter, and watched
Stephen grow into an outstanding young man. He had never failed to
provide for his family, and he furnished the guidance, necessary wisdom,
understanding, and patience the years had allowed him to acquire. Bob
had enjoyed much through hard work, dedication, and integrity, and he
had partnered a family of love that was built upon devotion. He had trusted
in others...and he had died unnecessarily and very, very badly. In examining
his life through the eyes of Alma, Debbie, and others, I discovered a legacy
and realized that the good accomplished by his acts will live on.

For me, the case emphasized that no matter the age, our most senior
citizens still possess hopes and dreams for the future. I more fully appreciated the meaning of living in the present, and I also comprehended the
more critical notion that no one is promised tomorrow. More importantly,
regardless of age, life and all of its dreams remain the most precious of
commodities. I came away from the Smith case knowing that the elderly
should always be revered as the most valuable masterpieces of our society.
Every single day of our lives, we should look upon our oldest people as a
significant and profound part of our culture, not some colorless or invisible
sector of humanity that can be pushed aside and forgotten. In youth-
oriented America, too often nursing and retirement communities prevent
contact and interaction with the fascinating people who have lived the
longest on this earth.

Often, I have found that the elderly possess the most wisdom. In the
traditions of many cultures, including the Native American heritage, the
oldest member of the tribe becomes the leader so that the wisdom, insight
and knowledge gained only through experience can be passed on to the
next generation. Bob Smith had become a "chief," not simply because of
his age, but also because of what he knew and had done with his life. His

worth as a husband, provider, and soulmate are memorialized by the carriage of justice in his case.

Bob proved that old age is nothing more than a state of mind. Alma continues to be a living example of that adage. Near eighty, Alma Smith could easily pass for a woman much, much younger. Her short, dark hair perfectly contrasts a smooth, ivory complexion, and her smile radiates the warmness of her heart. When she speaks of her husband, her doe-brown eyes still glisten with tears of love. "Bob was my whole life," she says with sincerity and affection. "I have not found anyone else, because I can never replace him. He was everything I ever wanted. The hardest thing I ever did in my life was say goodbye to him."

Bob Smith's wife, daughter, and their extended families are enjoying life and living well in Clearwater, Florida. Many people who witness their strength and happiness believe they are blessed by a very special angel. I believe them about the angel...and whenever I talk to him, I always call him Bob.

. . . .

In the Circuit Court of the Fifteenth Judicial Circuit
In and For the County of Palm Beach
State of Florida

The State of Florida,
Lawton M. Chiles Jr., Individually, and as
Governor of the State of Florida, et. al., Plaintiffs

Versus

The American Tobacco Company;
R. J. Reynolds Tobacco Company;
RJR Nabisco, Inc.,
Brown & Williamson Tobacco Corporation;
Philip Morris Companies, Inc.;
Philip Morris Incorporated
(Philip Morris U.S.A.); et. al., Defendants

. . .

CHAPTER EIGHT

The Tobacco Crusade:
Confronting the Devil

The Devil comes in many forms. In this case, he had no horns or shooting flames of fire. He hid in the cool shadows and sterile security of corporate boardrooms. He led a life of luxury, profit, and riches beyond imagination. And the price the public paid for his lavish lifestyle? Four hundred thousand American deaths a year, a broad range of illnesses, and the most horrendous forms of human suffering imaginable. The weapon the Devil used was nicotine addiction, and its power was overwhelming. Fueled in his success by the insatiable compulsion of need rather than choice, this modern-day Lucifer had become a dominant force in the world. His disciples came in pinstriped suits of blue and gray and fulfilled missions of profit on Wall Street. He owned enough city hall bureaucrats, state legislatures, congressmen, and senators to make himself immune from meaningful regulation, governance, or accountability.

The tobacco industry had been battling lawsuits in the courtroom since the early 1950s. There had never been a loss. Hundreds of lawsuits had been filed against various corporate entities on behalf of individual plaintiffs who had become ill or lost loved ones because of the dangerous and deadly effects of smoking. Still, the cigarette cartel had never paid a single dime as a result of the product-liability lawsuits brought against them. They had an unblemished record of more than eight hundred wins and no defeats. The Devil's advocates who defended the vast empire of "tobaccodom" were the best lawyers money could buy.

Most of the cases brought by tobacco plaintiffs never even went to court because the industry either exhausted or outlived the plaintiffs, their lawyers, and even surviving family members. The cigarette industry's legal strategy was to file every conceivable motion and take every possible deposition in order to bleed the plaintiff dry. Even for the few cases that survived long enough to make it to a courtroom, the defendants always had available the "blame the victim" approach. It had been simple: Just assert that the complaining smoker had assumed the risk, and success was guaranteed.

Then things went from bad to worse. Modernized production techniques that vastly increased the number of cigarettes being manufactured led to a more widespread form of satanic seduction that would ensnare more and more victims, one generation after another. Mass marketing exploited the public's innocence and astounding ignorance about the true danger of the product. Ads showed cigarette smokers as professional athletes, famous movie stars, and other heroes of our culture in order to attract younger and younger victims into the web of nicotine dependency. The devil was Joe Camel and the Marlboro Man or, at other times, a nameless young beauty who touted the allure of Virginia Slims.

Ironically, the cigarette manufacturers even marketed a brand named Eve. It was an appropriate Biblical reference for those old enough to choose between good and evil. But it was nothing more than a warped and perverted form of entrapment for the ten- and twelve-year-old children who were being targeted as replacement smokers for those individuals who had died from smoking-related illnesses. For all his beguiling names, I came to know the Devil simply as Big Tobacco, and eventually I would help to wage a war against these corporate giants, a battle that would save countless lives and change our society forever.

The legal case, which pitted the State of Florida against the entire tobacco industry, was extraordinary in the annals of American jurisprudence. It possessed the high drama that occurs only when good confronts evil. The three-year war of litigation that ensued took belief, courage, commitment, stamina, and almost every ounce of my being. The crusade in which I so eagerly enlisted extracted a tremendous toll on my personal and professional life. It began to put a strain on everything I treasured and I felt the increasing threat that I would be pulled into a black abyss of danger and destruction. There were even brief times when I abandoned the more noble notions of success and prayed for mere survival.

Conflicts raged among all the parties: the lawyers, the healthcare community, the politicians--and ultimately even invaded our attorney-client relationship. My experiences weave a tale of heroes and villains, truth and lies, trust and betrayal, and the most passionate of love that burned into cinders of hate.

And it all began with a simple telephone call.

1995
∙ ∙ ∙ ∙ ∙ ∙ ∙

From the twenty-first floor of my office building, I watched as massive freighters navigated the slim channels of Tampa Bay. Just moments earlier, I had hung up the telephone after speaking with Fred Levin, a well-known attorney from the panhandle town of Pensacola. He was one of the best trial lawyers in the country. I had just committed to taking on with him one of the biggest cases in the history of the legal world. As I stood at the window watching the ships move across the dark green waters of the Port of Tampa, I wondered if I had gone too far. My law practice had made me successful and financially secure. I had reached the point where I could pick and choose the cases I took. Why would I put everything on the line? Risk it all, and for what? A chance to take on well-moneyed corporate giants that had never lost? Then I went deeper.

This bastard addiction and its filthy industry had gone after our children. Fred Levin and the hand-picked legal team that was being assembled were the best chance to stop it all and take them down. It was the right thing to do. But at what price? The right thing to do had always been easy for me, because I had been taught well. Better still, I had not been required to learn much. I got an awful lot by just being born. I suspected my mother and father had simply passed the trait along genetically. Why was I so troubled about my decision to join the lawsuit? Before I could stop myself, I realized the thoughts that had been welling up inside had now begun to rush forward. These were the searing memories I tried so hard to forget but never could.

My father had been extremely handsome, smart, and a great athlete almost all of his life. Charlie Yerrid had been a man's man. He had fought for his country in the Pacific Theater during World War II. Working in the control tower at Nichols Air Field in Manila, Master Sergeant Yerrid had served in the Army Air Corps before he was even old enough to vote. After the Philippines were recaptured, the Japanese had launched a suicide raid on the airfield, and my father had been forced to kill. He always told me how much that changed his life.

During that time, he also fought in the ring. He distinguished himself as an undefeated heavyweight boxer in the military bouts that acted as a popular distraction from the agony of war. Halfway across the world from home, he had also picked up a habit of smoking unfiltered Camel cigarettes. The three-pack-a-day addiction killed him in 1982. He was fifty-eight years old and never lived to see his grandson, Gable. The coroner's report attributed his death to cerebral vascular disease. I knew better.

My mother's life was nine years longer than my father's—she was sixty-seven when she passed away. "Missy" Yerrid and I were very close, and I remember so well the last time I saw her. I had stopped by her home to deliver an airplane ticket for her annual trip to attend a family reunion in her hometown of Charleston, West Virginia. I arrived at her home on Davis Island, one of Tampa's waterfront neighborhoods, at 6:30 on a Friday evening. It was near the end of February in 1995, and the winter sun had already set. The house was dark when I pulled into the driveway. There was no sign of activity, although my mother's car was there. I knocked on the door and rang the doorbell, but no answer came.

Using the key my mother had given me long ago, I let myself in the door nearest the garage and walked past the dark screen of the large television she loved to watch so much. There was not a light on in the house, and my mother didn't answer as I called out her name. Her modest three-bedroom house was ranch-style, and the master bedroom was at the far end from where I had entered. Somehow, as I walked down the hallway, I already knew what I would find. I can never forget the fear I felt before I actually saw her.

My once-beautiful mother was lying back on the bed, her feet still on the floor as if she had just sat down and then decided to lie back, perhaps to take a nap. Her eyes were open and staring at the ceiling, but they held no life. An overwhelming sadness raced through me, and I reached out to hold her and close her eyelids. It was then that I noticed the insulated cup of water on her nightstand by the bed. It still contained small bits of ice. Beside the cup of water was her ever-present ashtray. The cigarette it held had burned all the way down to the filter, but the ash had remained intact. The gray profile of that long cylinder of death remained perfectly formed. My mother had died alongside the sinister addiction that had become her constant partner.

Mom was diagnosed as having died of a stroke. But her two and a half daily packs of Tareytons and I knew better.

Just a few months later as I stood at my office window, whatever doubts, fears, or hesitancy I harbored about taking the case Fred had discussed quickly left me. As so often in the past, my parents had told me all I ever needed to know. I had made the right decision. At the same time, I also knew that I could lose everything. But aren't there some things in life worth losing everything for?

And what a decision—and a gamble—it was. Fred had proposed that I, along with ten other high-profile trial lawyers, would go head to head and toe to toe against the rich, vast, and powerful cigarette cartel. The targets would be among the most cash-laden corporations in the world, with a base of operation, influence, control, and political power that was astounding. Fred and nationally renowned lawyer Ron Motley, from Charleston, South Carolina, had been working on a legislative bill with Florida's then-governor Lawton Chiles. The proposed law would allow lawyers to sue the tobacco industry on behalf of the State of Florida in order to retrieve all or even a portion of the money that had been spent on the medical care and treatment of people—particularly indigents supported by the state's Medicaid program—who had become sick or had died from using tobacco products. Fred had explained that it would be an undertaking of immeasurable proportions—worthy of being labeled a great cause. If the campaign was successful, it would change the tobacco industry forever. There could be no dispute that this was a renegade industry that was powerfully arrogant and needed to be reined in.

A lawsuit on behalf of the State of Florida was on the completely opposite end of the spectrum from an individual action. It would prevent the tobacco industry from employing some of the tactics it had employed so successfully for more than four decades. The theory of the case was simple: The cigarette industry had manufactured a product that, when used as directed, caused sickness and death.

When poor and indigent smokers became ill and in need of extensive medical care, the State of Florida had no choice: It was required to step in and provide care at taxpayer expense. In effect, the wrongdoers made the profit, and the citizens of Florida footed the bill. Taxpaying citizens had a right to get their money back.

Such a novel approach, especially in the form of a state law, had never been attempted, and it entailed certain risks. There would be constitutional challenges to the law itself, denial of due process arguments, and anything else the legal armada of the cigarette cartel could muster. Taking on Big Tobacco on its own would have been an overwhelming task for the State of Florida. Even armed with the new law, state officials realized they could not financially manage or provide the legal talent to prosecute the lawsuit without help. Trying to handle such massive litigation would have consumed literally hundreds of the state's staff lawyers. More than likely, such an approach would have expended most of the state's legal resources.

After much thought and deliberation, a decision was made to use lawyers from the private sector. Governor Chiles, his general counsel Dexter Douglass, and Fred Levin would select a team of trial lawyers with the necessary talent and financial resources to take on the Goliath of litigation. That's how I and the others had been pulled together. Many in the media immediately labeled us Florida's "Dream Team." Some defense lawyers called us the "Dirty Dozen"—and much worse. The newspapers thought of other names, like "the people's champions" and "warriors." But they also used such labels as "hired guns" and described us as "greedy," "overreaching," "litigious," "money-hungry," and the like.

Whatever you called us, the list of lawyers was impressive:
David Fonvielle of Tallahassee; W.C. Gentry of Jacksonville; Wayne Hogan of Jacksonville; Bob Kerrigan of Pensacola; Mike Maher of Orlando; Bob Montgomery, Jr. of West Palm Beach; Ron Motley of Charleston, South Carolina; Jim "Booty" Nance of Melbourne; Shelly Schlesinger of Fort Lauderdale; Dickie Scruggs of Pascagoula, Mississippi; Laurence Tribe of Cambridge, Massachusetts; Steve Yerrid of Tampa.

Governor Chiles' "Dream Team"

By Don Yaeger

Before she helped me out by calling each of the attorneys representing Florida to ask for a little professional background information, I suggested to my wife that she fill the paper cassette of our 100-page fax machine in anticipation of their responses. Being trial lawyers, most of them didn't disappoint. What we didn't expect, though, was that she would have to refill the cassette twice more before the day was out. Here, culled from more than 240 pages of detailed biographical information, are mini-profiles of Gov. Chiles' "Dream Team."

David Fonvielle

Fonvielle & Hinkle
(Tallahassee)

Practice focuses on personal injury and wrongful death claims. Has won large verdicts and settlements against such giants as A.H. Robbins and its Dalkon Shield intrauterine birth control device, which often necessitated surgery and caused infertility in hundreds of young women.

W.C. Gentry
Gentry, Phillips, Smith and Hodak
(Jacksonville)

Received national recognition in the 1970s when he established for the first time the right of abused children to hold governmental authorities accountable for failing to respond to child abuse complaints. Recovered the first multi-million dollar product liability verdict in Northeast Florida and a precedent-setting $10 million

punitive damages award against a corporation whose drunken employee caused two deaths after "engaging in corporately sanctioned entertainment of customers."

Wayne Hogan
Brown, Terrell, Hogan, Ellis, McClamma and Yegelwel
(Jacksonville)

Founding Chair of the Environmental Law Section of the Academy of Florida Trial Lawyers. Precedent-setting decisions include jury verdicts against Johns-Manville Sales Corp. and other asbestos manufacturers for causing disease and death.

Bob Kerrigan
Kerrigan Estess Rankin & McLeod
(Pensacola)

In 1984, firm secured a $28 million verdict against a drunken driver who killed a 10-year-old, the largest ever awarded on the Gulf Coast against an individual. Represented Michael Griffin, who was convicted in a high profile case of murdering an abortion doctor in Pensacola.

Mike Maher
Maher, Gibson and Guiley
(Orlando)

Selected by fellow Dream Teamers as the group's leader because, as one of his teammates said, "He handles all the egos perfectly." May explain why calls to Maher asking about his significant court victories yielded a cryptic, "I'd rather not talk about them." Bland bio boasts only of his election as President of the Association of Trial Lawyers of America.

Robert Montgomery, Jr.

Montgomery & Larmoyeux
(West Palm Beach)

Firm has won more than 46 verdicts or settlements of $1 million or more since 1979. Clients include relatives of victims killed in Delta and Air Florida crashes.

Ron Motley
Ness, Motley, Loadholt, Richardson & Poole (Charleston, S.C.)

Called by some "the Ralph Nader of Trial Lawyers." Best known for specialization in asbestos litigation, participating in more than 3,000 asbestos personal injury cases. Widely credited with bankrupting several asbestos companies. Powerful adversaries have included Pittsburgh Corning Corp., W.R. Grace & Co., and Raymark Industries. Now concentrating on tobacco companies.

Jim Nance
Nance, Cacciatore, Sisserson, Duryea & Hamilton (Melbourne)

Worked on the highly publicized 1981 tragedy when the Harbour Cay condominium project in Cocoa Beach collapsed, killing 11 workers and injuring 23; suits settled for $10 million. Won Florida's fourth million-dollar verdict in 1971 when a Sears, Roebuck and Co. roof collapsed leaving a young construction worker a paraplegic.

Shelly Schlesinger
Sheldon J. Schlesinger, P.A.
(Fort Lauderdale)

First lawyer ever to win a product-liability judgment against Toyota; has since won

large settlements from Ford and Federal Express. Once held the record for the single largest medical malpractice verdict in America: $12.5 million.

Dick Scruggs
Scruggs, Millette, Lawson, Bozeman and Dent
(Pascagoula, Miss.)

Played role in state of Mississippi's effort to recover public health expenditures from the tobacco industry. Leading an effort to reach a congressional settlement to the cigarette litigation. Specializes in tort cases for victims of asbestos and other occupational hazards. Won the first jury verdict for asbestos litigation against CSR Limited of Australia, $2 million.

Laurence Tribe
Professor at Harvard Law School
(Cambridge)

Though not a "paying" member of Chiles' Dream Team, considered by most of the team as a full partner because of the legal brilliance and credibility he adds to the process. Often a corporate attorney representing such giants as Bell Atlantic and Pennzoil. Tobacco suit takes him to the other side of the aisle. Has testified in 39 congressional hearings.

Steve Yerrid
Yerrid, Knopik & Mudano
(Tampa)

Has won more than 25 verdicts of $1 million or more against the likes of Ford, Allstate and State Farm. His $1 million verdict against Barnett Bank for a man assaulted while using an ATM caused banks to add lighting and security systems to protect ATM users.

OCTOBER 1996   OCTOBER 1996   ·65·   FLORIDA TREND

All had established reputations as leaders and men of conviction. More importantly, each one of us was known to be a high-stakes gambler when it came to the courtroom.

We unanimously agreed to aggressively pursue the cause using our own money, resources, law firms, and staff. At our first meeting, we came up with a name for our group. We would be known as the People's Trial Advocates, or PTA for short. The PTA would fund the entire litigation, take all of the risks, do all of the work, and if by some miracle we happened to win, we might even get paid. By structuring its legal representation in this manner, the State of Florida was able to take on the herculean task of bringing down Big Tobacco and, at the same time, shift the entire down-side of a bad result to us. Perfect.

Everyone involved knew we were jeopardizing our legal careers and our successful practices by taking on a case that many considered unwinnable. We all knew it could result in a bottomless pit of litigation expenses. But if we won—if we won—not only would our fees be huge, but the entire tobacco industry would also undergo a transformation unlike anything we could even imagine.

The deal was struck and the war began. We took hundreds of depositions, and tens of thousands of documents were discovered and produced. During motion hearings held in open court, one, two, or on very rare occasions all eleven of us often faced a hundred or more of tobacco's defense lawyers packing the courtroom.

Months of intense litigation turned into years, but we withstood the onslaught of the best defense money could buy, and we were still standing. Finally, three years after the lawsuit began, the trial itself commenced.

Three weeks into jury selection, the world was shocked when the leading cigarette companies in America agreed to settle and pay $13.6 billion dollars to the State of Florida rather than allow the case to go forward and have a jury decide the outcome. The money would compensate the state for public health costs caused by smoking-related illnesses. However, the terms of the settlement included other magnificent and unprecedented benefits. All cigarette billboards in the state would be taken

down within six months, beginning with signs within one thousand feet of schools; cigarette vending machines would be removed from places accessible to children; the usage of Joe Camel and the Marlboro Man would be permanently halted; outdoor advertising in sporting arenas and on mass transit would be banned; and a significant part of the settlement money would be earmarked for educating people about the dangers of smoking and addiction. Prevention campaigns would be created, funded and implemented. All of these huge reforms in advertising were voluntary concessions by the industry that would have been almost impossible to require legally.

Then the unthinkable happened. Even though the Dream Team had an absolutely unambiguous written, approved, signed, sealed, and delivered contingency fee contract with the State of Florida that entitled us to be paid twenty-five percent of any settlement amount recovered, we "got stiffed" (that's the only horribly inept expression I could ever come up with). The governor, the attorney general, and other members of our "client group" decided we should be paid by Big Tobacco, not the State of Florida.

As justification for the state's refusal to pay our legal fees, it was asserted that such an amount was simply too much money for the "greedy" trial lawyers we had suddenly become. Over the several years of the litigation and even for a short period of time after the victorious settlement, we had been labeled as advocates of the people, and we were welcomed, universally respected, and heralded as the courageous band of warrior Davids fighting the people's fight against the Goliaths of litigation.

What followed was the ugliest of legal battles pitting us against our own client in a life-and-death struggle for our professional—and in some cases, personal—survival. Friends were discovered to be false, and enemies sprang from every place imaginable. Dishonesty, betrayal, and deceit became all too familiar. Finally, after more than a year-long struggle that reached the Florida Supreme Court, the Dream Team went to arbitration and was awarded the largest legal fee in the history of our country: $3.4 billion, an amount ultimately paid by the wrongdoers themselves—the cigarette cartel.

But that is just the sequence of events as reported throughout the world. The real story and what has happened since is much, much more…but that is a very long tale that must be saved for another day. Suffice it to say that, for me, the true satisfaction was knowing that our efforts would ultimately save lives. For my parents, it was too late. But for many boys and girls who would no longer have to face the full, unrestrained onslaught of the Devil in a smoking jacket, the world would be a safer, healthier place. In this case, as in so many of my others, justice had indeed prevailed. A good lawyer can ask for nothing more.

. . . .

Photo of the "Dream Team's" last meeting, pictured here from left to right: Shelly Schlesinger, Bob Montgomery, David Fonvielle, W.C Gentry, Steve Yerrid, Joe Rice (Ron Motley's partner), Fred Levin, Mike Maher, "Booty" Nance, and Wayne Hogan. Not shown: Dickie Scruggs, Bob Kerrigan, and Ron Motley.

ACKNOWLEDGMENTS

This book is a tribute to the law of our great land, and it's also a deep personal tribute to the clients whom I've represented in the courtroom—especially those whose stories I tell here. These clients became friends and placed their trust in me. Some of the people in these chapters are no longer alive. My intention in writing about them has been to honor their memories. Those clients and family members who shared their experiences and gave interviews for this work have furthered the cause of keeping the hope of justice alive, and you have my deepest gratitude.

I am indebted to many people who helped me become a lawyer as well as a better person. The late Katherine Graham counseled me to attend Georgetown University Law Center, where so many outstanding professors—especially Richard Gordon, Bill McDaniels, David McCarthy, and Eugene Noonan—taught me everything about the law that I could hope to learn in a classroom.

During my early trial practice at the firm of Holland & Knight, I was fortunate to have mentors, law partners, and a talented staff who gave me invaluable advice, support, and encouragement. John Germany, Burke Kibler, Paul Hardy, John Arthur Jones, Chesterfield Smith, and many others—thank you all.

Thanks to my brothers and sisters in the Inner Circle for all of their brilliance and willingness to share. I am deeply appreciative of the members of my law firm, who are my professional family. My partners and each member of our staff have always been there for me to fight for our causes and, most importantly, our clients. For many years Cindy Heilman has been my special assistant, providing an invaluable source of support and encouragement in countless ways.

Becoming an author required me to learn a new set of skills, and many people contributed to that process. I'd like to specifically thank Bob Vito and Mary Ann Anderson for their help on the interviews and initial draft of the manuscript. For advice and comments at the early stages of this effort, my thanks to literary agents Peter Sawyer and the legendary Fifi Oscard. I found a unique publisher in Kate Hartson, an industry veteran who has formed her own publishing house and honored me with a position on her inaugural list. She has put together a first-rate team to produce this book, and I thank her and Bob Somerville for their fine editing, Tina Taylor for her exceptional design skills, and Sarah Sheehan for her production assistance.

Finally, thanks to my family and friends who believed in me even, at times, when I have doubted myself. Thank you, Uncle Nathan and my very special Aunt Izzy, for your love and help throughout my life and in the writing of these stories. I am especially thankful to my beautiful wife, Sharon, a great partner whose love, support, and patience helped me make this book a reality. And of course, many thanks to my wonderful son, Gable, for his loving heart and the inspiration he always provides.